ane & Hana

15

STORY AND ART BY

Yuki Shiwasu

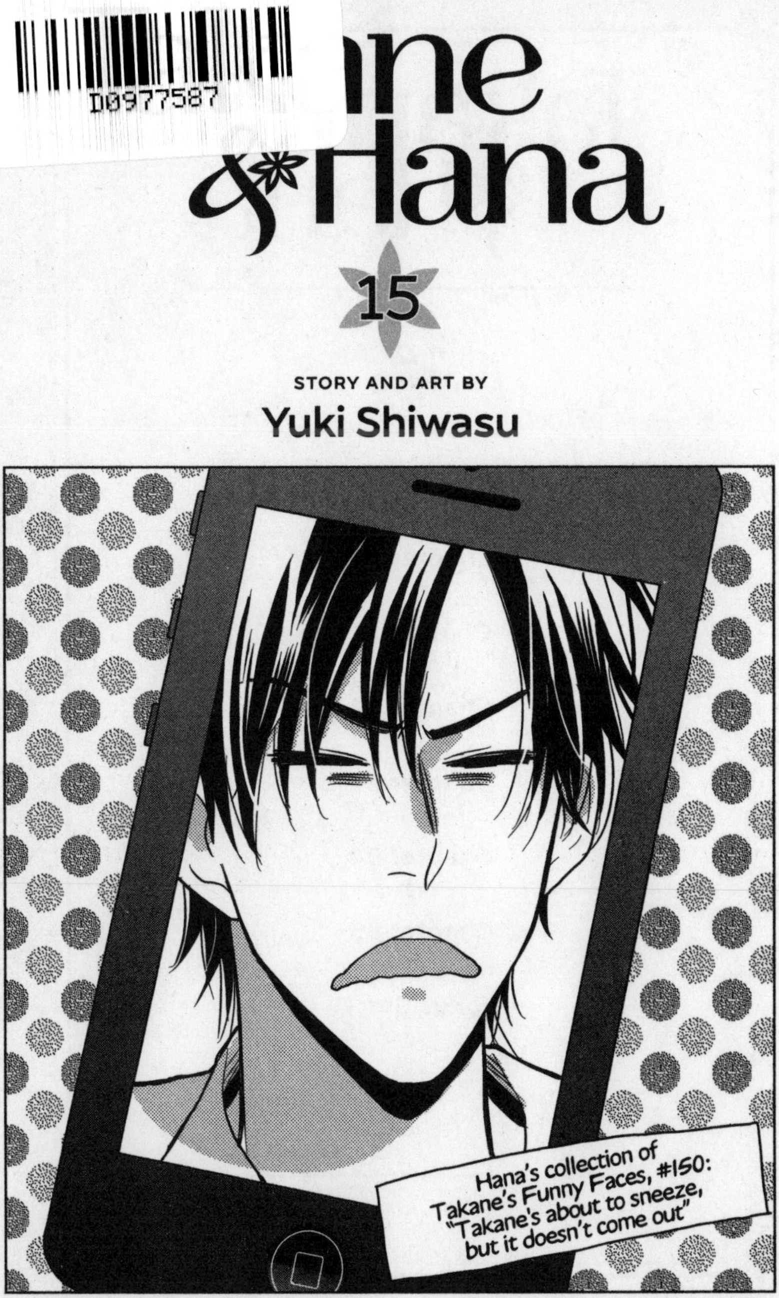
Hana's collection of
Takane's Funny Faces, #150:
"Takane's about to sneeze,
but it doesn't come out"

Takane & Hana

15

Chapter 80
~004~

Chapter 81
~037~

Chapter 82
~067~

Chapter 83
~099~

Chapter 84
~129~

Chapter 85
~159~

Bonus Story
~190~

Mistaken Identity

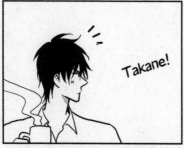

Takane!
CHAK
WHAT'S GOT YOU SOUNDING SO SWEET TODAY?
YOU'RE THAT DESPERATE...
...FOR ME TO HUG YOU?
...
Came to drop off his mail
...

Since she and Hana are sisters, they sometimes sound an awful lot alike.

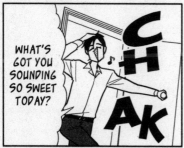

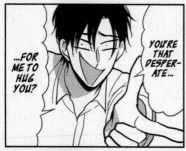

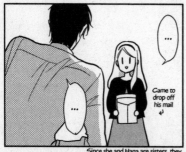

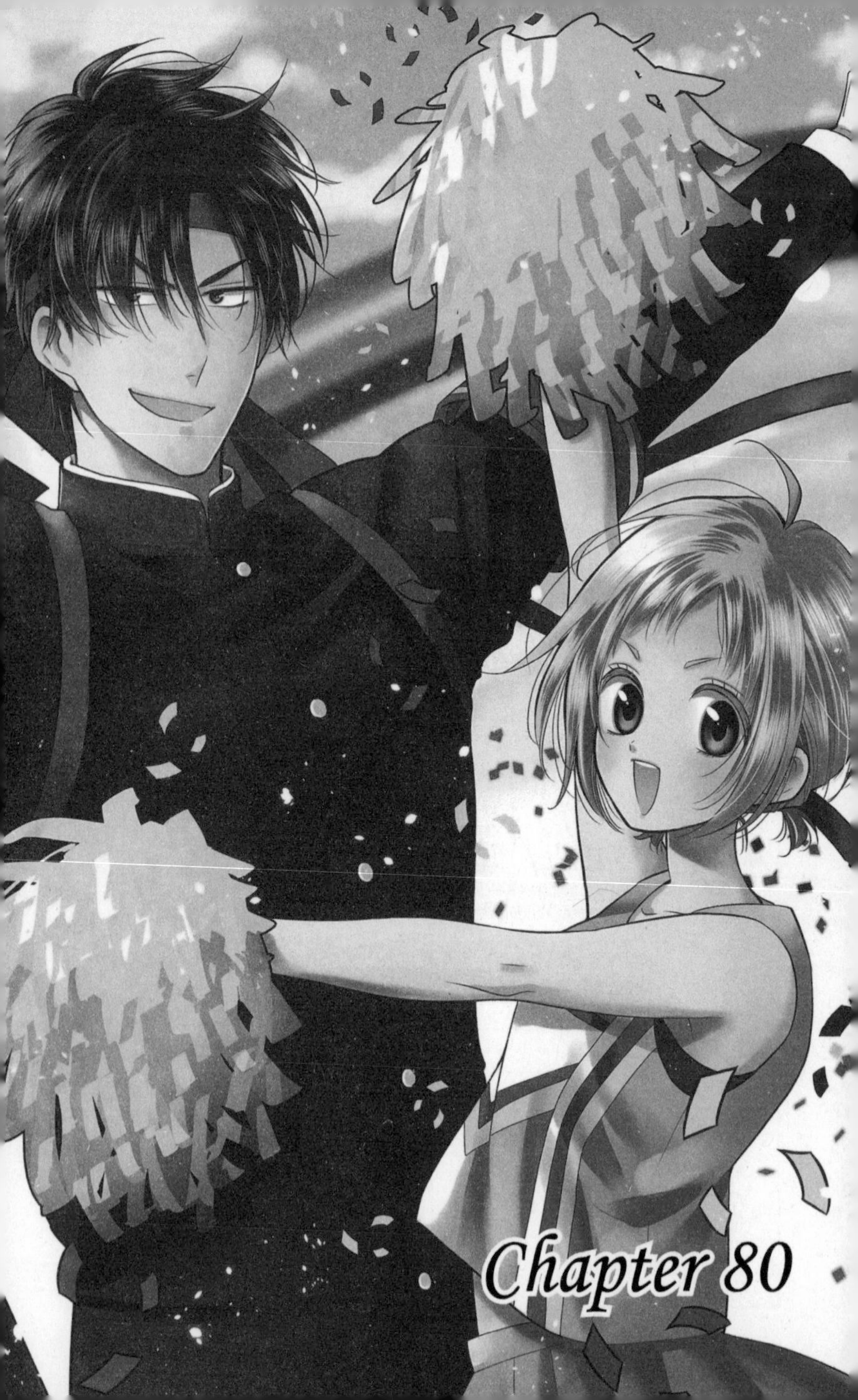
Chapter 80

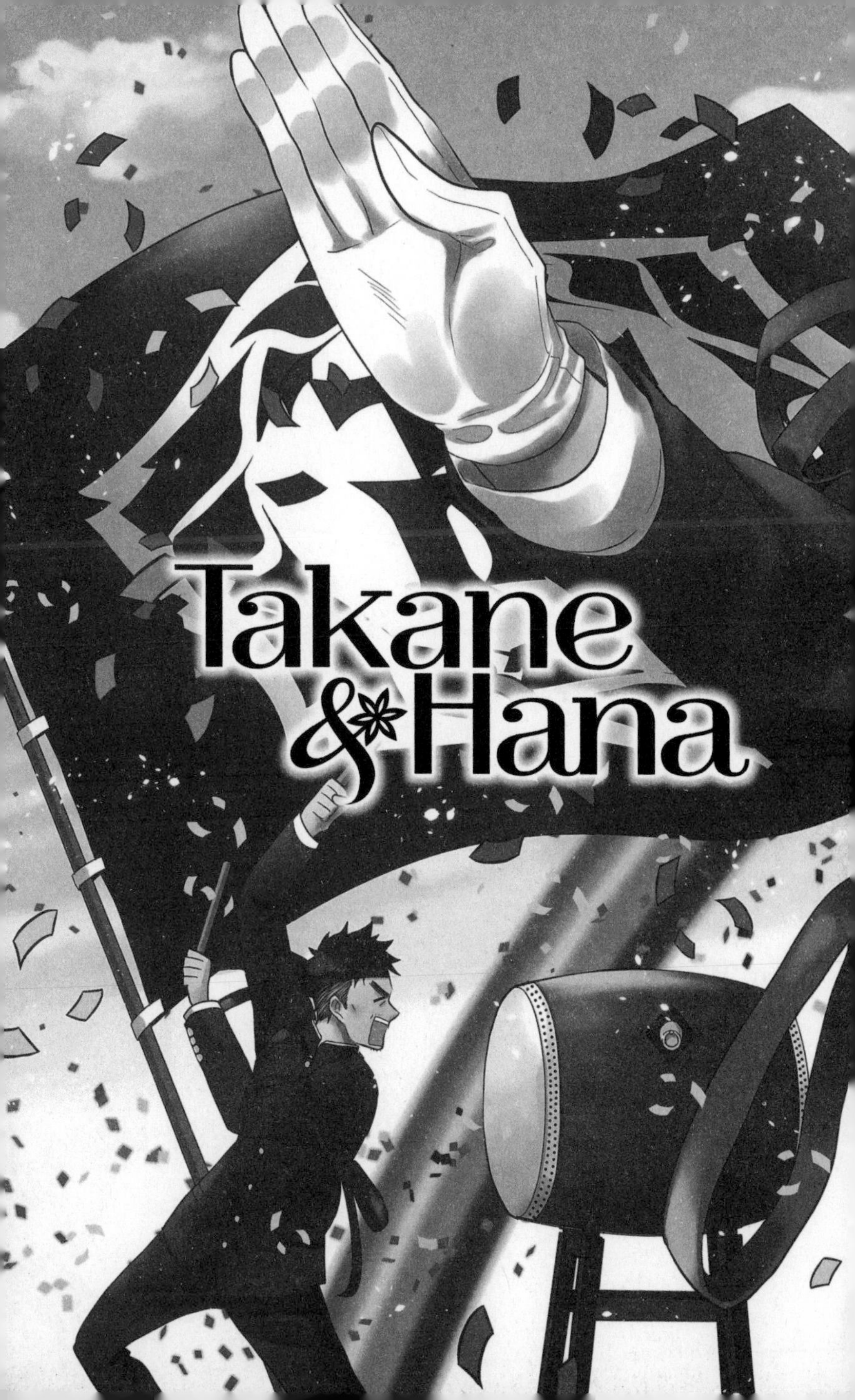
Takane & Hana

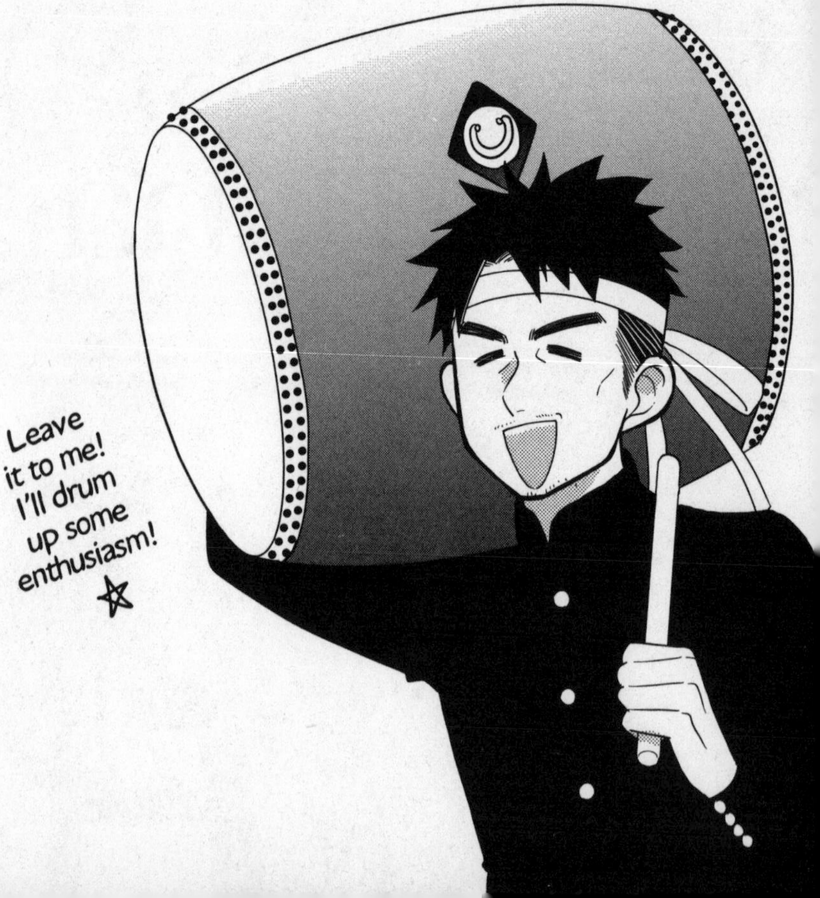
Leave it to me! I'll drum up some enthusiasm! ☆

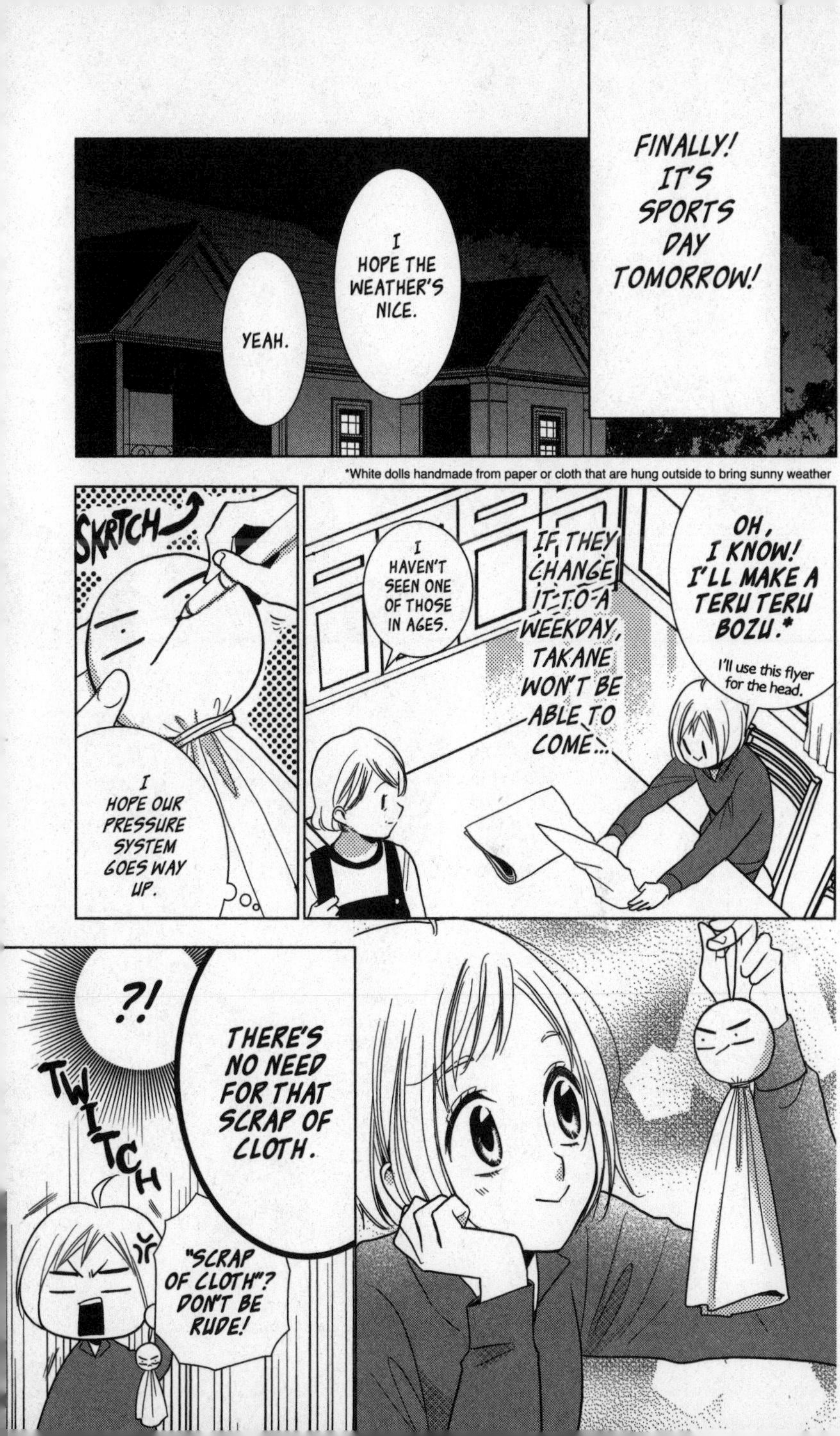
FINALLY! IT'S SPORTS DAY TOMORROW!
I HOPE THE WEATHER'S NICE.
YEAH.
OH, I KNOW! I'LL MAKE A TERU TERU BOZU.*
I'll use this flyer for the head.
IF THEY CHANGE IT TO A WEEKDAY, TAKANE WON'T BE ABLE TO COME...
I HAVEN'T SEEN ONE OF THOSE IN AGES.
SKRTCH
I HOPE OUR PRESSURE SYSTEM GOES WAY UP.
THERE'S NO NEED FOR THAT SCRAP OF CLOTH.
?!
TWITCH
"SCRAP OF CLOTH"? DON'T BE RUDE!

*White dolls handmade from paper or cloth that are hung outside to bring sunny weather

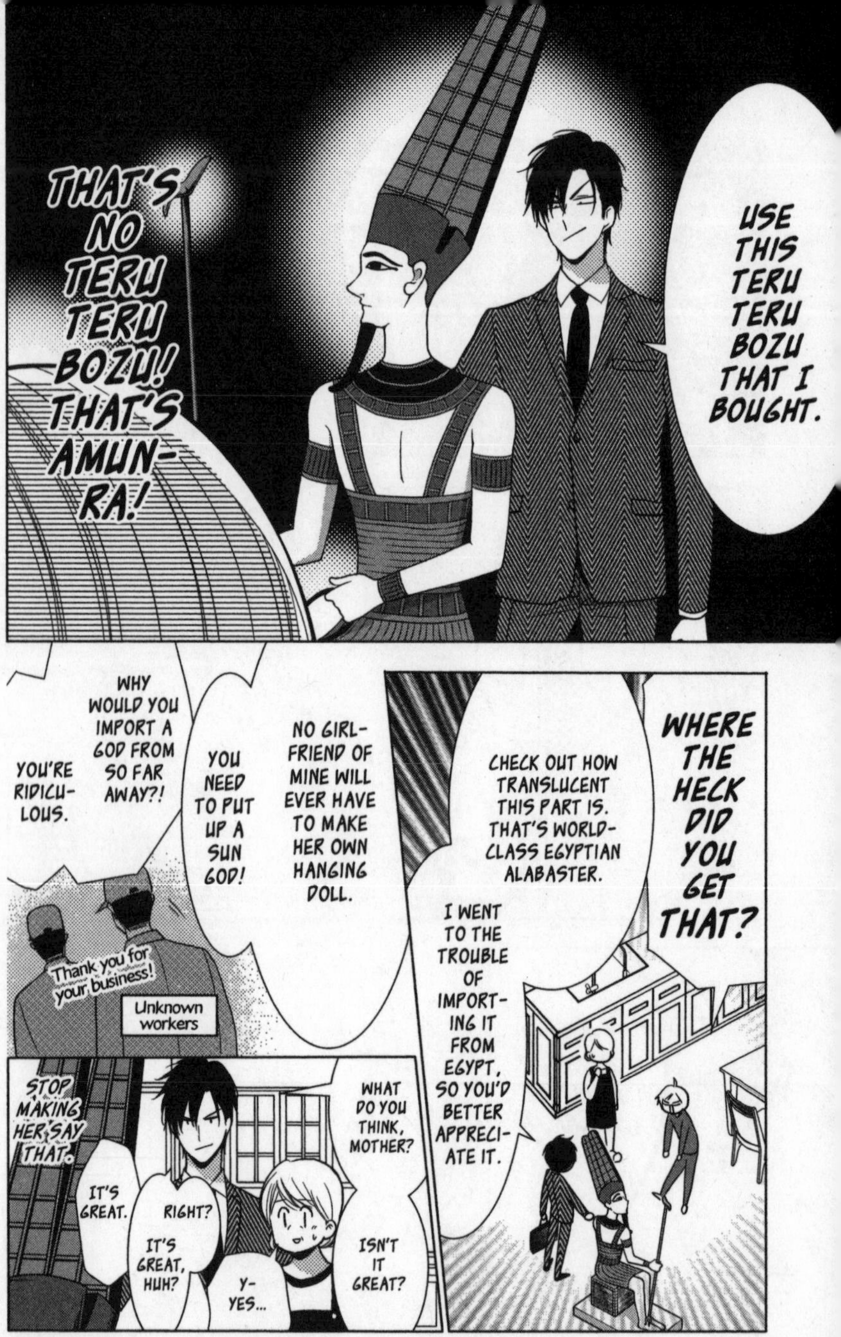
USE THIS TERU TERU BOZU THAT I BOUGHT.
THAT'S NO TERU TERU BOZU! THAT'S AMUN-RA!
WHERE THE HECK DID YOU GET THAT?
CHECK OUT HOW TRANSLUCENT THIS PART IS. THAT'S WORLD-CLASS EGYPTIAN ALABASTER.
I WENT TO THE TROUBLE OF IMPORTING IT FROM EGYPT, SO YOU'D BETTER APPRECIATE IT.
NO GIRLFRIEND OF MINE WILL EVER HAVE TO MAKE HER OWN HANGING DOLL.
YOU NEED TO PUT UP A SUN GOD!
WHY WOULD YOU IMPORT A GOD FROM SO FAR AWAY?!
YOU'RE RIDICULOUS.
Thank you for your business!
Unknown workers
WHAT DO YOU THINK, MOTHER?
ISN'T IT GREAT?
Y-YES...
RIGHT?
IT'S GREAT, HUH?
IT'S GREAT.
STOP MAKING HER SAY THAT.

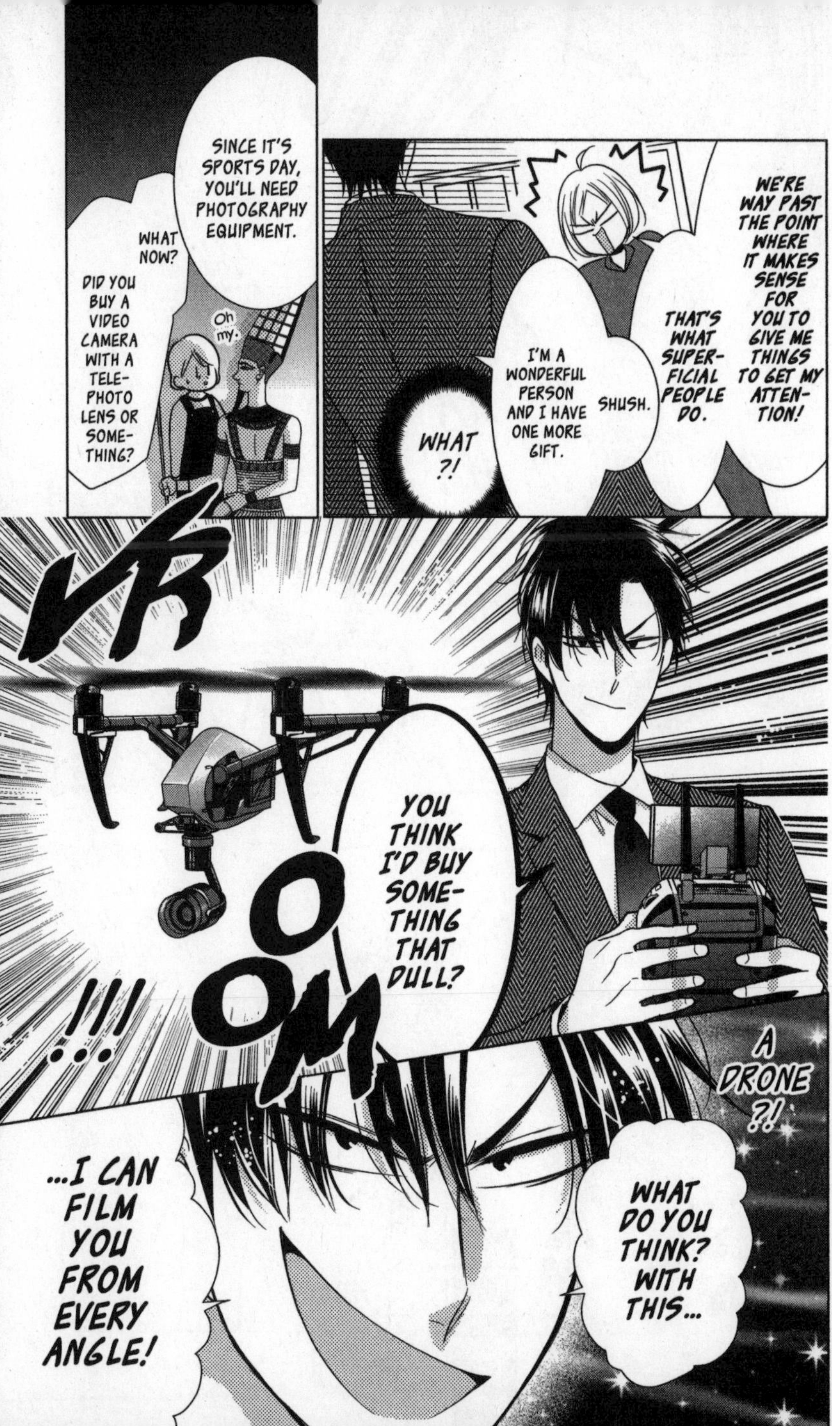
WE'RE WAY PAST THE POINT WHERE IT MAKES SENSE FOR YOU TO GIVE ME THINGS TO GET MY ATTENTION!
THAT'S WHAT SUPERFICIAL PEOPLE DO.
SHUSH.
I'M A WONDERFUL PERSON AND I HAVE ONE MORE GIFT.
WHAT?!
SINCE IT'S SPORTS DAY, YOU'LL NEED PHOTOGRAPHY EQUIPMENT.
WHAT NOW?
DID YOU BUY A VIDEO CAMERA WITH A TELEPHOTO LENS OR SOMETHING?
Oh my.
VROOM
YOU THINK I'D BUY SOMETHING THAT DULL?
...!!!
A DRONE?!
WHAT DO YOU THINK? WITH THIS...
...I CAN FILM YOU FROM EVERY ANGLE!

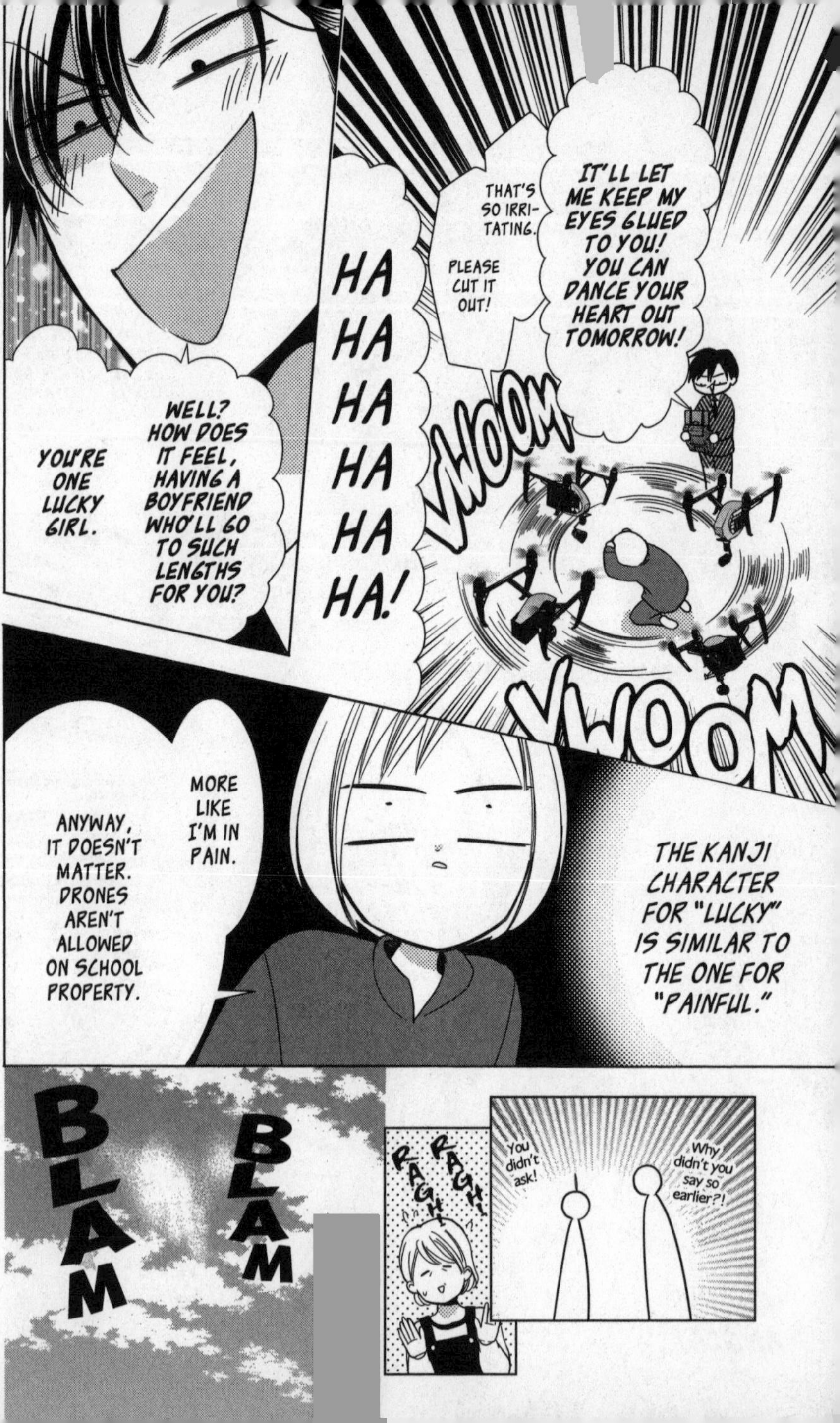
IT'LL LET ME KEEP MY EYES GLUED TO YOU! YOU CAN DANCE YOUR HEART OUT TOMORROW!
THAT'S SO IRRI-TATING.
PLEASE CUT IT OUT!
VWOOM
VWOOM
HA HA HA HA HA HA!
WELL? HOW DOES IT FEEL, HAVING A BOYFRIEND WHO'LL GO TO SUCH LENGTHS FOR YOU?
YOU'RE ONE LUCKY GIRL.
THE KANJI CHARACTER FOR "LUCKY" IS SIMILAR TO THE ONE FOR "PAINFUL."
MORE LIKE I'M IN PAIN.
ANYWAY, IT DOESN'T MATTER. DRONES AREN'T ALLOWED ON SCHOOL PROPERTY.
Why didn't you say so earlier?!
You didn't ask!
RAGH! RAGH!
BLAM
BLAM

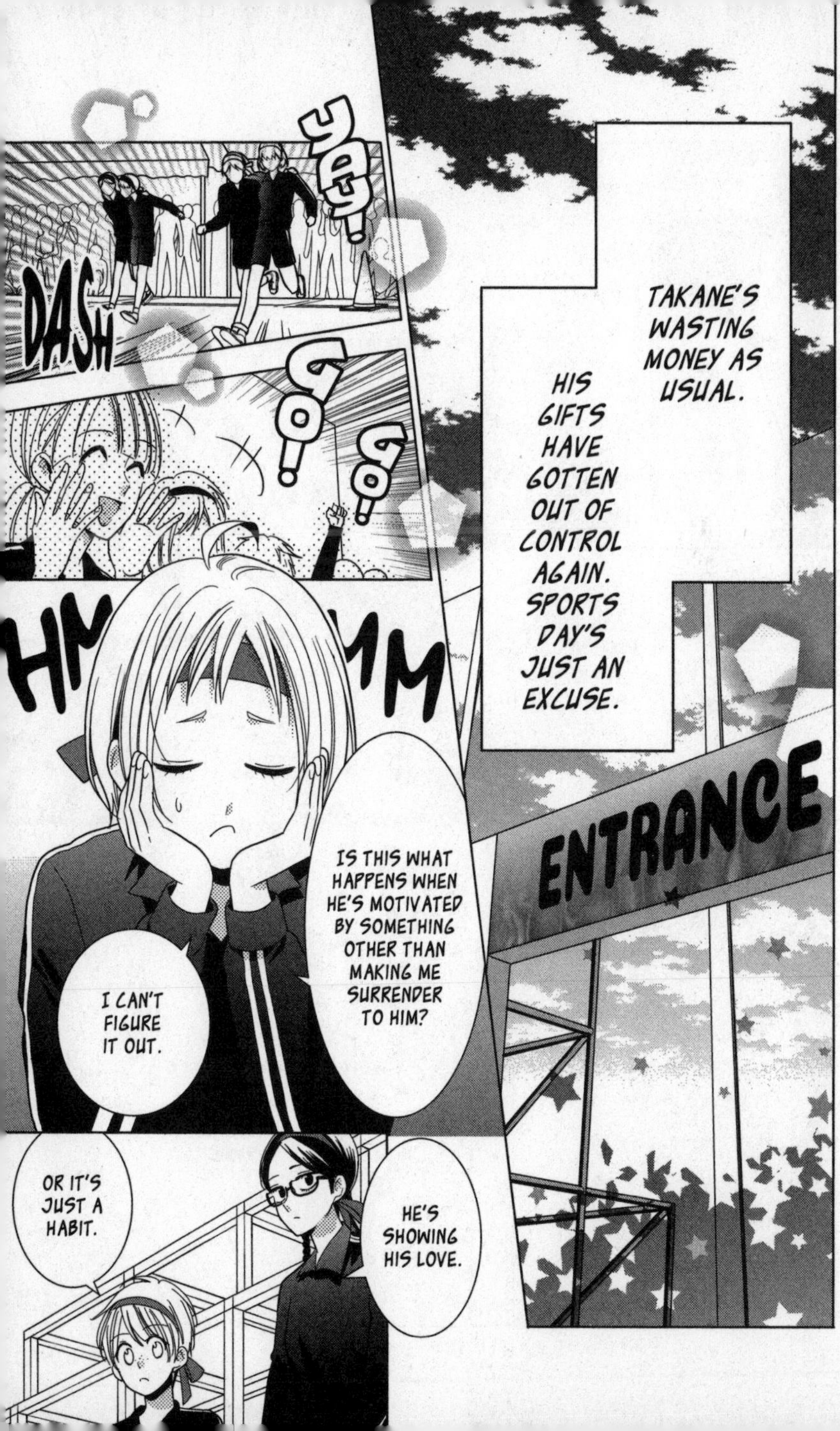
TAKANE'S WASTING MONEY AS USUAL.
HIS GIFTS HAVE GOTTEN OUT OF CONTROL AGAIN. SPORTS DAY'S JUST AN EXCUSE.
ENTRANCE
YAY!
DASH
GO! GO!
HM MM
IS THIS WHAT HAPPENS WHEN HE'S MOTIVATED BY SOMETHING OTHER THAN MAKING ME SURRENDER TO HIM?
I CAN'T FIGURE IT OUT.
HE'S SHOWING HIS LOVE.
OR IT'S JUST A HABIT.

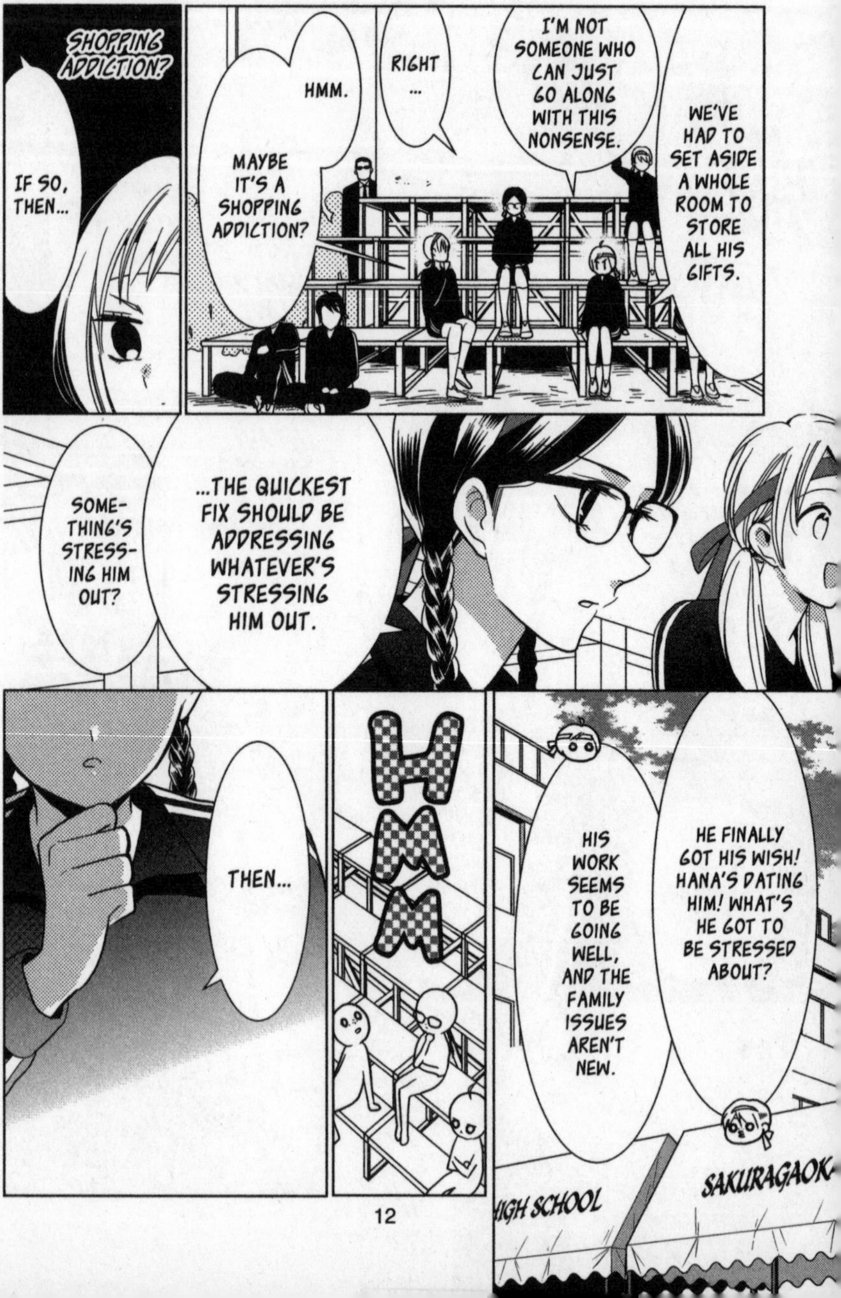
WE'VE HAD TO SET ASIDE A WHOLE ROOM TO STORE ALL HIS GIFTS.
I'M NOT SOMEONE WHO CAN JUST GO ALONG WITH THIS NONSENSE.
RIGHT ...
HMM.
MAYBE IT'S A SHOPPING ADDICTION?
SHOPPING ADDICTION?
IF SO, THEN...
...THE QUICKEST FIX SHOULD BE ADDRESSING WHATEVER'S STRESSING HIM OUT.
SOME-THING'S STRESS-ING HIM OUT?
HE FINALLY GOT HIS WISH! HANA'S DATING HIM! WHAT'S HE GOT TO BE STRESSED ABOUT?
HIS WORK SEEMS TO BE GOING WELL, AND THE FAMILY ISSUES AREN'T NEW.
SAKURAGAOK
HIGH SCHOOL
HMM
THEN...

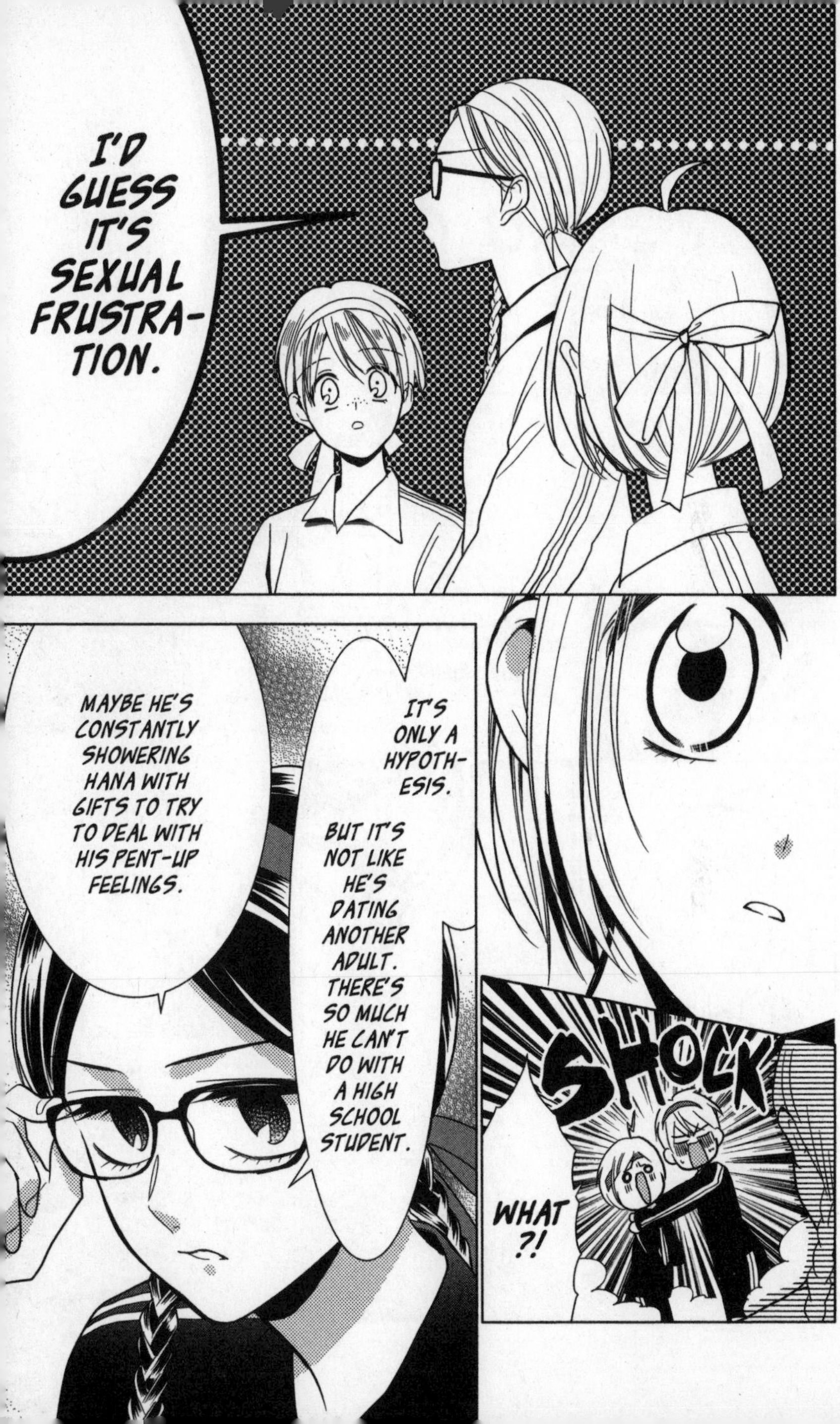
I'D GUESS IT'S SEXUAL FRUSTRA-TION.
SHOCK
WHAT ?!
IT'S ONLY A HYPOTH-ESIS.
BUT IT'S NOT LIKE HE'S DATING ANOTHER ADULT. THERE'S SO MUCH HE CAN'T DO WITH A HIGH SCHOOL STUDENT.
MAYBE HE'S CONSTANTLY SHOWERING HANA WITH GIFTS TO TRY TO DEAL WITH HIS PENT-UP FEELINGS.

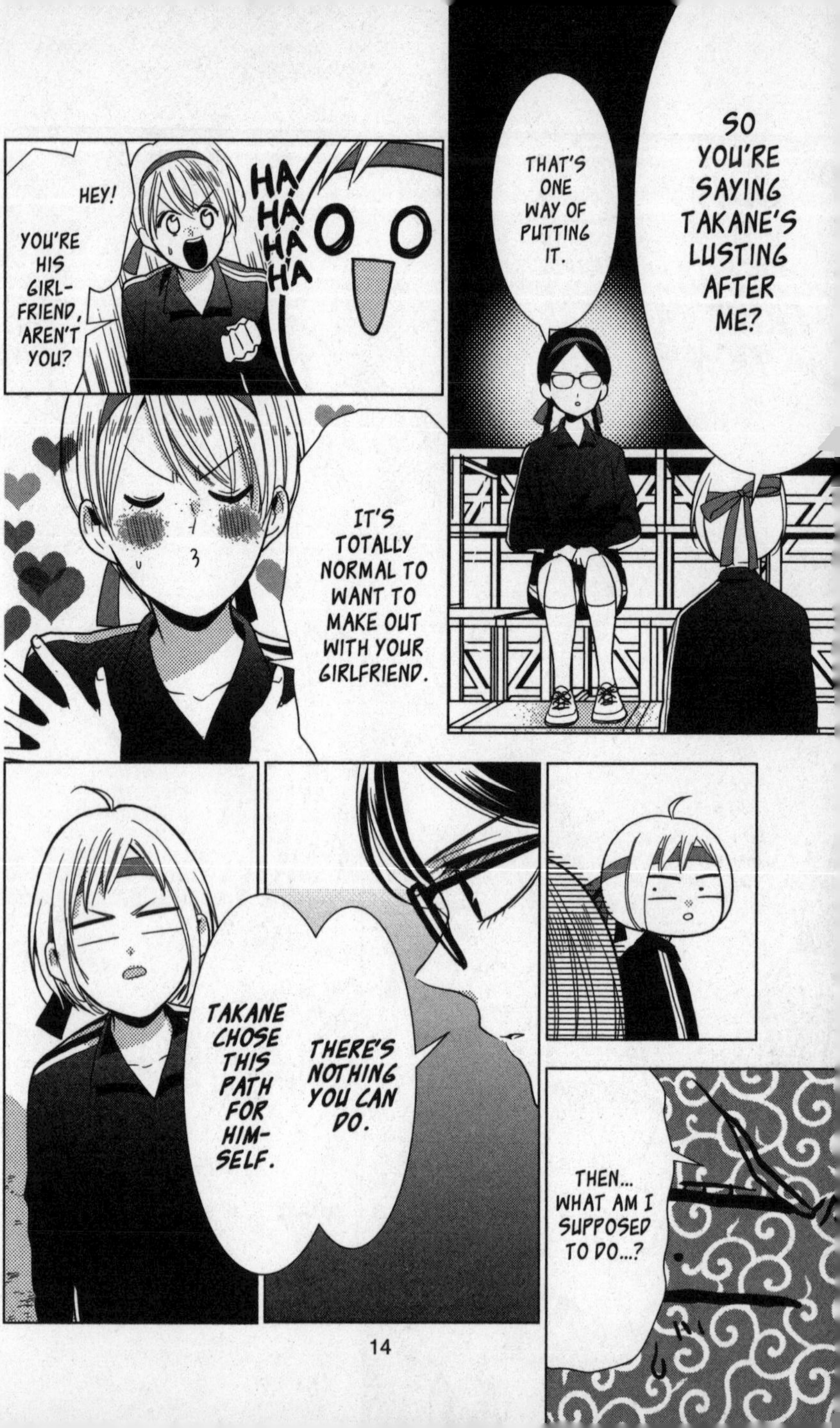
SO YOU'RE SAYING TAKANE'S LUSTING AFTER ME?
THAT'S ONE WAY OF PUTTING IT.
HEY!
YOU'RE HIS GIRL-FRIEND, AREN'T YOU?
HA HA HA HA
IT'S TOTALLY NORMAL TO WANT TO MAKE OUT WITH YOUR GIRLFRIEND.
THERE'S NOTHING YOU CAN DO.
TAKANE CHOSE THIS PATH FOR HIM-SELF.
THEN... WHAT AM I SUPPOSED TO DO...?

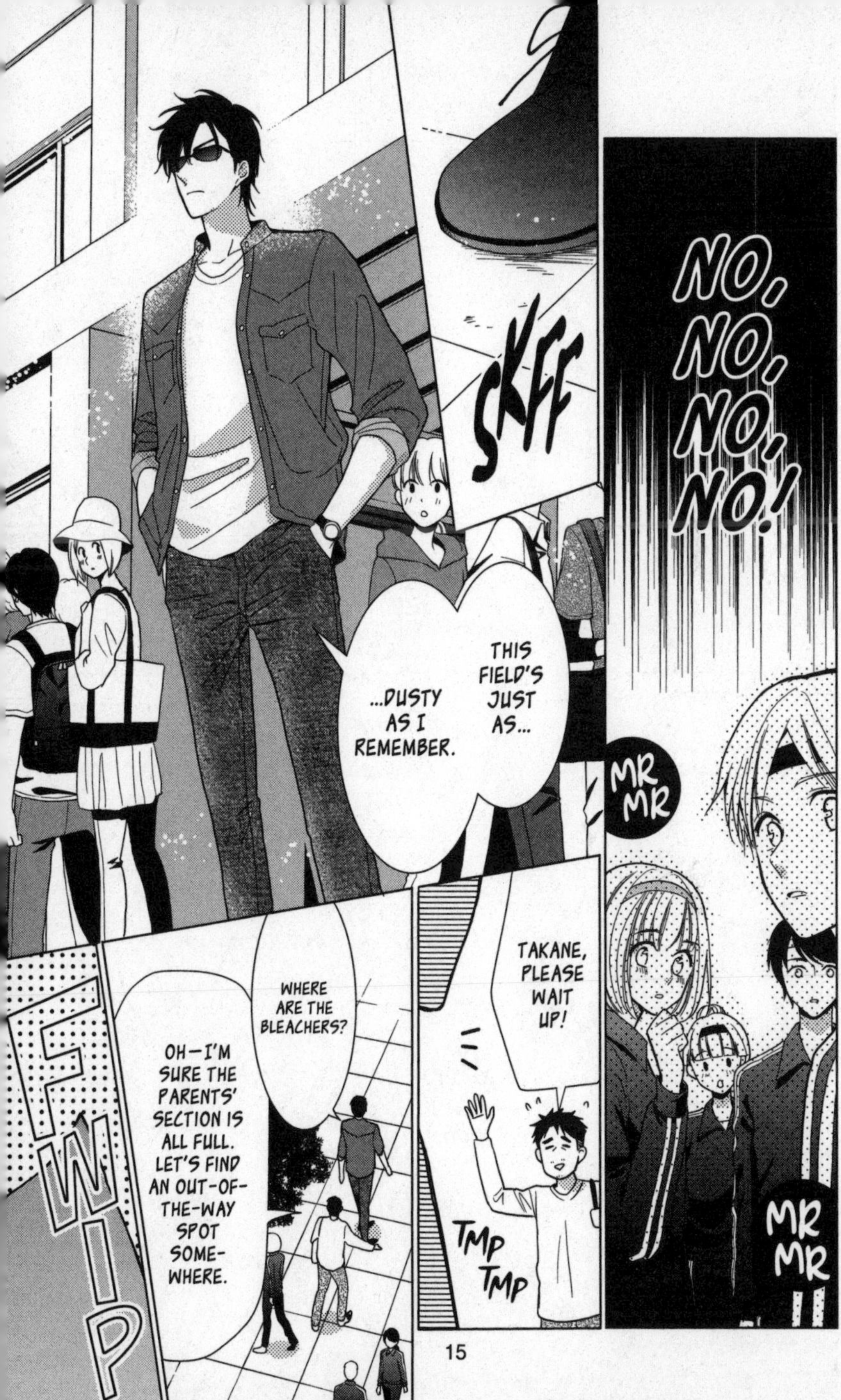
NO, NO, NO, NO!
MR MR
MR MR
SKFF
THIS FIELD'S JUST AS...
...DUSTY AS I REMEMBER.
TAKANE, PLEASE WAIT UP!
TMP TMP
WHERE ARE THE BLEACHERS?
OH—I'M SURE THE PARENTS' SECTION IS ALL FULL. LET'S FIND AN OUT-OF-THE-WAY SPOT SOME-WHERE.
FWIP

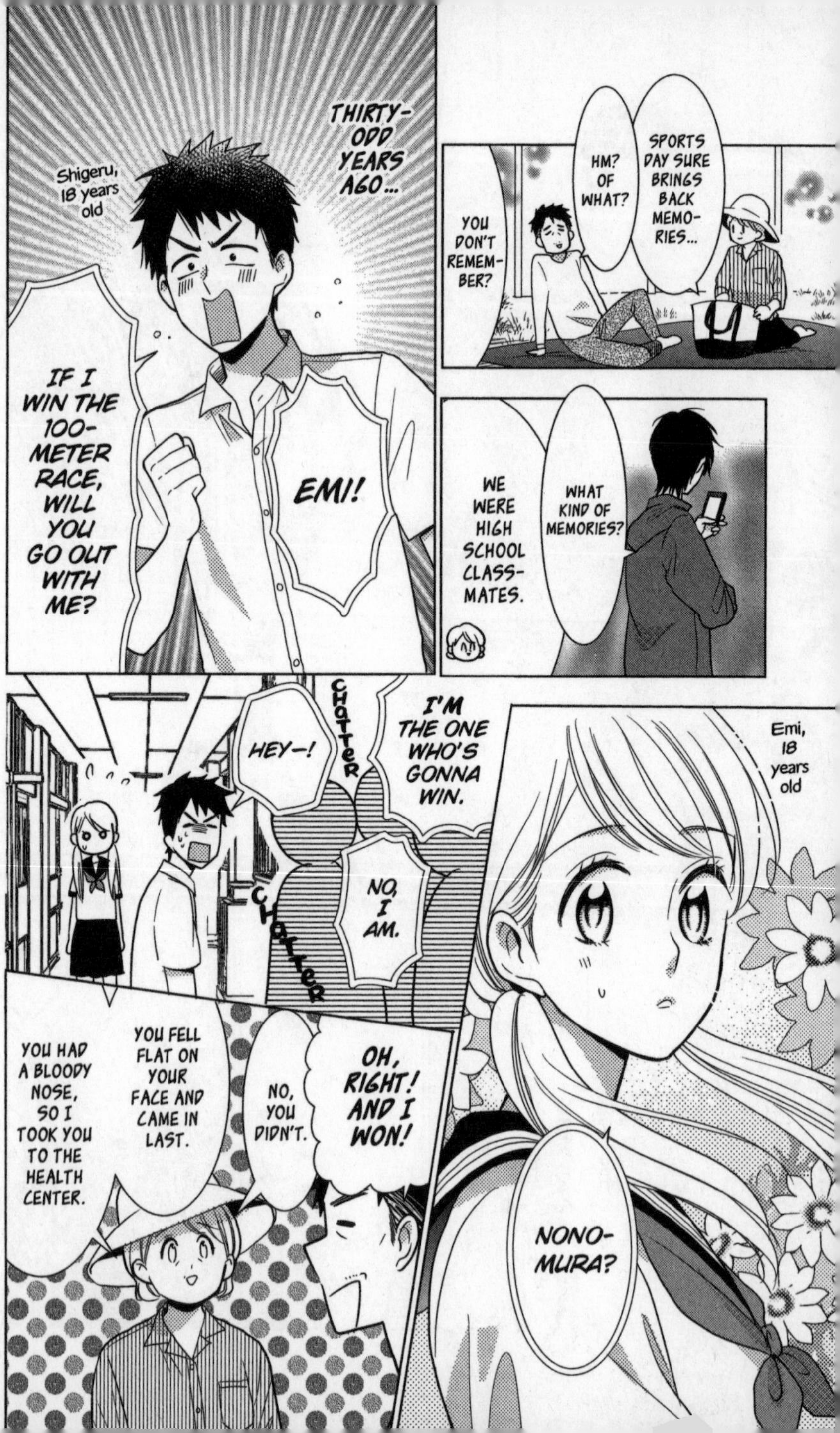
SPORTS DAY SURE BRINGS BACK MEMORIES...
HM? OF WHAT?
YOU DON'T REMEMBER?
WHAT KIND OF MEMORIES?
WE WERE HIGH SCHOOL CLASSMATES.
THIRTY-ODD YEARS AGO...
Shigeru, 18 years old
EMI!
IF I WIN THE 100-METER RACE, WILL YOU GO OUT WITH ME?
Emi, 18 years old
NONO-MURA?
I'M THE ONE WHO'S GONNA WIN.
CHATTER
HEY-!
NO, I AM.
CHATTER
OH, RIGHT! AND I WON!
NO, YOU DIDN'T.
YOU FELL FLAT ON YOUR FACE AND CAME IN LAST.
YOU HAD A BLOODY NOSE, SO I TOOK YOU TO THE HEALTH CENTER.

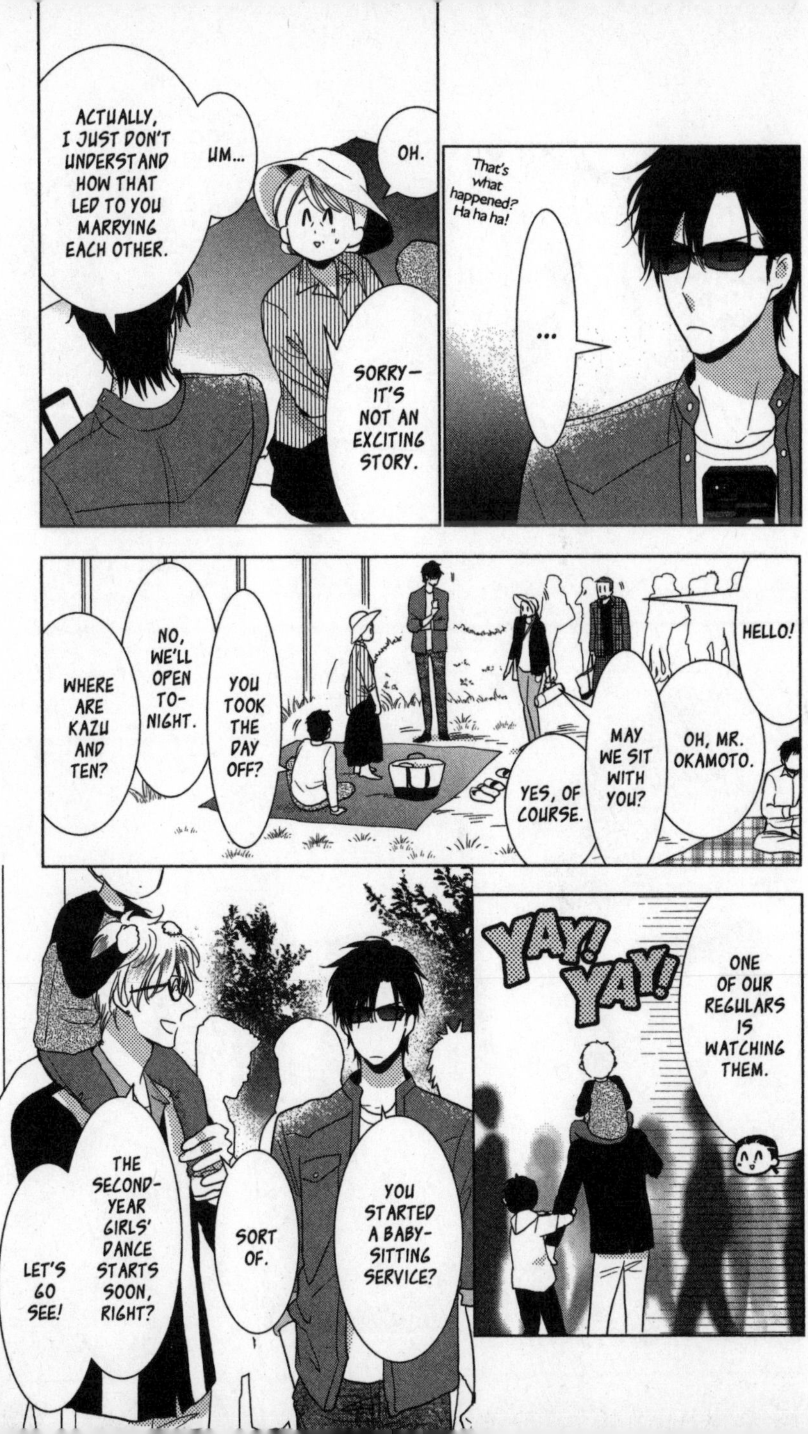
That's what happened? Ha ha ha!
...
OH.
UM...
ACTUALLY, I JUST DON'T UNDERSTAND HOW THAT LED TO YOU MARRYING EACH OTHER.
SORRY— IT'S NOT AN EXCITING STORY.
HELLO!
OH, MR. OKAMOTO.
MAY WE SIT WITH YOU?
YES, OF COURSE.
YOU TOOK THE DAY OFF?
NO, WE'LL OPEN TO-NIGHT.
WHERE ARE KAZU AND TEN?
YAY! YAY!
ONE OF OUR REGULARS IS WATCHING THEM.
YOU STARTED A BABY-SITTING SERVICE?
SORT OF.
THE SECOND-YEAR GIRLS' DANCE STARTS SOON, RIGHT?
LET'S GO SEE!

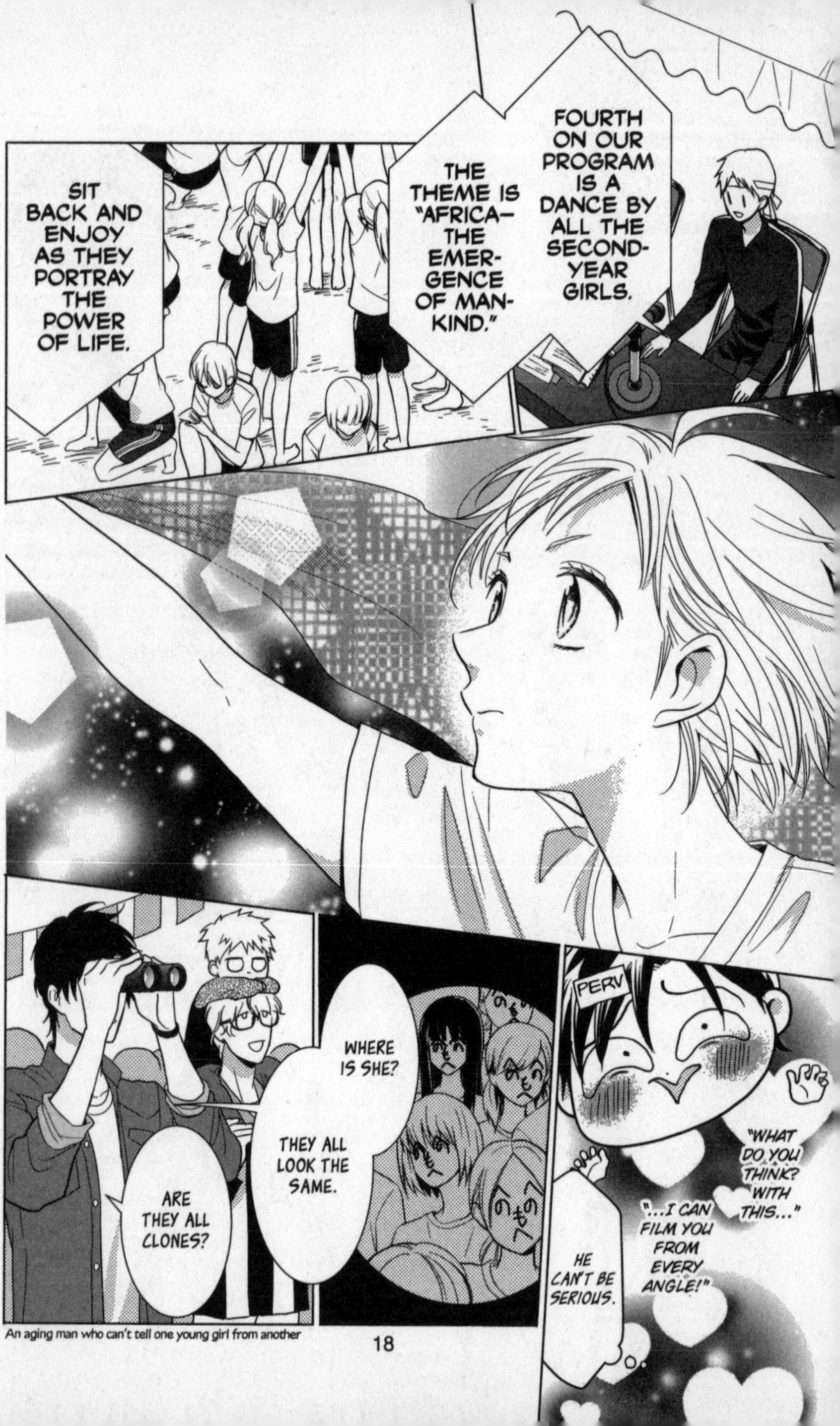
FOURTH ON OUR PROGRAM IS A DANCE BY ALL THE SECOND-YEAR GIRLS.
THE THEME IS "AFRICA—THE EMERGENCE OF MANKIND."
SIT BACK AND ENJOY AS THEY PORTRAY THE POWER OF LIFE.
PERV
"WHAT DO YOU THINK? WITH THIS..."
"...I CAN FILM YOU FROM EVERY ANGLE!"
HE CAN'T BE SERIOUS.
WHERE IS SHE?
THEY ALL LOOK THE SAME.
ARE THEY ALL CLONES?
An aging man who can't tell one young girl from another

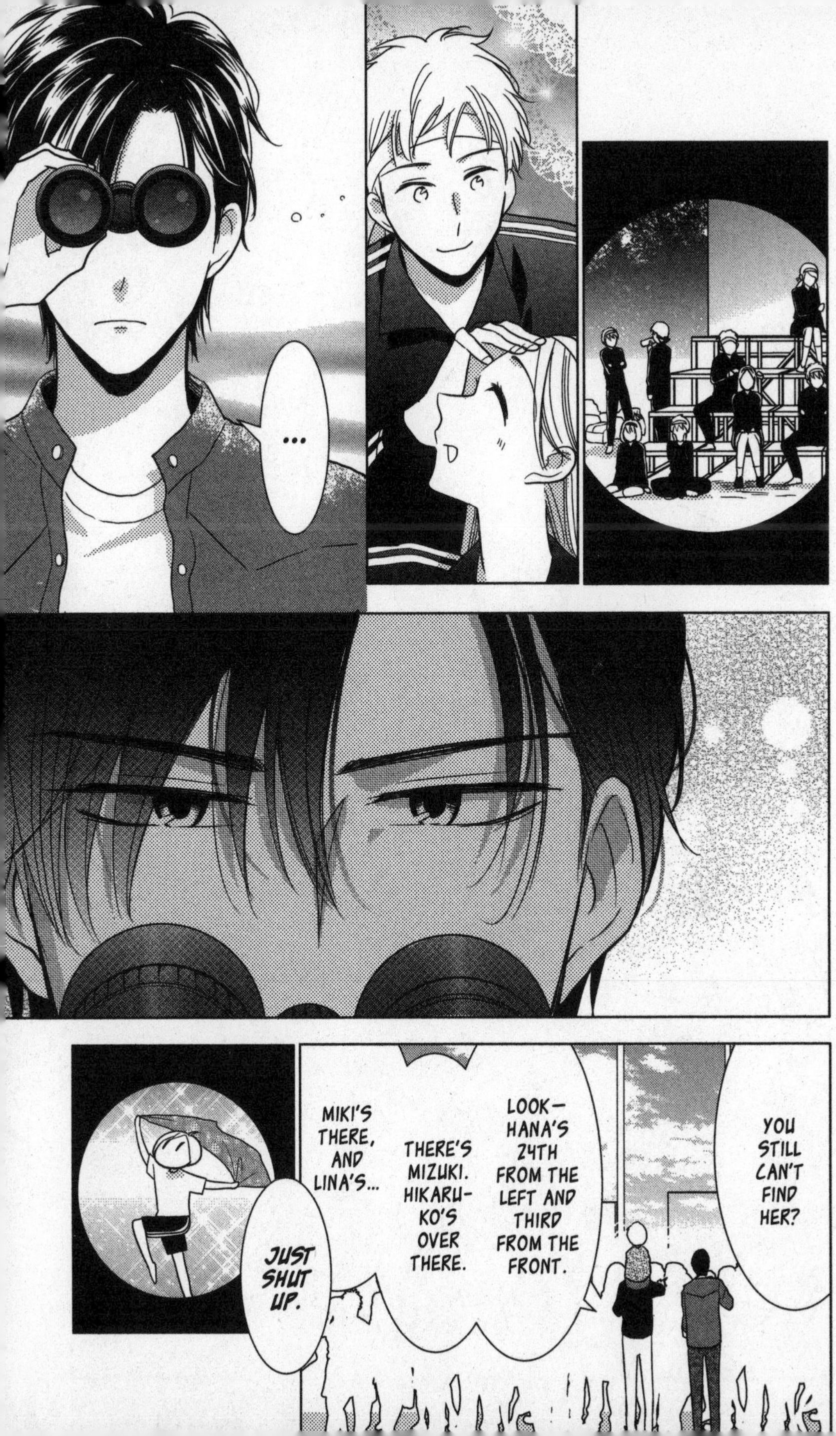
...
YOU STILL CAN'T FIND HER?
LOOK—HANA'S 24TH FROM THE LEFT AND THIRD FROM THE FRONT.
THERE'S MIZUKI. HIKARU-KO'S OVER THERE.
MIKI'S THERE, AND LINA'S...
JUST SHUT UP.

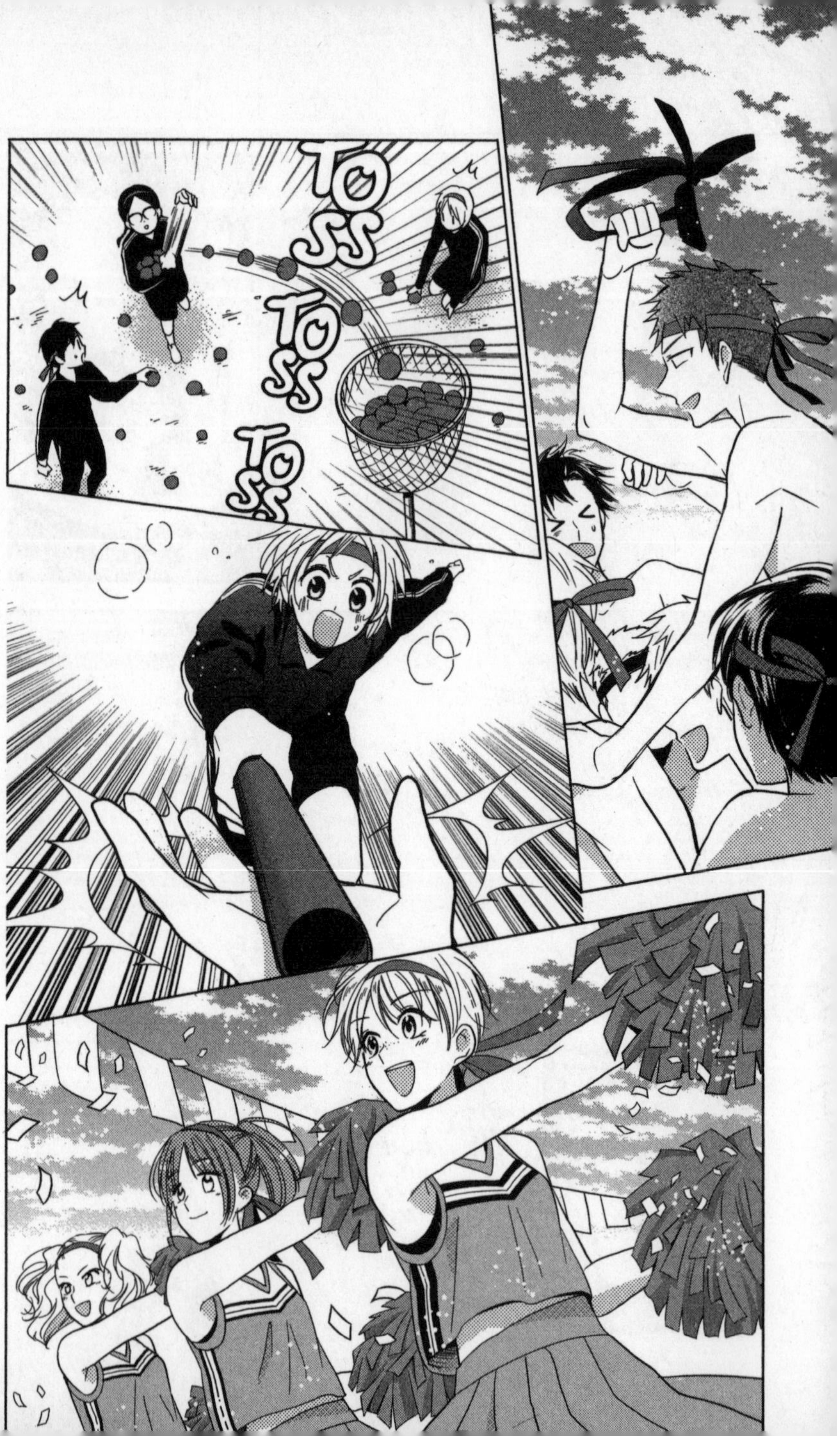
TOSS
TOSS
TOSS

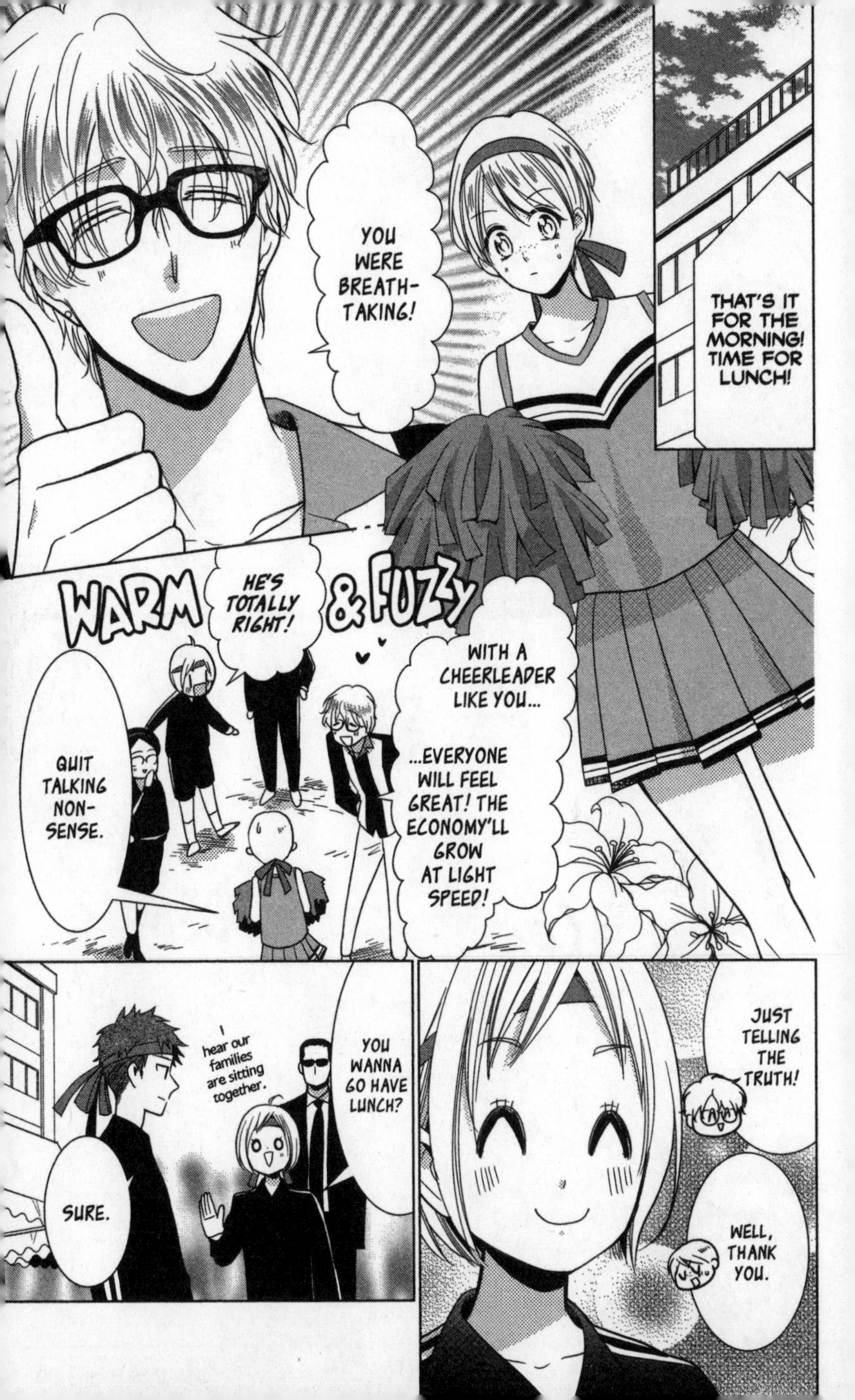
THAT'S IT FOR THE MORNING! TIME FOR LUNCH!
YOU WERE BREATH-TAKING!
WITH A CHEERLEADER LIKE YOU...
...EVERYONE WILL FEEL GREAT! THE ECONOMY'LL GROW AT LIGHT SPEED!
WARM & FUZZy
HE'S TOTALLY RIGHT!
QUIT TALKING NON-SENSE.
JUST TELLING THE TRUTH!
WELL, THANK YOU.
YOU WANNA GO HAVE LUNCH?
I hear our families are sitting together.
SURE.

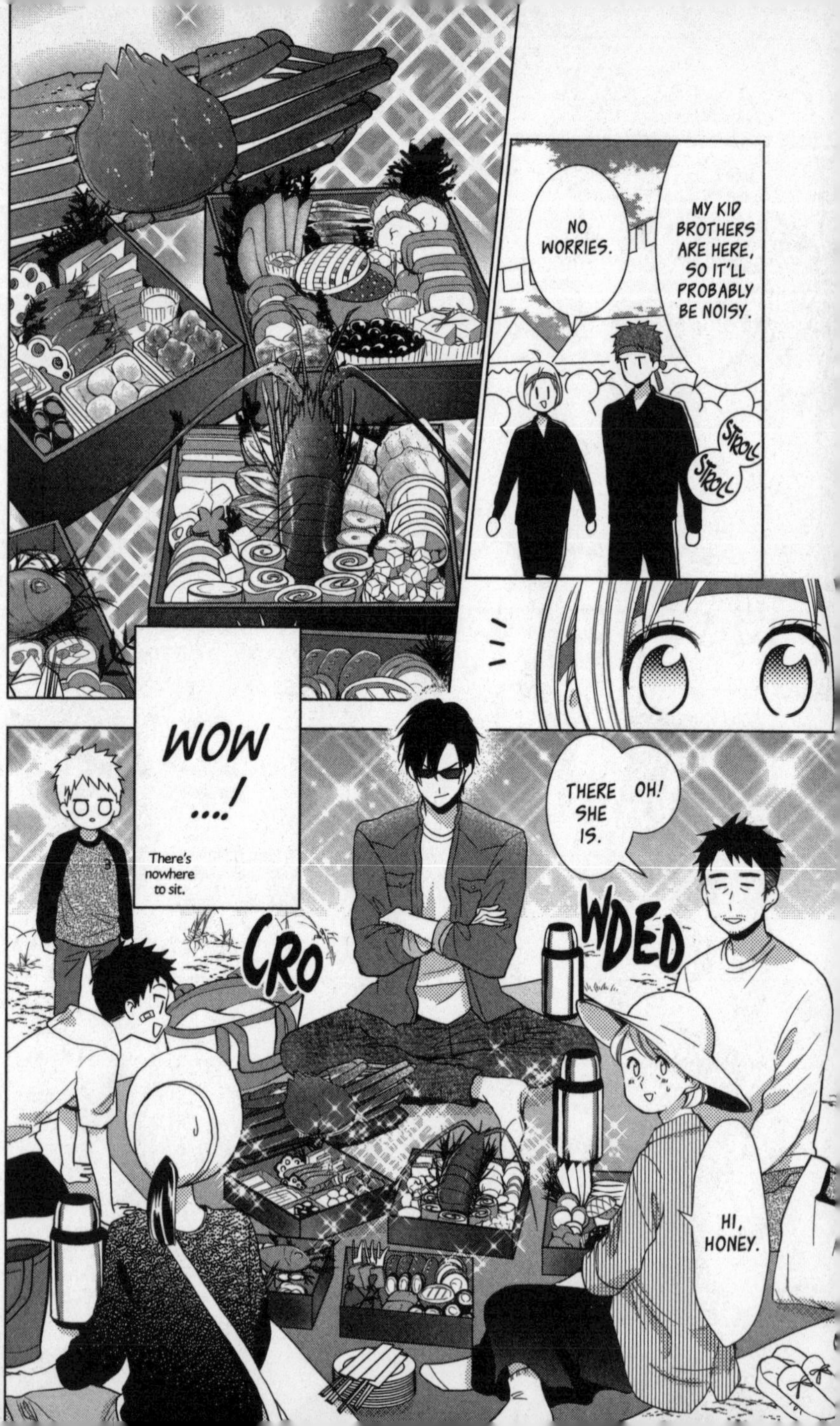
MY KID BROTHERS ARE HERE, SO IT'LL PROBABLY BE NOISY.
NO WORRIES.
STROLL STROLL
WOW ....!
There's nowhere to sit.
OH! THERE SHE IS.
CROWDED
HI, HONEY.

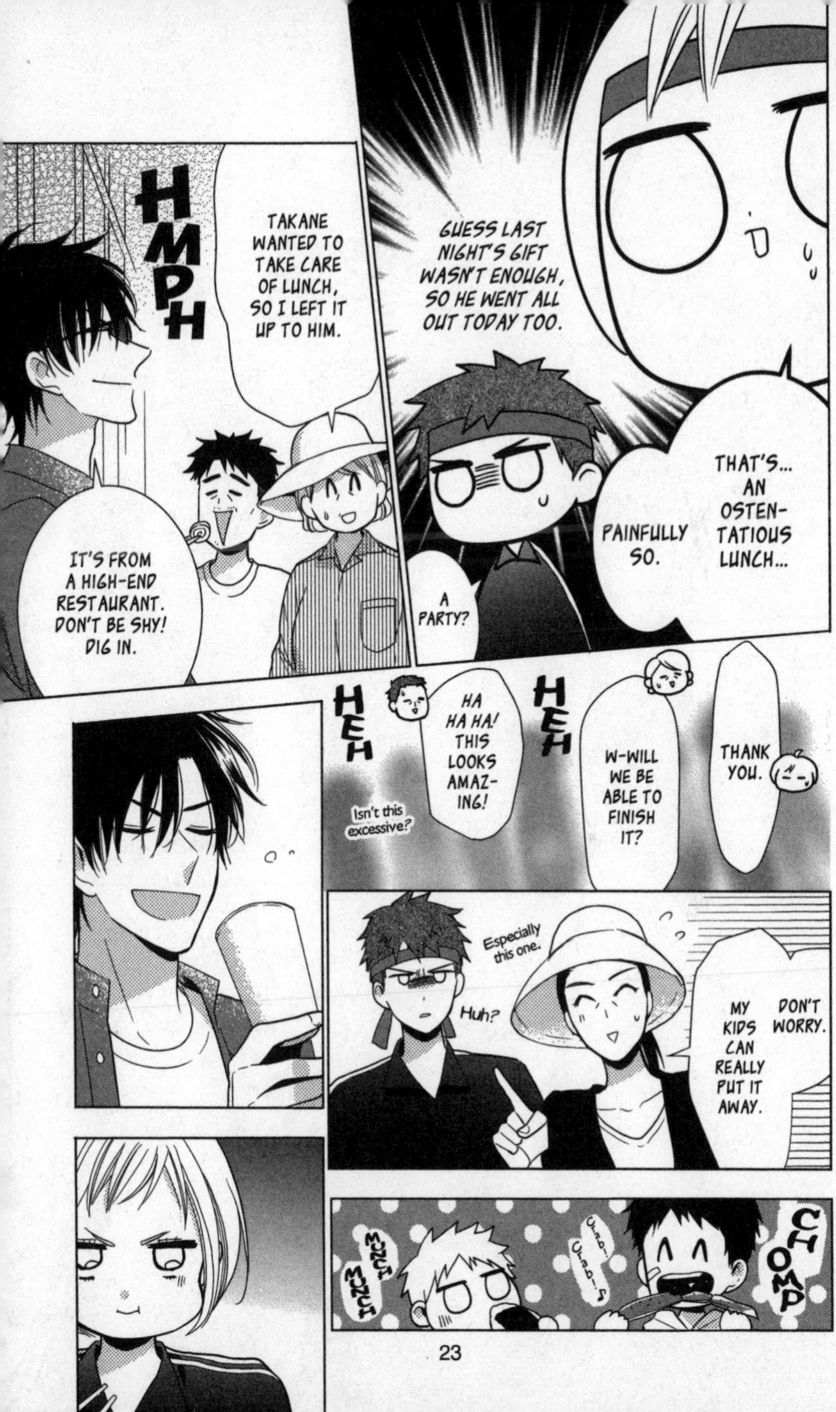
GUESS LAST NIGHT'S GIFT WASN'T ENOUGH, SO HE WENT ALL OUT TODAY TOO.
THAT'S... AN OSTEN-TATIOUS LUNCH...
PAINFULLY SO.
A PARTY?
TAKANE WANTED TO TAKE CARE OF LUNCH, SO I LEFT IT UP TO HIM.
HMPH
IT'S FROM A HIGH-END RESTAURANT. DON'T BE SHY! DIG IN.
THANK YOU.
W-WILL WE BE ABLE TO FINISH IT?
HEH
HA HA HA! THIS LOOKS AMAZ-ING!
HEH
Isn't this excessive?
DON'T WORRY.
MY KIDS CAN REALLY PUT IT AWAY.
Especially this one.
Huh?
CHOMP
Crab! Crab!♪
MUNCH MUNCH

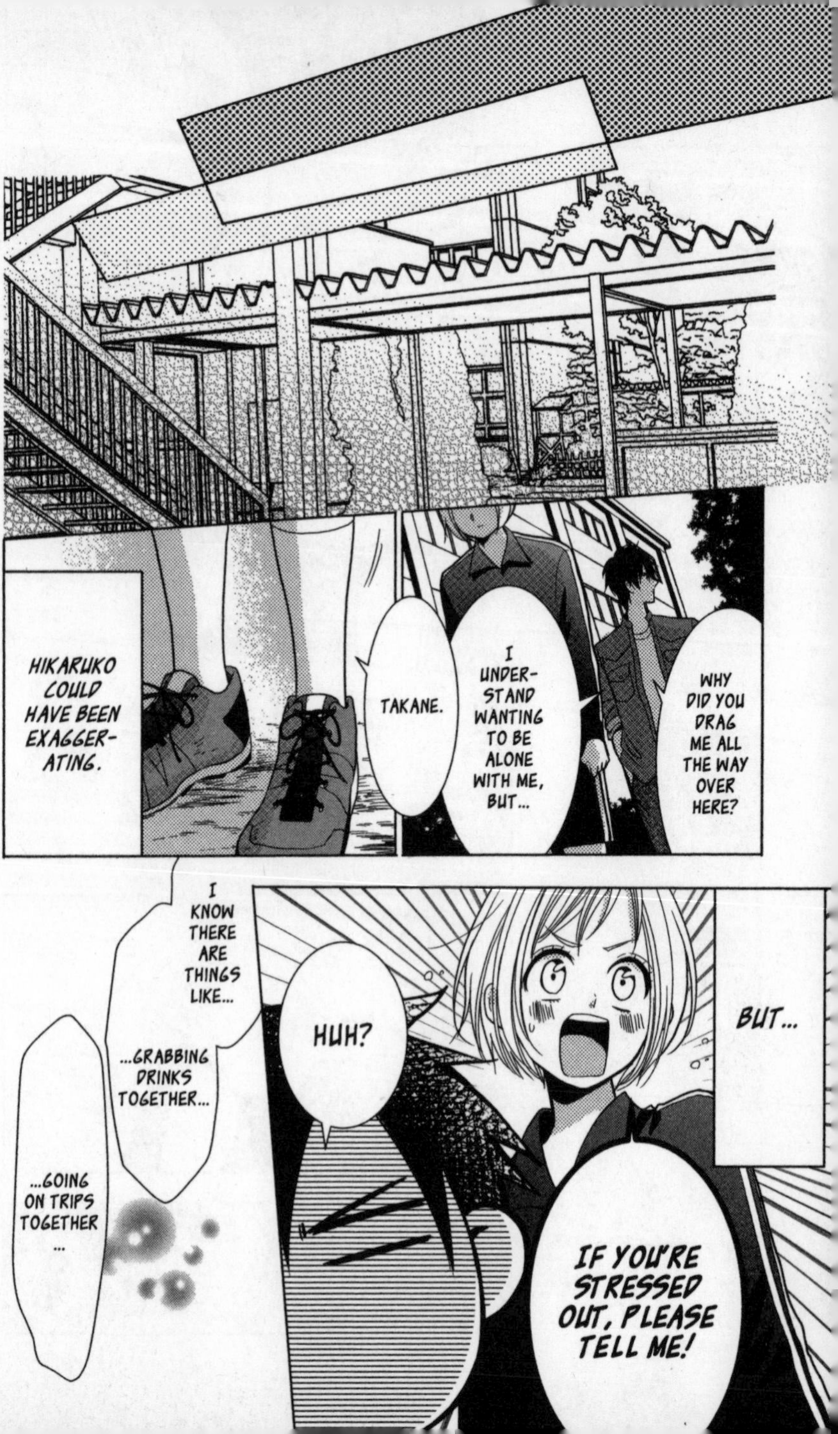
WHY DID YOU DRAG ME ALL THE WAY OVER HERE?
I UNDER-STAND WANTING TO BE ALONE WITH ME, BUT...
TAKANE.
HIKARUKO COULD HAVE BEEN EXAGGER-ATING.
BUT...
IF YOU'RE STRESSED OUT, PLEASE TELL ME!
HUH?
I KNOW THERE ARE THINGS LIKE...
...GRABBING DRINKS TOGETHER...
...GOING ON TRIPS TOGETHER ...

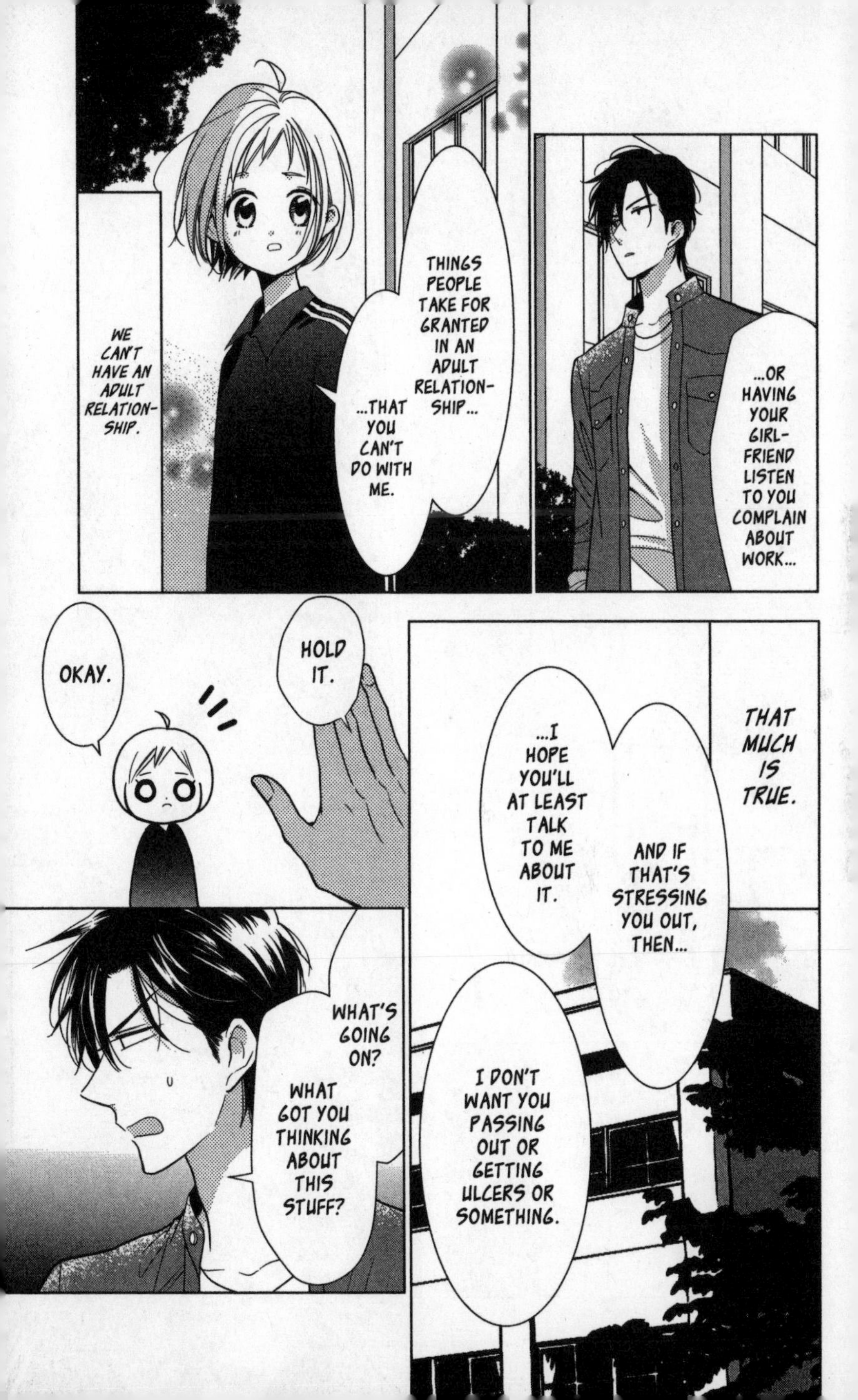
...OR HAVING YOUR GIRLFRIEND LISTEN TO YOU COMPLAIN ABOUT WORK...
THINGS PEOPLE TAKE FOR GRANTED IN AN ADULT RELATIONSHIP...
...THAT YOU CAN'T DO WITH ME.
WE CAN'T HAVE AN ADULT RELATIONSHIP.
THAT MUCH IS TRUE.
AND IF THAT'S STRESSING YOU OUT, THEN...
...I HOPE YOU'LL AT LEAST TALK TO ME ABOUT IT.
I DON'T WANT YOU PASSING OUT OR GETTING ULCERS OR SOMETHING.
HOLD IT.
OKAY.
WHAT'S GOING ON?
WHAT GOT YOU THINKING ABOUT THIS STUFF?

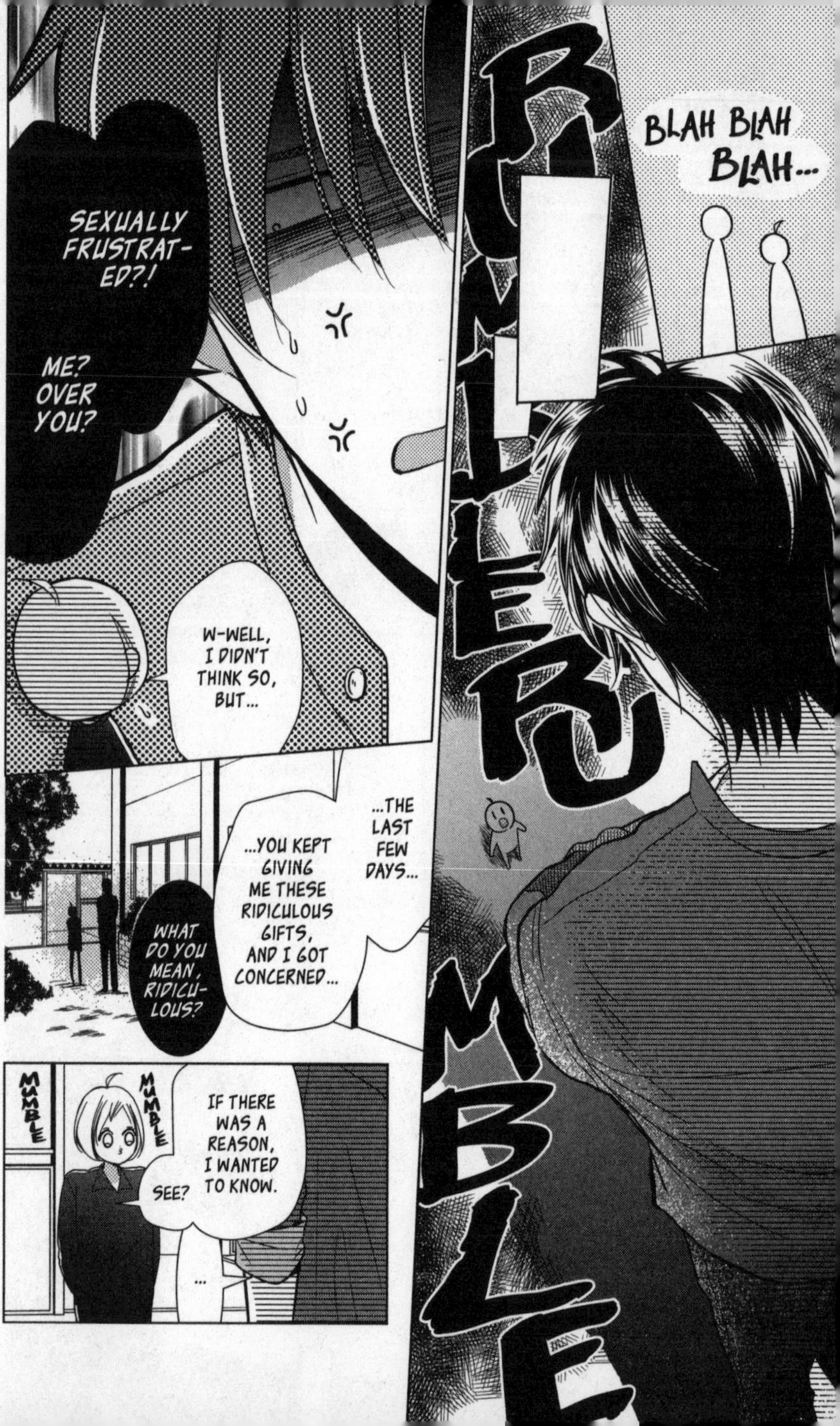
BLAH BLAH BLAH...
SEXUALLY FRUSTRAT-ED?!
ME? OVER YOU?
W-WELL, I DIDN'T THINK SO, BUT...
...THE LAST FEW DAYS...
...YOU KEPT GIVING ME THESE RIDICULOUS GIFTS, AND I GOT CONCERNED...
WHAT DO YOU MEAN, RIDICU-LOUS?
IF THERE WAS A REASON, I WANTED TO KNOW.
MUMBLE
SEE?
MUMBLE
...

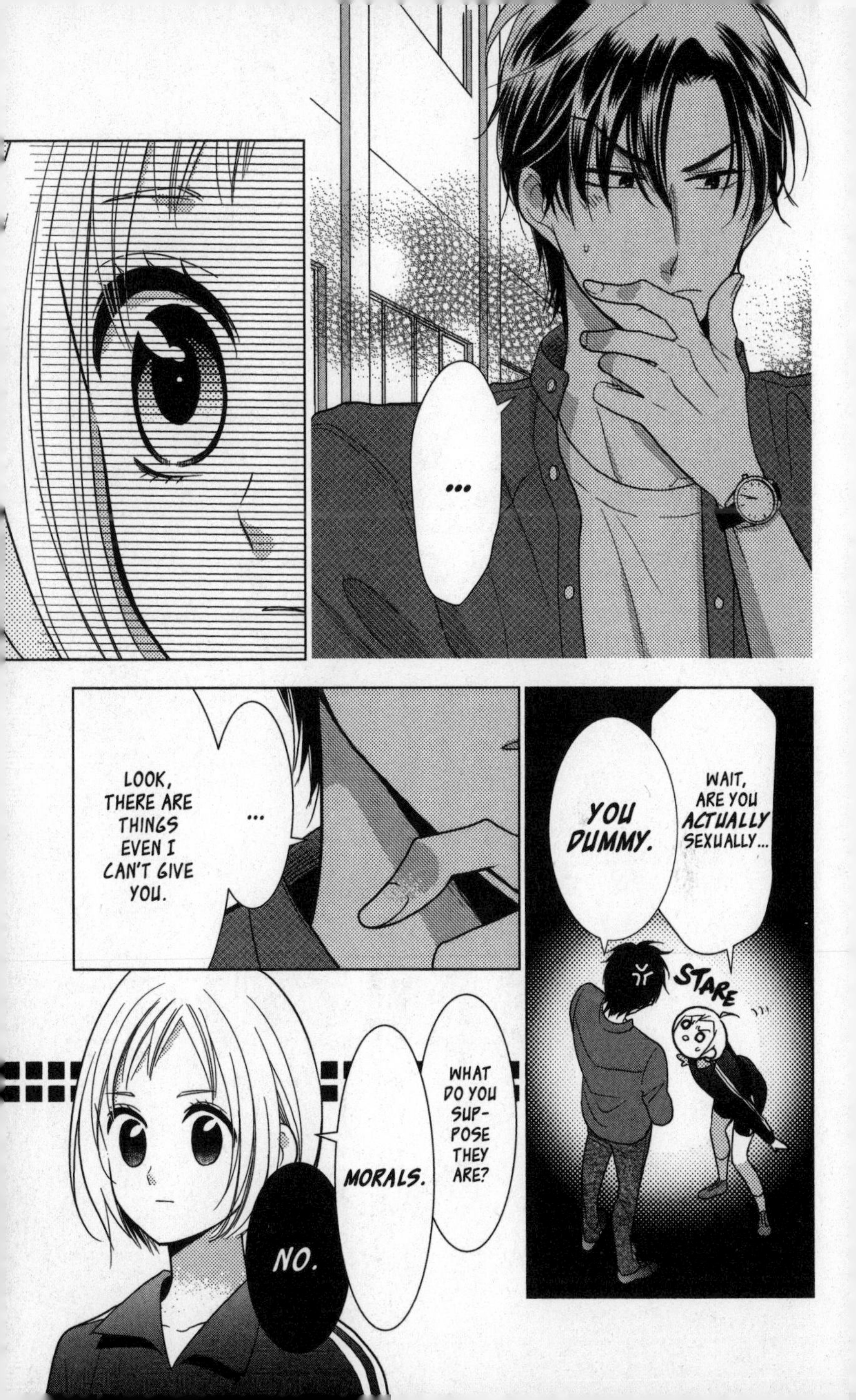
...
WAIT, ARE YOU ACTUALLY SEXUALLY...
YOU DUMMY.
STARE
...
LOOK, THERE ARE THINGS EVEN I CAN'T GIVE YOU.
WHAT DO YOU SUP-POSE THEY ARE?
MORALS.
NO.

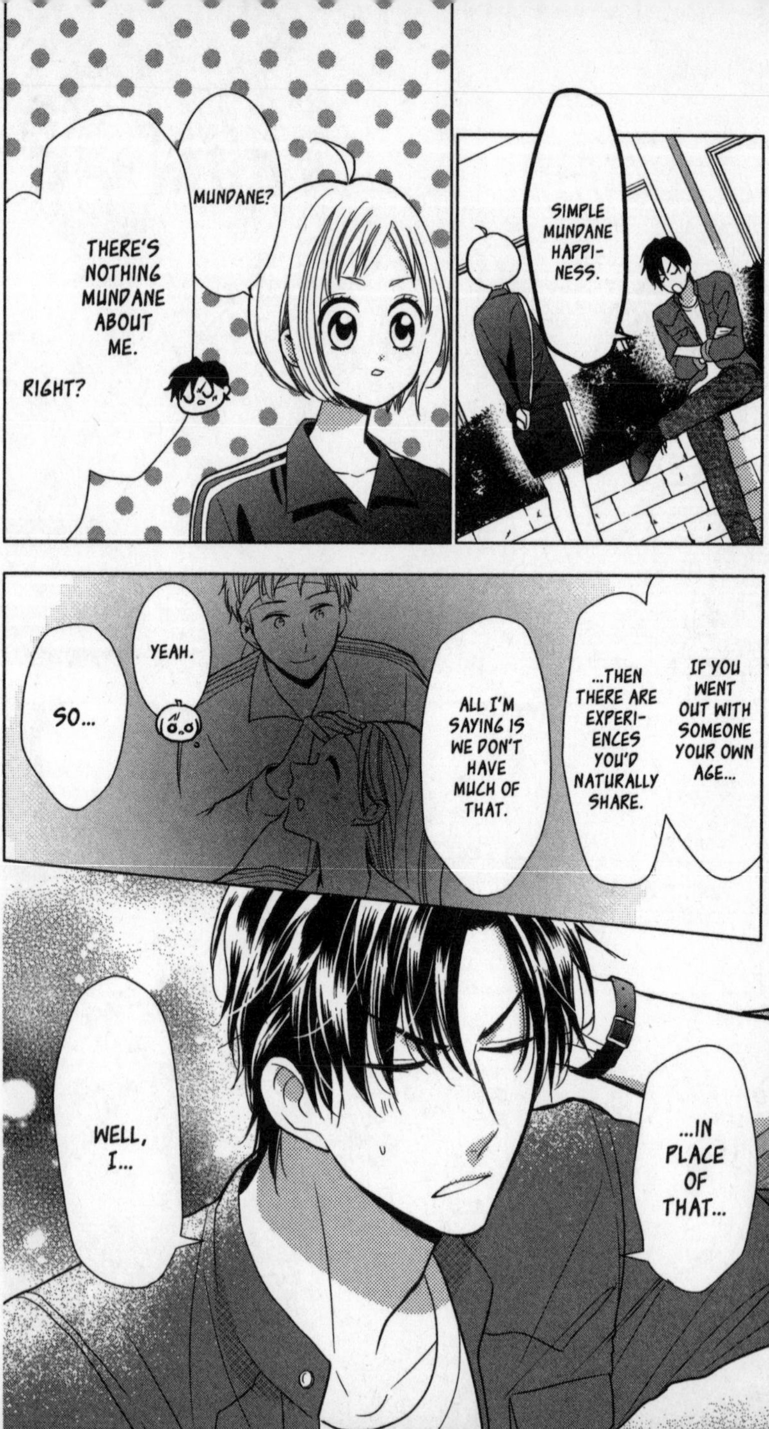
SIMPLE MUNDANE HAPPINESS.
MUNDANE?
THERE'S NOTHING MUNDANE ABOUT ME.
RIGHT?
IF YOU WENT OUT WITH SOMEONE YOUR OWN AGE...
...THEN THERE ARE EXPERIENCES YOU'D NATURALLY SHARE.
ALL I'M SAYING IS WE DON'T HAVE MUCH OF THAT.
YEAH.
SO...
...IN PLACE OF THAT...
WELL, I...

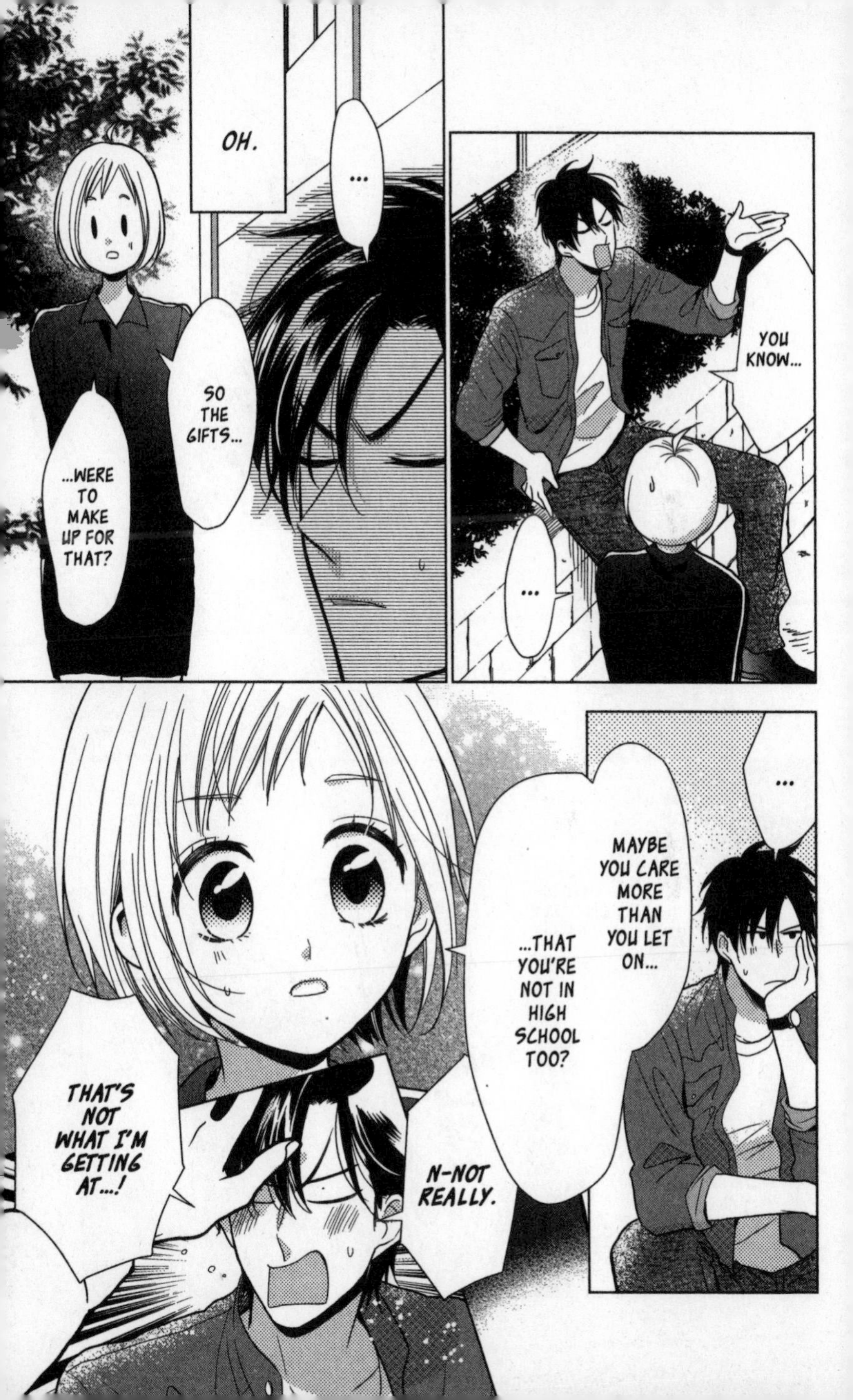
YOU KNOW...
...
OH.
...
SO THE GIFTS...
...WERE TO MAKE UP FOR THAT?
...
MAYBE YOU CARE MORE THAN YOU LET ON...
...THAT YOU'RE NOT IN HIGH SCHOOL TOO?
N-NOT REALLY.
THAT'S NOT WHAT I'M GETTING AT...!

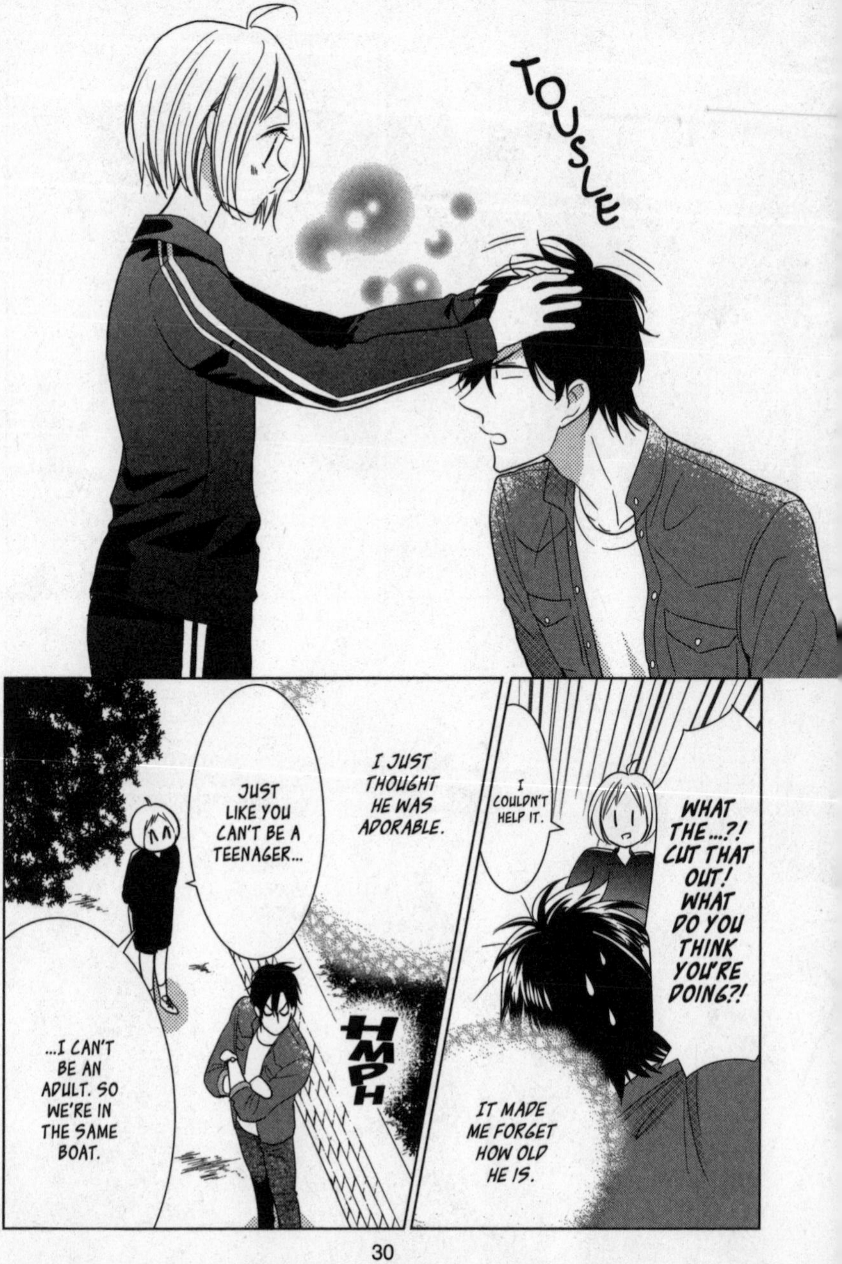
TOUSLE
WHAT THE...?! CUT THAT OUT! WHAT DO YOU THINK YOU'RE DOING?!
I COULDN'T HELP IT.
IT MADE ME FORGET HOW OLD HE IS.
I JUST THOUGHT HE WAS ADORABLE.
JUST LIKE YOU CAN'T BE A TEENAGER...
HMPH
...I CAN'T BE AN ADULT. SO WE'RE IN THE SAME BOAT.

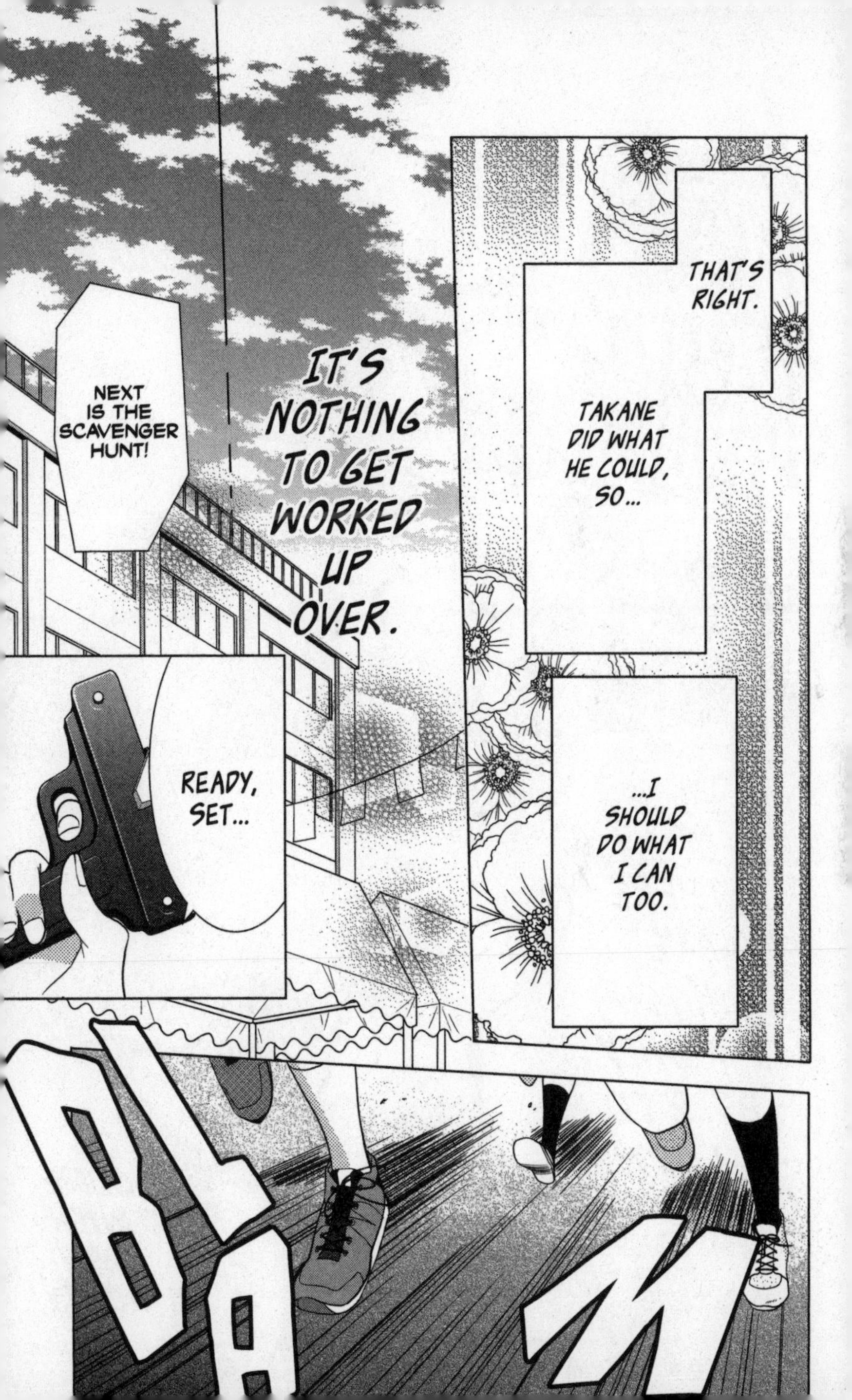
THAT'S RIGHT.
TAKANE DID WHAT HE COULD, SO...
...I SHOULD DO WHAT I CAN TOO.
IT'S NOTHING TO GET WORKED UP OVER.
NEXT IS THE SCAVENGER HUNT!
READY, SET...
BLAM

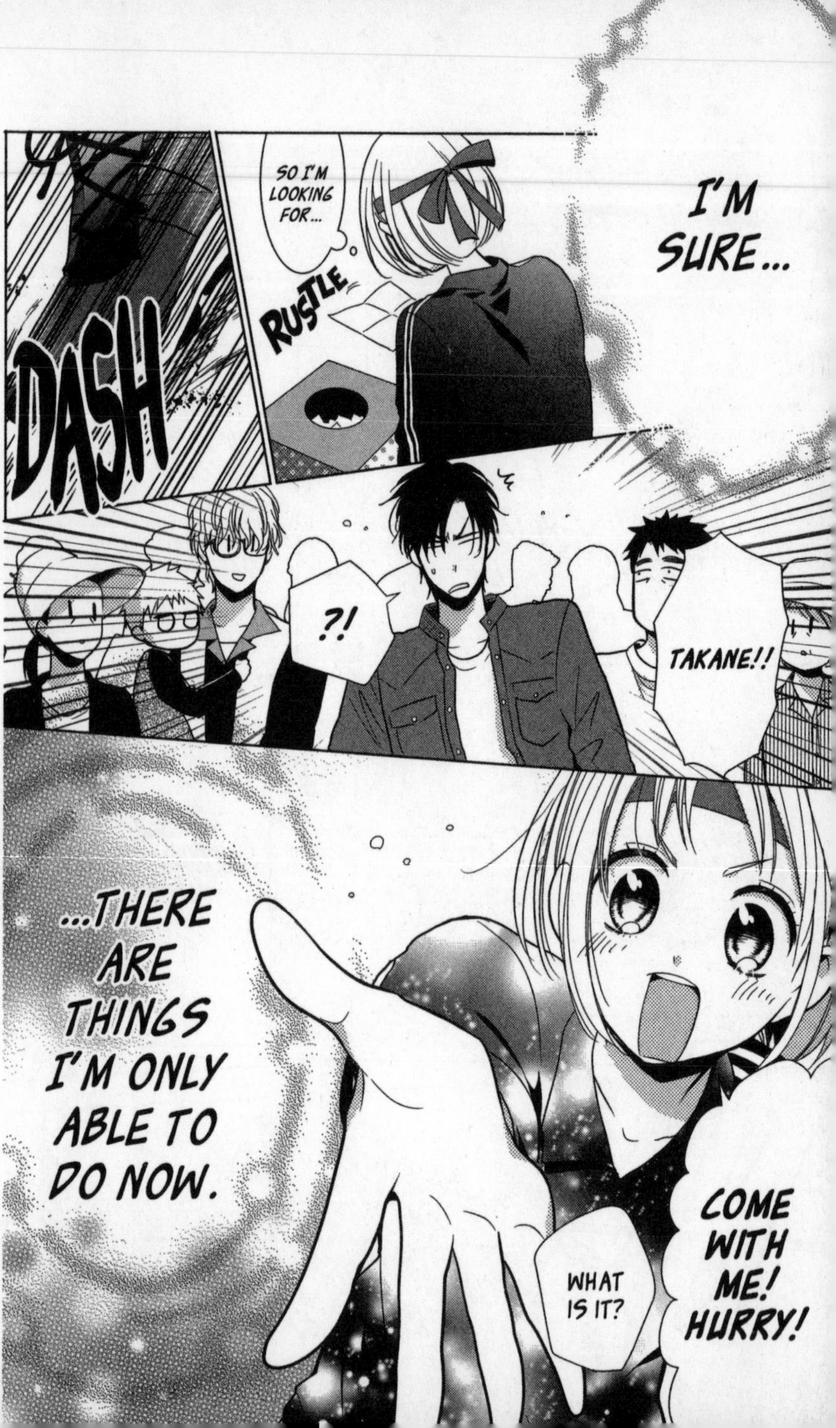
I'M SURE...
SO I'M LOOKING FOR...
RUSTLE
DASH
TAKANE!!
?!
COME WITH ME! HURRY!
WHAT IS IT?
...THERE ARE THINGS I'M ONLY ABLE TO DO NOW.

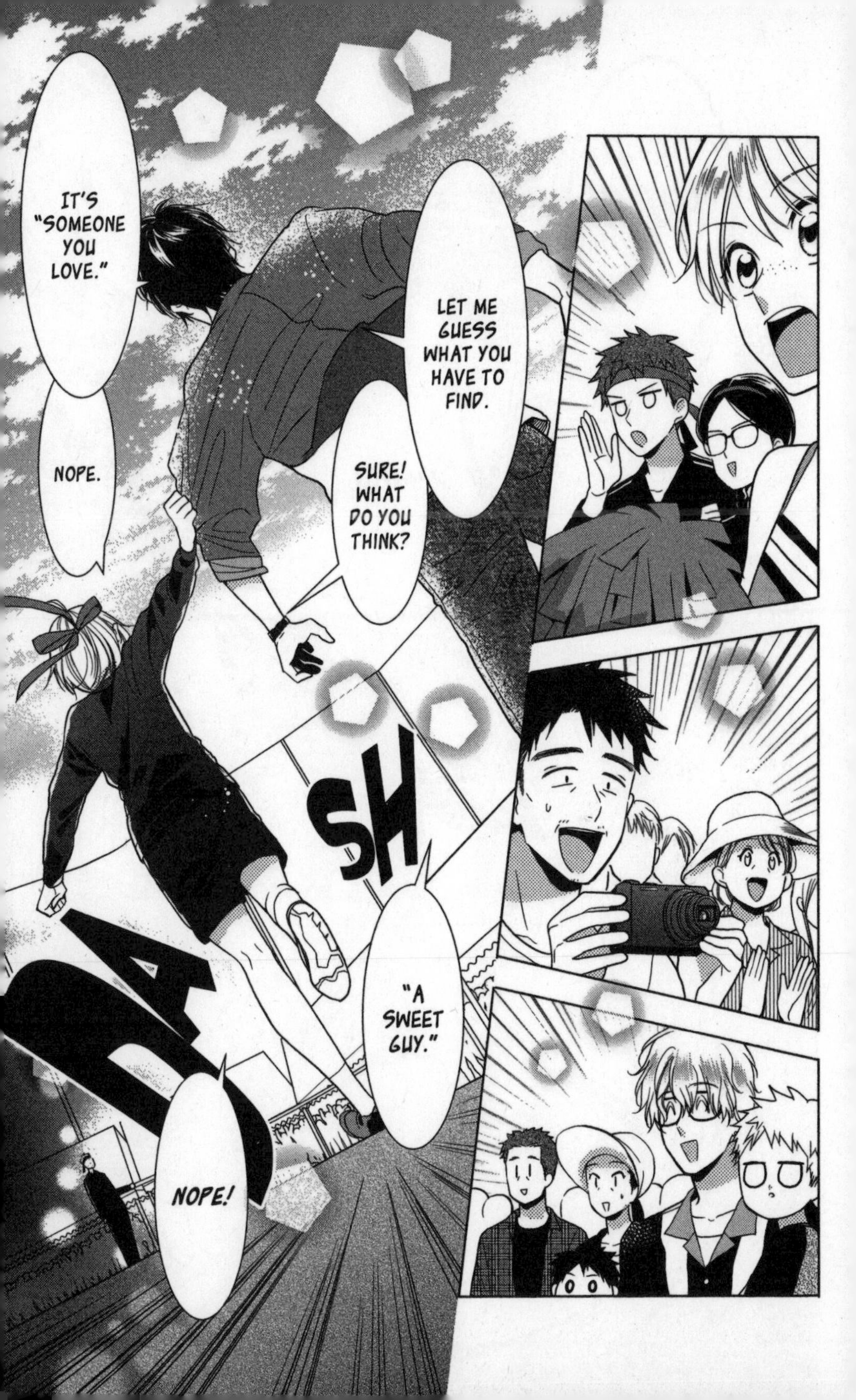
LET ME GUESS WHAT YOU HAVE TO FIND.
SURE! WHAT DO YOU THINK?
IT'S "SOMEONE YOU LOVE."
NOPE.
SH
"A SWEET GUY."
NOPE!

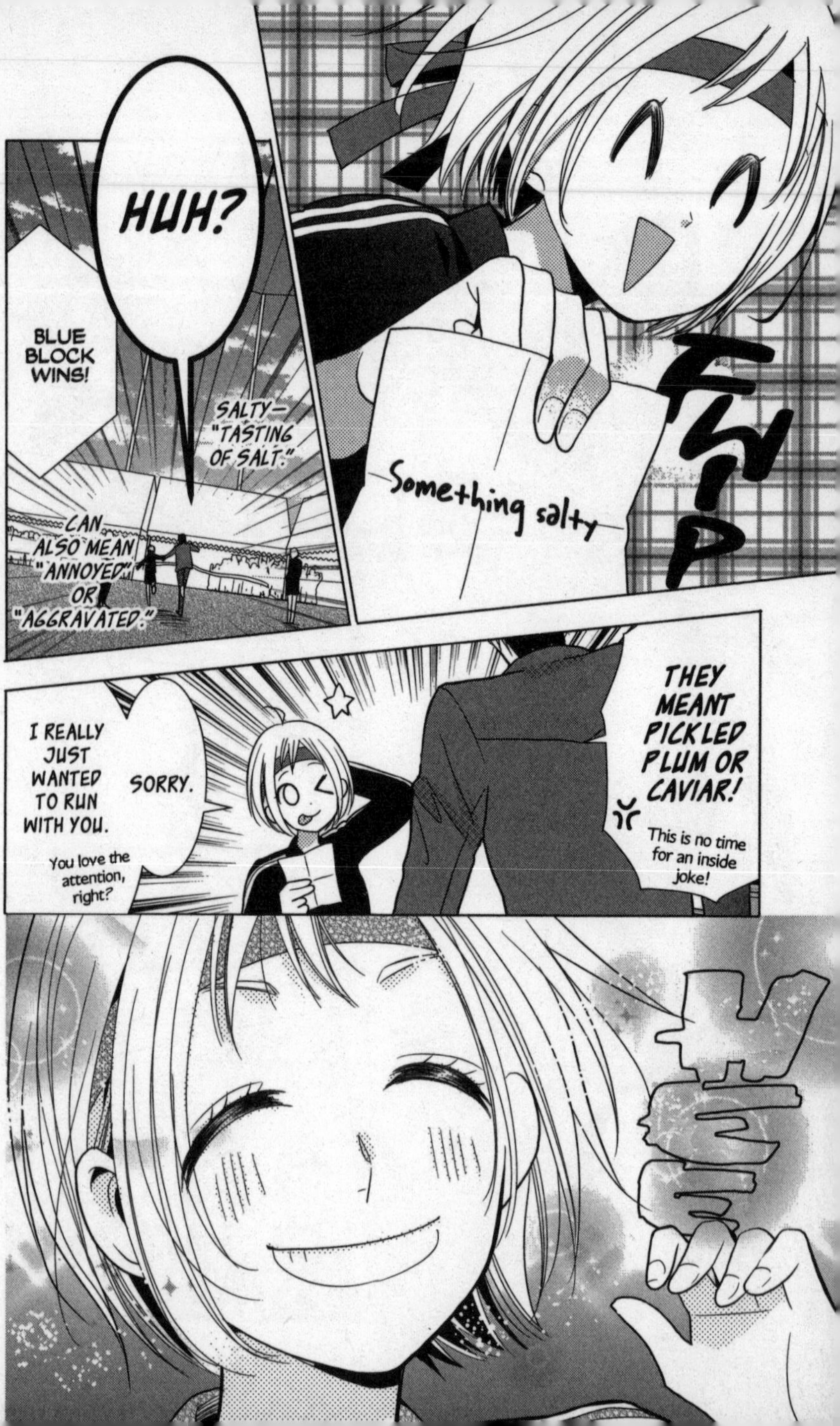
Something salty
FWIP
HUH?
SALTY—"TASTING OF SALT." CAN ALSO MEAN "ANNOYED" OR "AGGRAVATED."
BLUE BLOCK WINS!
THEY MEANT PICKLED PLUM OR CAVIAR!
This is no time for an inside joke!
SORRY.
I REALLY JUST WANTED TO RUN WITH YOU.
You love the attention, right?

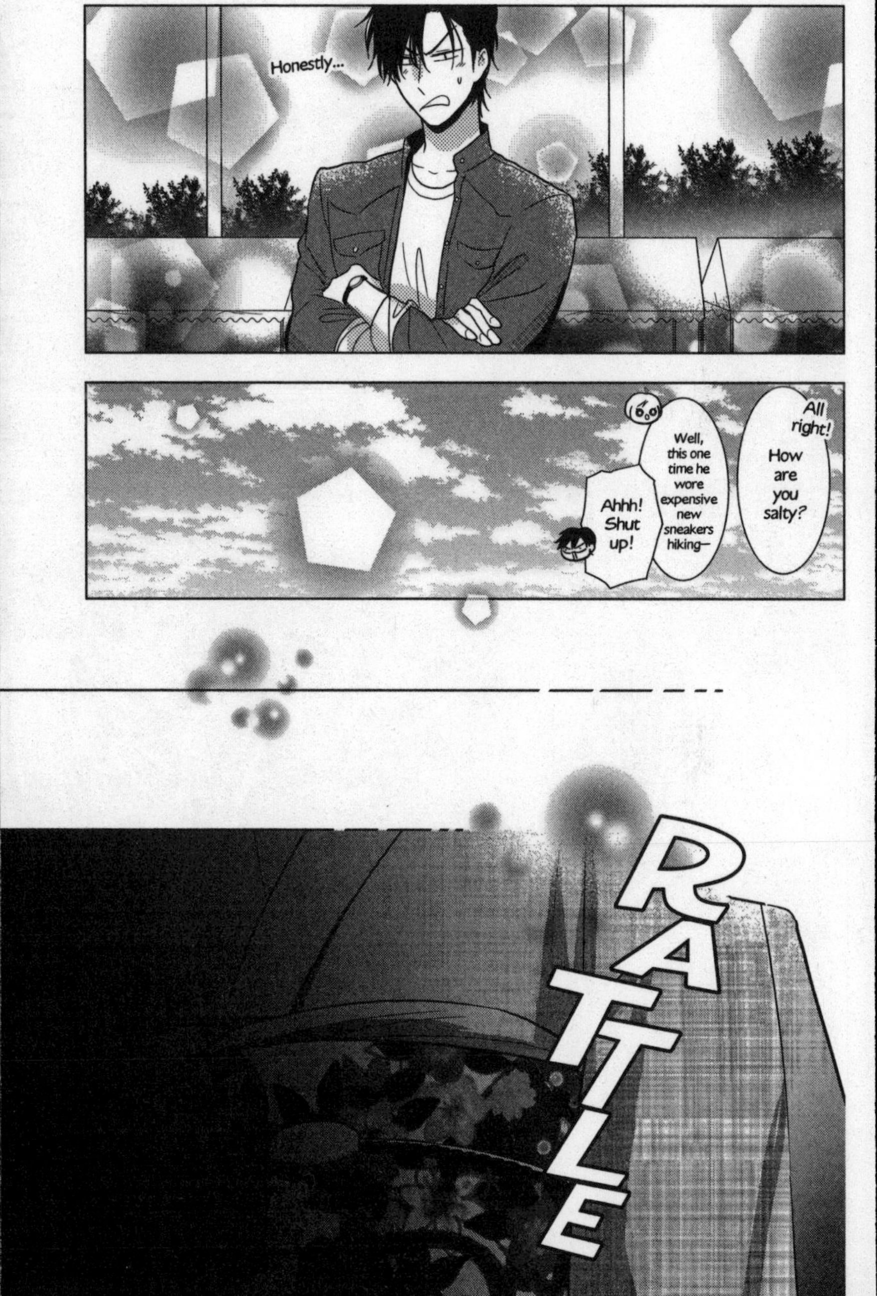
Honestly...
All right! How are you salty?
Well, this one time he wore expensive new sneakers hiking—
Ahhh! Shut up!
RATTLE

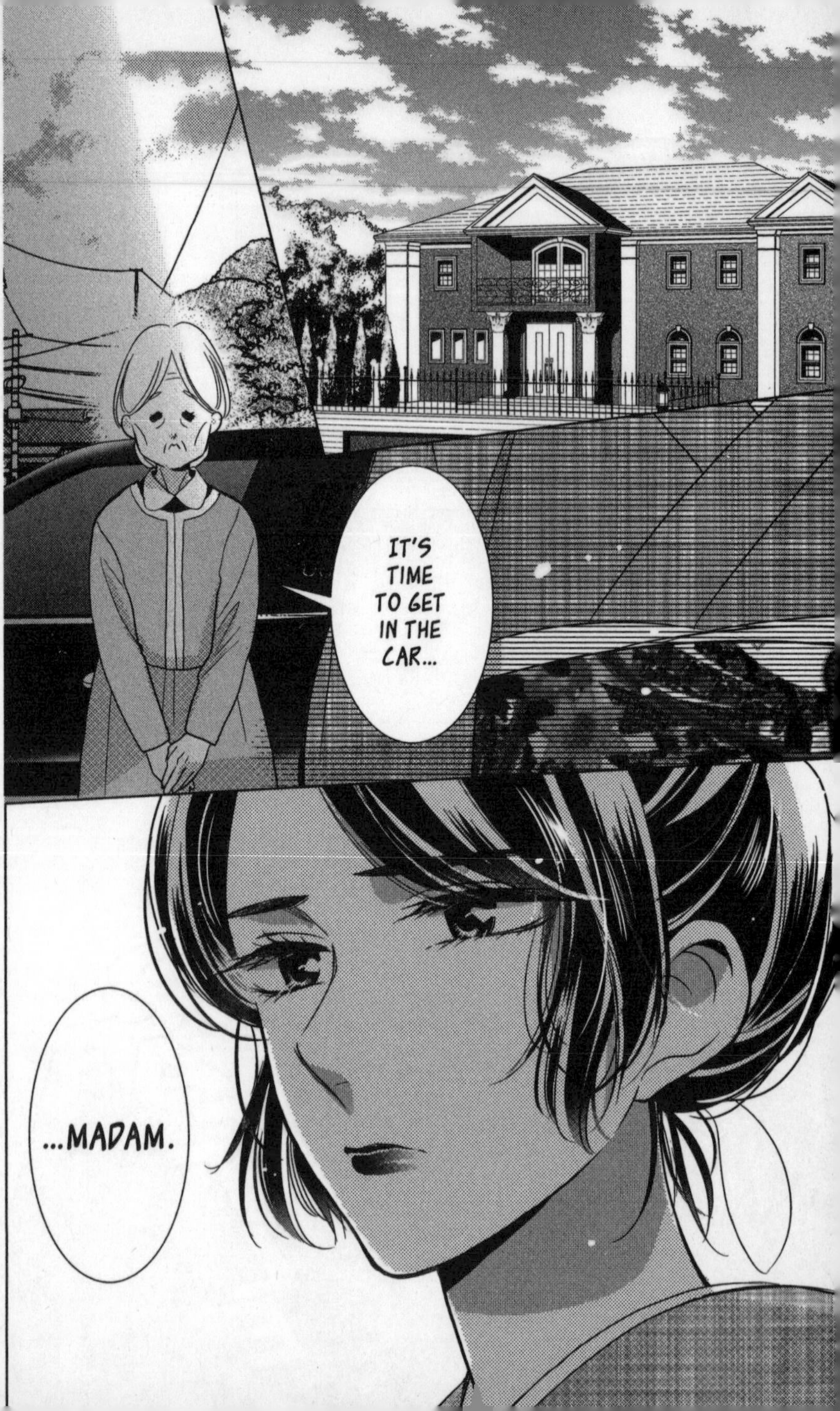
IT'S TIME TO GET IN THE CAR...
...MADAM.

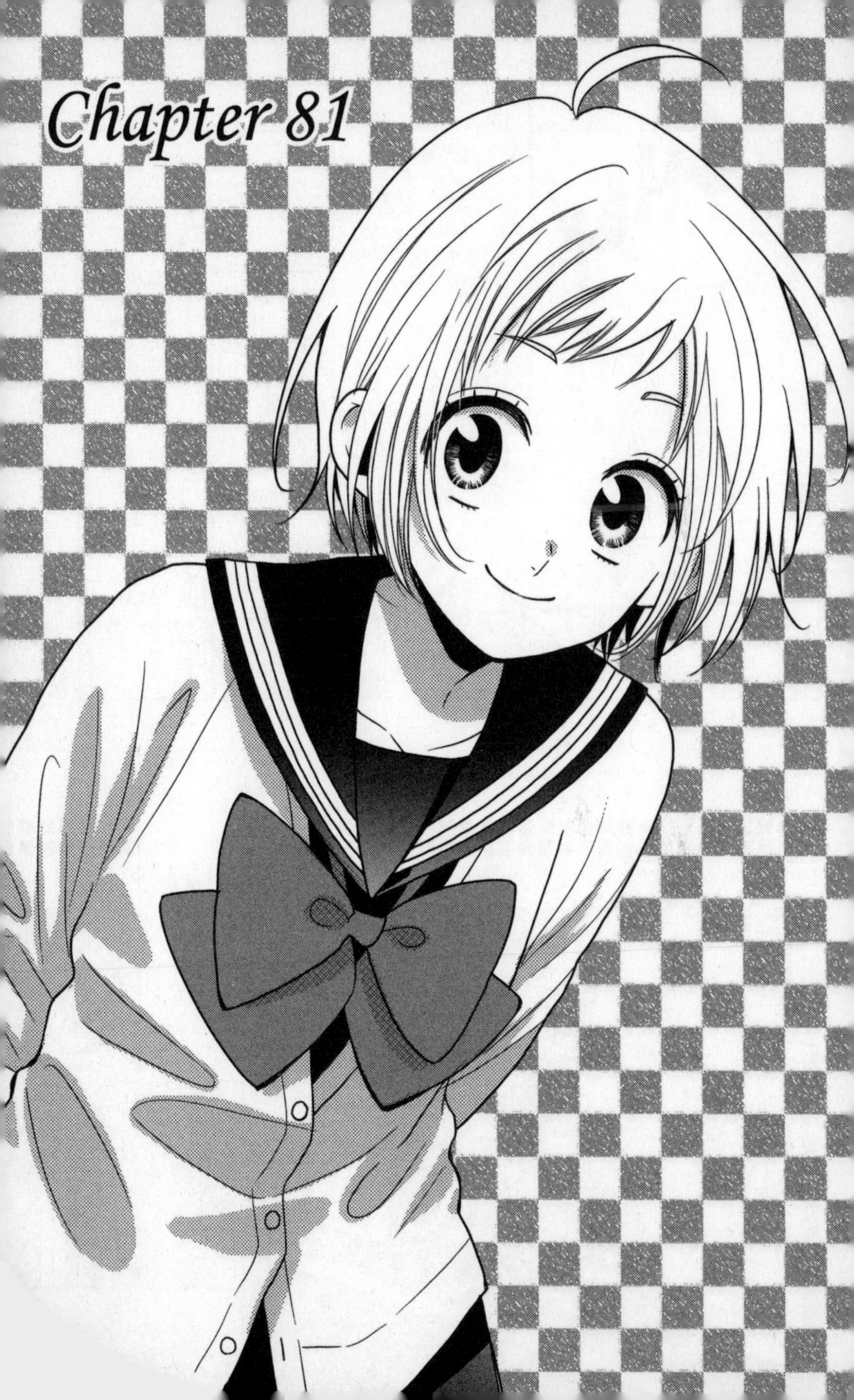
Chapter 81

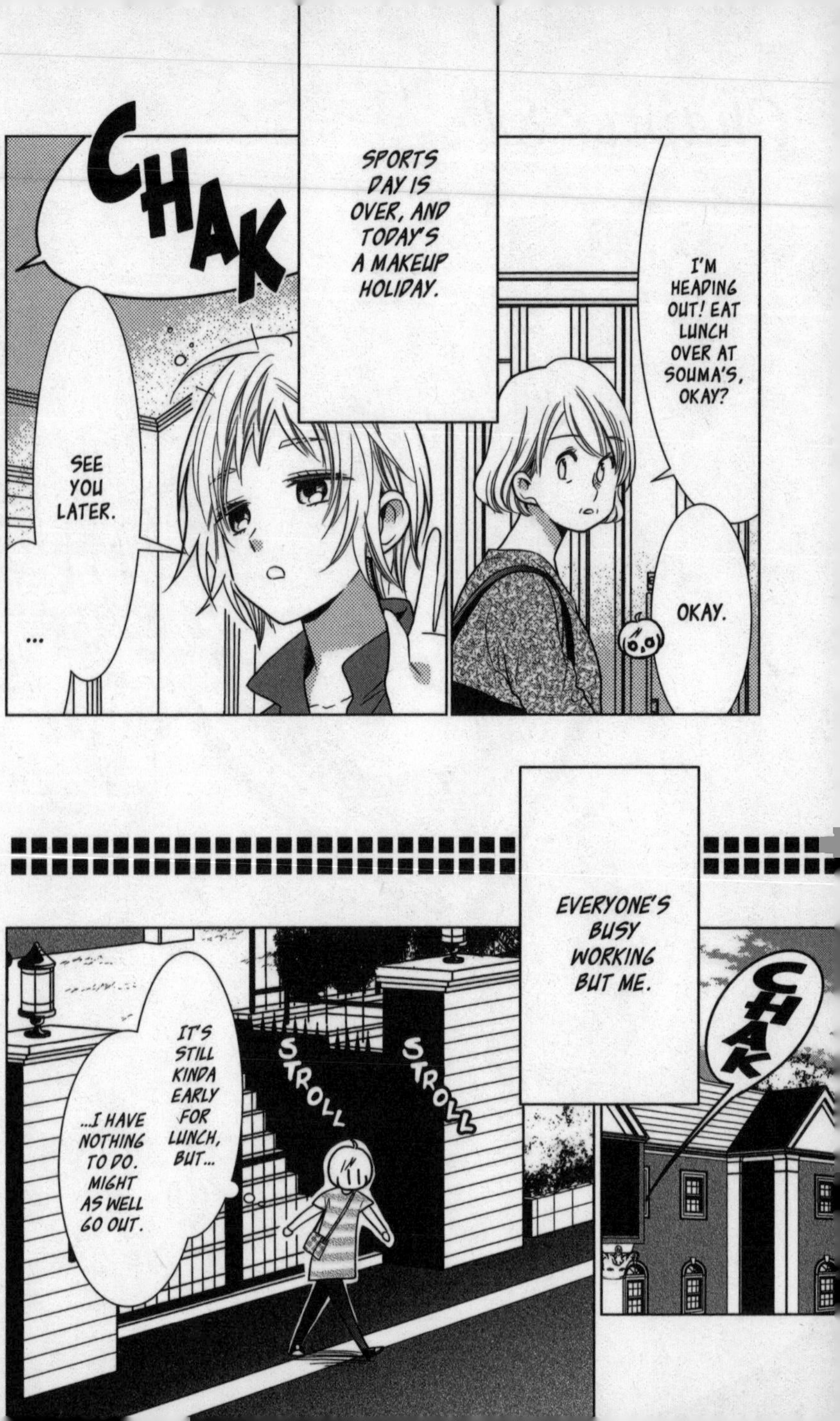
SPORTS DAY IS OVER, AND TODAY'S A MAKEUP HOLIDAY.
I'M HEADING OUT! EAT LUNCH OVER AT SOUMA'S, OKAY?
OKAY.
CHAK
SEE YOU LATER.
...
EVERYONE'S BUSY WORKING BUT ME.
CHAK
STROLL
STROLL
IT'S STILL KINDA EARLY FOR LUNCH, BUT...
...I HAVE NOTHING TO DO. MIGHT AS WELL GO OUT.

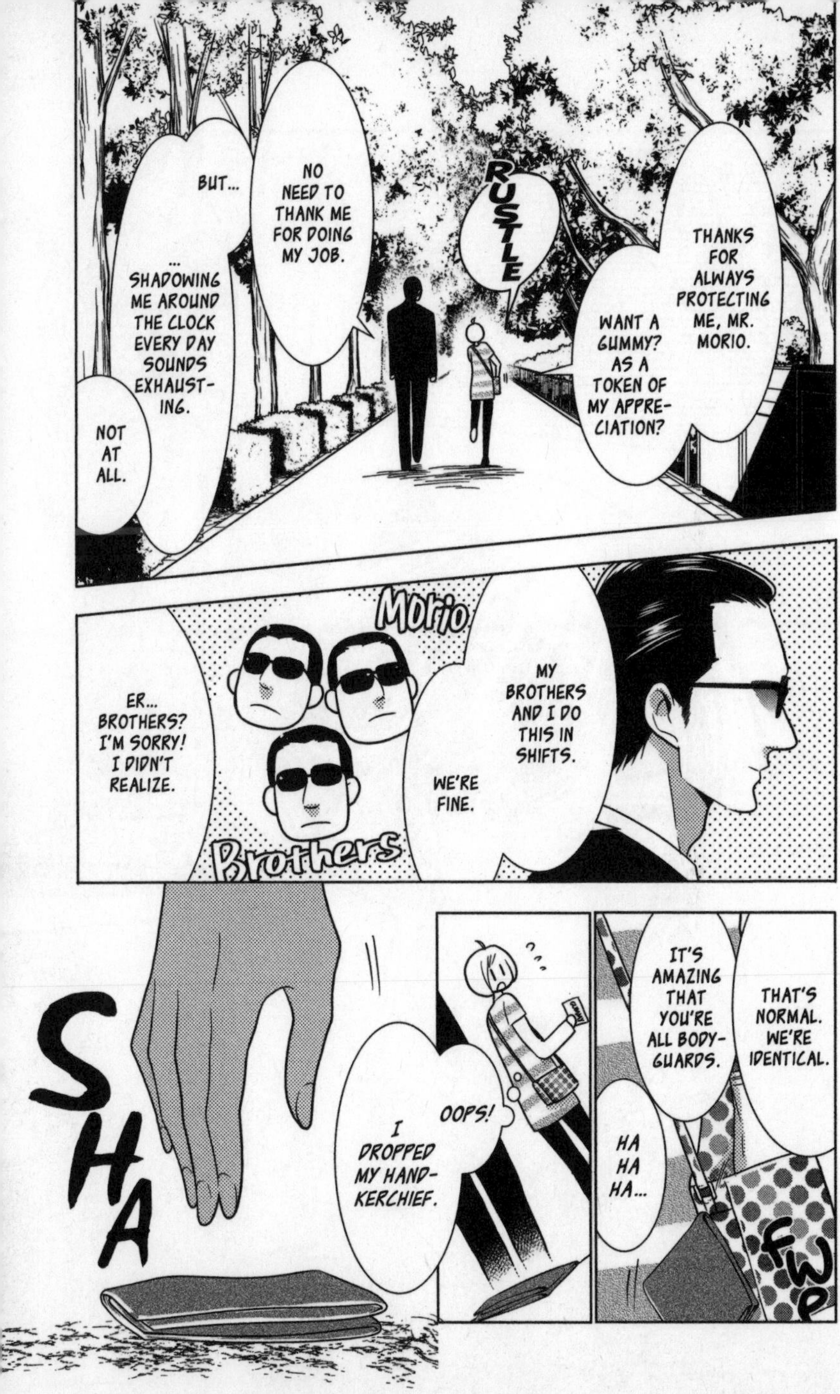
THANKS FOR ALWAYS PROTECTING ME, MR. MORIO.
WANT A GUMMY? AS A TOKEN OF MY APPRECIATION?
RUSTLE
NO NEED TO THANK ME FOR DOING MY JOB.
BUT...
...SHADOWING ME AROUND THE CLOCK EVERY DAY SOUNDS EXHAUSTING.
NOT AT ALL.
MY BROTHERS AND I DO THIS IN SHIFTS.
WE'RE FINE.
Morio
Brothers
ER... BROTHERS? I'M SORRY! I DIDN'T REALIZE.
THAT'S NORMAL. WE'RE IDENTICAL.
IT'S AMAZING THAT YOU'RE ALL BODYGUARDS.
HA HA HA...
FWP
OOPS!
I DROPPED MY HANDKERCHIEF.
SHA

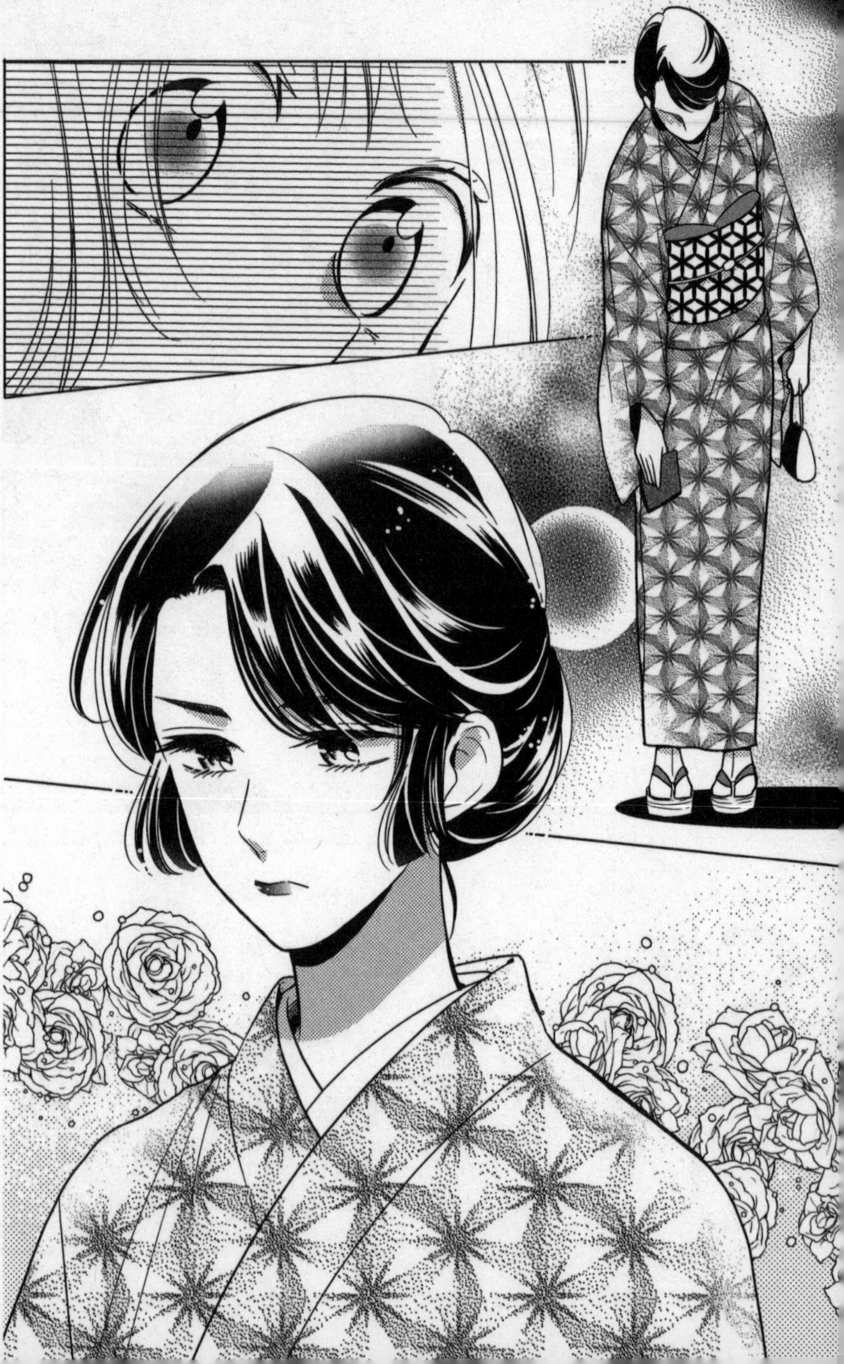

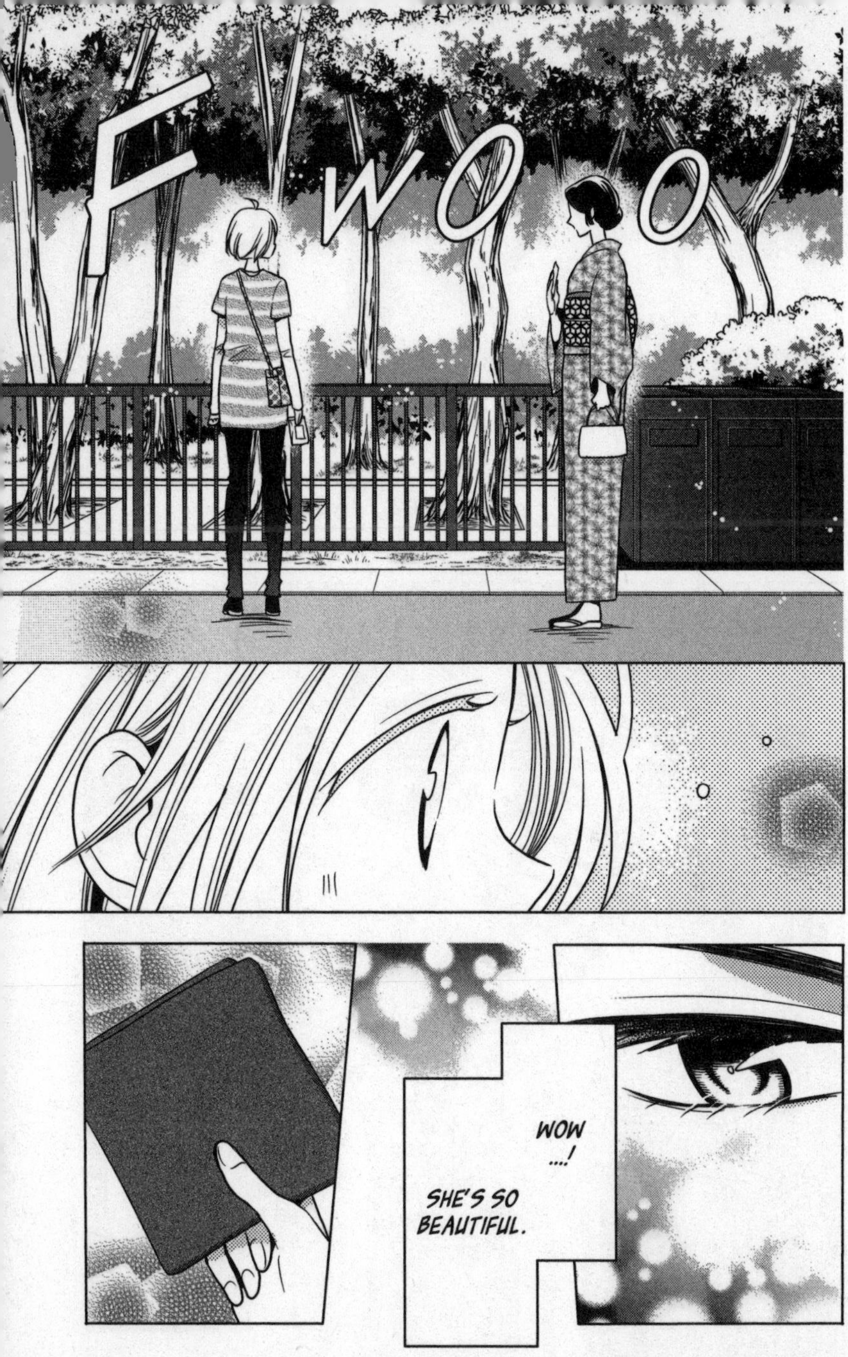
FWOO
WOW ...!
SHE'S SO BEAUTIFUL.

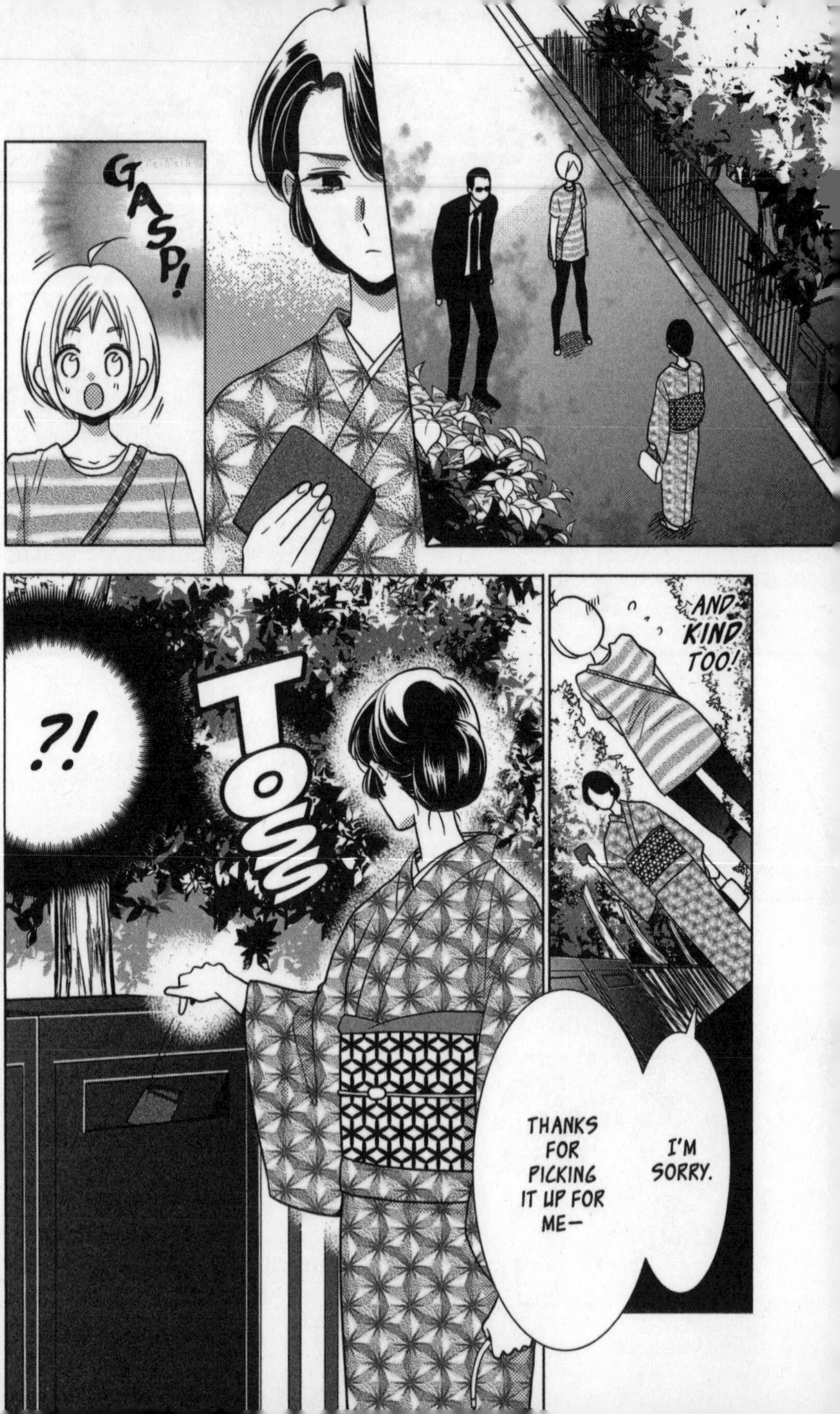
GASP!
AND KIND TOO!
?!
TOSS
I'M SORRY.
THANKS FOR PICKING IT UP FOR ME—

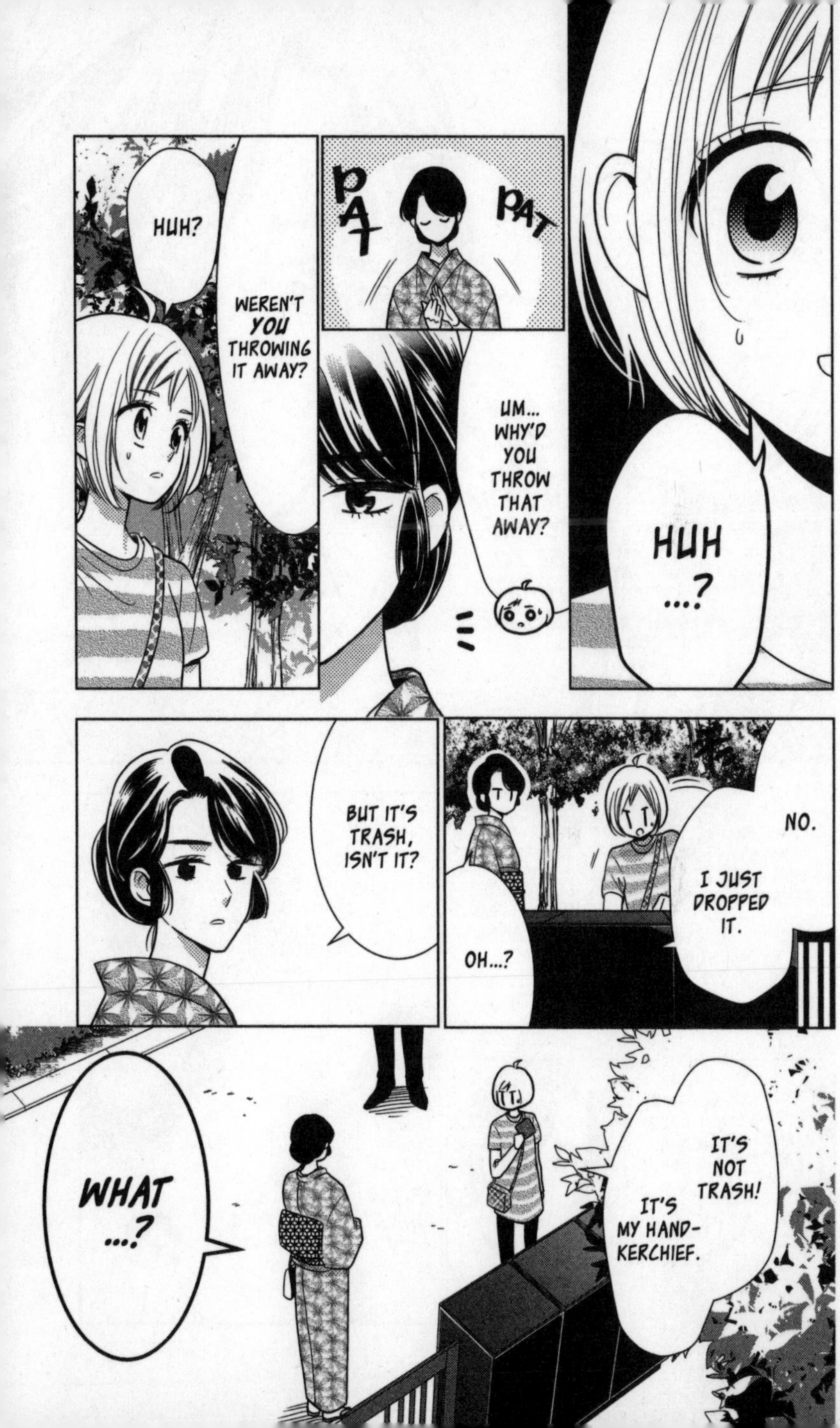
HUH ...?
PAT
PAT
UM... WHY'D YOU THROW THAT AWAY?
HUH?
WEREN'T YOU THROWING IT AWAY?
NO.
I JUST DROPPED IT.
OH...?
BUT IT'S TRASH, ISN'T IT?
IT'S NOT TRASH!
IT'S MY HAND-KERCHIEF.
WHAT ...?

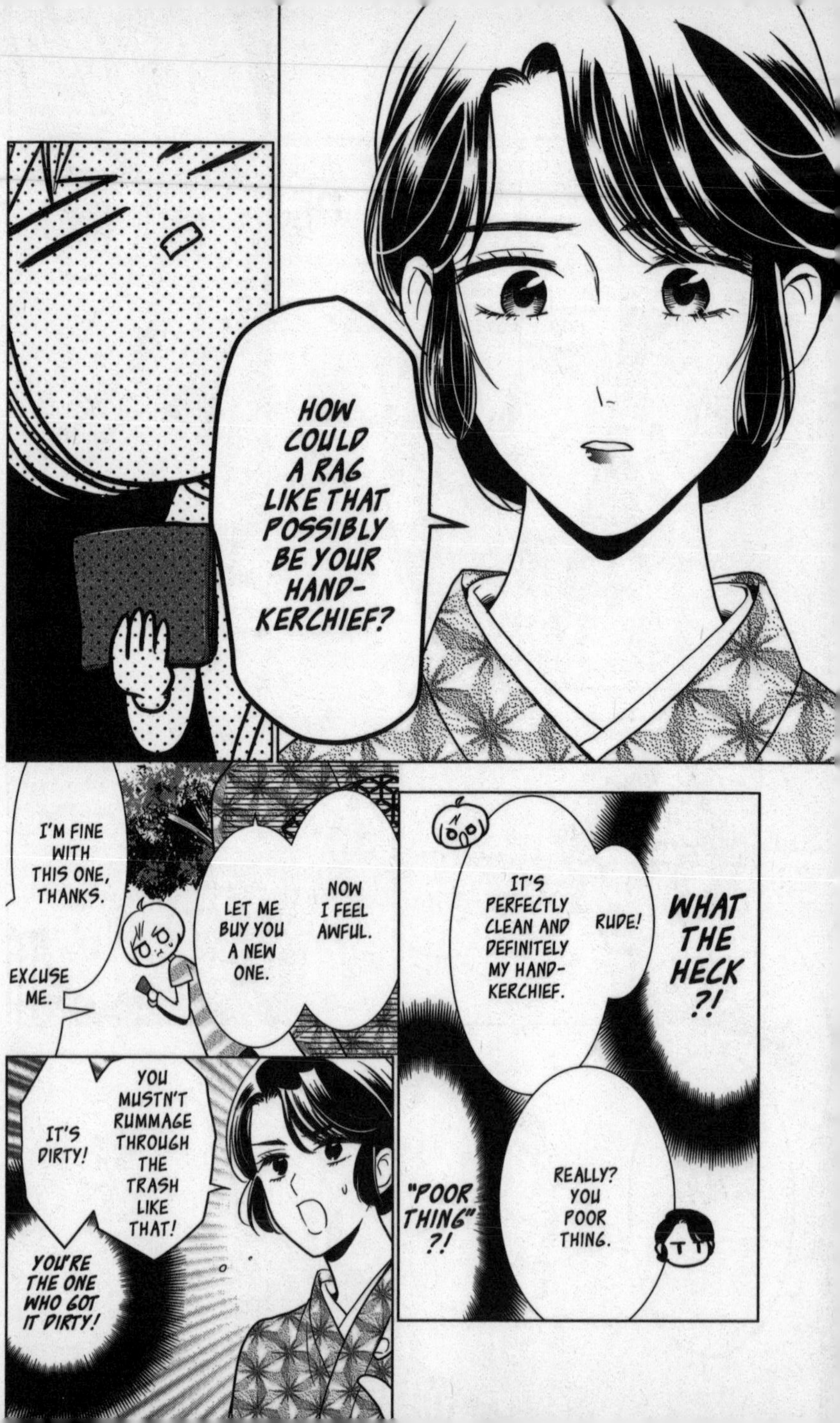
HOW COULD A RAG LIKE THAT POSSIBLY BE YOUR HAND-KERCHIEF?
WHAT THE HECK ?!
RUDE!
IT'S PERFECTLY CLEAN AND DEFINITELY MY HAND-KERCHIEF.
REALLY? YOU POOR THING.
"POOR THING" ?!
NOW I FEEL AWFUL.
LET ME BUY YOU A NEW ONE.
I'M FINE WITH THIS ONE, THANKS.
EXCUSE ME.
YOU MUSTN'T RUMMAGE THROUGH THE TRASH LIKE THAT!
IT'S DIRTY!
YOU'RE THE ONE WHO GOT IT DIRTY!

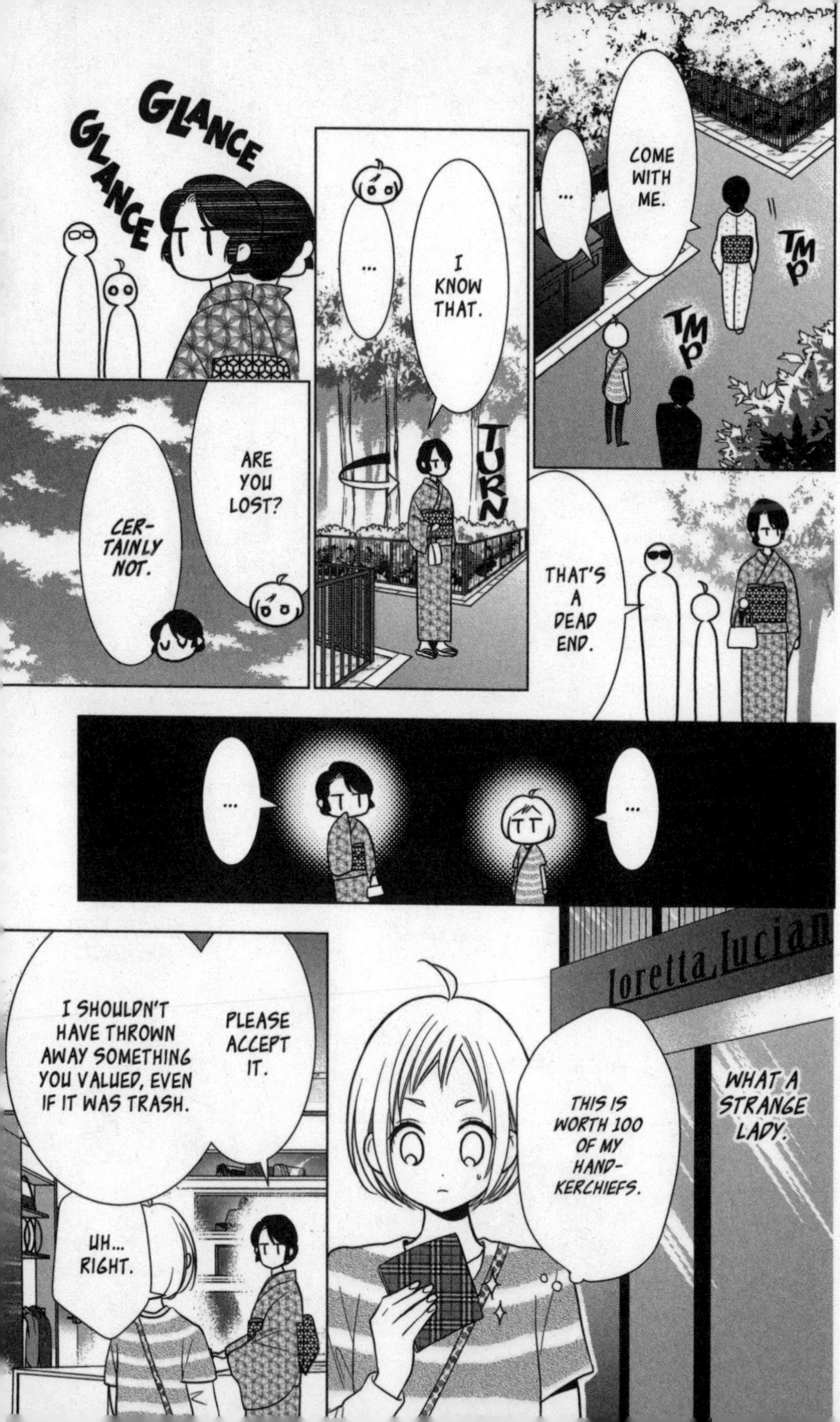
GLANCE
GLANCE
ARE YOU LOST?
CERTAINLY NOT.
THAT'S A DEAD END.
TURN
I KNOW THAT.
...
COME WITH ME.
...
TMP
TMP
...
...
I SHOULDN'T HAVE THROWN AWAY SOMETHING YOU VALUED, EVEN IF IT WAS TRASH.
PLEASE ACCEPT IT.
UH... RIGHT.
loretta lucian
THIS IS WORTH 100 OF MY HANDKERCHIEFS.
WHAT A STRANGE LADY.

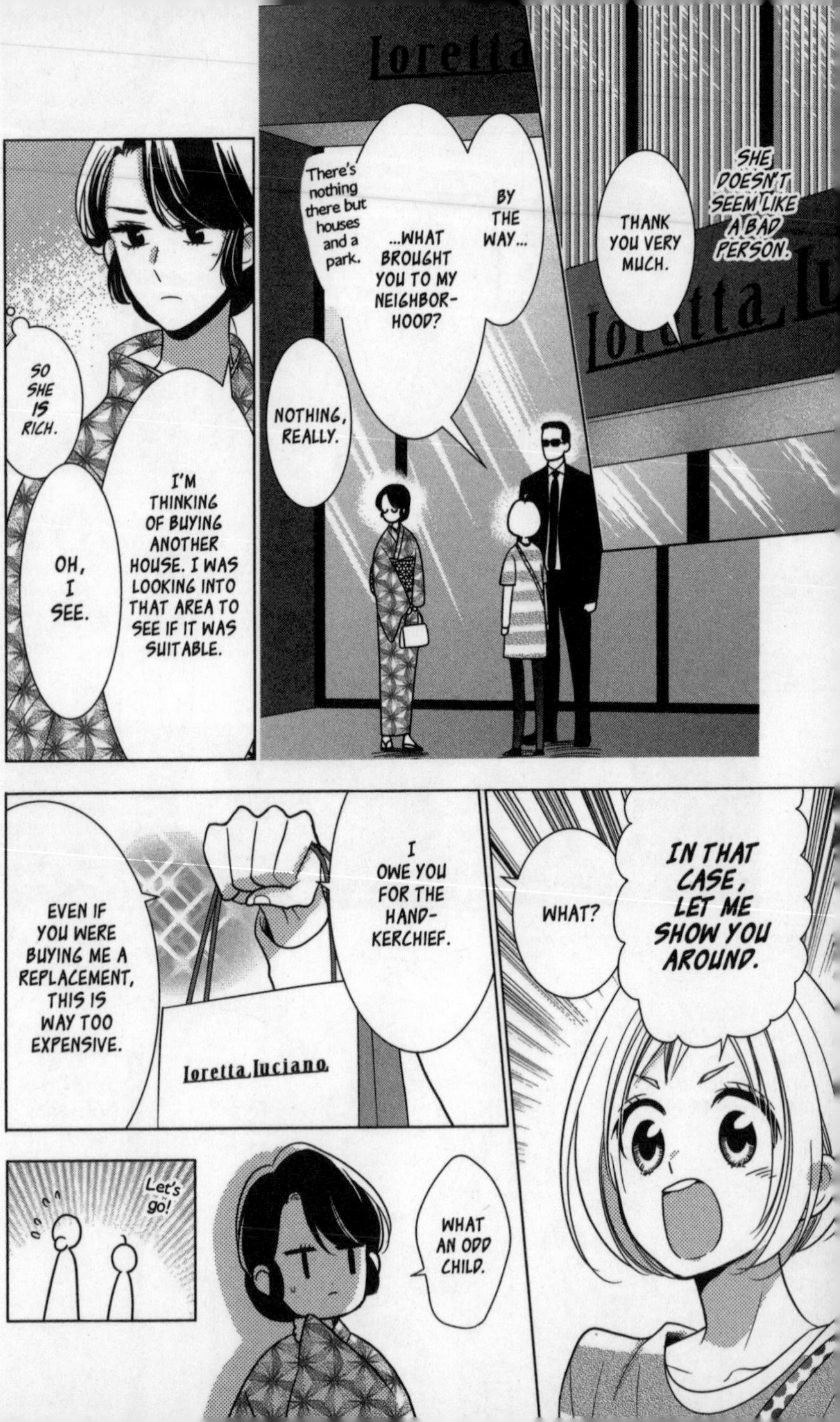

loretta
SHE DOESN'T SEEM LIKE A BAD PERSON.
THANK YOU VERY MUCH.
loretta lu
BY THE WAY...
...WHAT BROUGHT YOU TO MY NEIGHBOR-HOOD?
There's nothing there but houses and a park.
NOTHING, REALLY.
I'M THINKING OF BUYING ANOTHER HOUSE. I WAS LOOKING INTO THAT AREA TO SEE IF IT WAS SUITABLE.
OH, I SEE.
SO SHE IS RICH.
IN THAT CASE, LET ME SHOW YOU AROUND.
WHAT?
I OWE YOU FOR THE HAND-KERCHIEF.
EVEN IF YOU WERE BUYING ME A REPLACEMENT, THIS IS WAY TOO EXPENSIVE.
loretta luciano
WHAT AN ODD CHILD.
Let's go!

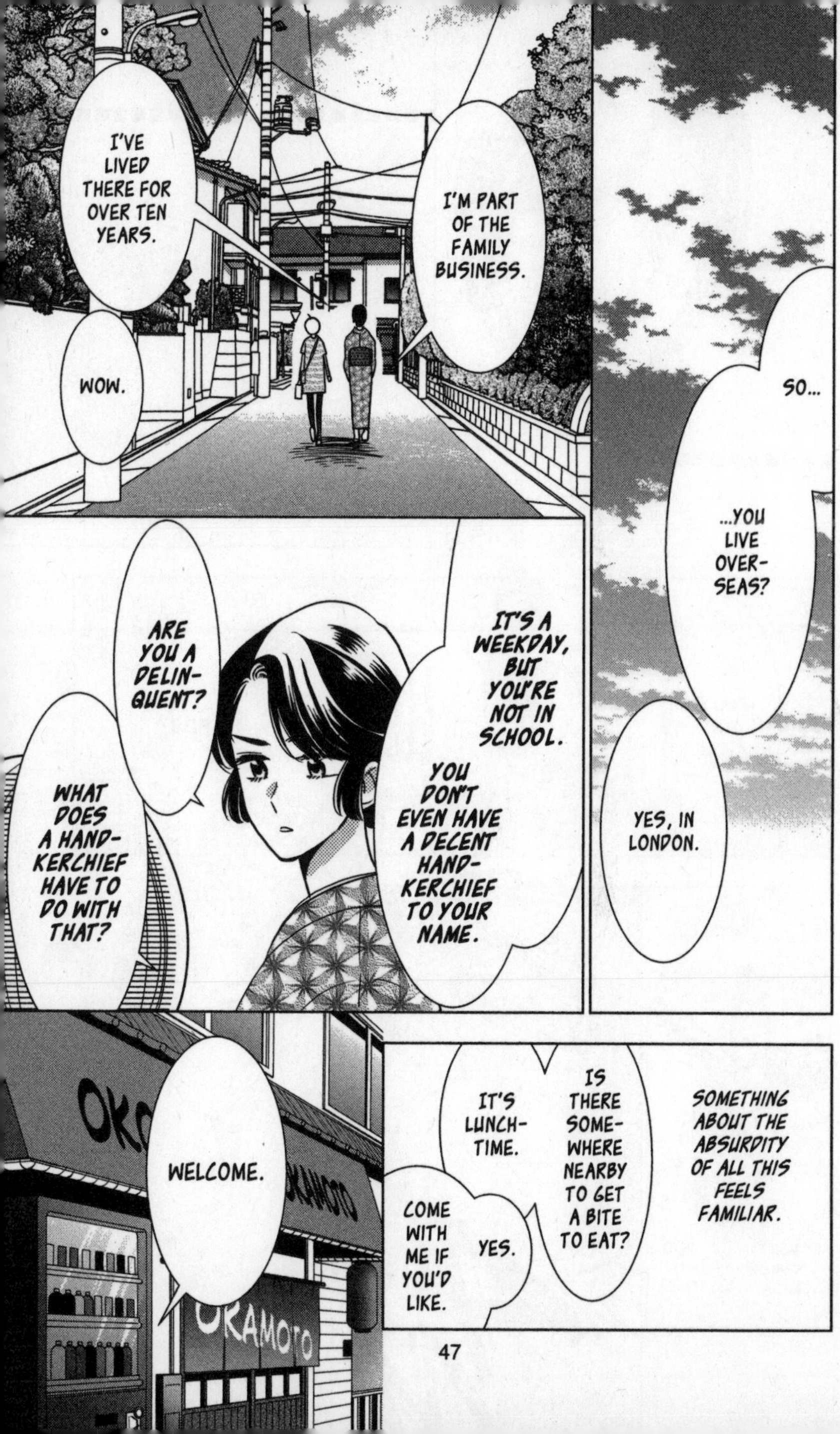
SO...
...YOU LIVE OVER-SEAS?
YES, IN LONDON.
I'M PART OF THE FAMILY BUSINESS.
I'VE LIVED THERE FOR OVER TEN YEARS.
WOW.
IT'S A WEEKDAY, BUT YOU'RE NOT IN SCHOOL.
YOU DON'T EVEN HAVE A DECENT HAND-KERCHIEF TO YOUR NAME.
ARE YOU A DELIN-QUENT?
WHAT DOES A HAND-KERCHIEF HAVE TO DO WITH THAT?
SOMETHING ABOUT THE ABSURDITY OF ALL THIS FEELS FAMILIAR.
IS THERE SOME-WHERE NEARBY TO GET A BITE TO EAT?
IT'S LUNCH-TIME.
YES.
COME WITH ME IF YOU'D LIKE.
WELCOME.

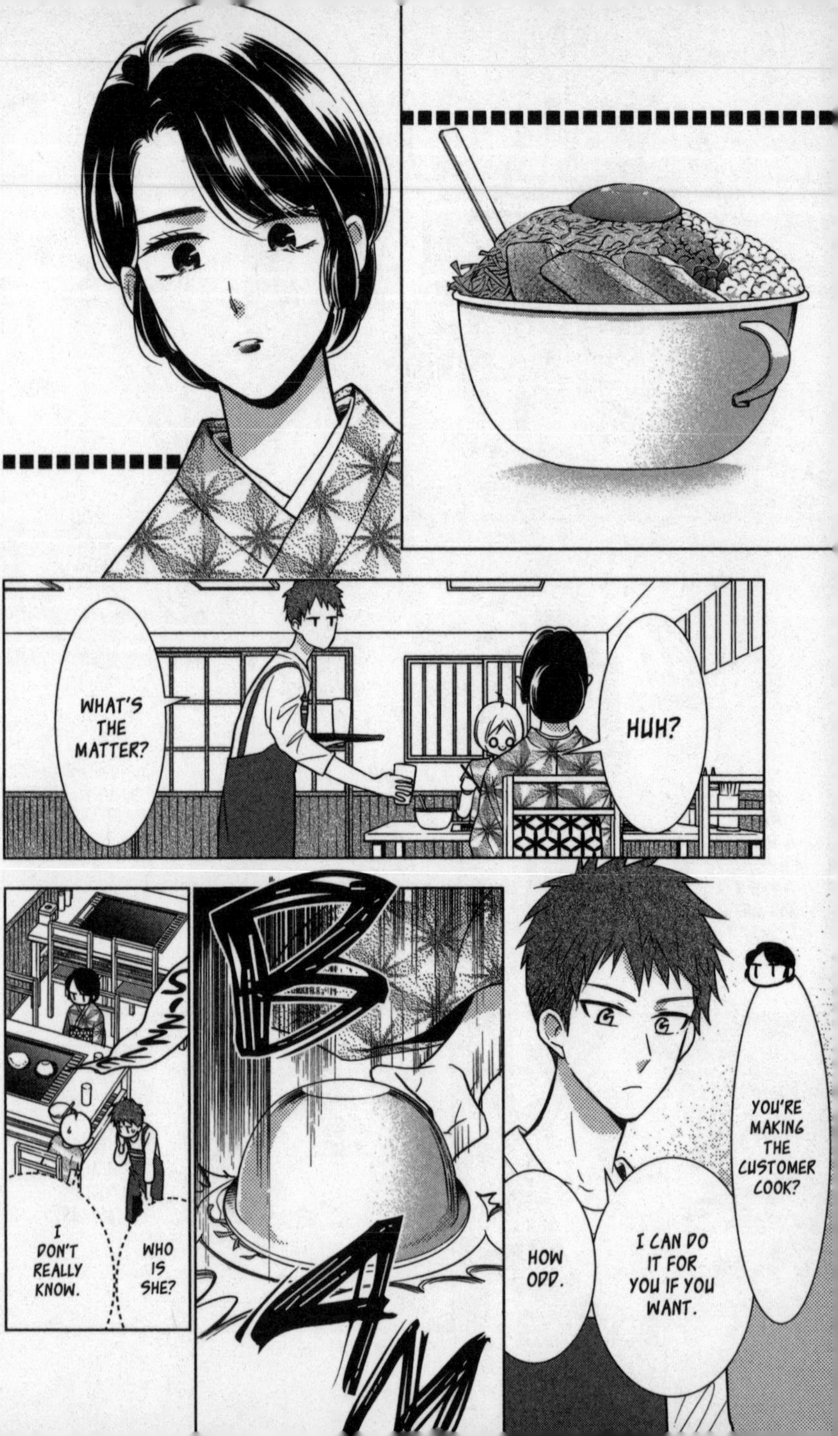
HUH?
WHAT'S THE MATTER?
YOU'RE MAKING THE CUSTOMER COOK?
I CAN DO IT FOR YOU IF YOU WANT.
HOW ODD.
BAM
WHO IS SHE?
I DON'T REALLY KNOW.

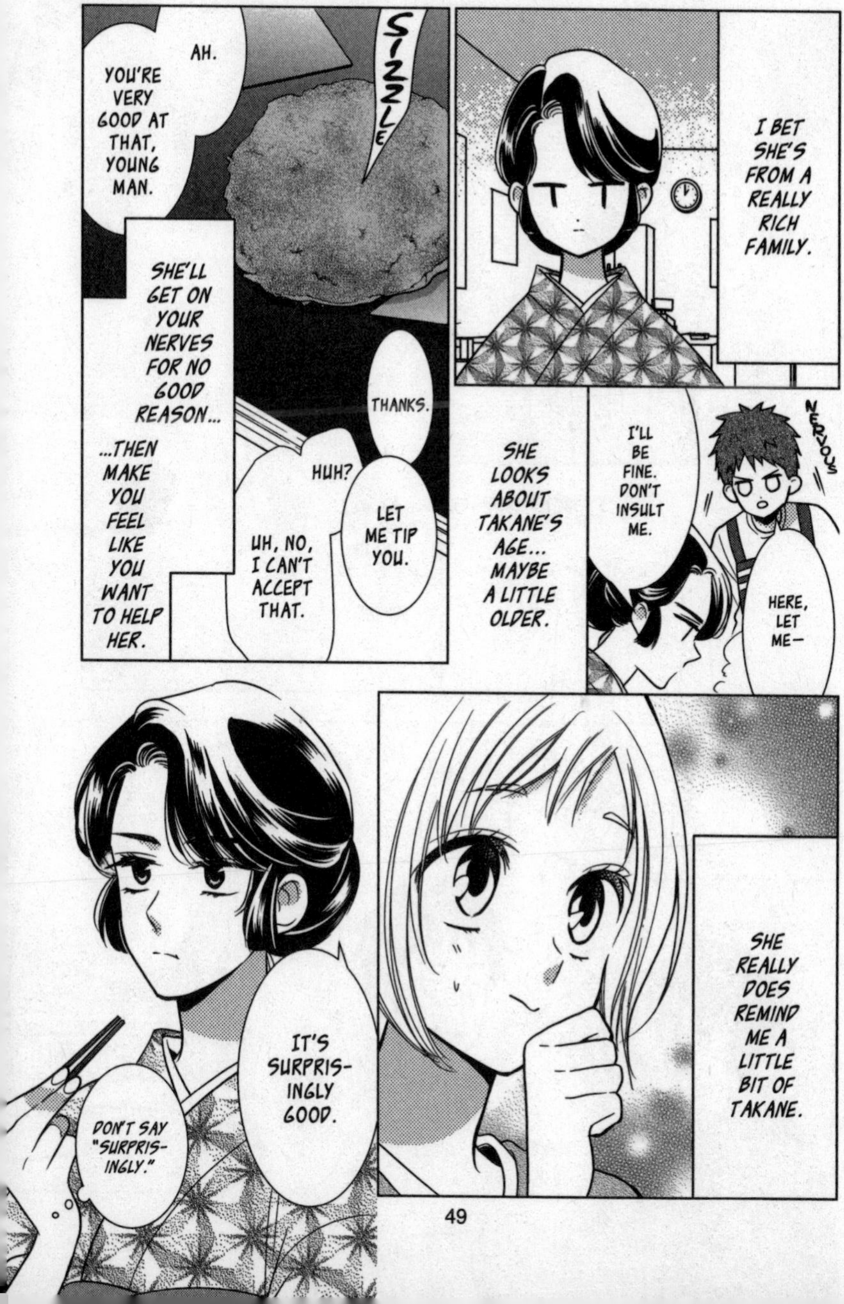
I BET SHE'S FROM A REALLY RICH FAMILY.
HERE, LET ME—
NERVOUS
I'LL BE FINE. DON'T INSULT ME.
SHE LOOKS ABOUT TAKANE'S AGE... MAYBE A LITTLE OLDER.
SIZZLE
AH.
YOU'RE VERY GOOD AT THAT, YOUNG MAN.
THANKS.
HUH?
LET ME TIP YOU.
UH, NO, I CAN'T ACCEPT THAT.
SHE'LL GET ON YOUR NERVES FOR NO GOOD REASON...
...THEN MAKE YOU FEEL LIKE YOU WANT TO HELP HER.
SHE REALLY DOES REMIND ME A LITTLE BIT OF TAKANE.
IT'S SURPRIS-INGLY GOOD.
DON'T SAY "SURPRIS-INGLY."

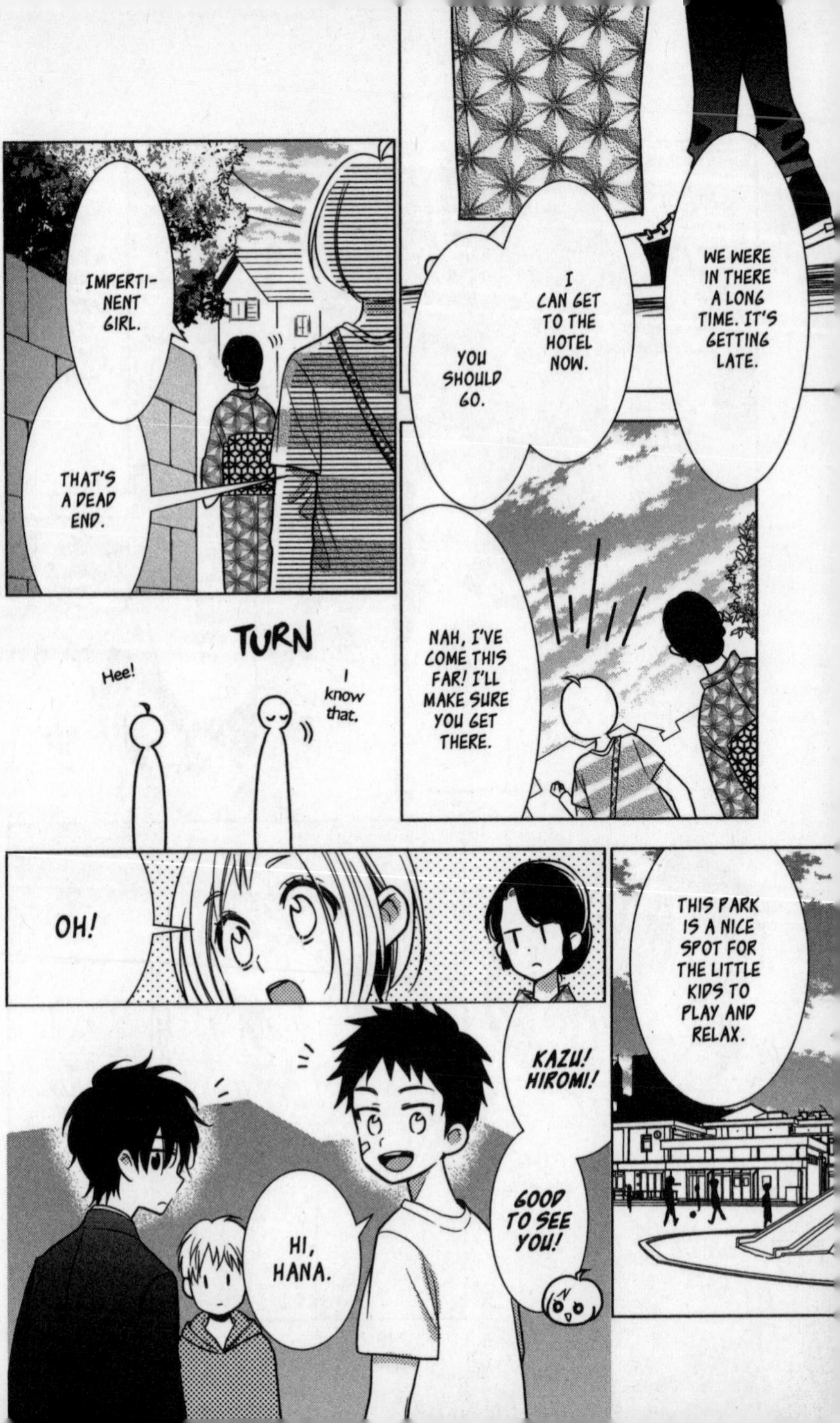
WE WERE IN THERE A LONG TIME. IT'S GETTING LATE.
I CAN GET TO THE HOTEL NOW.
YOU SHOULD GO.
NAH, I'VE COME THIS FAR! I'LL MAKE SURE YOU GET THERE.
IMPERTI- NENT GIRL.
THAT'S A DEAD END.
TURN
I know that.
Hee!
THIS PARK IS A NICE SPOT FOR THE LITTLE KIDS TO PLAY AND RELAX.
OH!
KAZU! HIROMI!
GOOD TO SEE YOU!
HI, HANA.

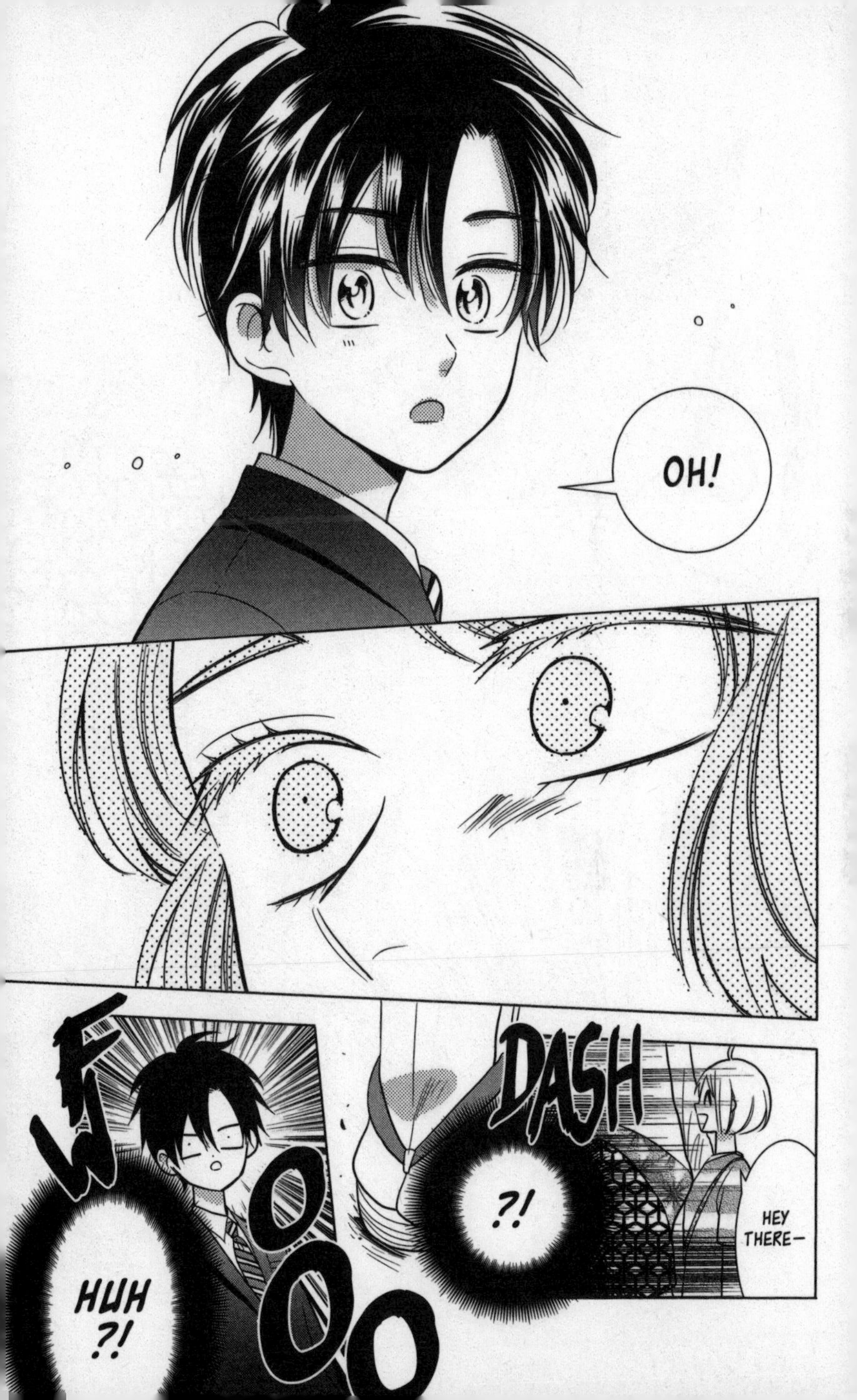
OH!
HEY THERE—
DASH
?!
FWOOOO
HUH ?!

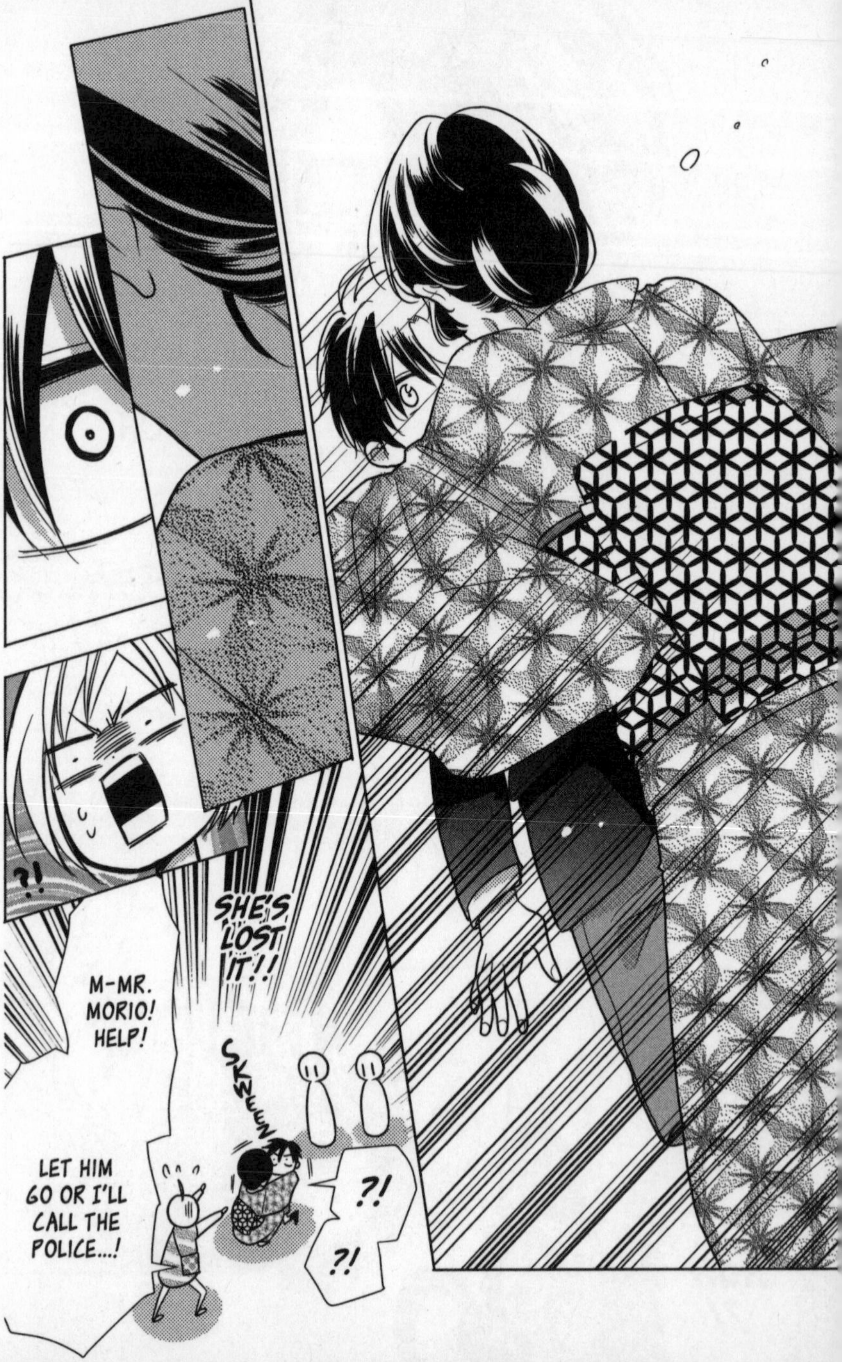
?!
SHE'S LOST IT!!
SKWEEZ
?!
?!
M-MR. MORIO! HELP!
LET HIM GO OR I'LL CALL THE POLICE...!

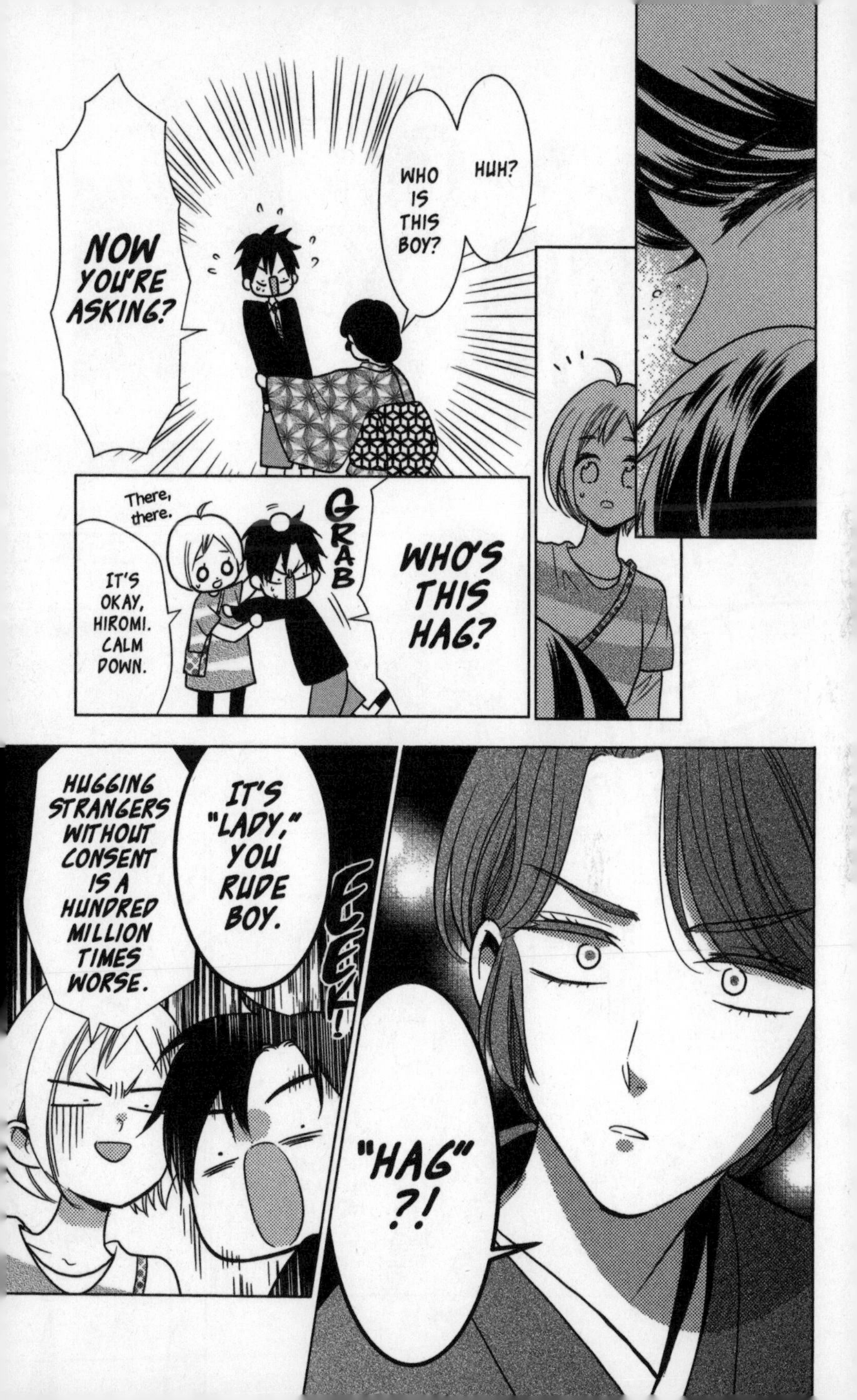
HUH? WHO IS THIS BOY?
NOW YOU'RE ASKING?
WHO'S THIS HAG?
GRAB
There, there.
IT'S OKAY, HIROMI. CALM DOWN.
"HAG"?!
IT'S "LADY," YOU RUDE BOY.
HUGGING STRANGERS WITHOUT CONSENT IS A HUNDRED MILLION TIMES WORSE.

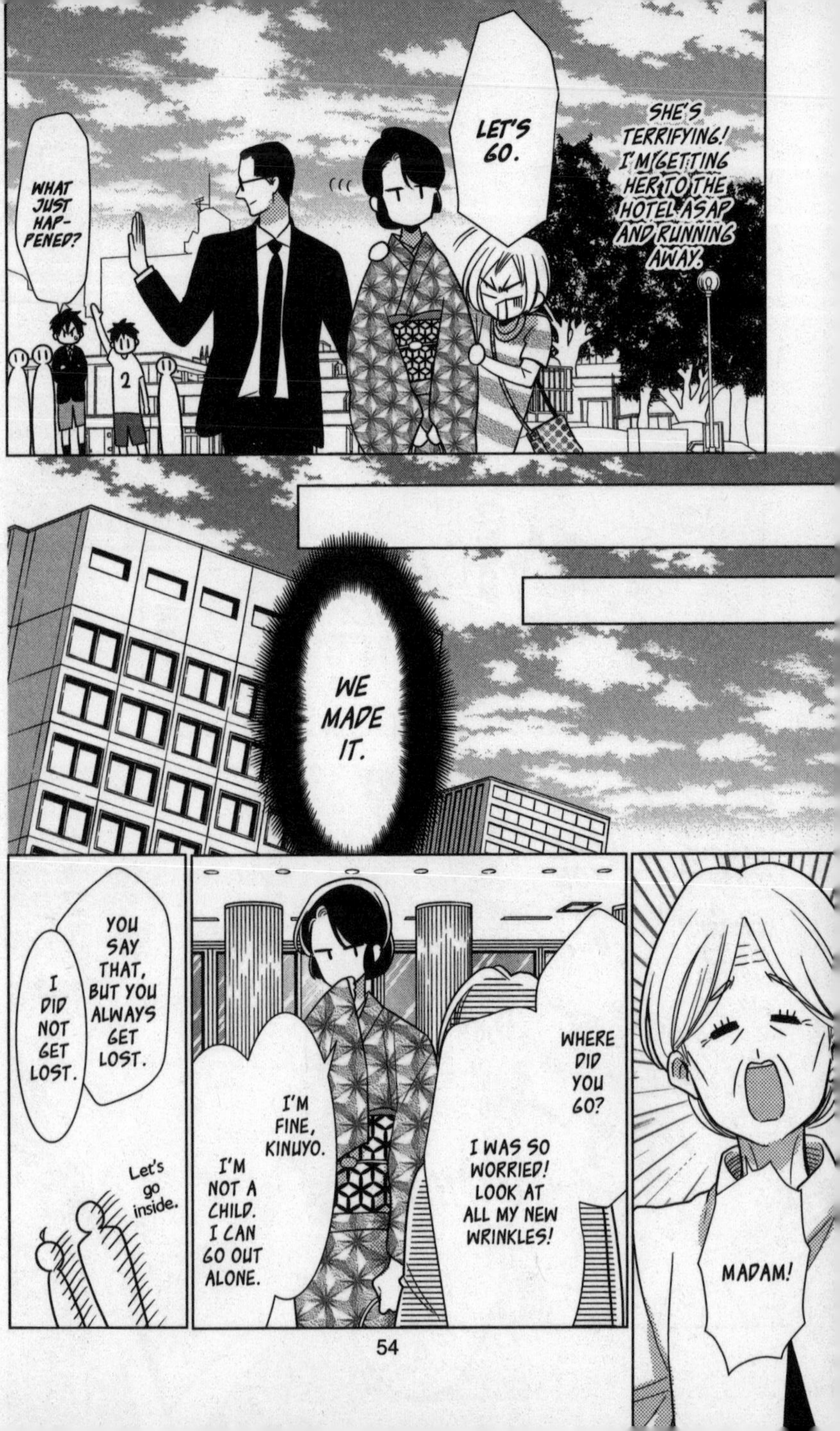
SHE'S TERRIFYING! I'M GETTING HER TO THE HOTEL ASAP AND RUNNING AWAY.
LET'S GO.
WHAT JUST HAP-PENED?
WE MADE IT.
MADAM!
WHERE DID YOU GO?
I WAS SO WORRIED! LOOK AT ALL MY NEW WRINKLES!
I'M FINE, KINUYO.
I'M NOT A CHILD. I CAN GO OUT ALONE.
YOU SAY THAT, BUT YOU ALWAYS GET LOST.
I DID NOT GET LOST.
Let's go inside.

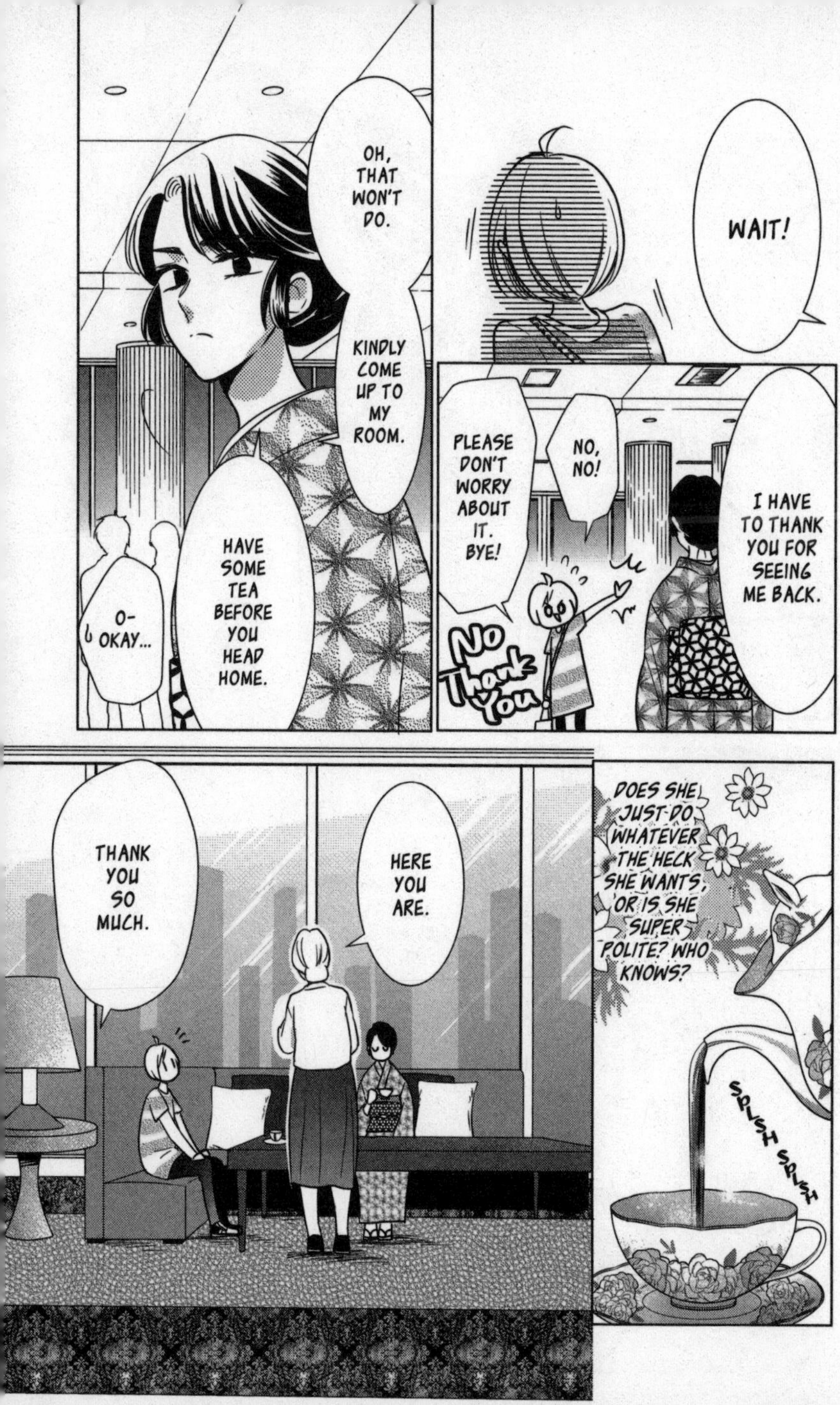
WAIT!
I HAVE TO THANK YOU FOR SEEING ME BACK.
NO, NO!
PLEASE DON'T WORRY ABOUT IT. BYE!
No Thank You
OH, THAT WON'T DO.
KINDLY COME UP TO MY ROOM.
HAVE SOME TEA BEFORE YOU HEAD HOME.
O-OKAY...
DOES SHE JUST DO WHATEVER THE HECK SHE WANTS, OR IS SHE SUPER POLITE? WHO KNOWS?
SPLSH SPLSH
HERE YOU ARE.
THANK YOU SO MUCH.

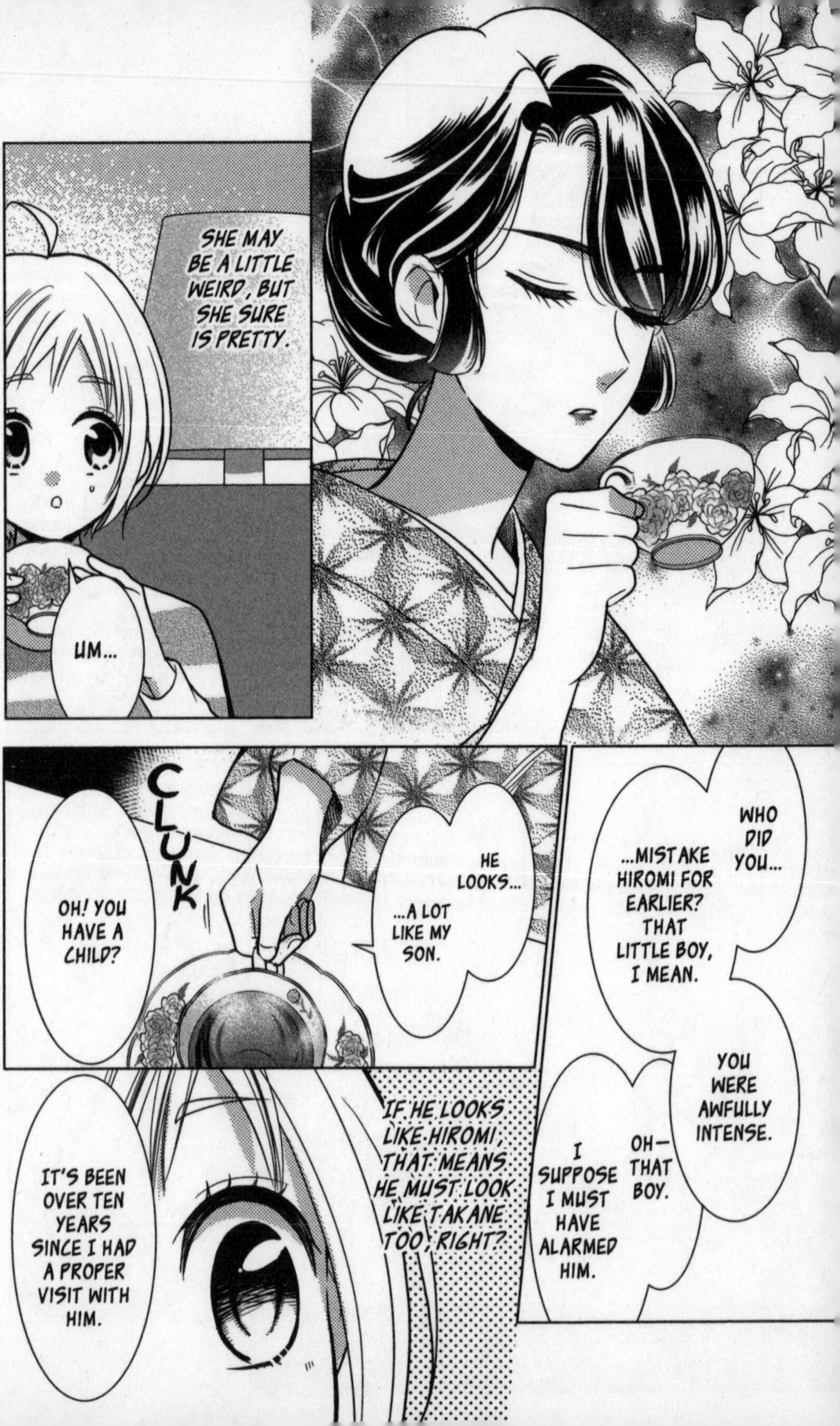
SHE MAY BE A LITTLE WEIRD, BUT SHE SURE IS PRETTY.
UM...
WHO DID YOU...
...MISTAKE HIROMI FOR EARLIER? THAT LITTLE BOY, I MEAN.
YOU WERE AWFULLY INTENSE.
OH— THAT BOY.
I SUPPOSE I MUST HAVE ALARMED HIM.
CLUNK
HE LOOKS...
...A LOT LIKE MY SON.
OH! YOU HAVE A CHILD?
IF HE LOOKS LIKE HIROMI, THAT MEANS HE MUST LOOK LIKE TAKANE TOO, RIGHT?
IT'S BEEN OVER TEN YEARS SINCE I HAD A PROPER VISIT WITH HIM.

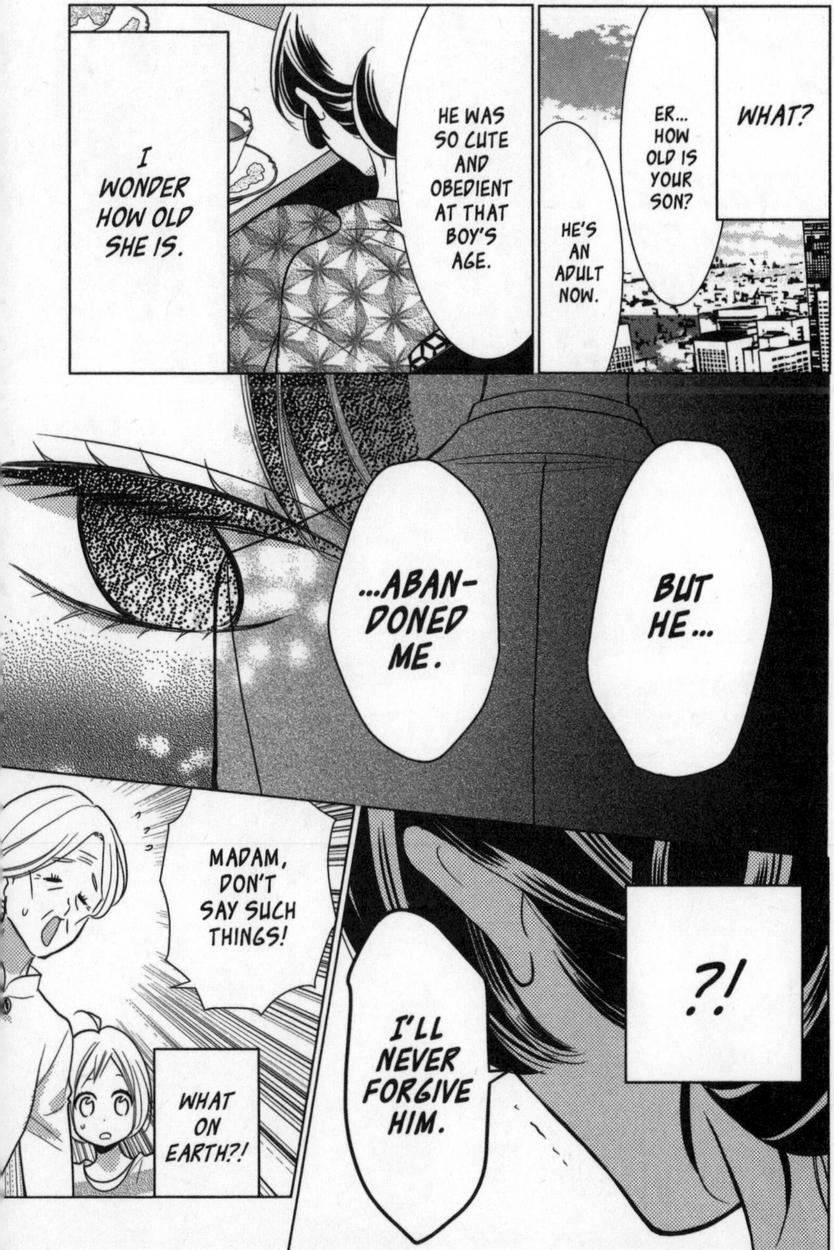
WHAT?
ER... HOW OLD IS YOUR SON?
HE'S AN ADULT NOW.
HE WAS SO CUTE AND OBEDIENT AT THAT BOY'S AGE.
I WONDER HOW OLD SHE IS.
BUT HE...
...ABAN-DONED ME.
?!
I'LL NEVER FORGIVE HIM.
MADAM, DON'T SAY SUCH THINGS!
WHAT ON EARTH?!

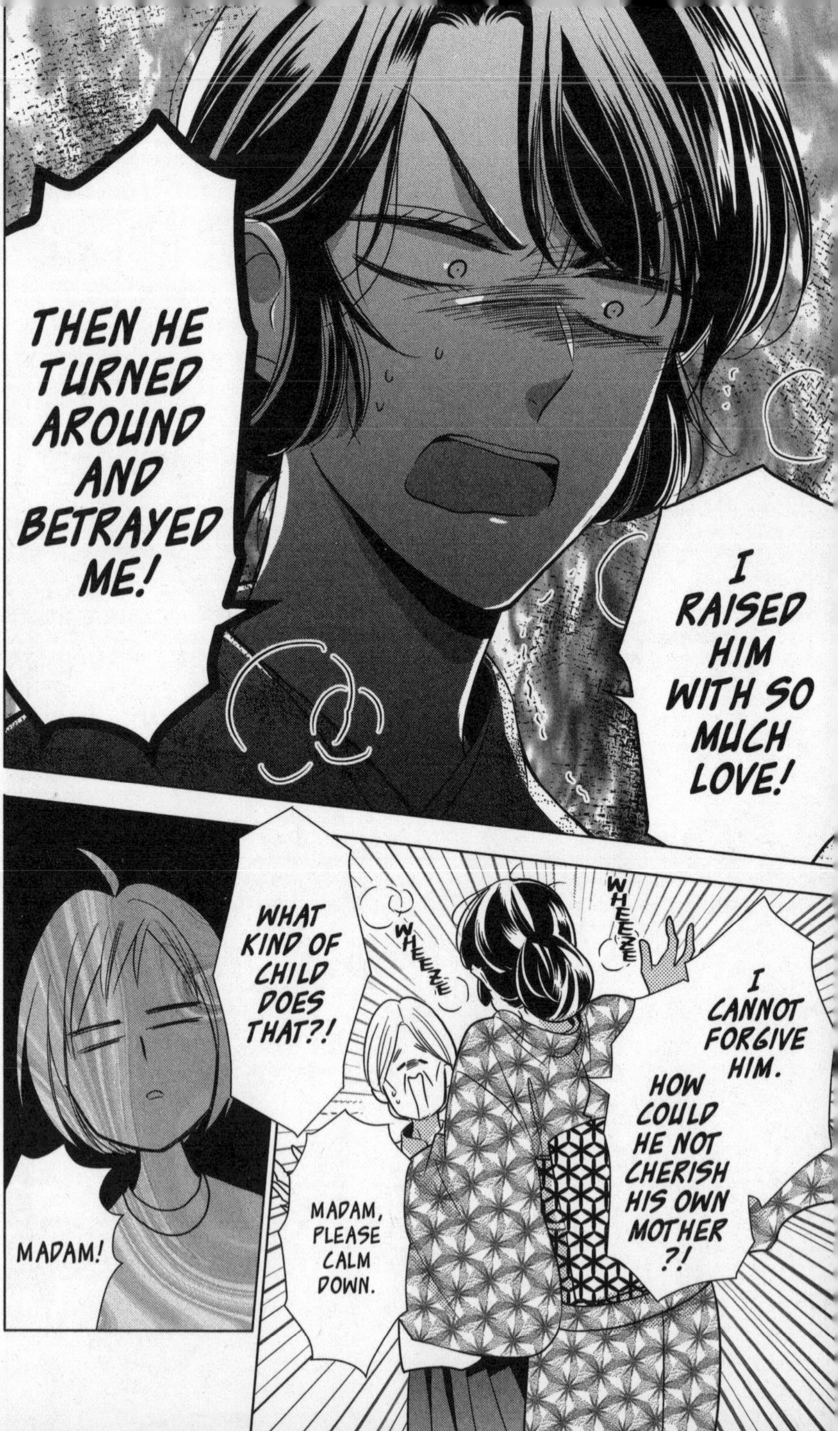
I RAISED HIM WITH SO MUCH LOVE!
THEN HE TURNED AROUND AND BETRAYED ME!
WHEEZE
WHEEZE
I CANNOT FORGIVE HIM.
HOW COULD HE NOT CHERISH HIS OWN MOTHER?!
WHAT KIND OF CHILD DOES THAT?!
MADAM, PLEASE CALM DOWN.
MADAM!

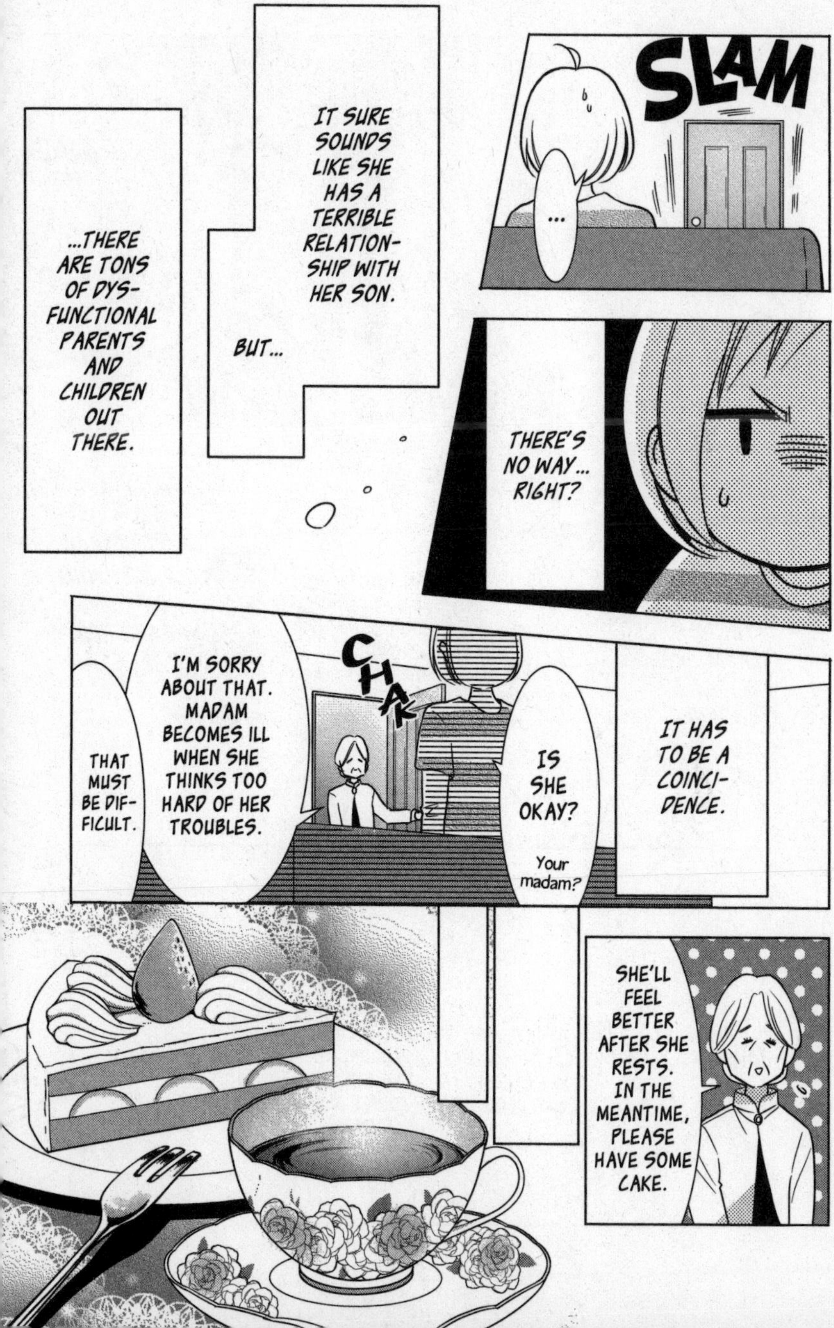
SLAM
...
IT SURE SOUNDS LIKE SHE HAS A TERRIBLE RELATIONSHIP WITH HER SON.
BUT...
...THERE ARE TONS OF DYSFUNCTIONAL PARENTS AND CHILDREN OUT THERE.
THERE'S NO WAY... RIGHT?
IT HAS TO BE A COINCIDENCE.
IS SHE OKAY?
Your madam?
CHAK
I'M SORRY ABOUT THAT. MADAM BECOMES ILL WHEN SHE THINKS TOO HARD OF HER TROUBLES.
THAT MUST BE DIFFICULT.
SHE'LL FEEL BETTER AFTER SHE RESTS. IN THE MEANTIME, PLEASE HAVE SOME CAKE.

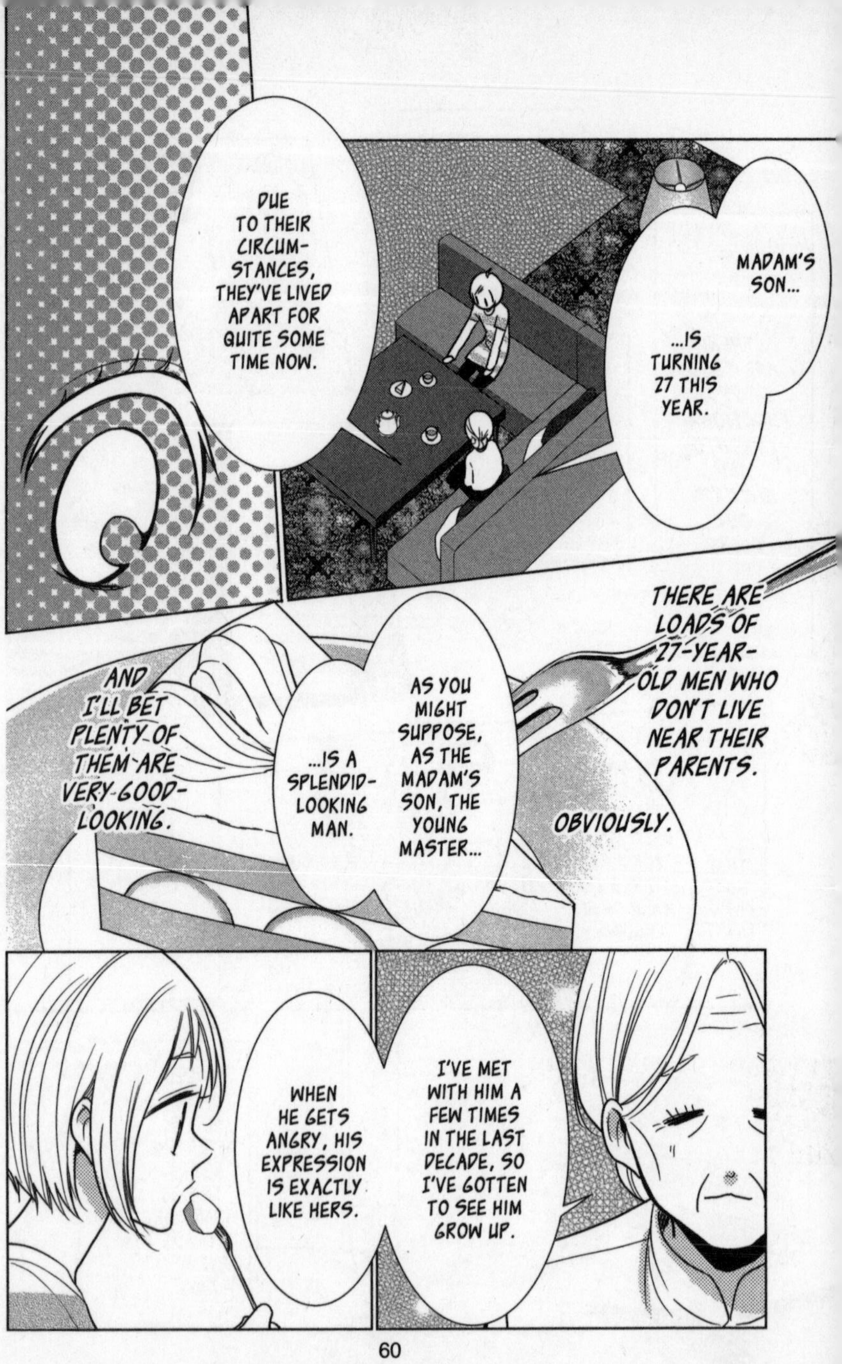
MADAM'S SON...
...IS TURNING 27 THIS YEAR.
DUE TO THEIR CIRCUM-STANCES, THEY'VE LIVED APART FOR QUITE SOME TIME NOW.
THERE ARE LOADS OF 27-YEAR-OLD MEN WHO DON'T LIVE NEAR THEIR PARENTS.
OBVIOUSLY.
AS YOU MIGHT SUPPOSE, AS THE MADAM'S SON, THE YOUNG MASTER...
...IS A SPLENDID-LOOKING MAN.
AND I'LL BET PLENTY OF THEM ARE VERY GOOD-LOOKING.
I'VE MET WITH HIM A FEW TIMES IN THE LAST DECADE, SO I'VE GOTTEN TO SEE HIM GROW UP.
WHEN HE GETS ANGRY, HIS EXPRESSION IS EXACTLY LIKE HERS.

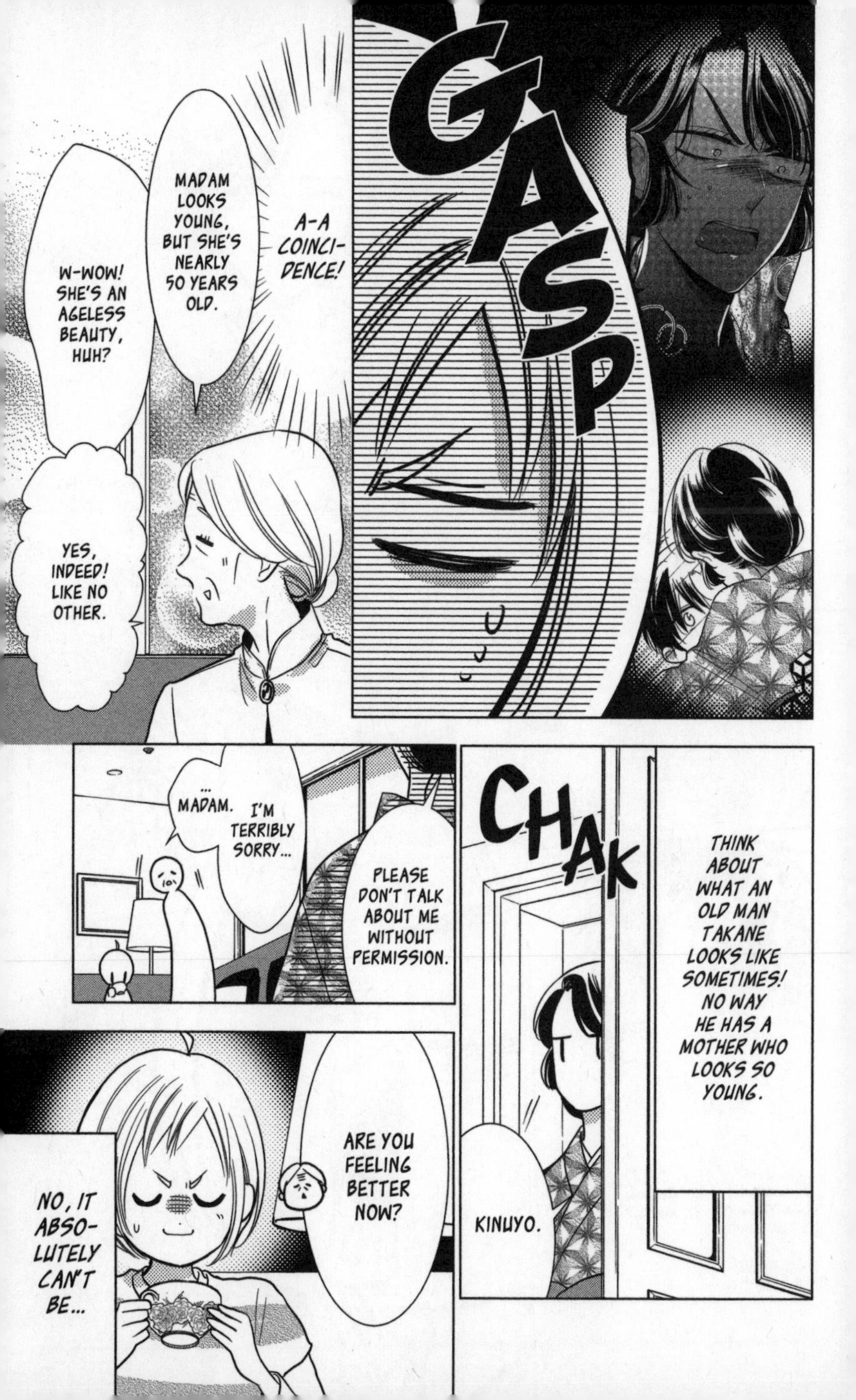
GASP
A-A COINCI-DENCE!
MADAM LOOKS YOUNG, BUT SHE'S NEARLY 50 YEARS OLD.
W-WOW! SHE'S AN AGELESS BEAUTY, HUH?
YES, INDEED! LIKE NO OTHER.
CHAK
THINK ABOUT WHAT AN OLD MAN TAKANE LOOKS LIKE SOMETIMES! NO WAY HE HAS A MOTHER WHO LOOKS SO YOUNG.
KINUYO.
PLEASE DON'T TALK ABOUT ME WITHOUT PERMISSION.
... MADAM. I'M TERRIBLY SORRY...
ARE YOU FEELING BETTER NOW?
NO, IT ABSO-LUTELY CAN'T BE...

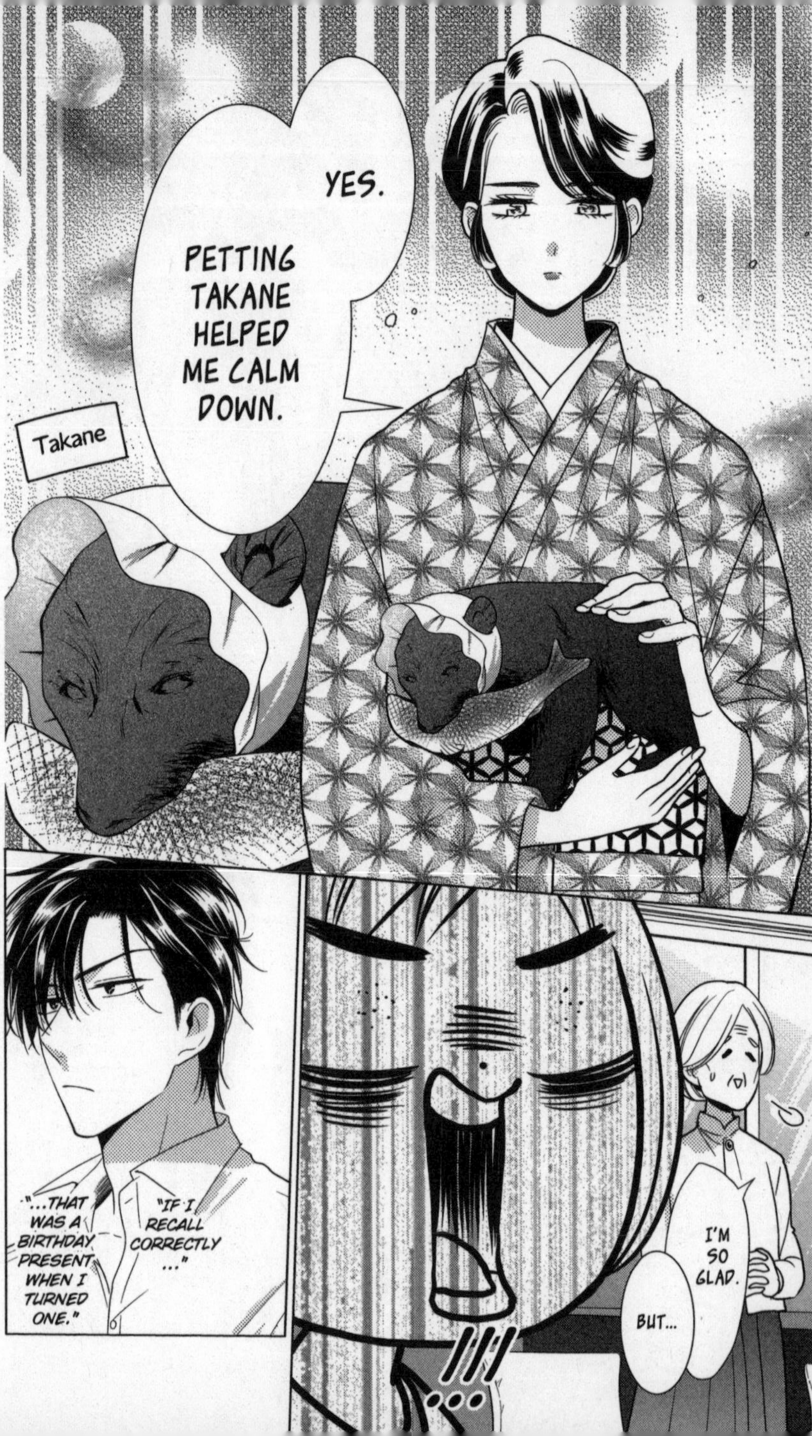
YES.
PETTING TAKANE HELPED ME CALM DOWN.
Takane
I'M SO GLAD.
BUT...
...
"IF I RECALL CORRECTLY..."
"...THAT WAS A BIRTHDAY PRESENT WHEN I TURNED ONE."

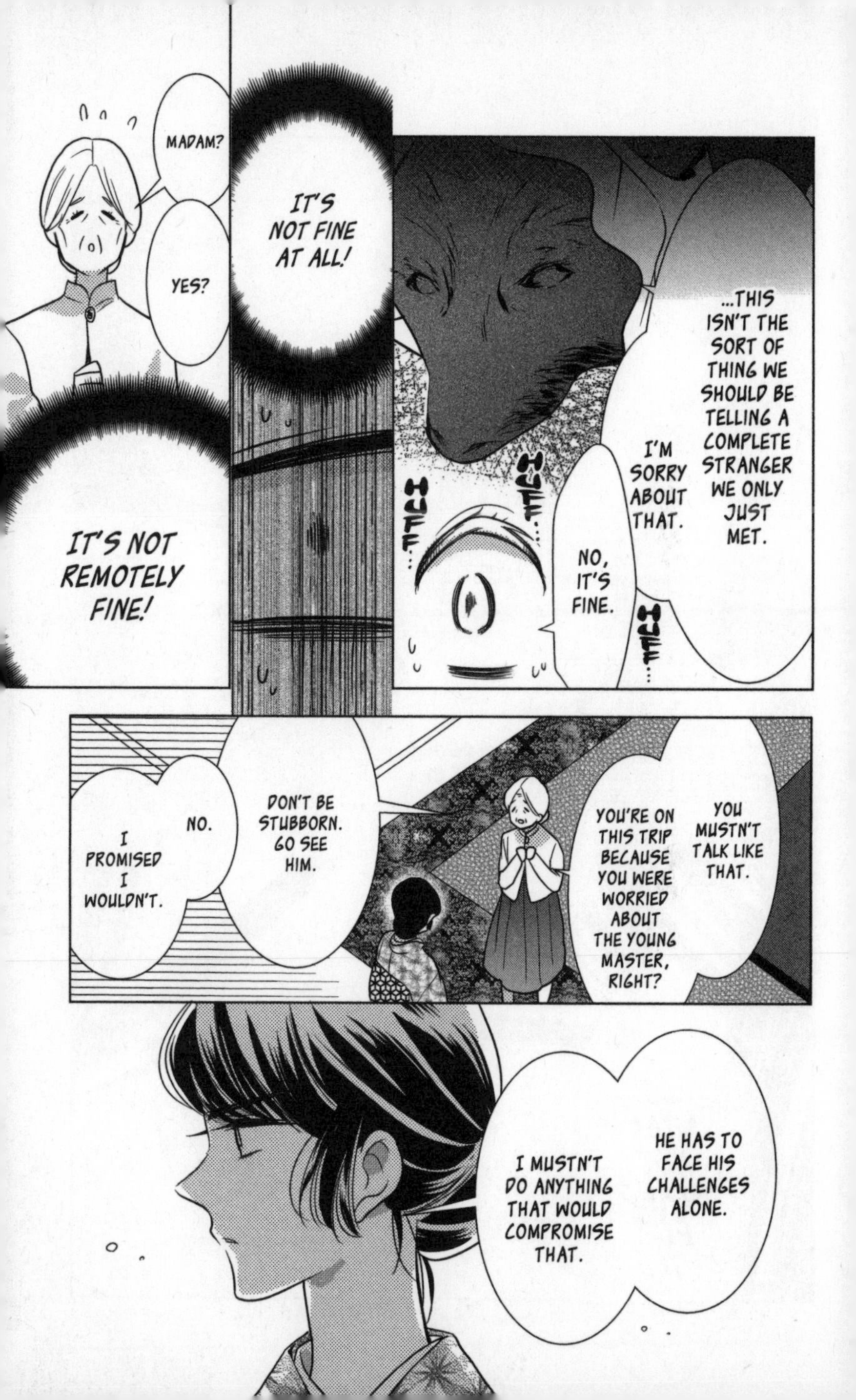
...THIS ISN'T THE SORT OF THING WE SHOULD BE TELLING A COMPLETE STRANGER WE ONLY JUST MET.
I'M SORRY ABOUT THAT.
HUFF...
HUFF...
NO, IT'S FINE.
HUFF...
IT'S NOT FINE AT ALL!
MADAM?
YES?
IT'S NOT REMOTELY FINE!
YOU MUSTN'T TALK LIKE THAT.
YOU'RE ON THIS TRIP BECAUSE YOU WERE WORRIED ABOUT THE YOUNG MASTER, RIGHT?
DON'T BE STUBBORN. GO SEE HIM.
NO.
I PROMISED I WOULDN'T.
HE HAS TO FACE HIS CHALLENGES ALONE.
I MUSTN'T DO ANYTHING THAT WOULD COMPROMISE THAT.

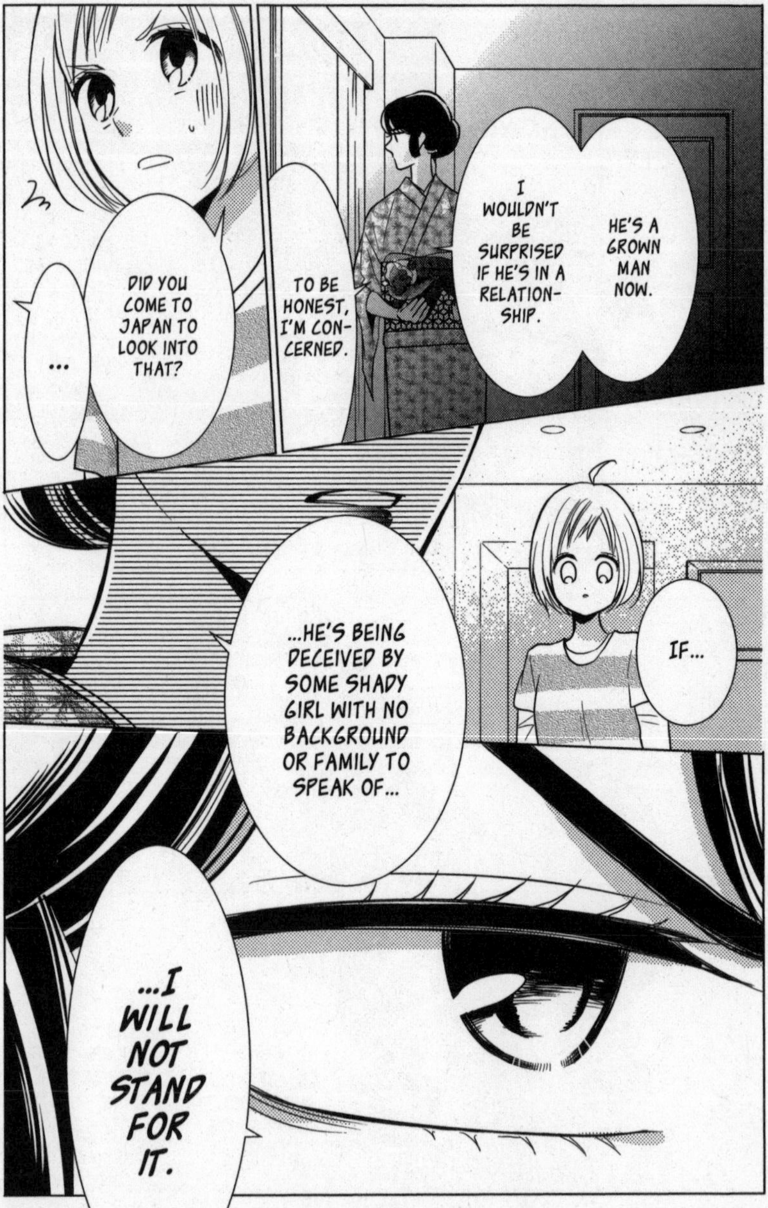
HE'S A GROWN MAN NOW.
I WOULDN'T BE SURPRISED IF HE'S IN A RELATION-SHIP.
TO BE HONEST, I'M CON-CERNED.
DID YOU COME TO JAPAN TO LOOK INTO THAT?
...
IF...
...HE'S BEING DECEIVED BY SOME SHADY GIRL WITH NO BACKGROUND OR FAMILY TO SPEAK OF...
...I WILL NOT STAND FOR IT.

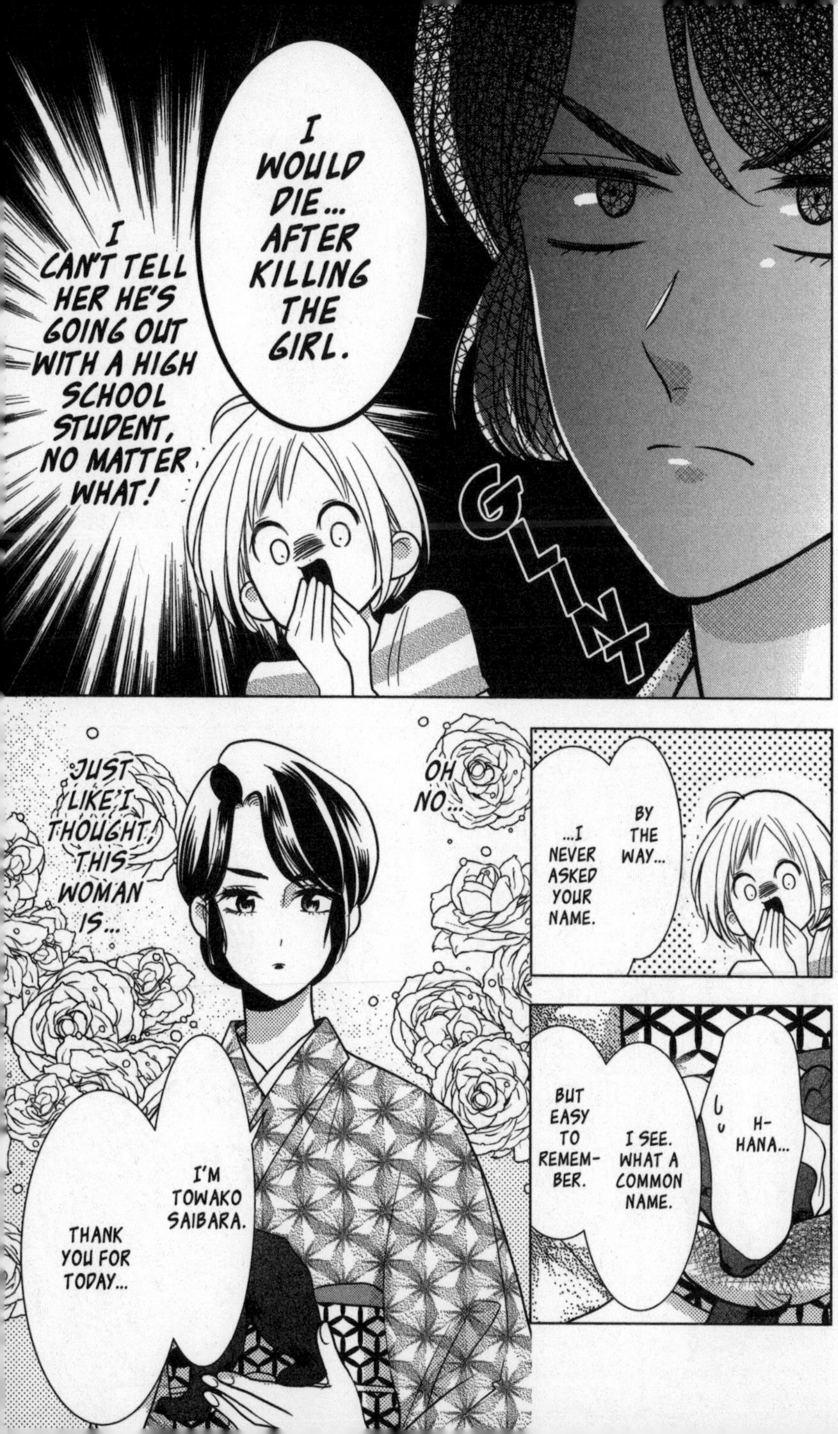
I WOULD DIE... AFTER KILLING THE GIRL.
GLINT
I CAN'T TELL HER HE'S GOING OUT WITH A HIGH SCHOOL STUDENT, NO MATTER WHAT!
BY THE WAY...
...I NEVER ASKED YOUR NAME.
H-HANA...
I SEE. WHAT A COMMON NAME.
BUT EASY TO REMEMBER.
I'M TOWAKO SAIBARA.
THANK YOU FOR TODAY...
OH NO...
JUST LIKE I THOUGHT, THIS WOMAN IS...

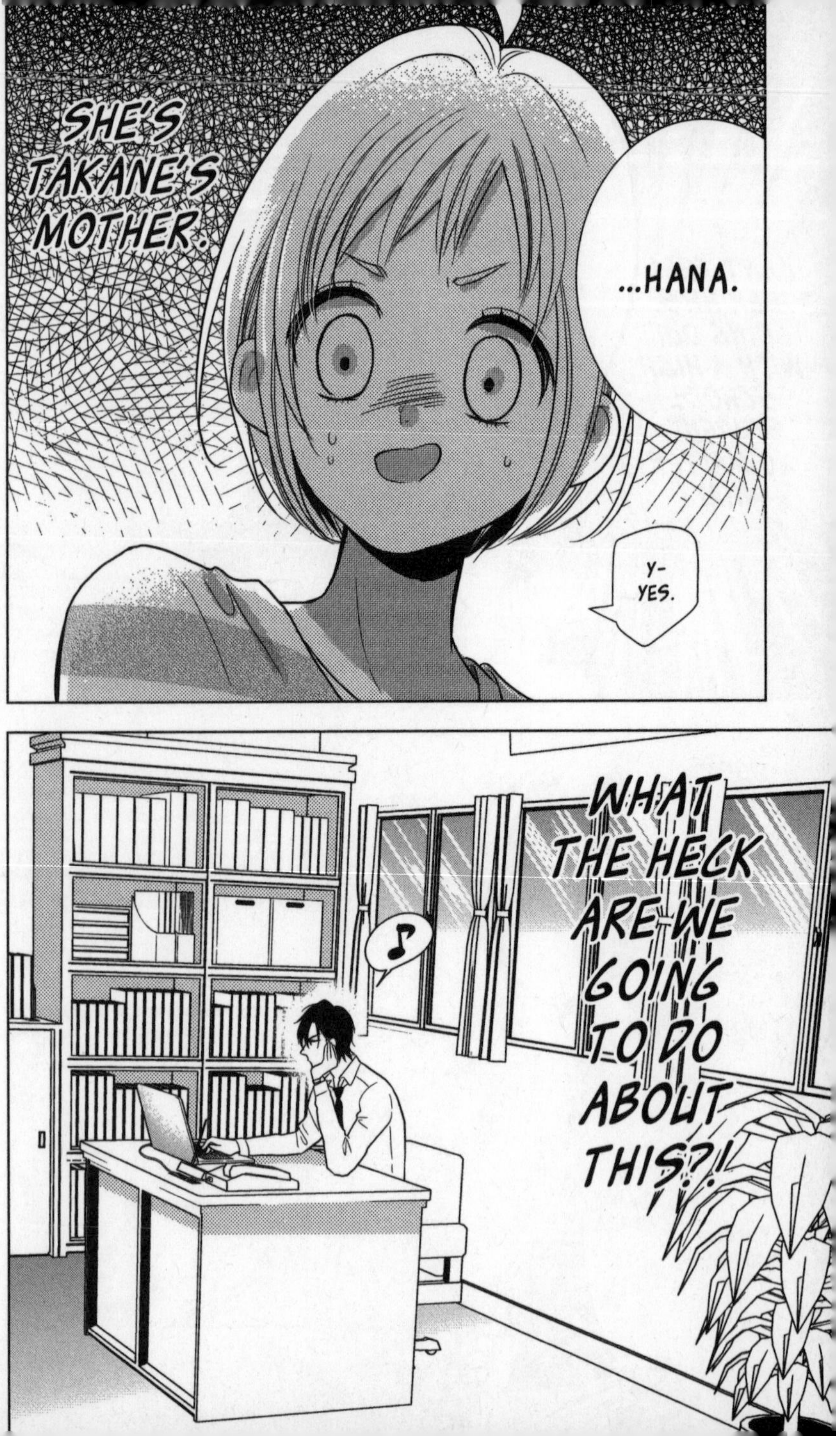
...HANA.
Y-YES.
SHE'S TAKANE'S MOTHER.
♪
WHAT THE HECK ARE WE GOING TO DO ABOUT THIS?!

Chapter 82

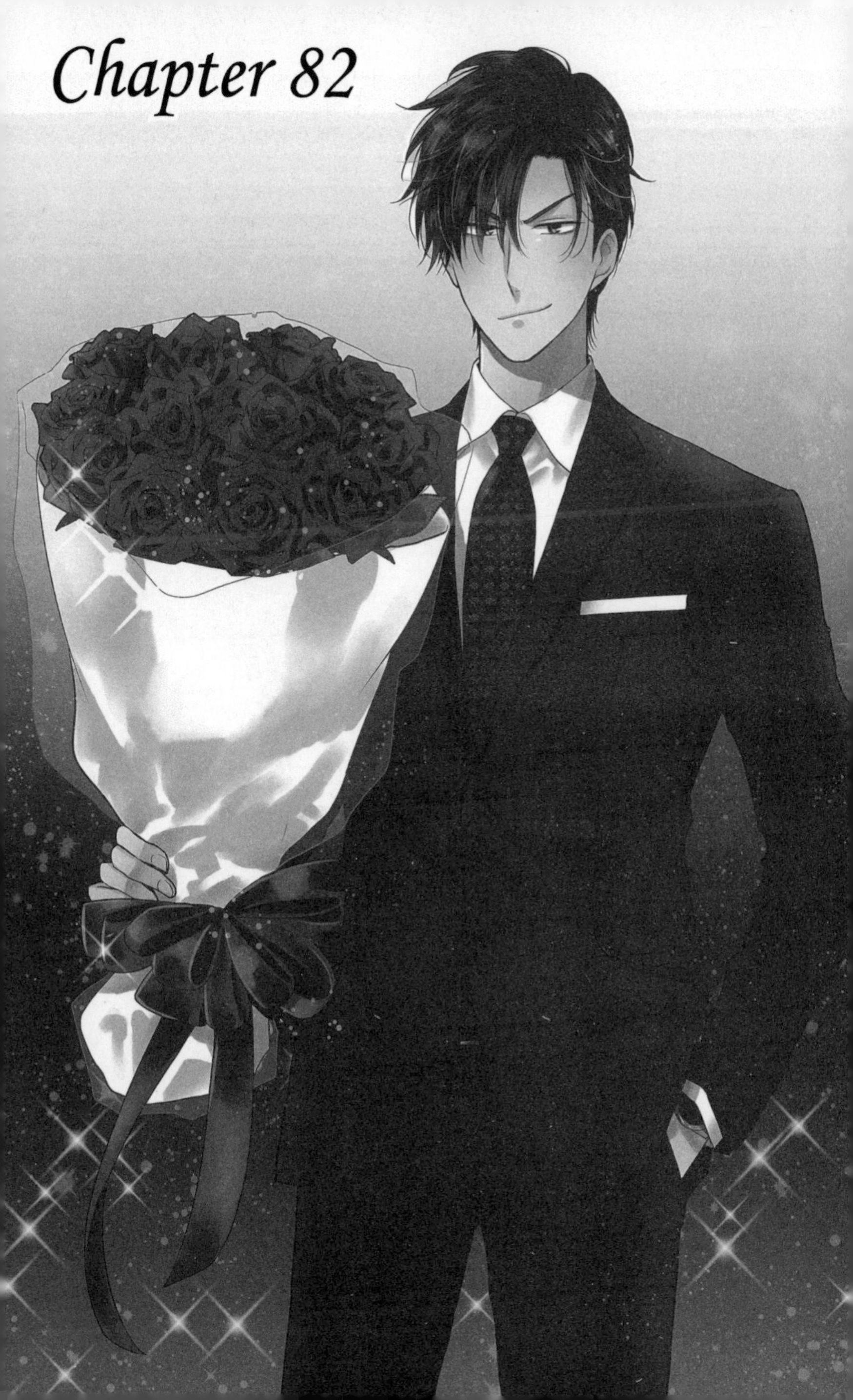

MAKEOVER

Short hair

Can't quite pull off the fresh, youthful look

Pigtails

Childish

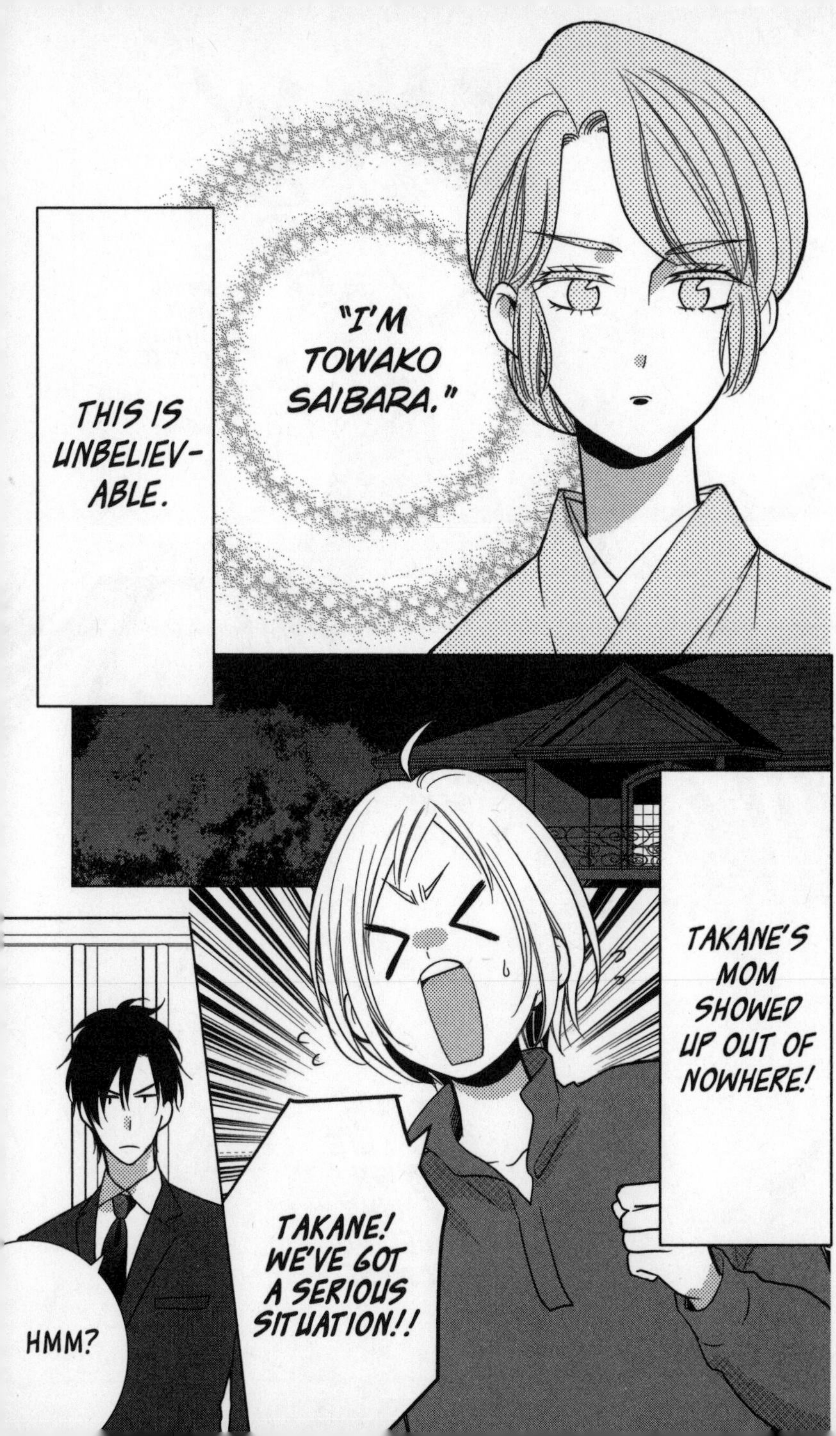
"I'M TOWAKO SAIBARA."
THIS IS UNBELIEVABLE.
TAKANE'S MOM SHOWED UP OUT OF NOWHERE!
TAKANE! WE'VE GOT A SERIOUS SITUATION!!
HMM?

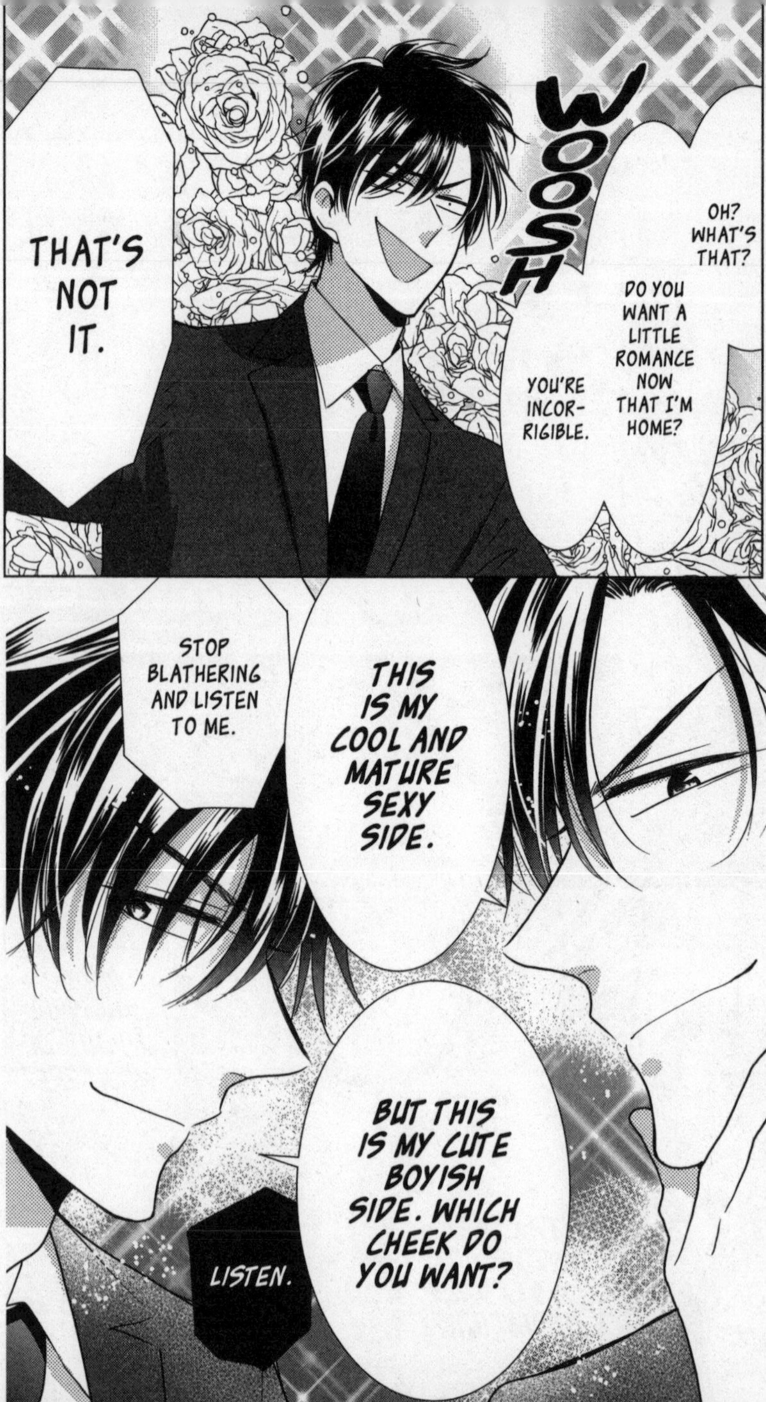
OH? WHAT'S THAT?
DO YOU WANT A LITTLE ROMANCE NOW THAT I'M HOME?
YOU'RE INCORRIGIBLE.
WOOSH
THAT'S NOT IT.
THIS IS MY COOL AND MATURE SEXY SIDE.
STOP BLATHERING AND LISTEN TO ME.
BUT THIS IS MY CUTE BOYISH SIDE. WHICH CHEEK DO YOU WANT?
LISTEN.

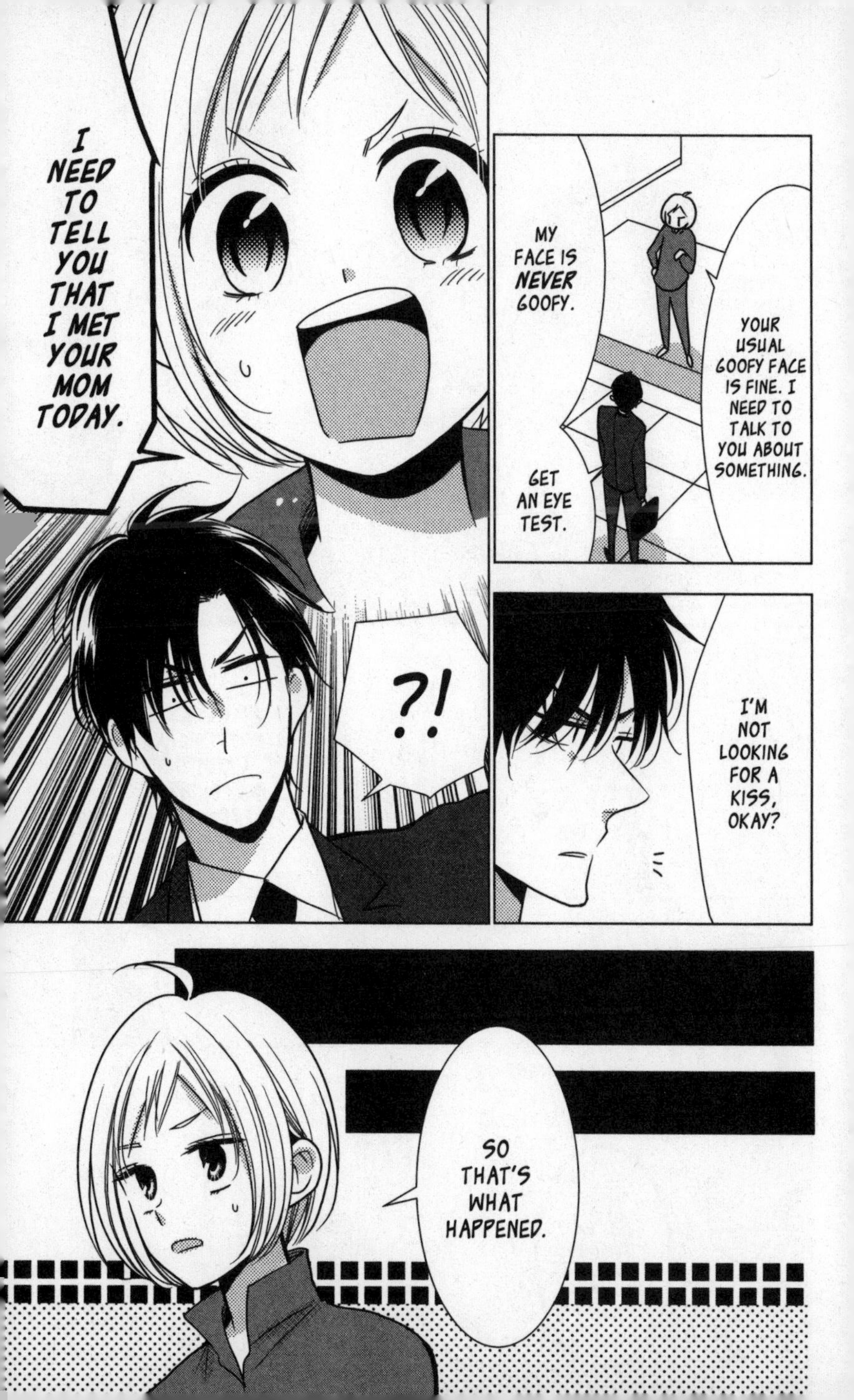
YOUR USUAL GOOFY FACE IS FINE. I NEED TO TALK TO YOU ABOUT SOMETHING.
MY FACE IS NEVER GOOFY.
GET AN EYE TEST.
I'M NOT LOOKING FOR A KISS, OKAY?
I NEED TO TELL YOU THAT I MET YOUR MOM TODAY.
?!
SO THAT'S WHAT HAPPENED.

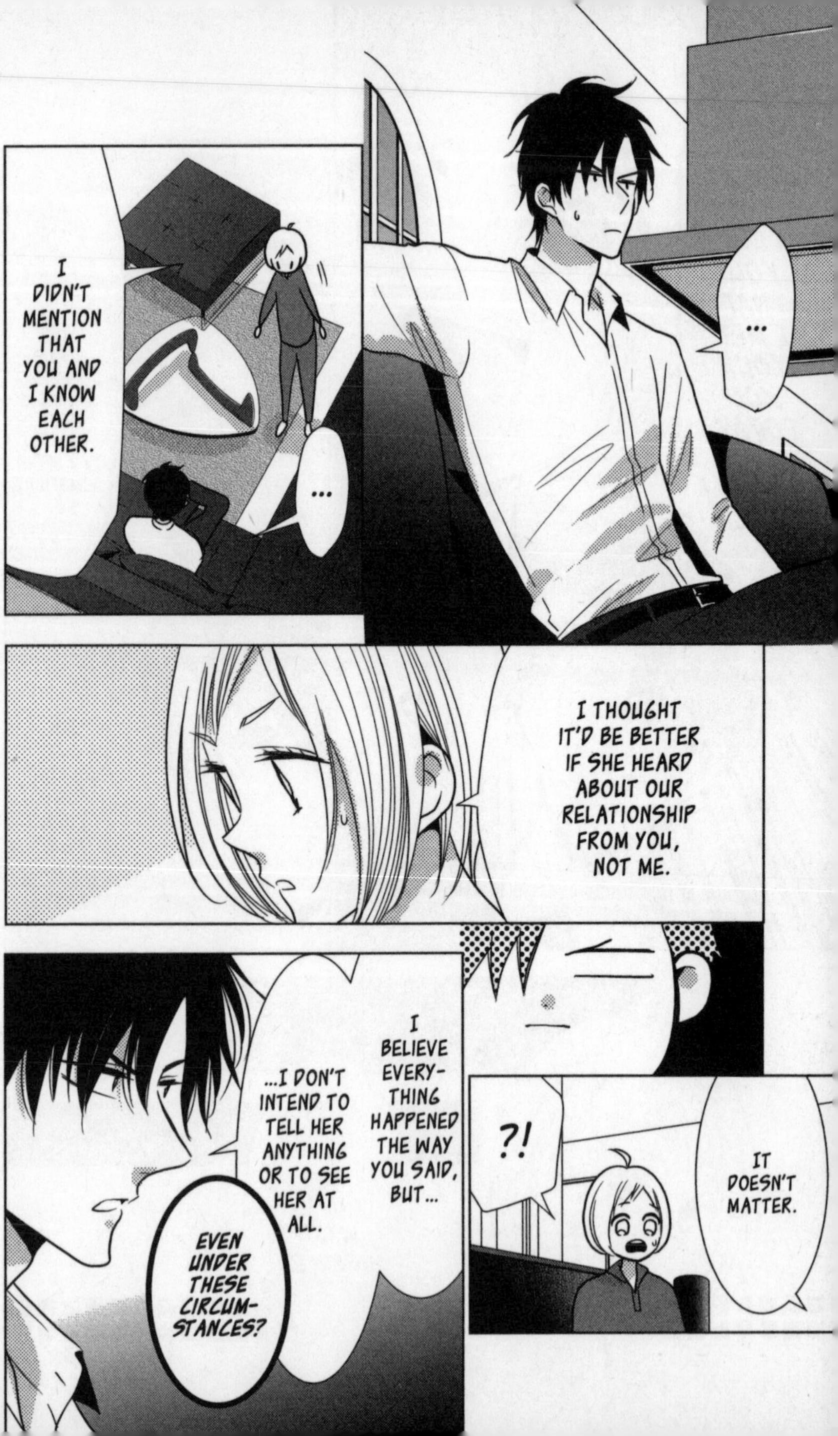
...
I DIDN'T MENTION THAT YOU AND I KNOW EACH OTHER.
...
I THOUGHT IT'D BE BETTER IF SHE HEARD ABOUT OUR RELATIONSHIP FROM YOU, NOT ME.
IT DOESN'T MATTER.
?!
I BELIEVE EVERYTHING HAPPENED THE WAY YOU SAID, BUT...
...I DON'T INTEND TO TELL HER ANYTHING OR TO SEE HER AT ALL.
EVEN UNDER THESE CIRCUMSTANCES?

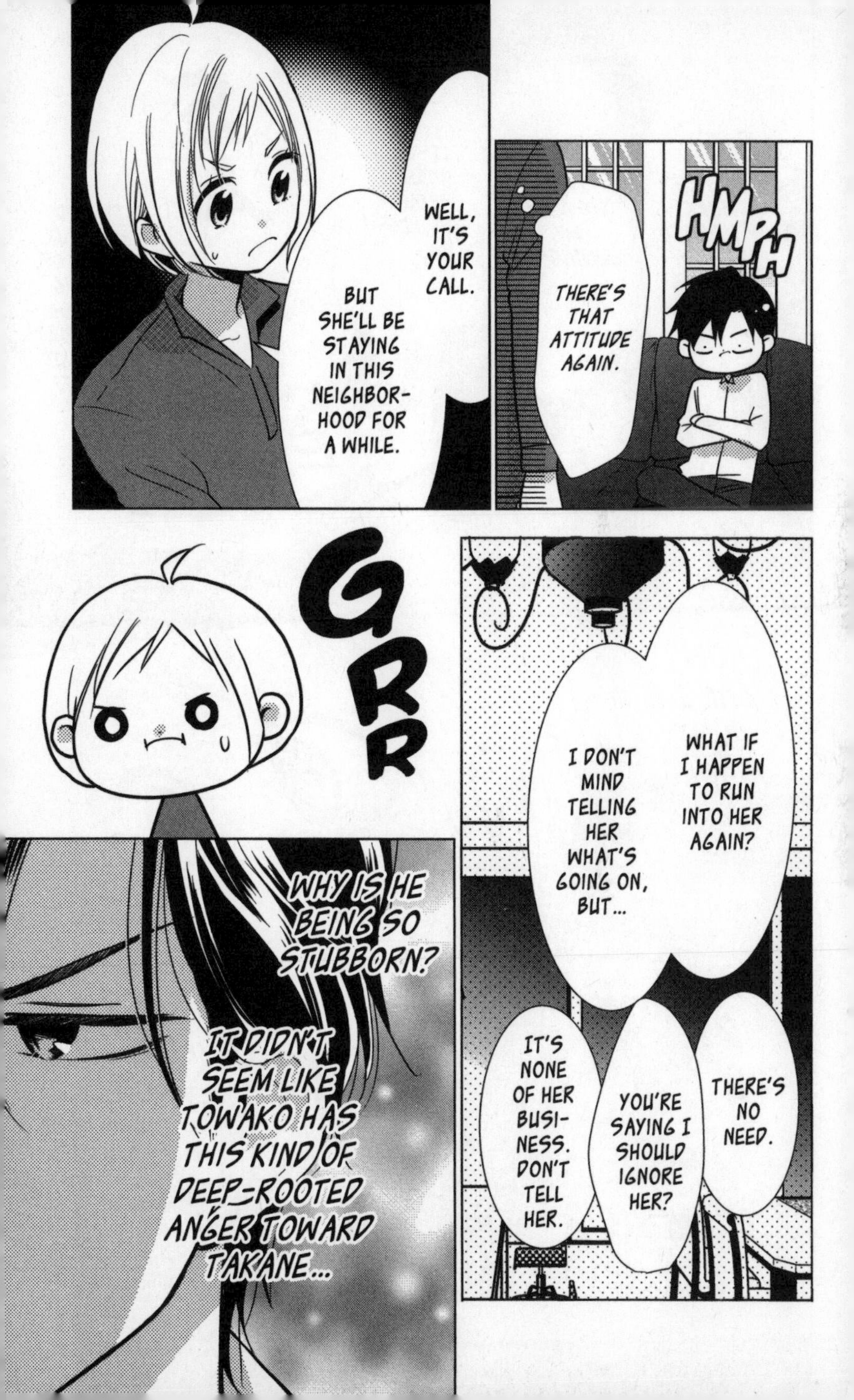
HMPH
THERE'S THAT ATTITUDE AGAIN.
WELL, IT'S YOUR CALL.
BUT SHE'LL BE STAYING IN THIS NEIGHBOR-HOOD FOR A WHILE.
WHAT IF I HAPPEN TO RUN INTO HER AGAIN?
I DON'T MIND TELLING HER WHAT'S GOING ON, BUT...
THERE'S NO NEED.
YOU'RE SAYING I SHOULD IGNORE HER?
IT'S NONE OF HER BUSINESS. DON'T TELL HER.
GRR
WHY IS HE BEING SO STUBBORN?
IT DIDN'T SEEM LIKE TOWAKO HAS THIS KIND OF DEEP-ROOTED ANGER TOWARD TAKANE...

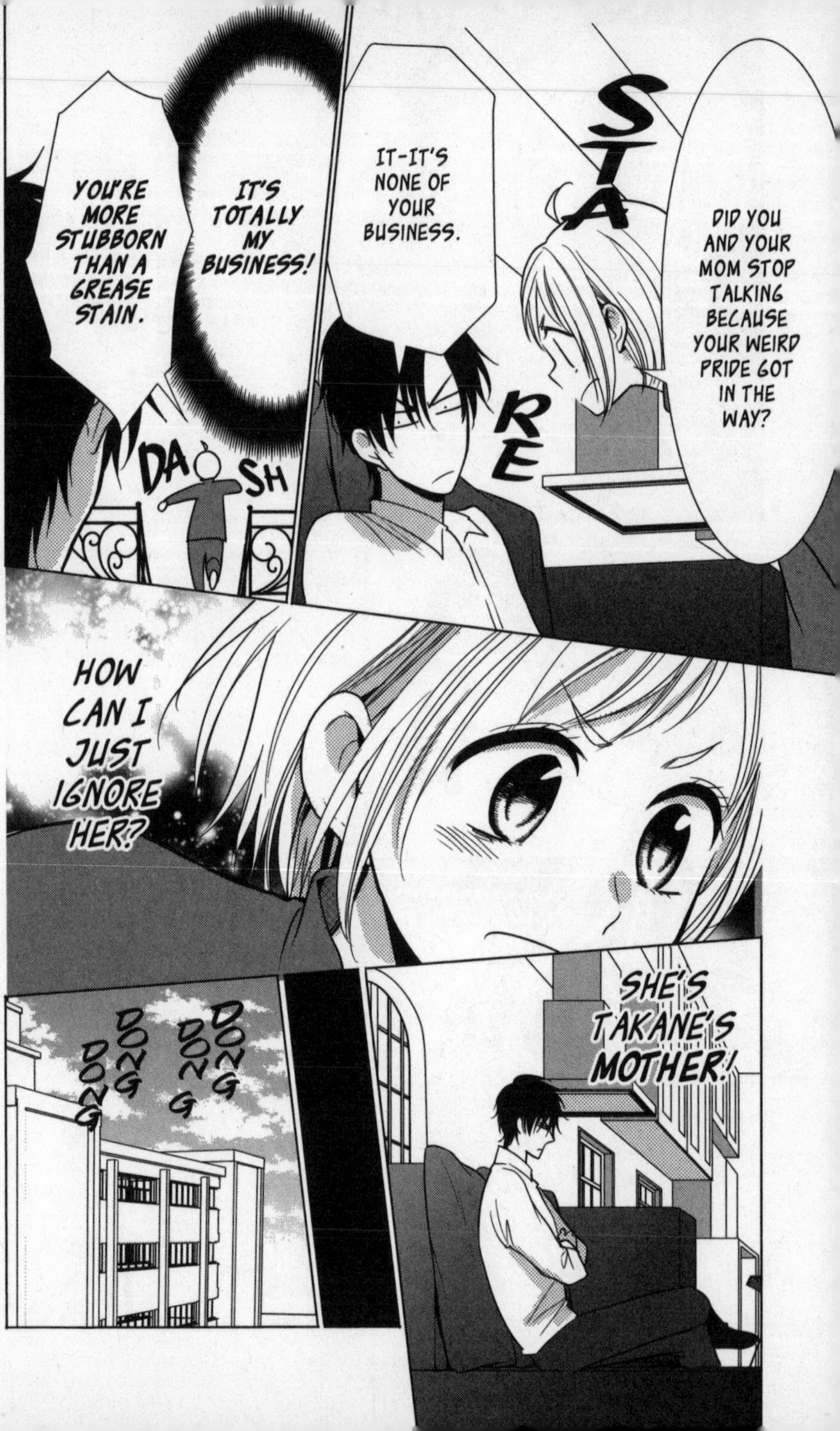
DID YOU AND YOUR MOM STOP TALKING BECAUSE YOUR WEIRD PRIDE GOT IN THE WAY?
STARE
IT-IT'S NONE OF YOUR BUSINESS.
IT'S TOTALLY MY BUSINESS!
YOU'RE MORE STUBBORN THAN A GREASE STAIN.
DASH
HOW CAN I JUST IGNORE HER?
SHE'S TAKANE'S MOTHER!
DONG DONG DONG
DONG

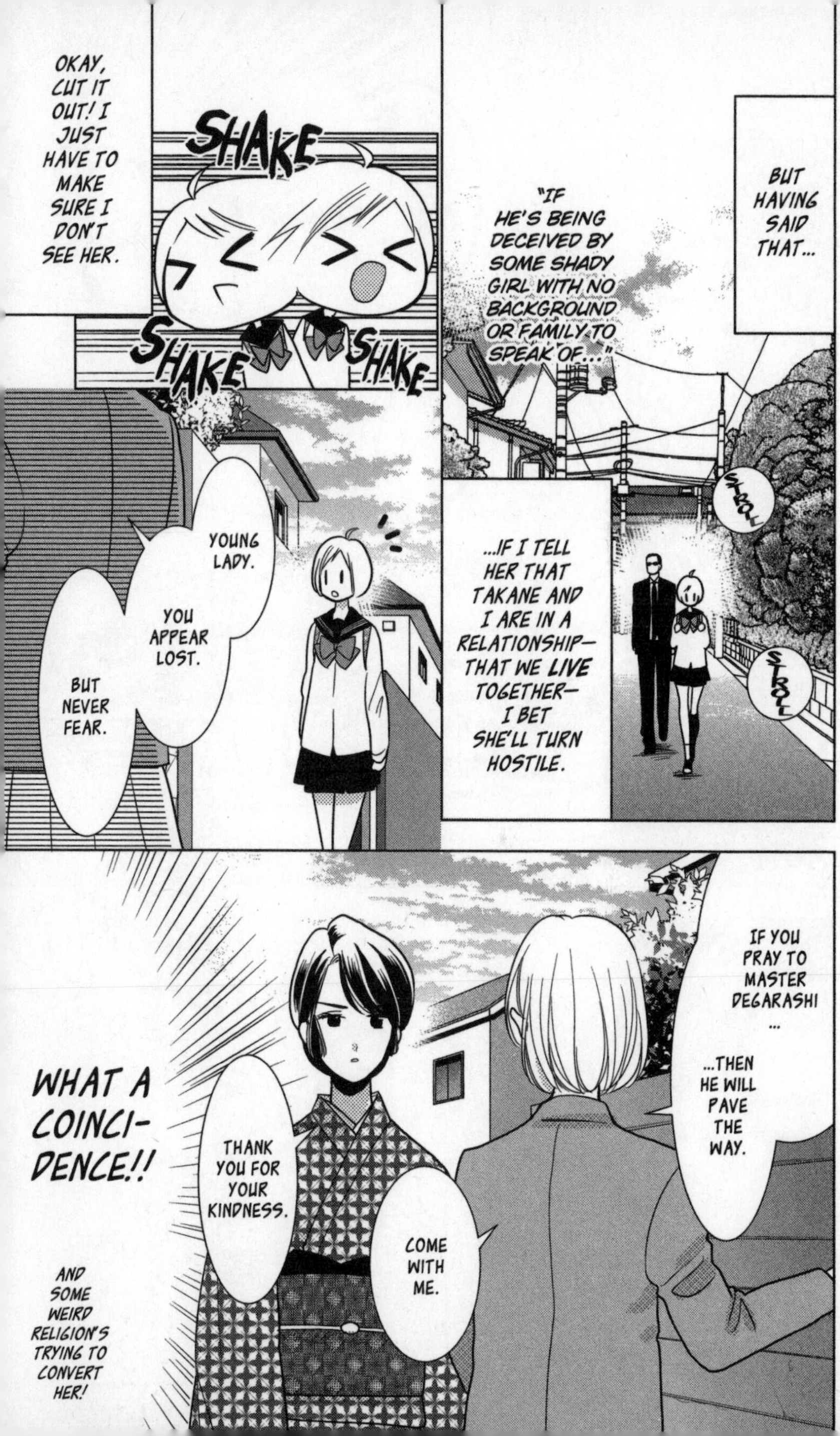
BUT HAVING SAID THAT...
"IF HE'S BEING DECEIVED BY SOME SHADY GIRL WITH NO BACKGROUND OR FAMILY TO SPEAK OF..."
...IF I TELL HER THAT TAKANE AND I ARE IN A RELATIONSHIP— THAT WE *LIVE* TOGETHER— I BET SHE'LL TURN HOSTILE.
STROLL
STROLL
OKAY, CUT IT OUT! I JUST HAVE TO MAKE SURE I DON'T SEE HER.
SHAKE
SHAKE
SHAKE
YOUNG LADY.
YOU APPEAR LOST.
BUT NEVER FEAR.
IF YOU PRAY TO MASTER DEGARASHI ...
...THEN HE WILL PAVE THE WAY.
COME WITH ME.
THANK YOU FOR YOUR KINDNESS.
WHAT A COINCI- DENCE!!
AND SOME WEIRD RELIGION'S TRYING TO CONVERT HER!

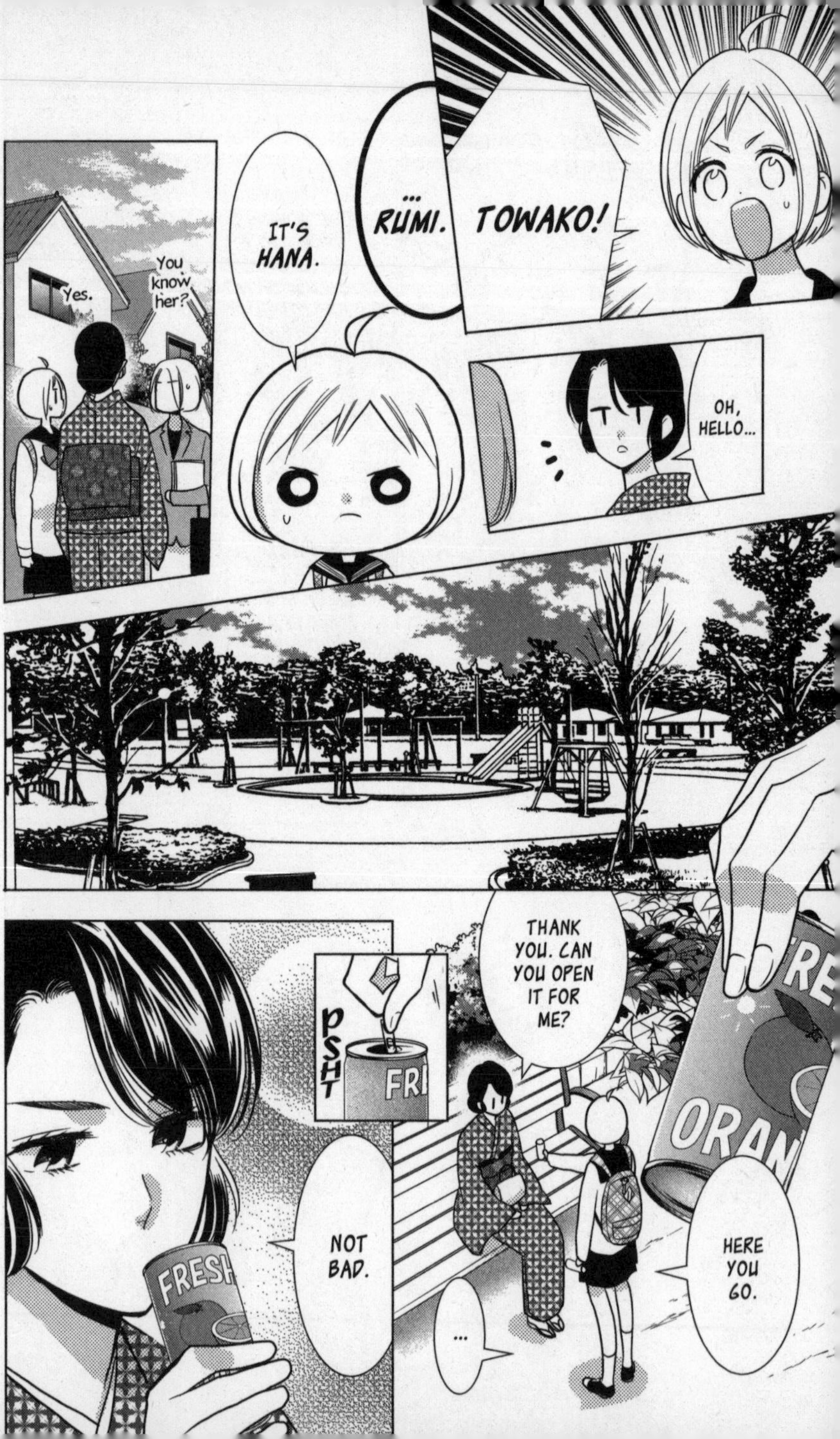
TOWAKO!
OH, HELLO...
... RÜMI.
IT'S HANA.
You know her?
Yes.
TRE
ORAN
HERE YOU GO.
THANK YOU. CAN YOU OPEN IT FOR ME?
...
PSHT
FRI
NOT BAD.
FRESH

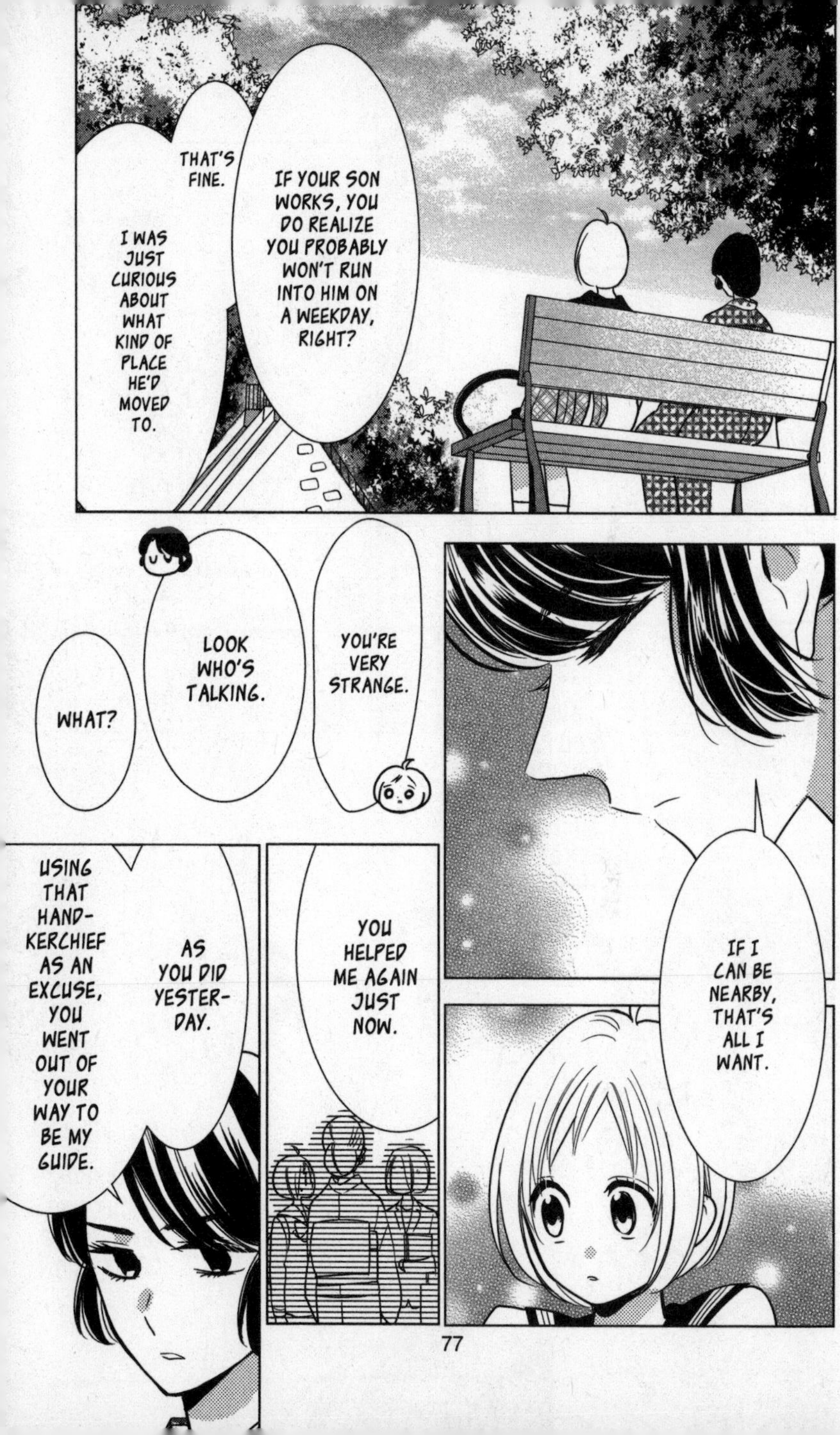
IF YOUR SON WORKS, YOU DO REALIZE YOU PROBABLY WON'T RUN INTO HIM ON A WEEKDAY, RIGHT?
THAT'S FINE.
I WAS JUST CURIOUS ABOUT WHAT KIND OF PLACE HE'D MOVED TO.
IF I CAN BE NEARBY, THAT'S ALL I WANT.
YOU'RE VERY STRANGE.
LOOK WHO'S TALKING.
WHAT?
YOU HELPED ME AGAIN JUST NOW.
AS YOU DID YESTER-DAY.
USING THAT HAND-KERCHIEF AS AN EXCUSE, YOU WENT OUT OF YOUR WAY TO BE MY GUIDE.

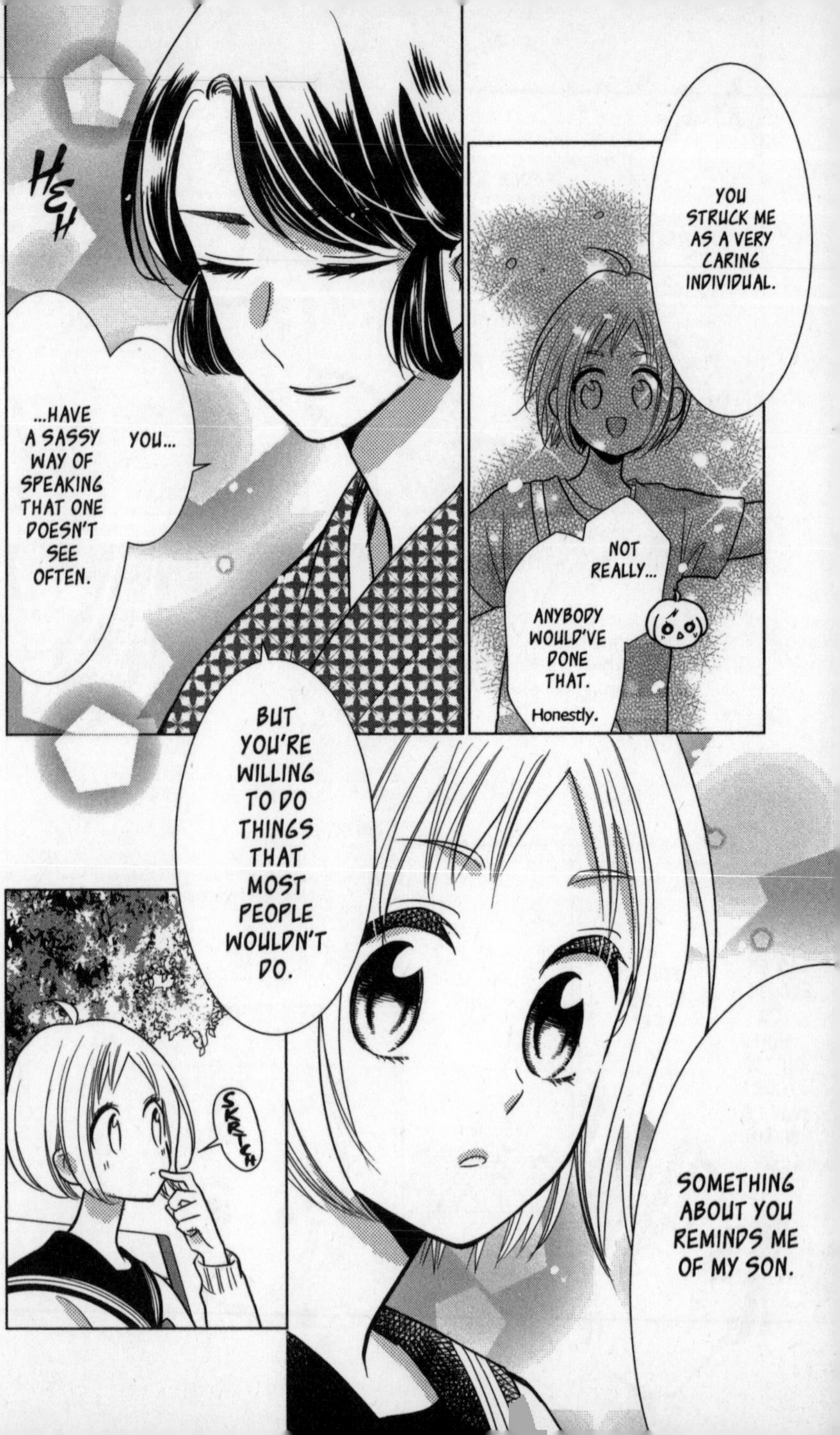
YOU STRUCK ME AS A VERY CARING INDIVIDUAL.
NOT REALLY...
ANYBODY WOULD'VE DONE THAT.
Honestly.
HEH
YOU...
...HAVE A SASSY WAY OF SPEAKING THAT ONE DOESN'T SEE OFTEN.
BUT YOU'RE WILLING TO DO THINGS THAT MOST PEOPLE WOULDN'T DO.
SOMETHING ABOUT YOU REMINDS ME OF MY SON.
SKRTCH

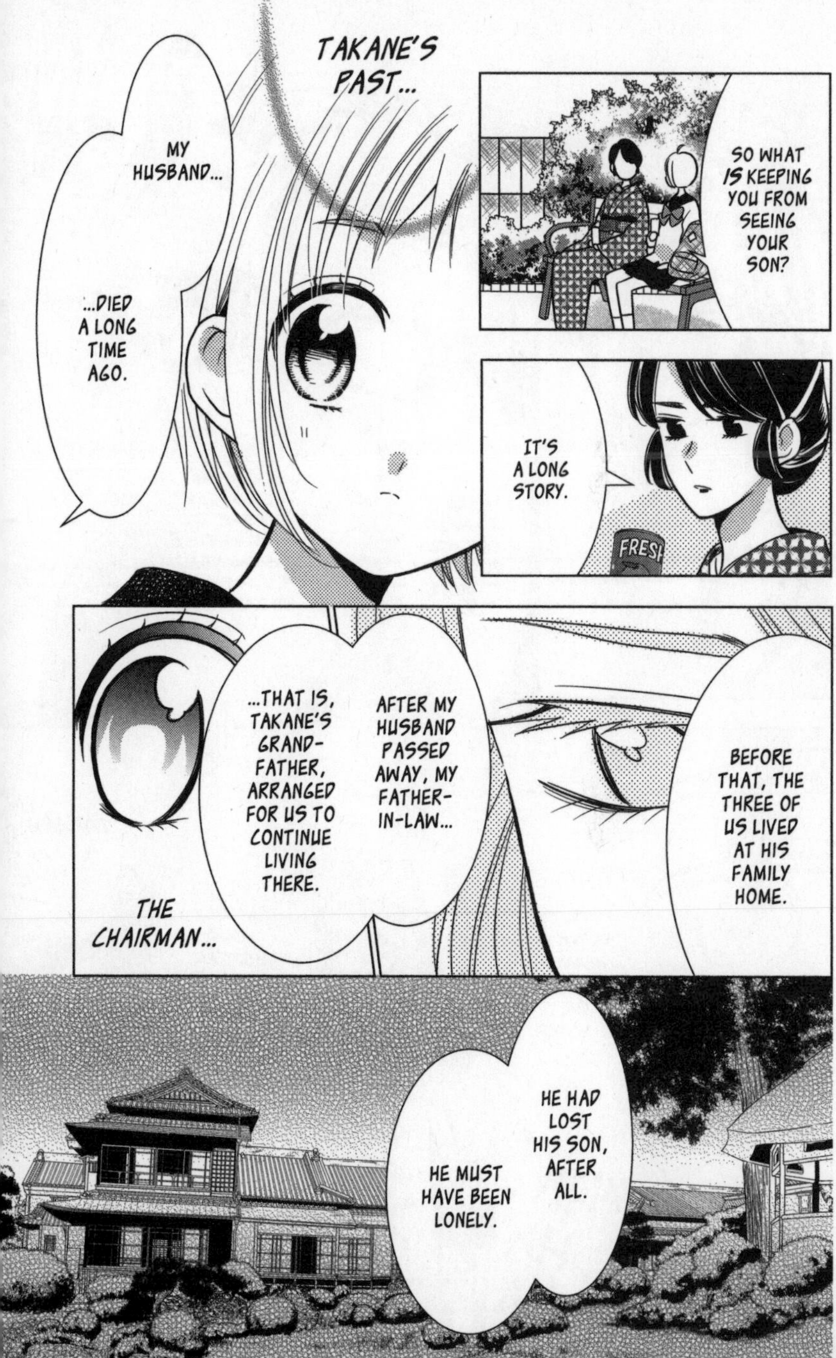
SO WHAT IS KEEPING YOU FROM SEEING YOUR SON?
IT'S A LONG STORY.
TAKANE'S PAST...
MY HUSBAND...
...DIED A LONG TIME AGO.
BEFORE THAT, THE THREE OF US LIVED AT HIS FAMILY HOME.
AFTER MY HUSBAND PASSED AWAY, MY FATHER-IN-LAW...
...THAT IS, TAKANE'S GRANDFATHER, ARRANGED FOR US TO CONTINUE LIVING THERE.
THE CHAIRMAN...
HE HAD LOST HIS SON, AFTER ALL.
HE MUST HAVE BEEN LONELY.

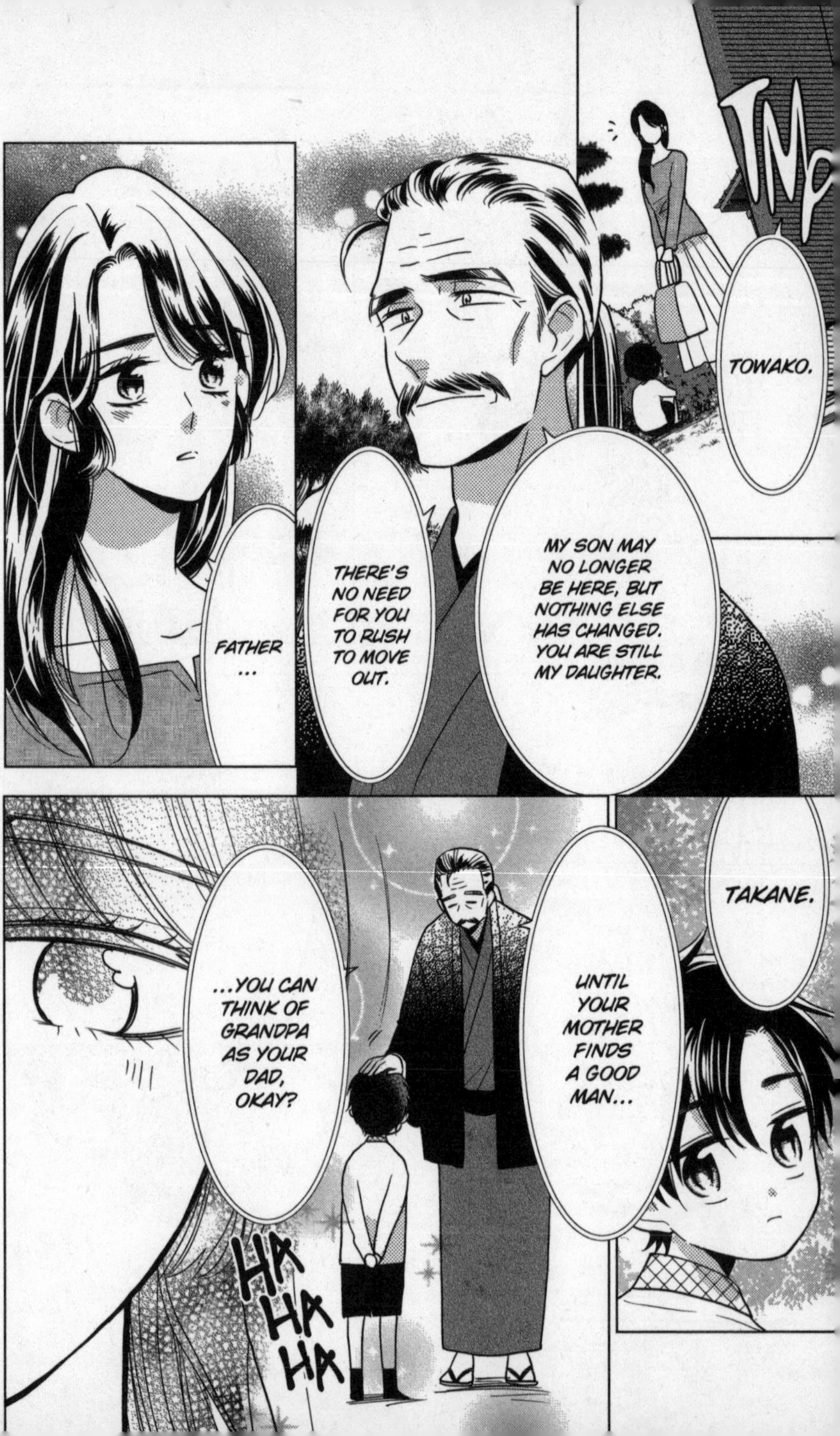
TOWAKO.
MY SON MAY NO LONGER BE HERE, BUT NOTHING ELSE HAS CHANGED. YOU ARE STILL MY DAUGHTER.
THERE'S NO NEED FOR YOU TO RUSH TO MOVE OUT.
FATHER ...
TAKANE.
UNTIL YOUR MOTHER FINDS A GOOD MAN...
...YOU CAN THINK OF GRANDPA AS YOUR DAD, OKAY?
HA HA HA

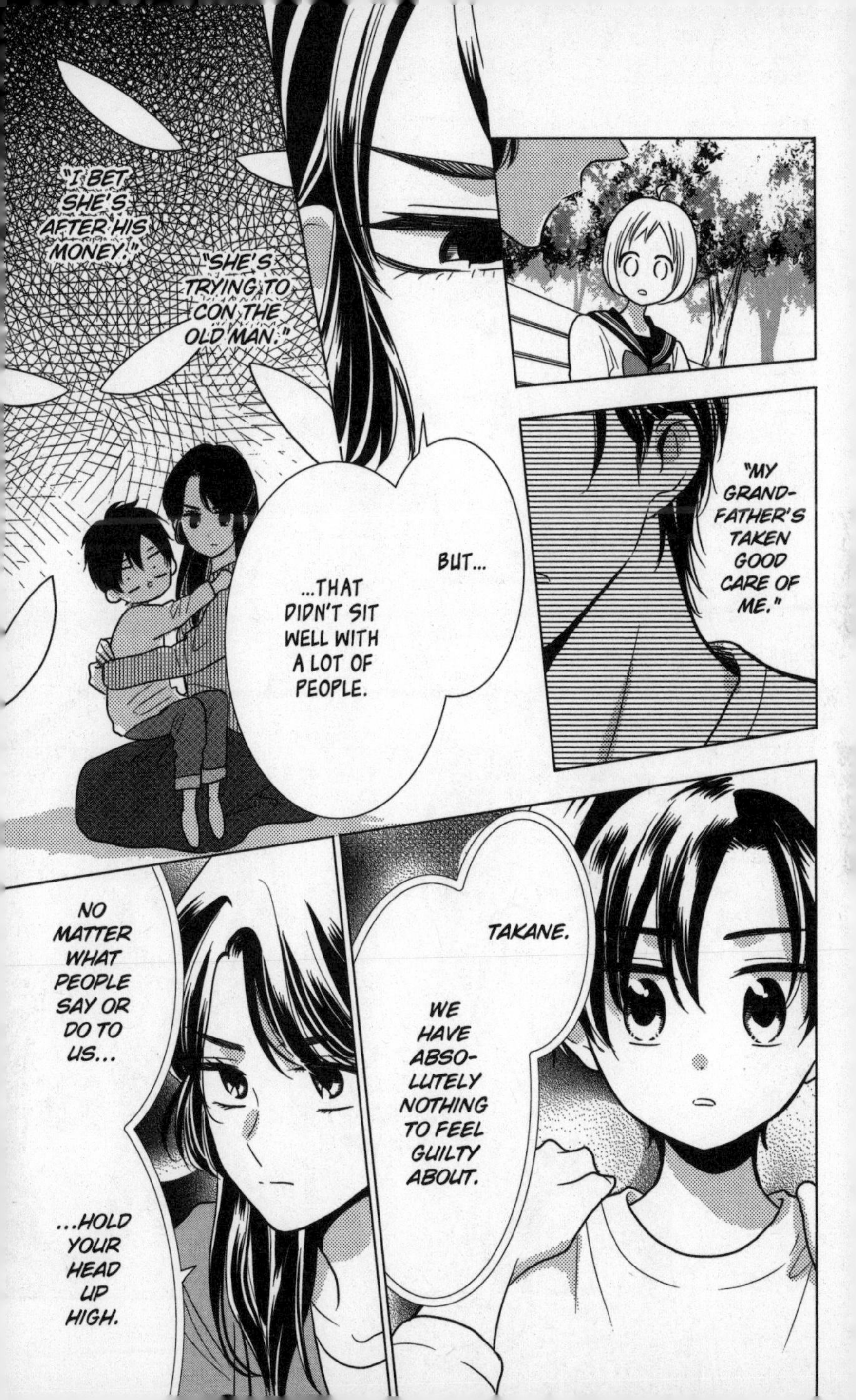
"MY GRAND-FATHER'S TAKEN GOOD CARE OF ME."
BUT...
...THAT DIDN'T SIT WELL WITH A LOT OF PEOPLE.
"I BET SHE'S AFTER HIS MONEY."
"SHE'S TRYING TO CON THE OLD MAN."
TAKANE.
WE HAVE ABSO-LUTELY NOTHING TO FEEL GUILTY ABOUT.
NO MATTER WHAT PEOPLE SAY OR DO TO US...
...HOLD YOUR HEAD UP HIGH.

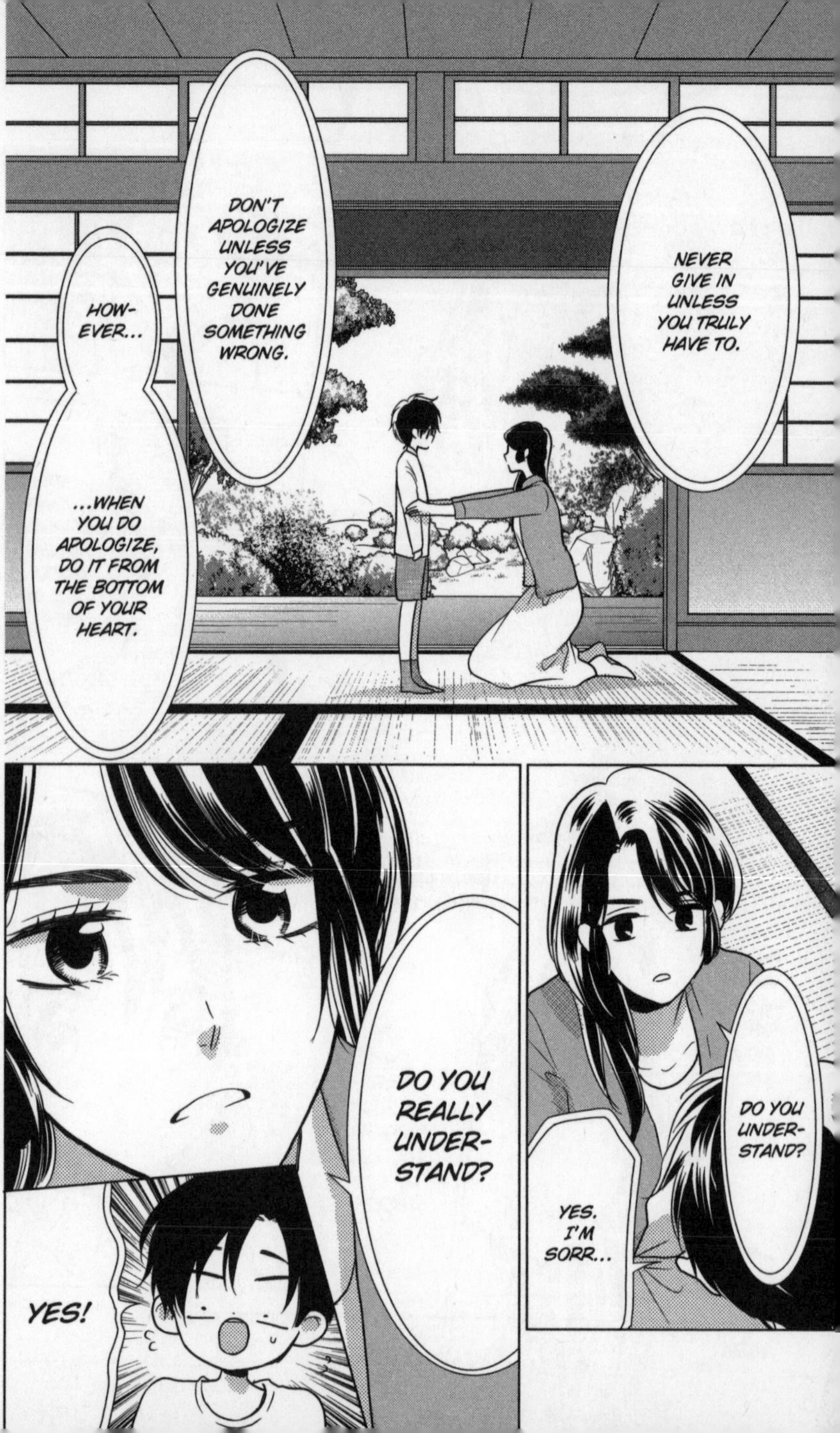
NEVER GIVE IN UNLESS YOU TRULY HAVE TO.
DON'T APOLOGIZE UNLESS YOU'VE GENUINELY DONE SOMETHING WRONG.
HOW-EVER...
...WHEN YOU DO APOLOGIZE, DO IT FROM THE BOTTOM OF YOUR HEART.
DO YOU UNDER-STAND?
YES. I'M SORR...
DO YOU REALLY UNDER-STAND?
YES!

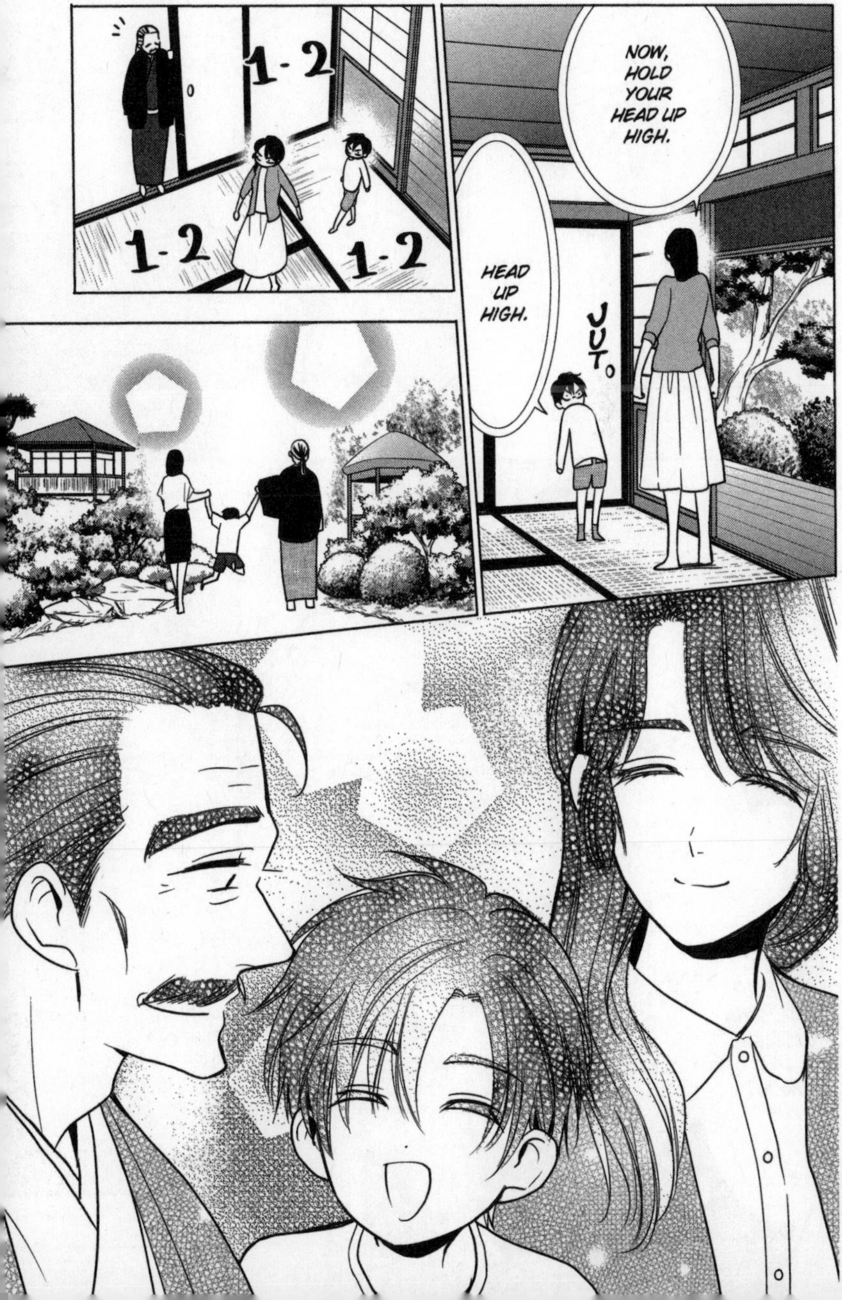
NOW, HOLD YOUR HEAD UP HIGH.
HEAD UP HIGH.
JUT
1-2
1-2
1-2

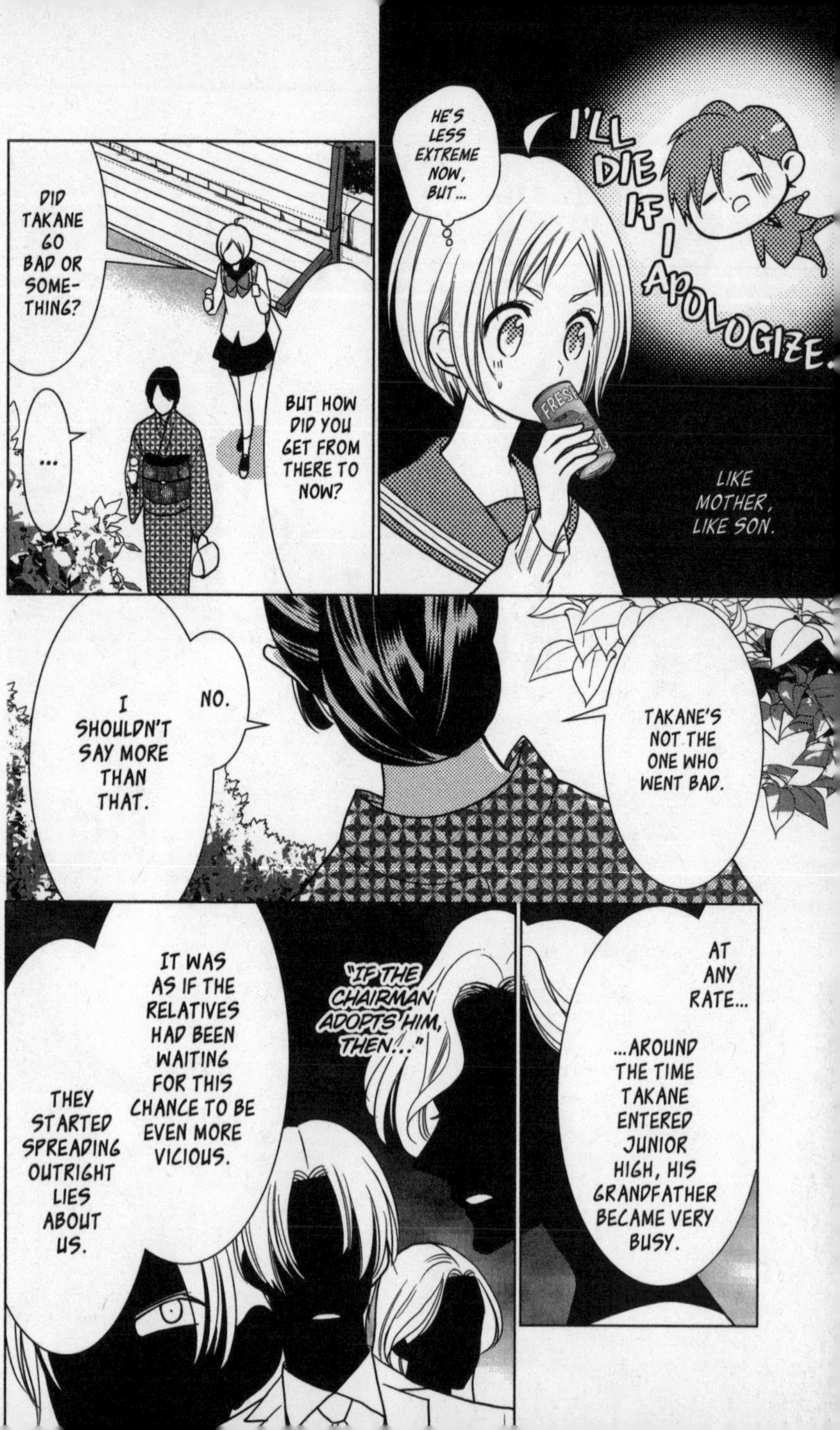
HE'S LESS EXTREME NOW, BUT...
I'LL DIE IF I APOLOGIZE.
LIKE MOTHER, LIKE SON.
DID TAKANE GO BAD OR SOME-THING?
BUT HOW DID YOU GET FROM THERE TO NOW?
...
TAKANE'S NOT THE ONE WHO WENT BAD.
NO.
I SHOULDN'T SAY MORE THAN THAT.
AT ANY RATE...
...AROUND THE TIME TAKANE ENTERED JUNIOR HIGH, HIS GRANDFATHER BECAME VERY BUSY.
"IF THE CHAIRMAN ADOPTS HIM, THEN..."
IT WAS AS IF THE RELATIVES HAD BEEN WAITING FOR THIS CHANCE TO BE EVEN MORE VICIOUS.
THEY STARTED SPREADING OUTRIGHT LIES ABOUT US.

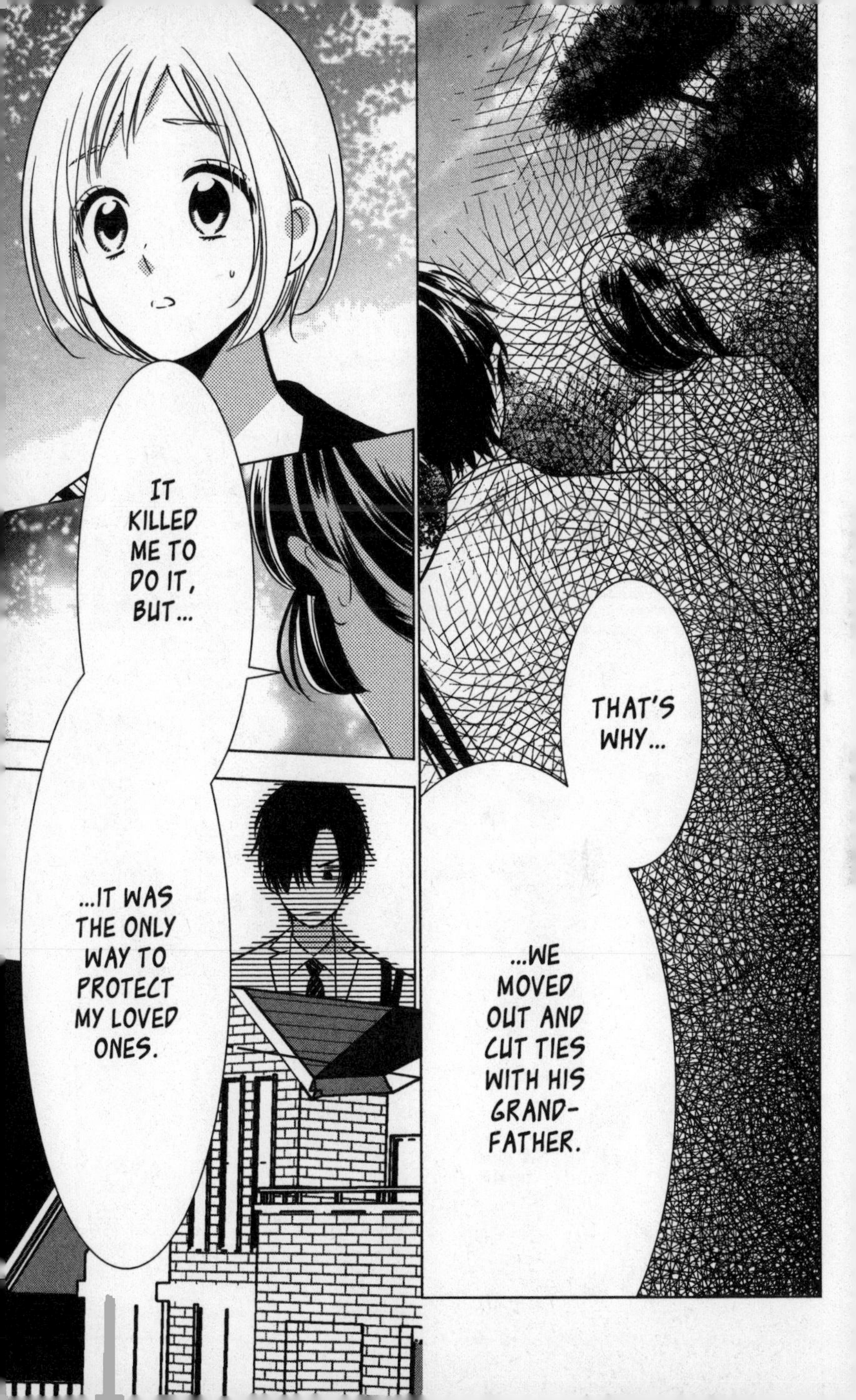
THAT'S WHY...
...WE MOVED OUT AND CUT TIES WITH HIS GRANDFATHER.
IT KILLED ME TO DO IT, BUT...
...IT WAS THE ONLY WAY TO PROTECT MY LOVED ONES.

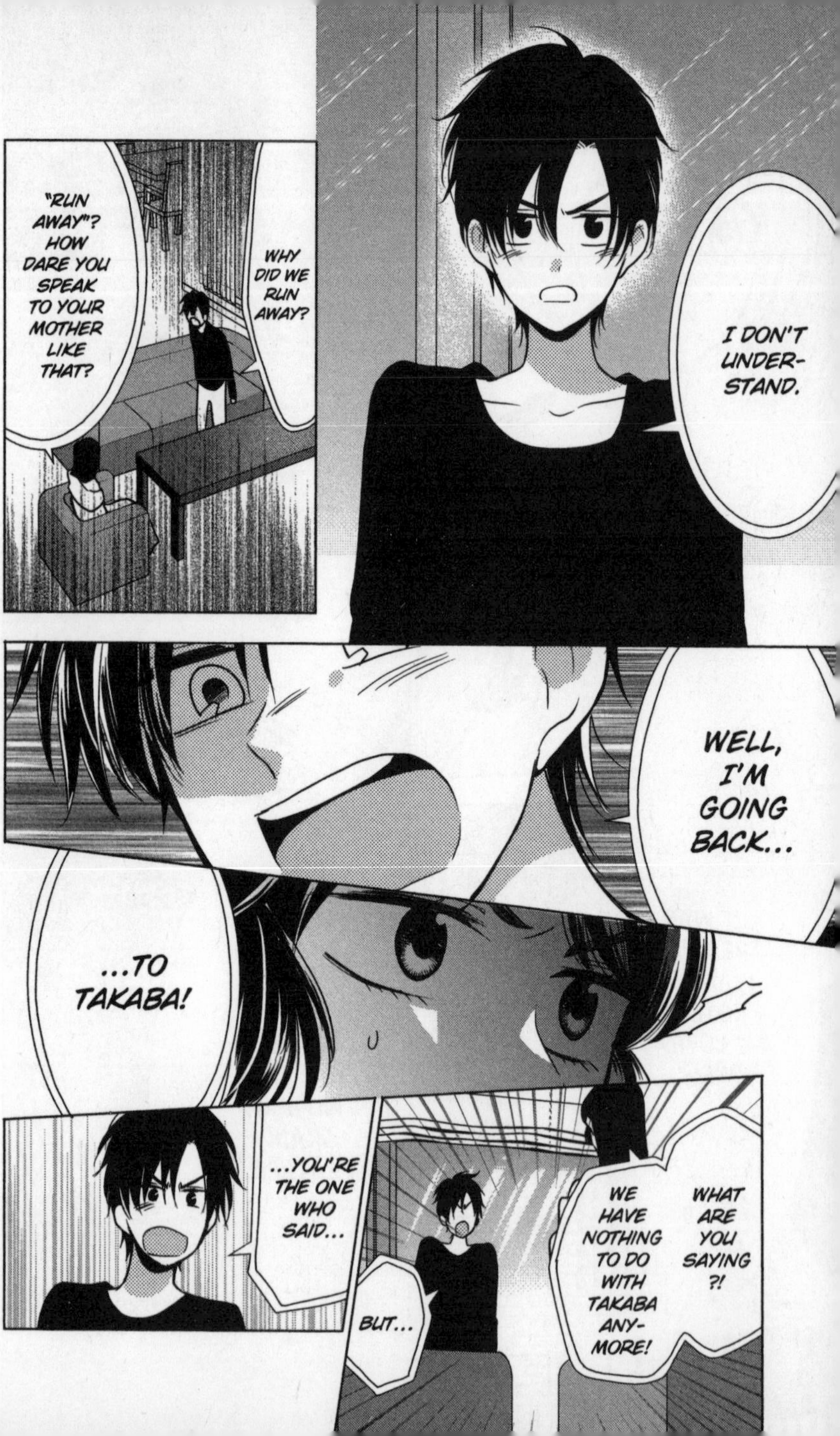
I DON'T UNDER-STAND.
WHY DID WE RUN AWAY?
"RUN AWAY"? HOW DARE YOU SPEAK TO YOUR MOTHER LIKE THAT?
WELL, I'M GOING BACK...
...TO TAKABA!
WHAT ARE YOU SAYING?!
WE HAVE NOTHING TO DO WITH TAKABA ANY-MORE!
BUT...
...YOU'RE THE ONE WHO SAID...

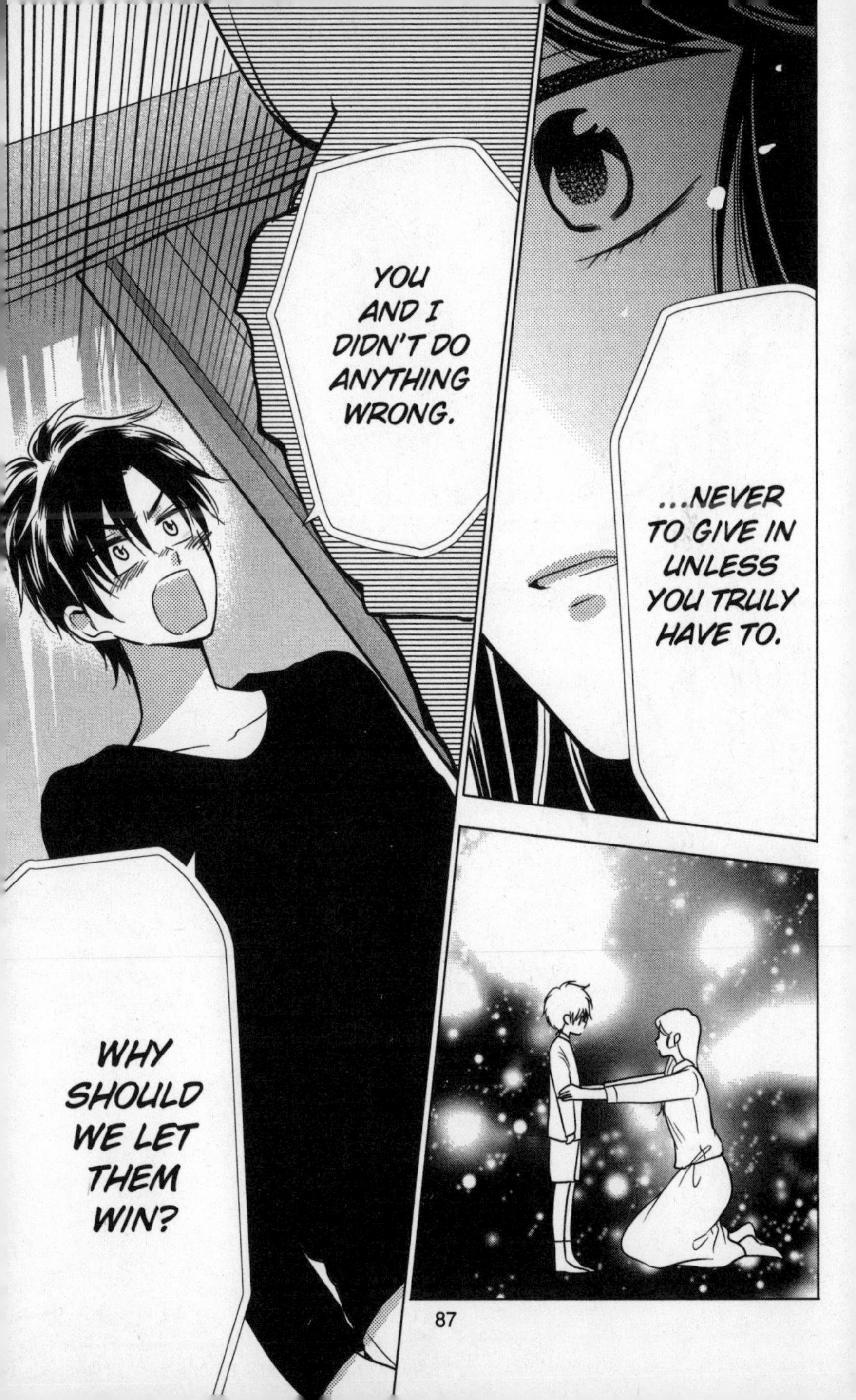
...NEVER TO GIVE IN UNLESS YOU TRULY HAVE TO.
YOU AND I DIDN'T DO ANYTHING WRONG.
WHY SHOULD WE LET THEM WIN?

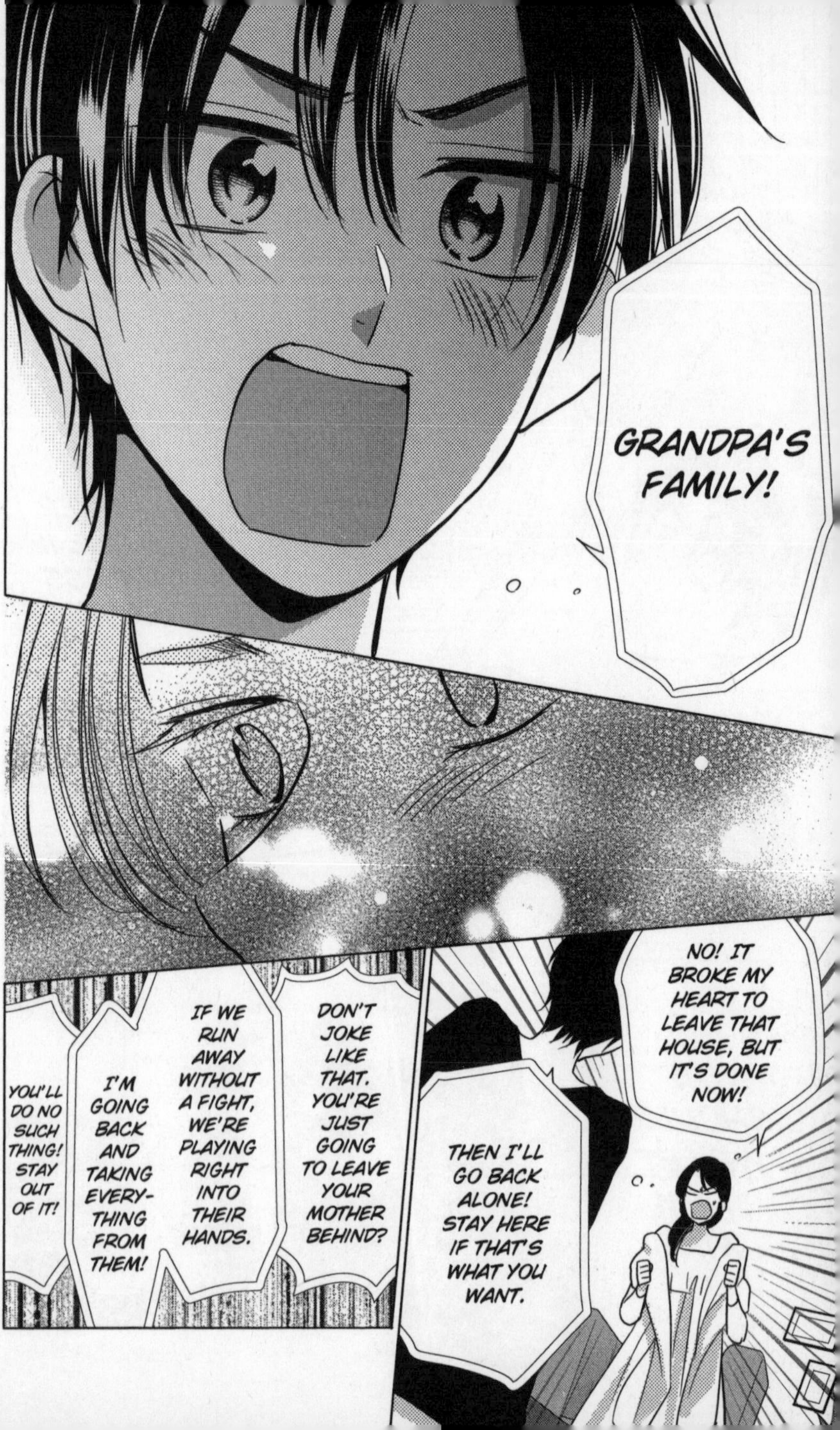
GRANDPA'S FAMILY!
NO! IT BROKE MY HEART TO LEAVE THAT HOUSE, BUT IT'S DONE NOW!
THEN I'LL GO BACK ALONE! STAY HERE IF THAT'S WHAT YOU WANT.
DON'T JOKE LIKE THAT. YOU'RE JUST GOING TO LEAVE YOUR MOTHER BEHIND?
IF WE RUN AWAY WITHOUT A FIGHT, WE'RE PLAYING RIGHT INTO THEIR HANDS.
I'M GOING BACK AND TAKING EVERY-THING FROM THEM!
YOU'LL DO NO SUCH THING! STAY OUT OF IT!

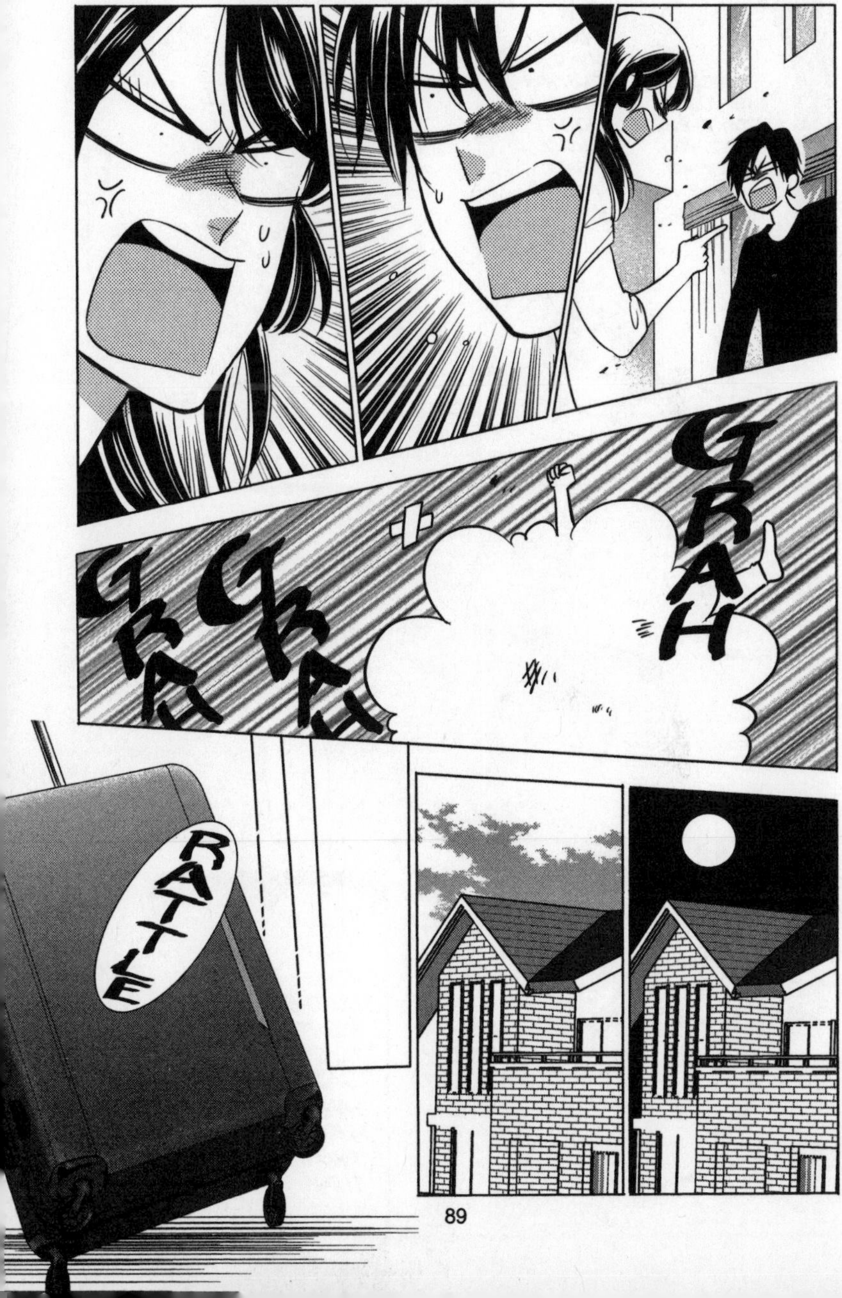
GRAH
GRAH
GRAH
RATTLE

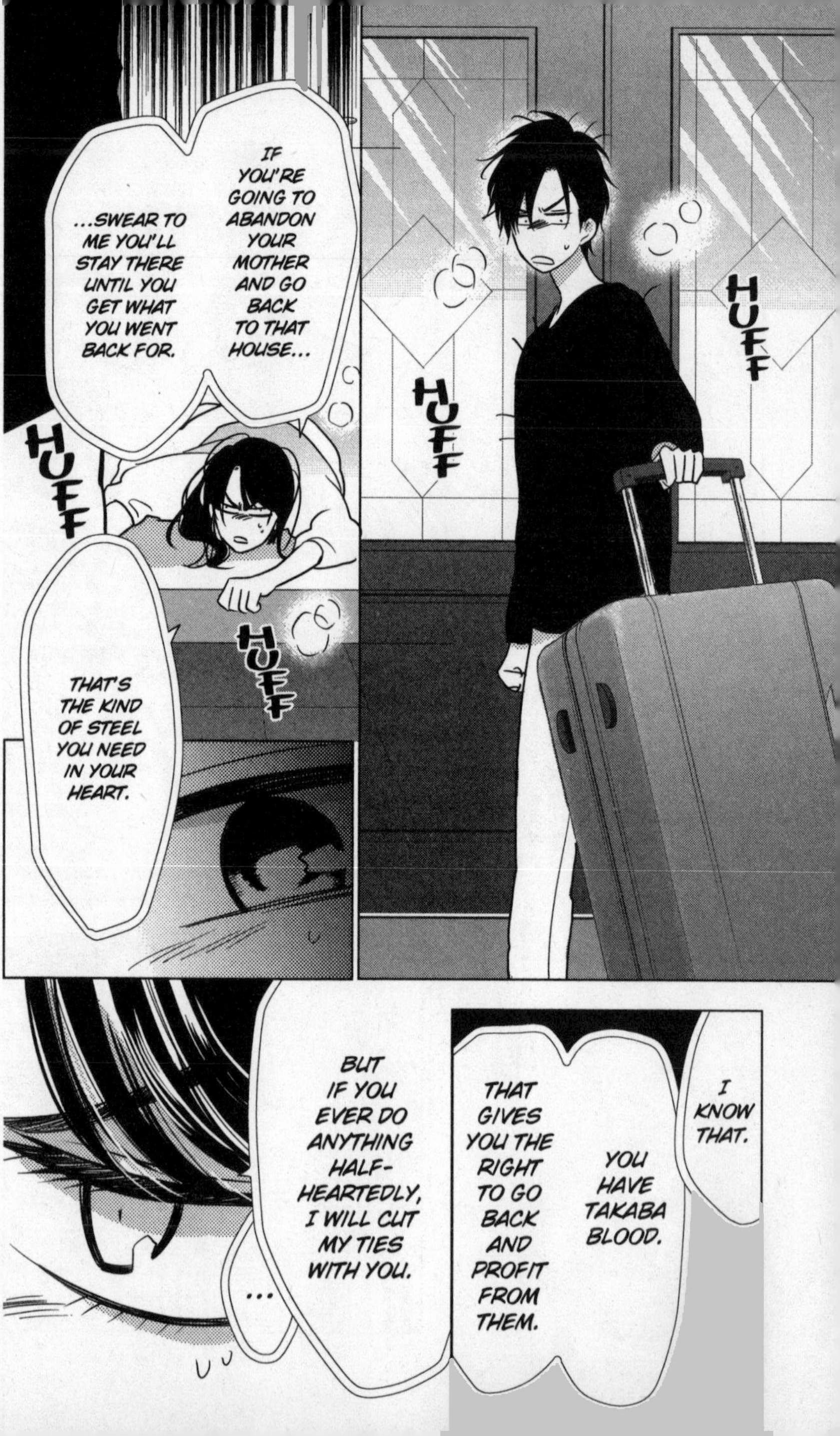
HUFF
HUFF
IF YOU'RE GOING TO ABANDON YOUR MOTHER AND GO BACK TO THAT HOUSE...
...SWEAR TO ME YOU'LL STAY THERE UNTIL YOU GET WHAT YOU WENT BACK FOR.
HUFF
HUFF
THAT'S THE KIND OF STEEL YOU NEED IN YOUR HEART.
I KNOW THAT.
YOU HAVE TAKABA BLOOD.
THAT GIVES YOU THE RIGHT TO GO BACK AND PROFIT FROM THEM.
BUT IF YOU EVER DO ANYTHING HALF-HEARTEDLY, I WILL CUT MY TIES WITH YOU.
...

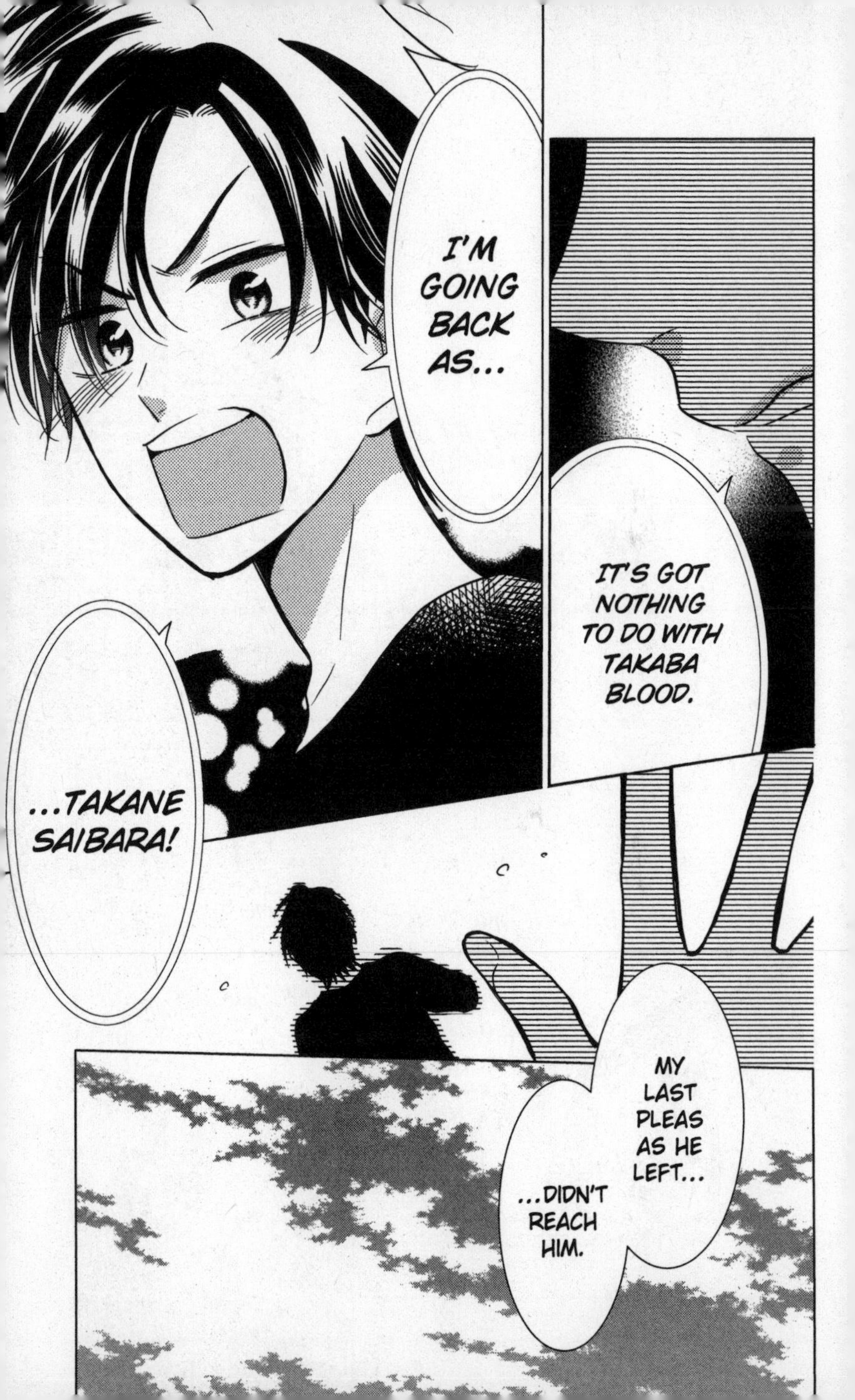
IT'S GOT NOTHING TO DO WITH TAKABA BLOOD.
I'M GOING BACK AS...
...TAKANE SAIBARA!
MY LAST PLEAS AS HE LEFT...
...DIDN'T REACH HIM.

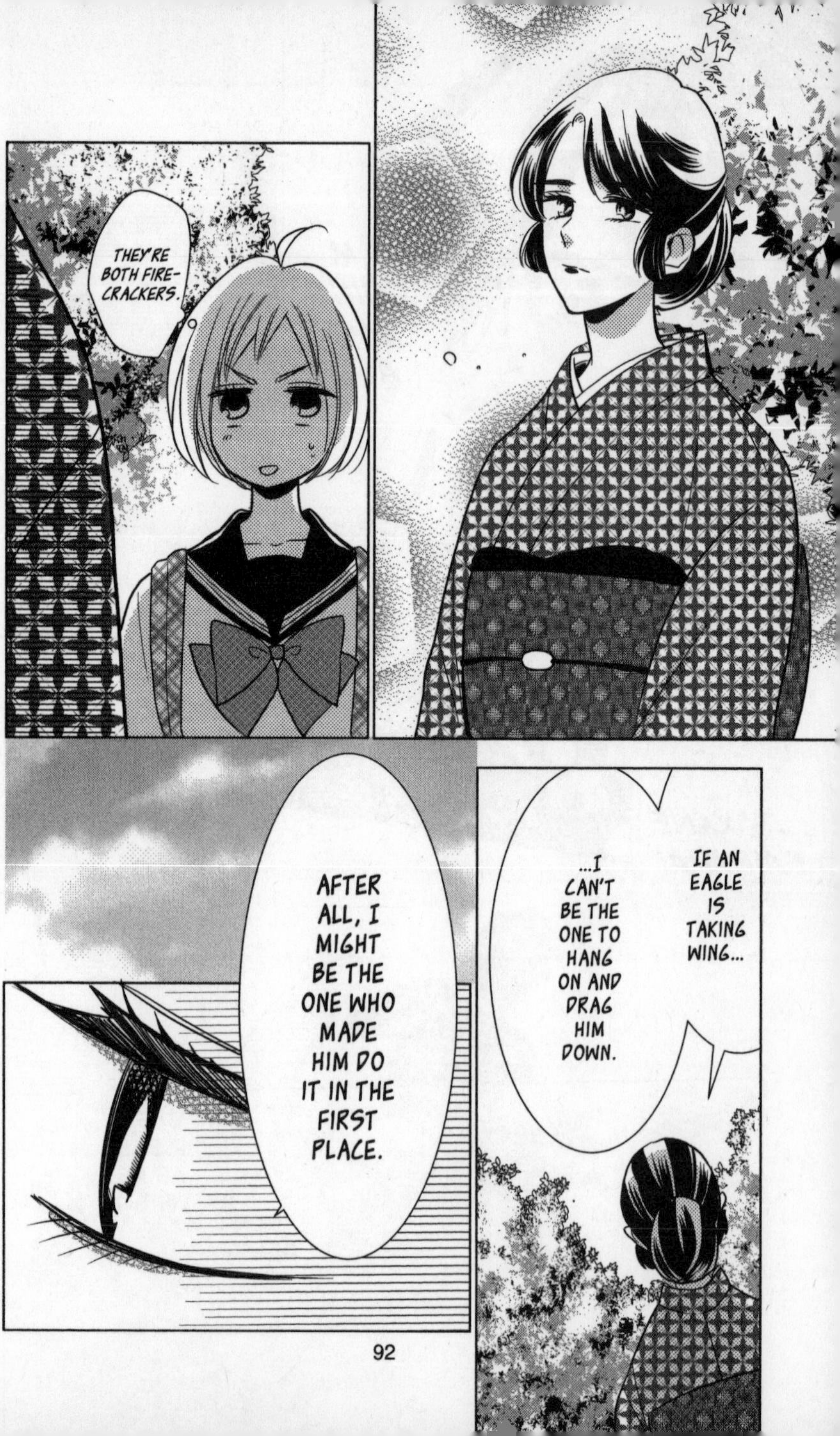
THEY'RE BOTH FIRE-CRACKERS.
IF AN EAGLE IS TAKING WING...
...I CAN'T BE THE ONE TO HANG ON AND DRAG HIM DOWN.
AFTER ALL, I MIGHT BE THE ONE WHO MADE HIM DO IT IN THE FIRST PLACE.

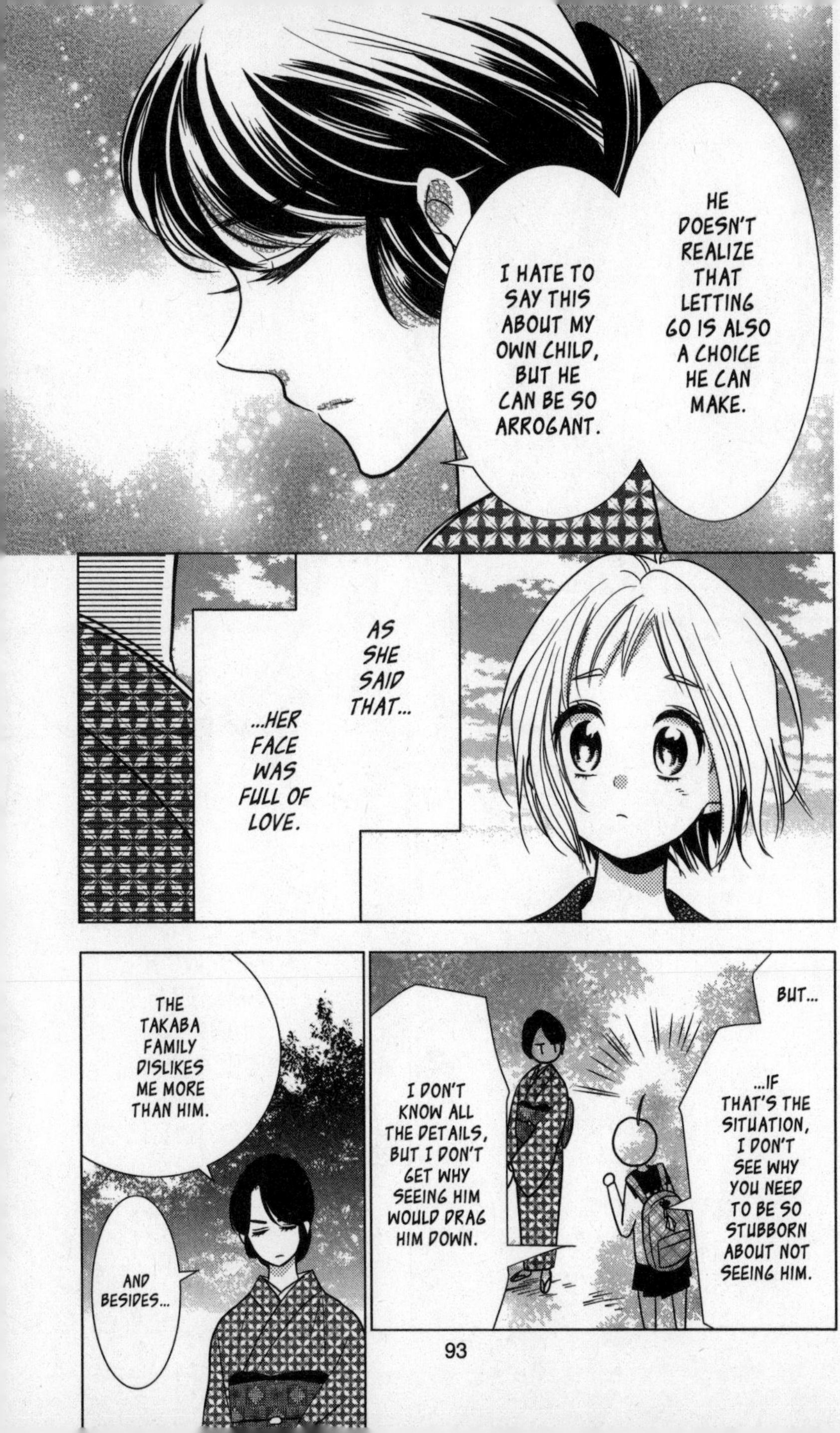
HE DOESN'T REALIZE THAT LETTING GO IS ALSO A CHOICE HE CAN MAKE.
I HATE TO SAY THIS ABOUT MY OWN CHILD, BUT HE CAN BE SO ARROGANT.
AS SHE SAID THAT...
...HER FACE WAS FULL OF LOVE.
BUT...
...IF THAT'S THE SITUATION, I DON'T SEE WHY YOU NEED TO BE SO STUBBORN ABOUT NOT SEEING HIM.
I DON'T KNOW ALL THE DETAILS, BUT I DON'T GET WHY SEEING HIM WOULD DRAG HIM DOWN.
THE TAKABA FAMILY DISLIKES ME MORE THAN HIM.
AND BESIDES...

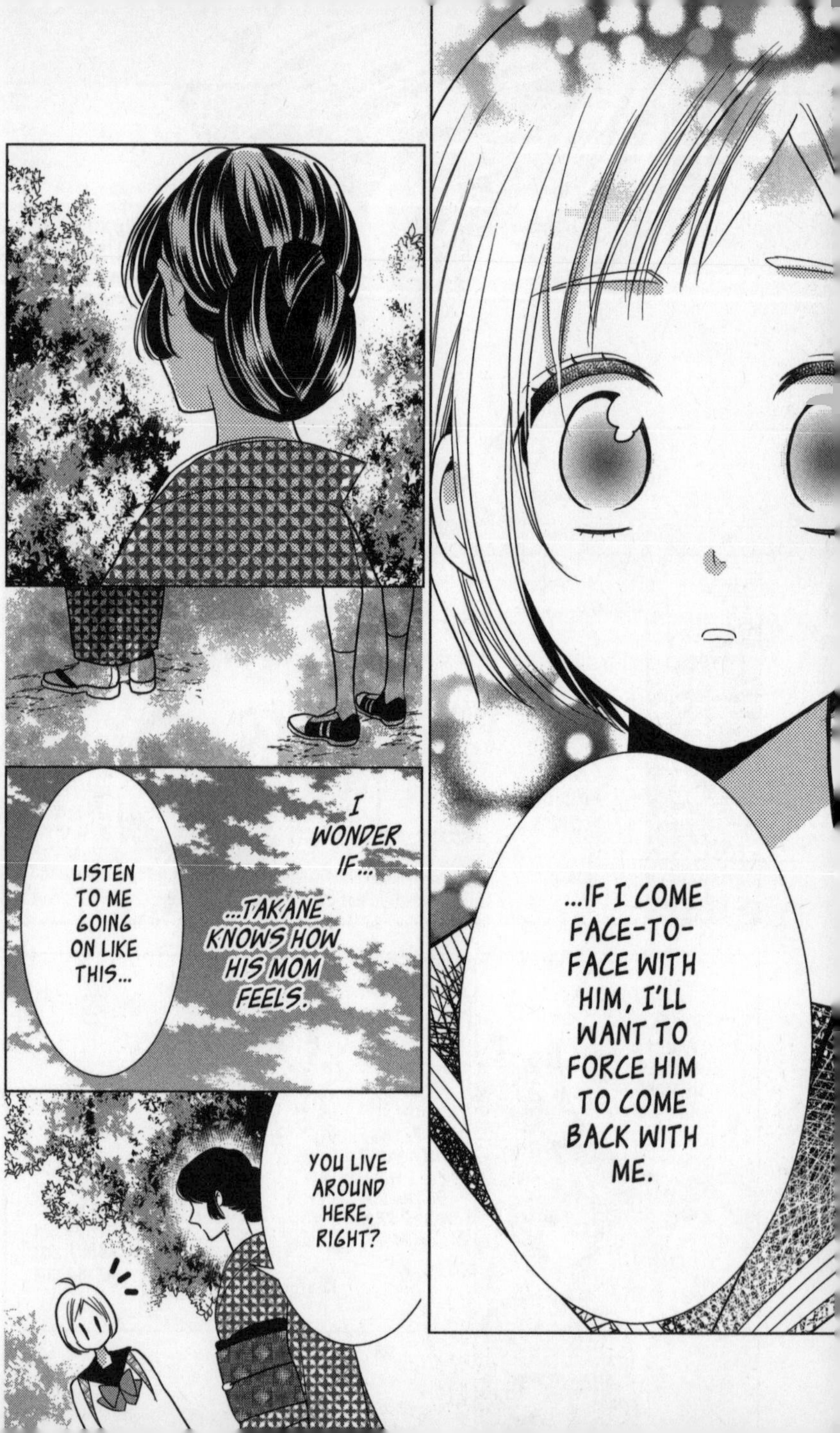
...IF I COME FACE-TO-FACE WITH HIM, I'LL WANT TO FORCE HIM TO COME BACK WITH ME.
I WONDER IF...
...TAKANE KNOWS HOW HIS MOM FEELS.
LISTEN TO ME GOING ON LIKE THIS...
YOU LIVE AROUND HERE, RIGHT?

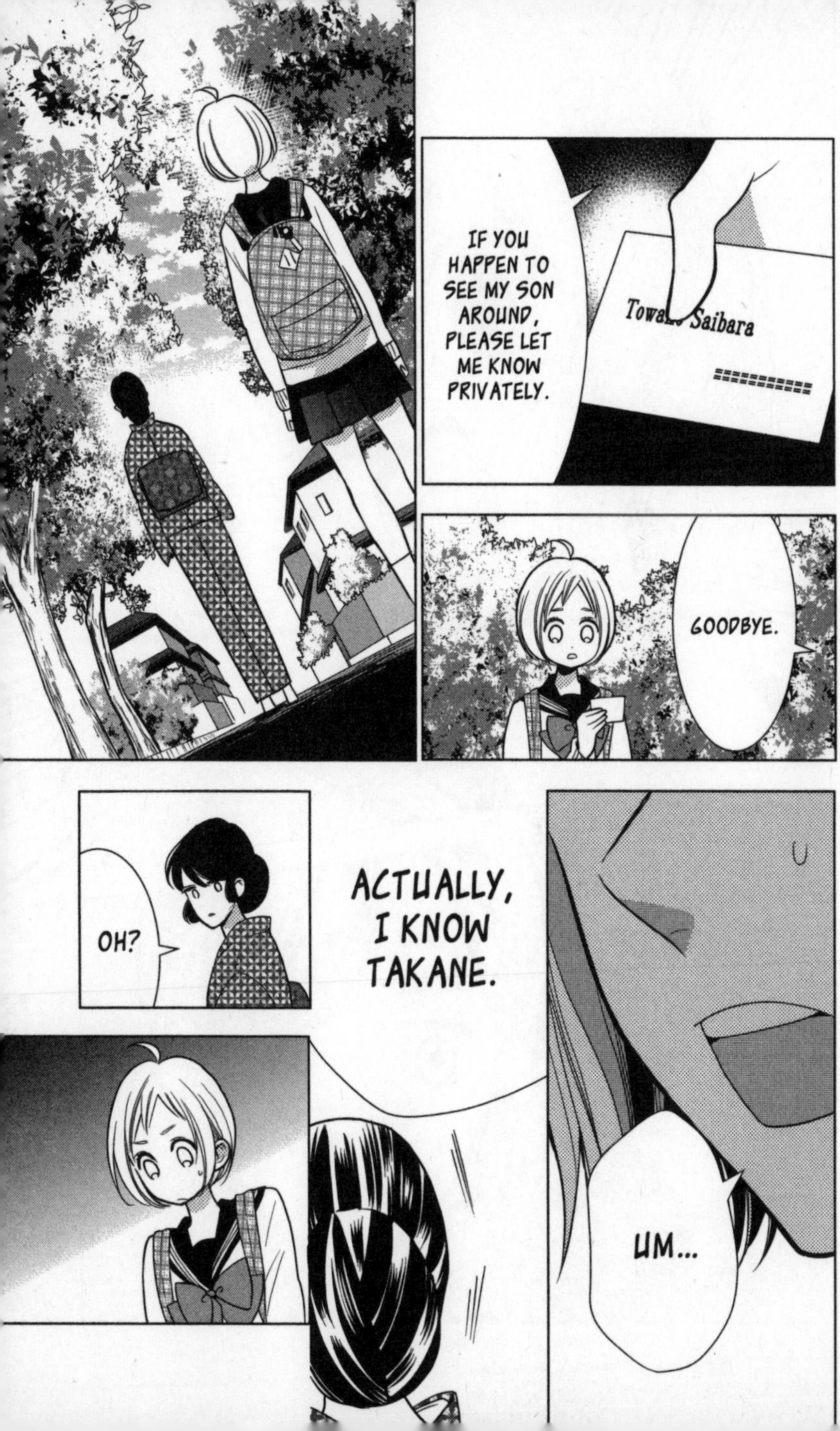
IF YOU HAPPEN TO SEE MY SON AROUND, PLEASE LET ME KNOW PRIVATELY.
Saibara
GOODBYE.
UM...
OH?
ACTUALLY, I KNOW TAKANE.

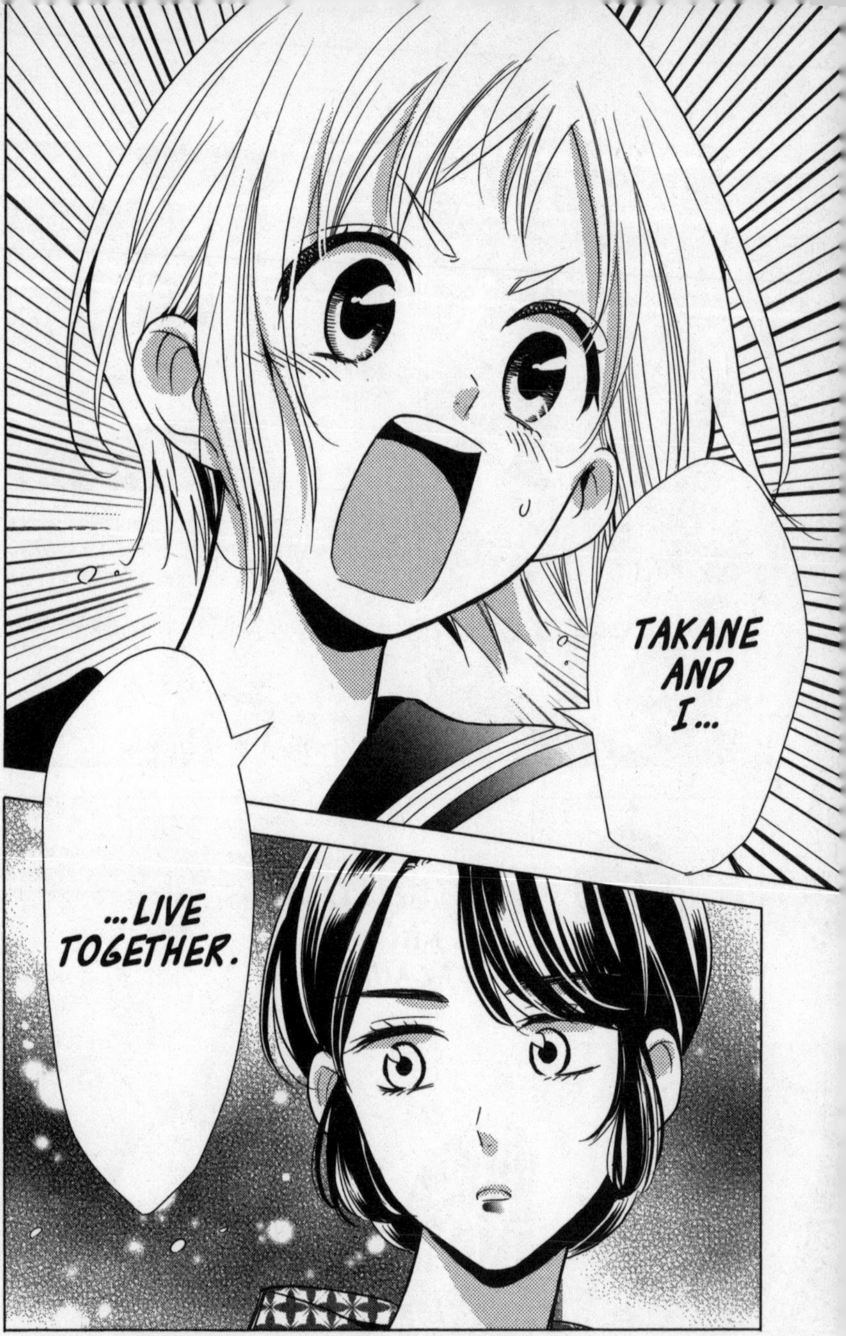
TAKANE AND I...
...LIVE TOGETHER.

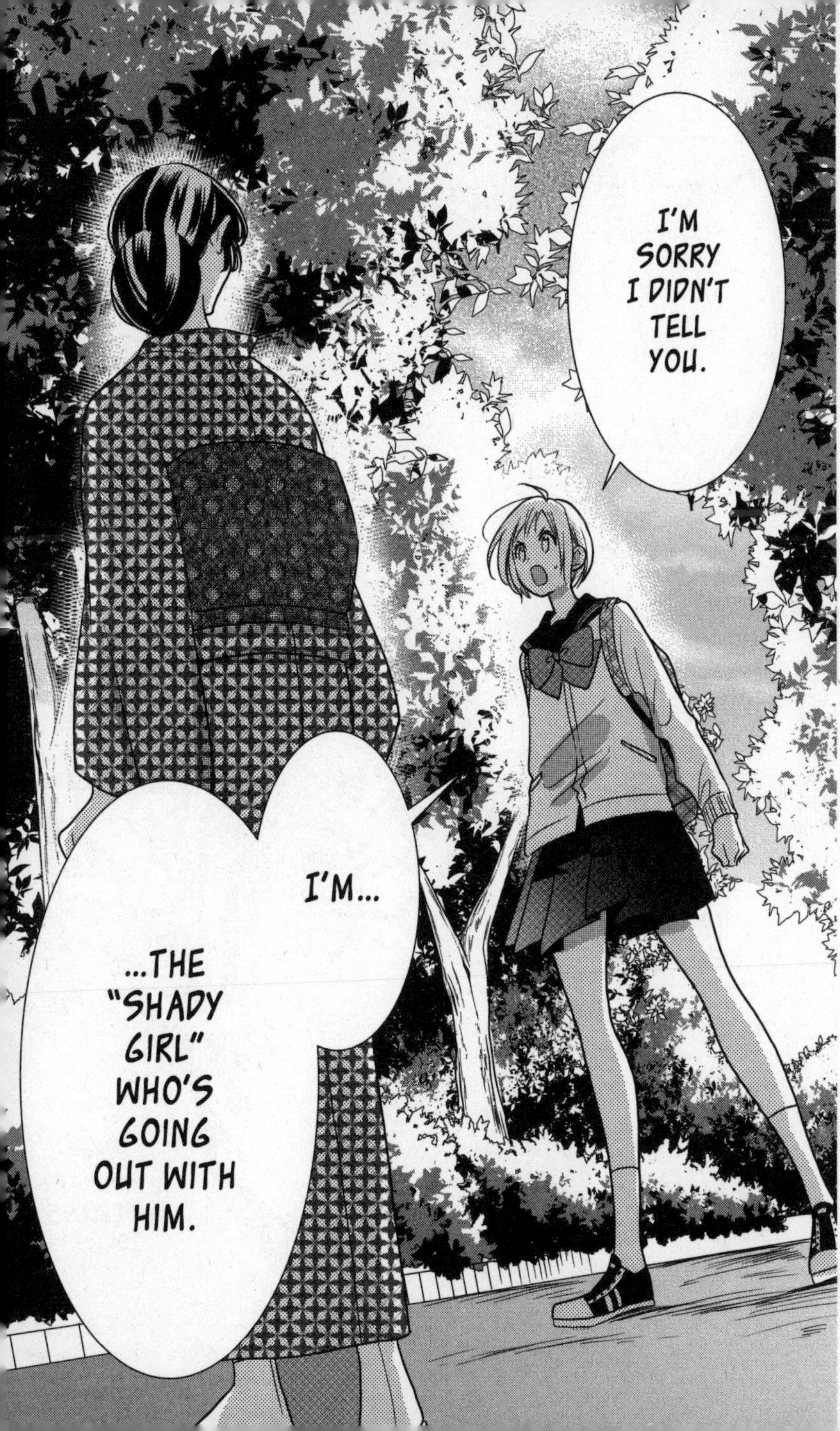
I'M SORRY I DIDN'T TELL YOU.
I'M...
..."THE "SHADY GIRL" WHO'S GOING OUT WITH HIM.

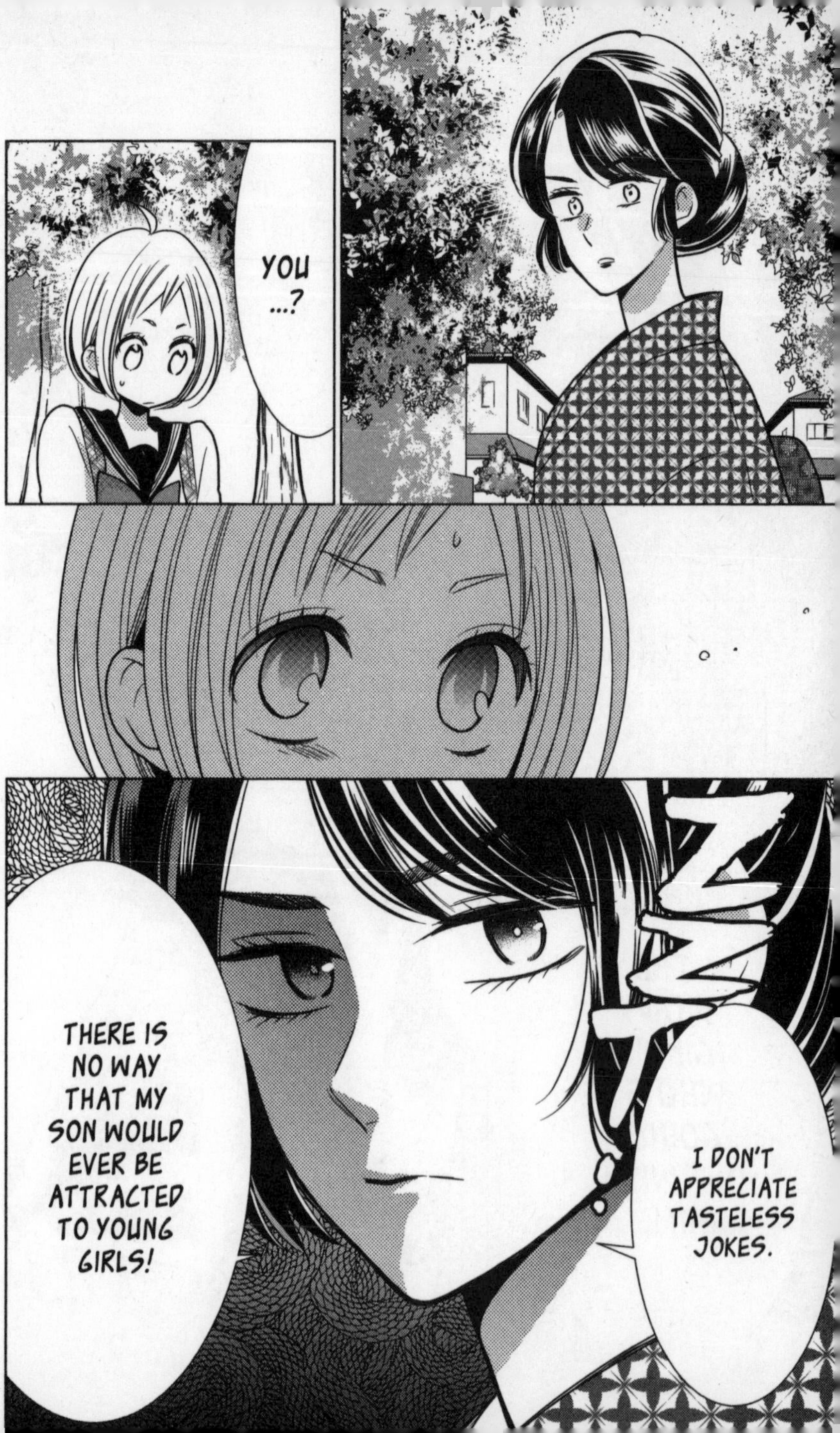
YOU ...?
I DON'T APPRECIATE TASTELESS JOKES.
THERE IS NO WAY THAT MY SON WOULD EVER BE ATTRACTED TO YOUNG GIRLS!

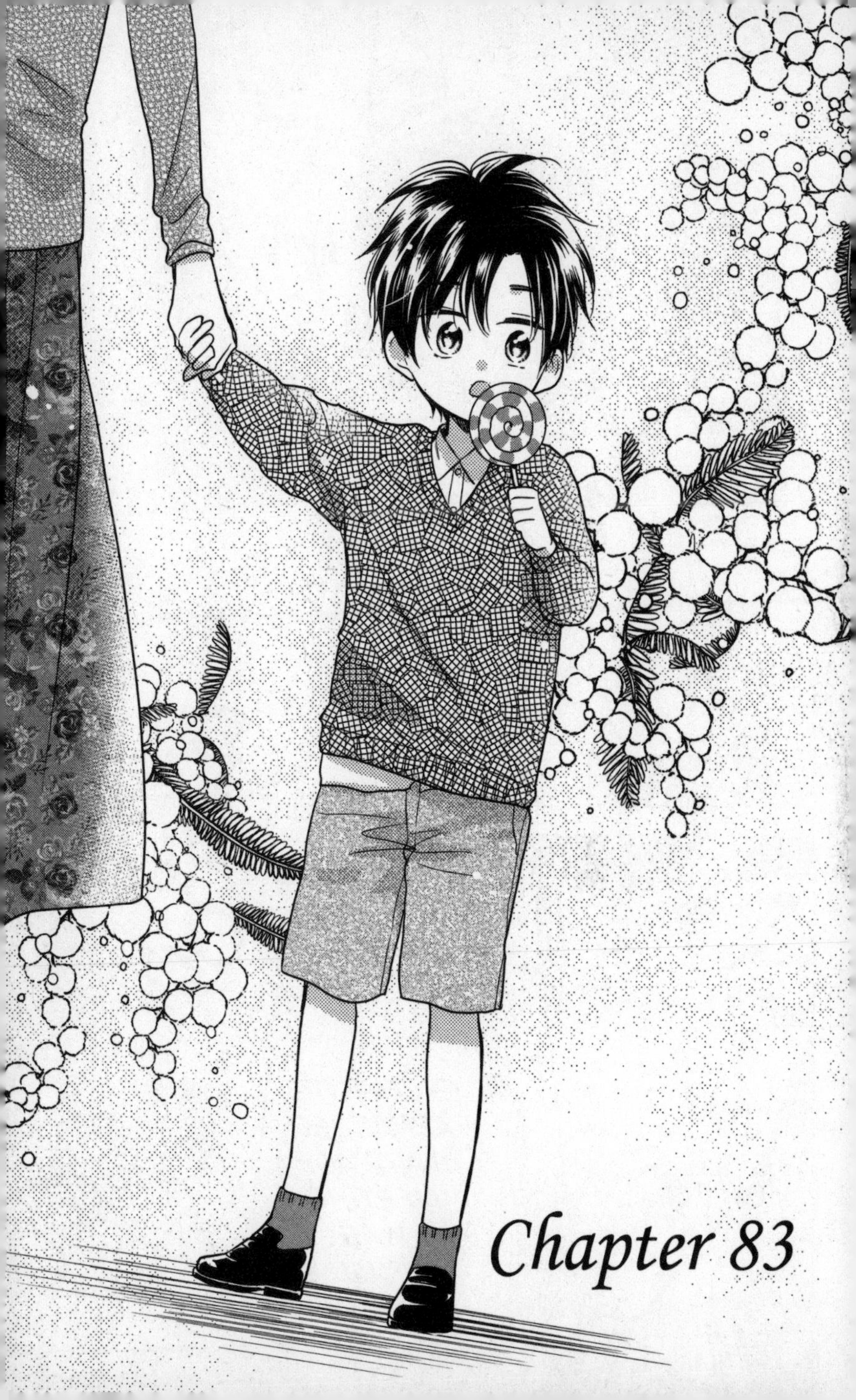

Chapter 83

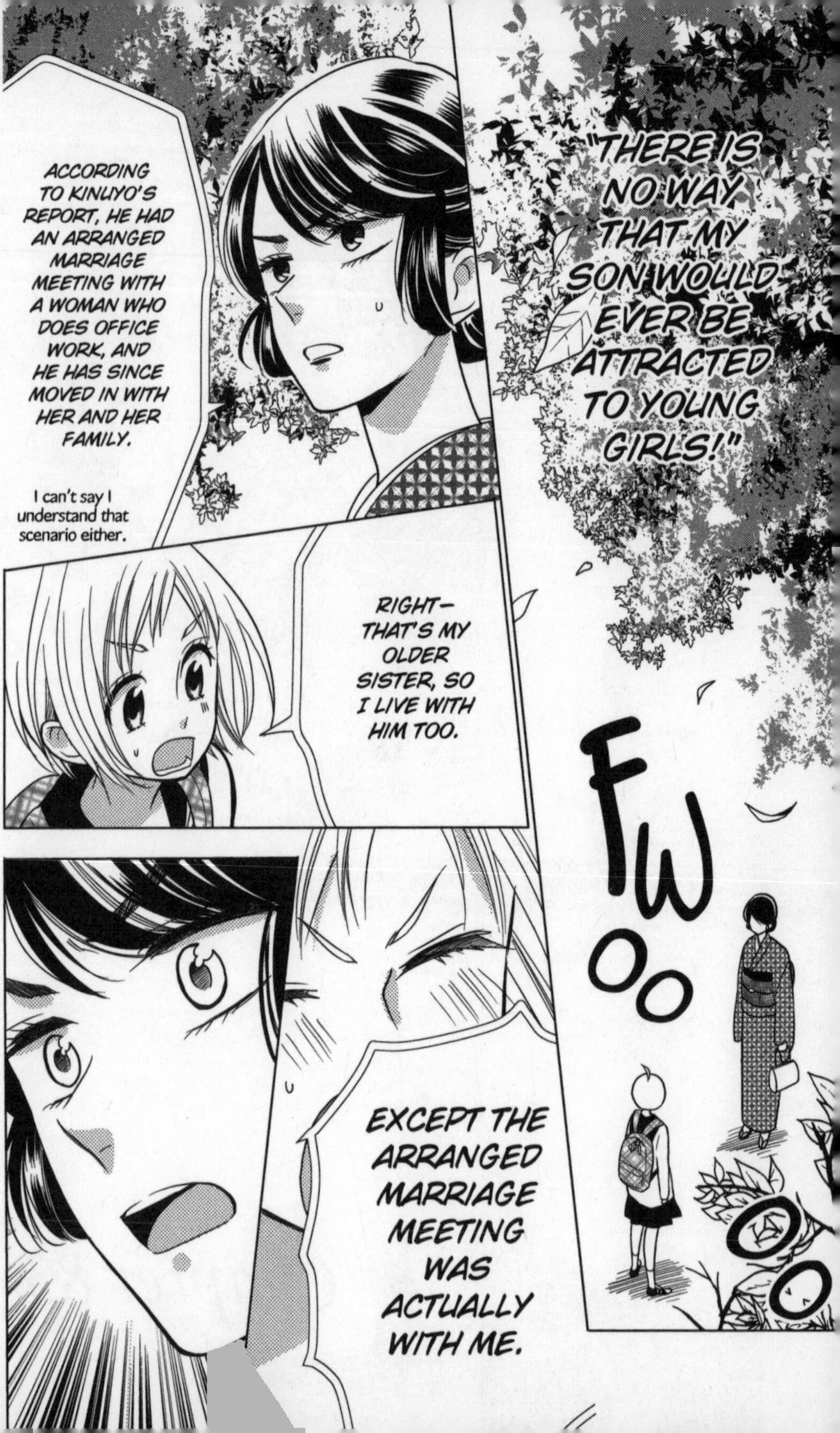
"THERE IS NO WAY THAT MY SON WOULD EVER BE ATTRACTED TO YOUNG GIRLS!"
FWOO
OO
ACCORDING TO KINUYO'S REPORT, HE HAD AN ARRANGED MARRIAGE MEETING WITH A WOMAN WHO DOES OFFICE WORK, AND HE HAS SINCE MOVED IN WITH HER AND HER FAMILY.
I can't say I understand that scenario either.
RIGHT—THAT'S MY OLDER SISTER, SO I LIVE WITH HIM TOO.
EXCEPT THE ARRANGED MARRIAGE MEETING WAS ACTUALLY WITH ME.

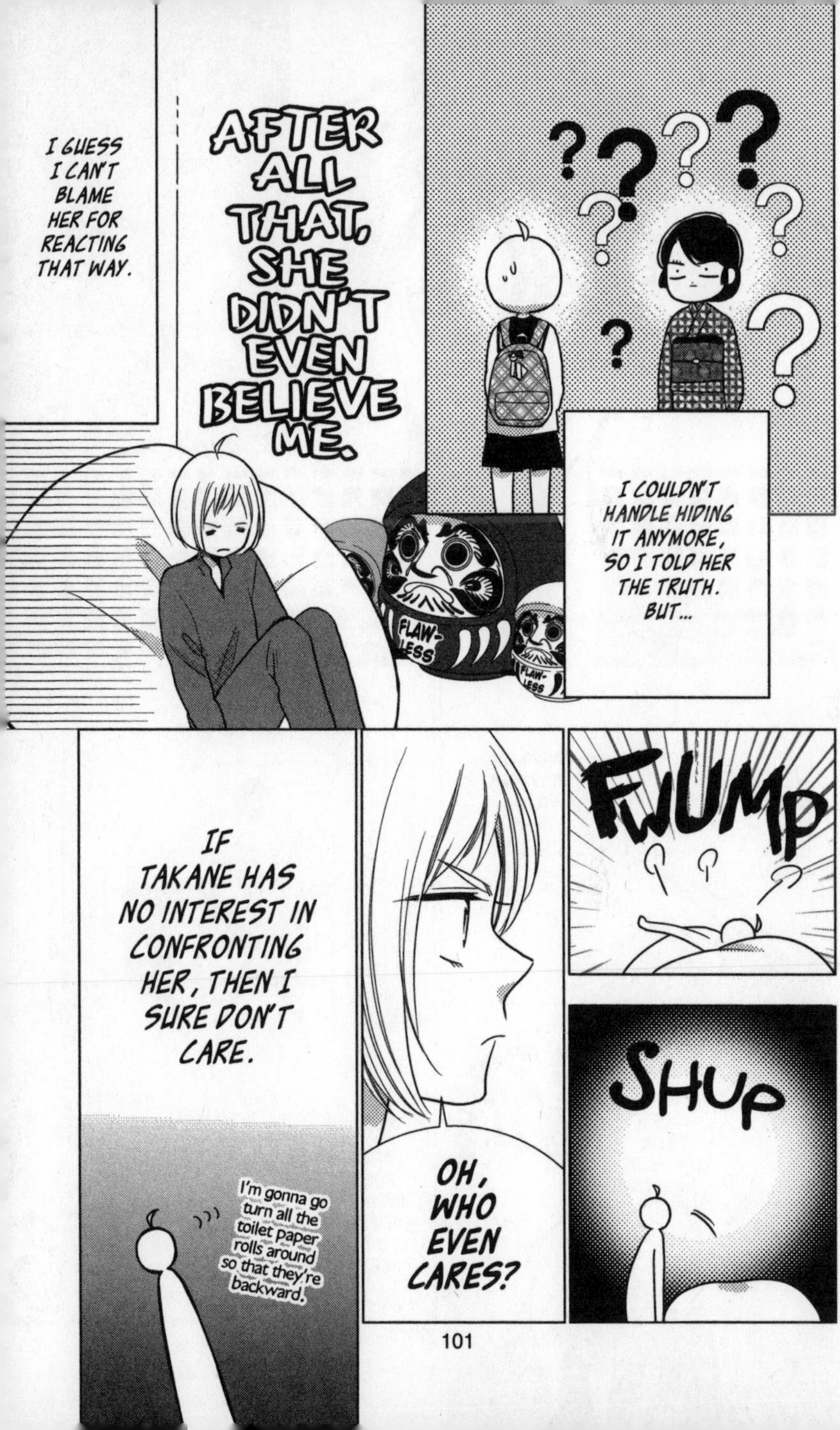
I COULDN'T HANDLE HIDING IT ANYMORE, SO I TOLD HER THE TRUTH. BUT...
AFTER ALL THAT, SHE DIDN'T EVEN BELIEVE ME.
I GUESS I CAN'T BLAME HER FOR REACTING THAT WAY.
FLAW-LESS
FLAW-LESS
FWUMP
SHUP
OH, WHO EVEN CARES?
IF TAKANE HAS NO INTEREST IN CONFRONTING HER, THEN I SURE DON'T CARE.
I'm gonna go turn all the toilet paper rolls around so that they're backward.

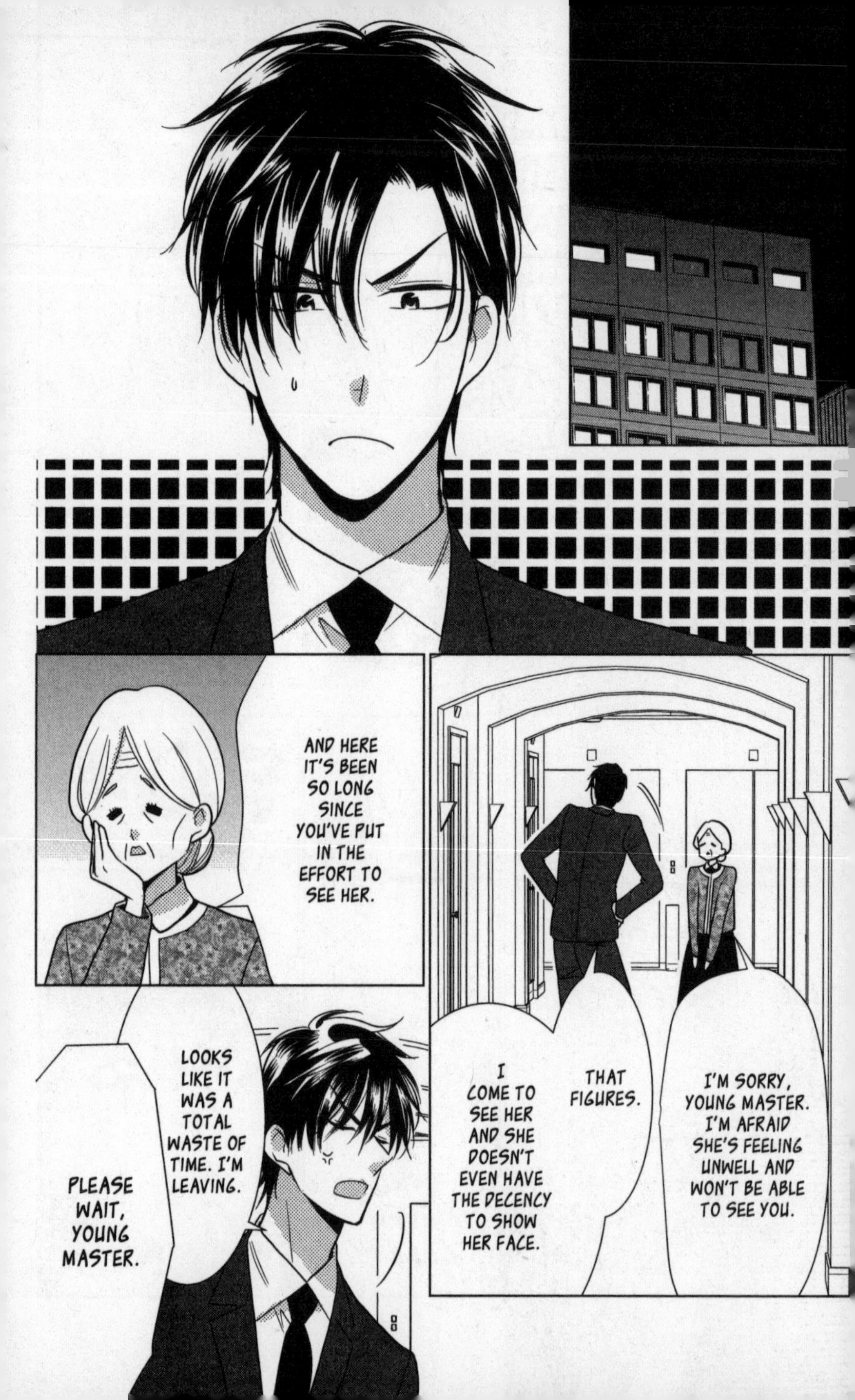
I'M SORRY, YOUNG MASTER. I'M AFRAID SHE'S FEELING UNWELL AND WON'T BE ABLE TO SEE YOU.
THAT FIGURES.
I COME TO SEE HER AND SHE DOESN'T EVEN HAVE THE DECENCY TO SHOW HER FACE.
AND HERE IT'S BEEN SO LONG SINCE YOU'VE PUT IN THE EFFORT TO SEE HER.
LOOKS LIKE IT WAS A TOTAL WASTE OF TIME. I'M LEAVING.
PLEASE WAIT, YOUNG MASTER.

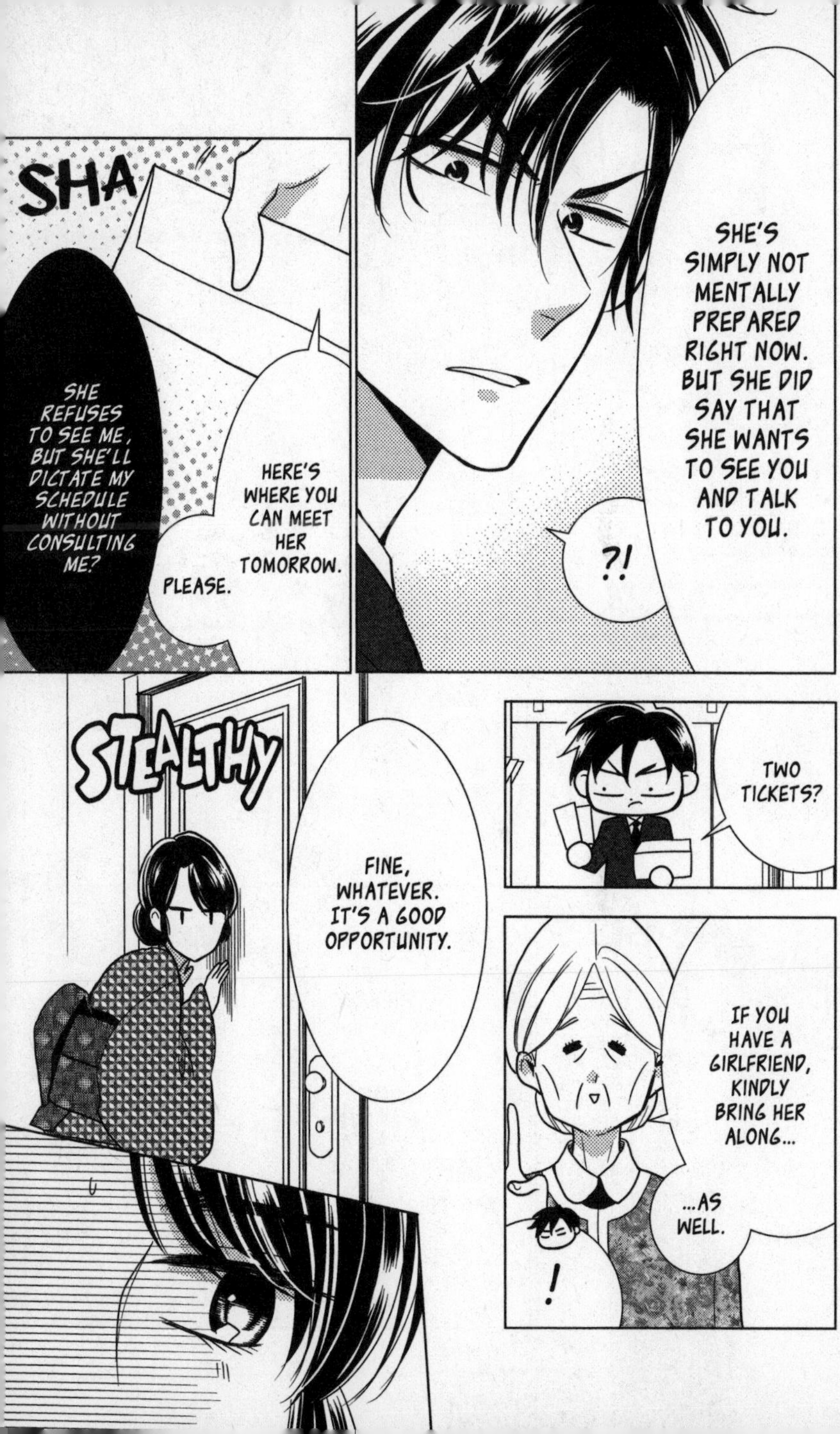
SHE'S SIMPLY NOT MENTALLY PREPARED RIGHT NOW. BUT SHE DID SAY THAT SHE WANTS TO SEE YOU AND TALK TO YOU.
?!
SHA
HERE'S WHERE YOU CAN MEET HER TOMORROW.
PLEASE.
SHE REFUSES TO SEE ME, BUT SHE'LL DICTATE MY SCHEDULE WITHOUT CONSULTING ME?
TWO TICKETS?
IF YOU HAVE A GIRLFRIEND, KINDLY BRING HER ALONG...
...AS WELL.
!
FINE, WHATEVER. IT'S A GOOD OPPORTUNITY.
STEALTHY

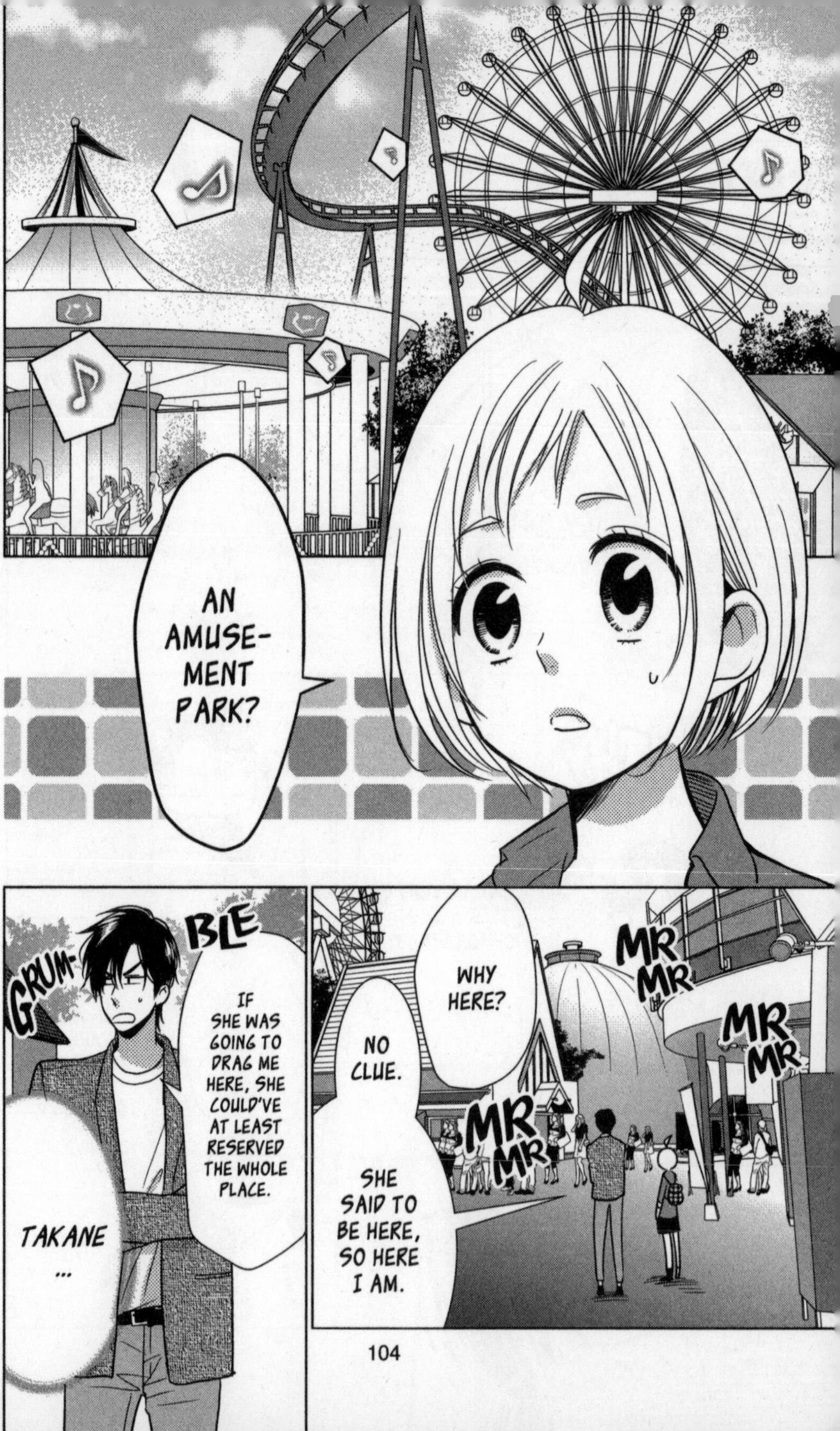
AN AMUSEMENT PARK?
MR MR
WHY HERE?
MR MR
NO CLUE.
MR MR
SHE SAID TO BE HERE, SO HERE I AM.
GRUMBLE
IF SHE WAS GOING TO DRAG ME HERE, SHE COULD'VE AT LEAST RESERVED THE WHOLE PLACE.
TAKANE ...

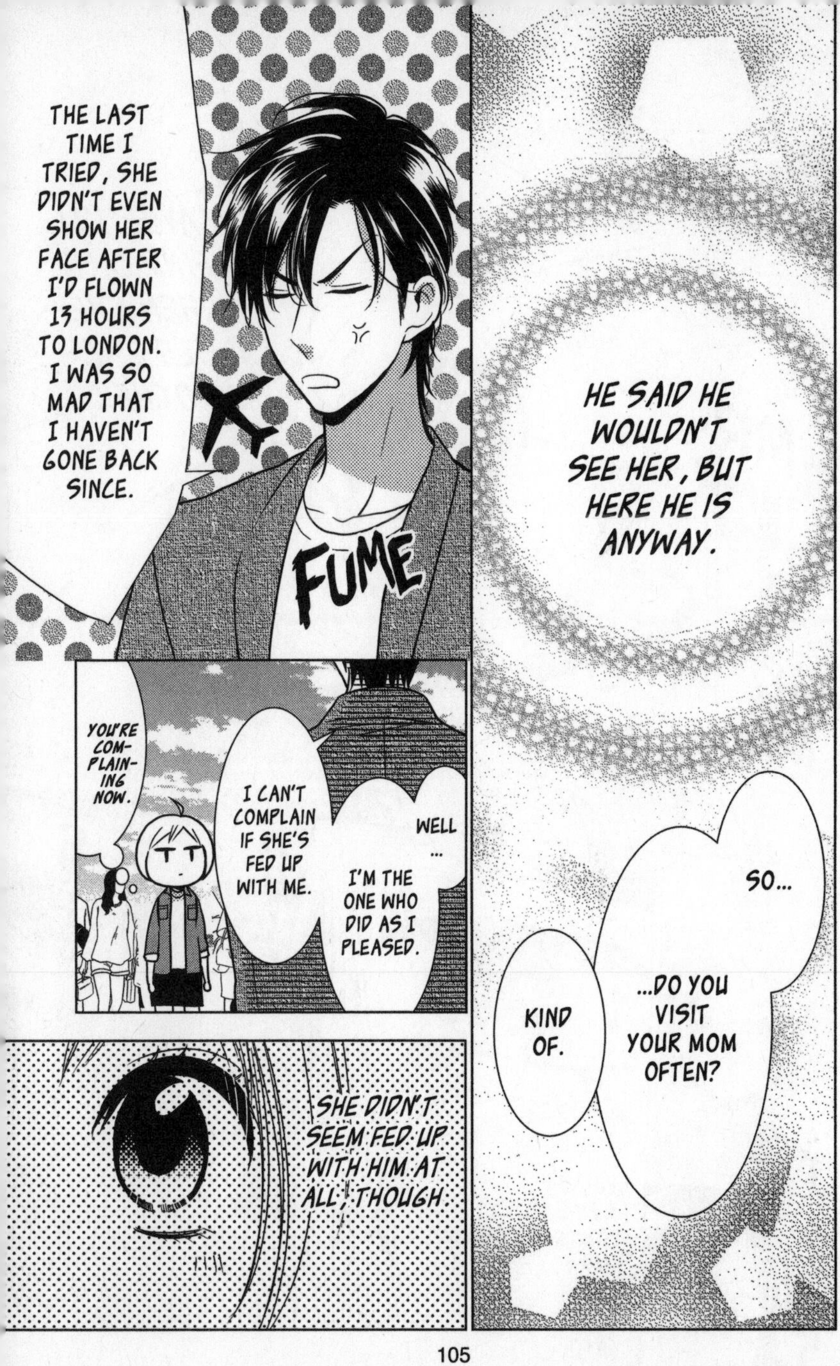
HE SAID HE WOULDN'T SEE HER, BUT HERE HE IS ANYWAY.
SO...
...DO YOU VISIT YOUR MOM OFTEN?
KIND OF.
THE LAST TIME I TRIED, SHE DIDN'T EVEN SHOW HER FACE AFTER I'D FLOWN 13 HOURS TO LONDON. I WAS SO MAD THAT I HAVEN'T GONE BACK SINCE.
FUME
WELL...
I'M THE ONE WHO DID AS I PLEASED.
I CAN'T COMPLAIN IF SHE'S FED UP WITH ME.
YOU'RE COM-PLAIN-ING NOW.
SHE DIDN'T SEEM FED UP WITH HIM AT ALL, THOUGH.

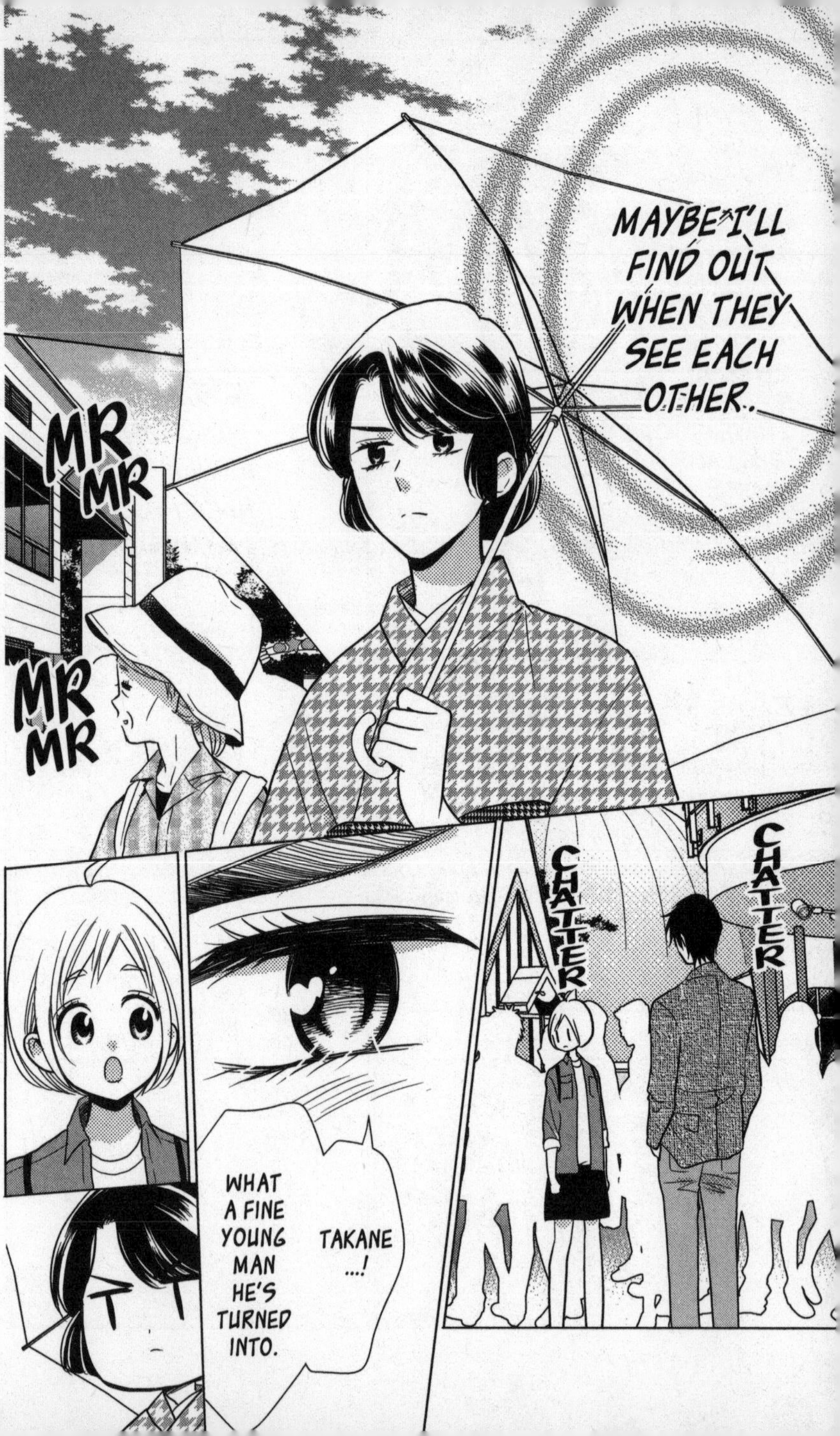
MAYBE I'LL FIND OUT WHEN THEY SEE EACH OTHER..
MR MR
MR MR
CHATTER
CHATTER
TAKANE ...!
WHAT A FINE YOUNG MAN HE'S TURNED INTO.

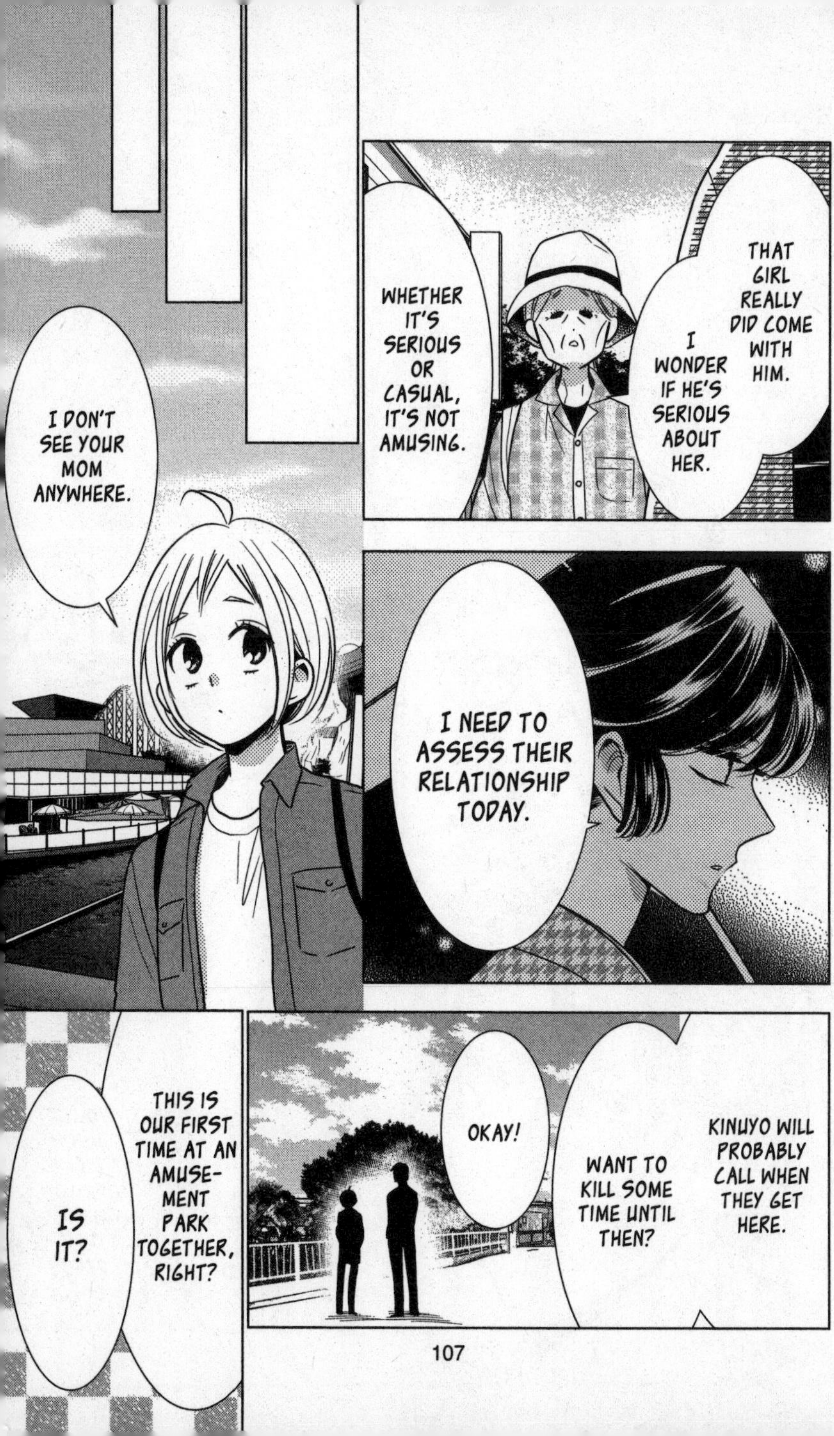
THAT GIRL REALLY DID COME WITH HIM.
I WONDER IF HE'S SERIOUS ABOUT HER.
WHETHER IT'S SERIOUS OR CASUAL, IT'S NOT AMUSING.
I NEED TO ASSESS THEIR RELATIONSHIP TODAY.
I DON'T SEE YOUR MOM ANYWHERE.
KINUYO WILL PROBABLY CALL WHEN THEY GET HERE.
WANT TO KILL SOME TIME UNTIL THEN?
OKAY!
THIS IS OUR FIRST TIME AT AN AMUSEMENT PARK TOGETHER, RIGHT?
IS IT?

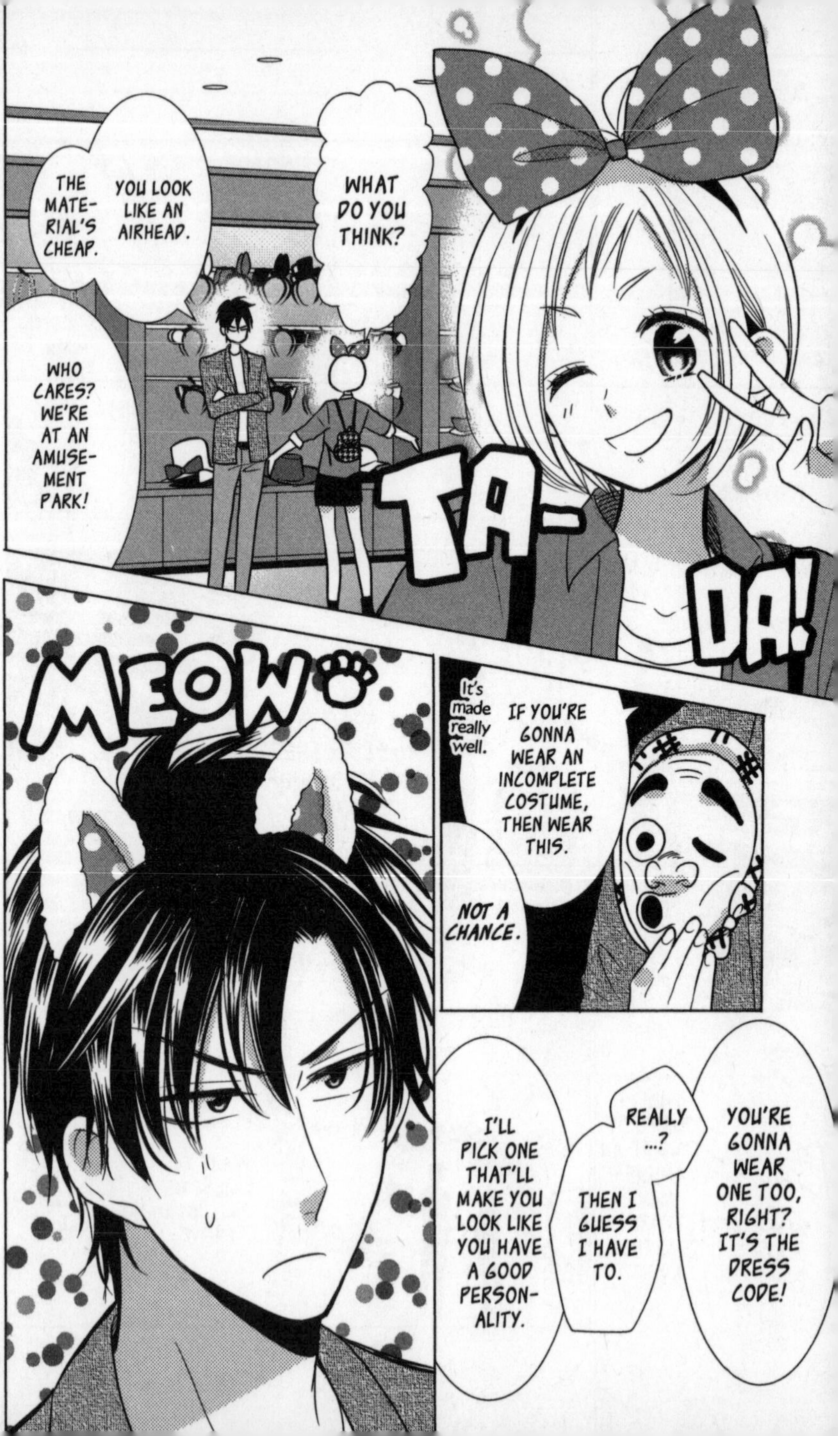
TA-DA!
WHAT DO YOU THINK?
YOU LOOK LIKE AN AIRHEAD.
THE MATERIAL'S CHEAP.
WHO CARES? WE'RE AT AN AMUSEMENT PARK!
IF YOU'RE GONNA WEAR AN INCOMPLETE COSTUME, THEN WEAR THIS.
It's made really well.
NOT A CHANCE.
YOU'RE GONNA WEAR ONE TOO, RIGHT? IT'S THE DRESS CODE!
REALLY...?
THEN I GUESS I HAVE TO.
I'LL PICK ONE THAT'LL MAKE YOU LOOK LIKE YOU HAVE A GOOD PERSONALITY.
MEOW

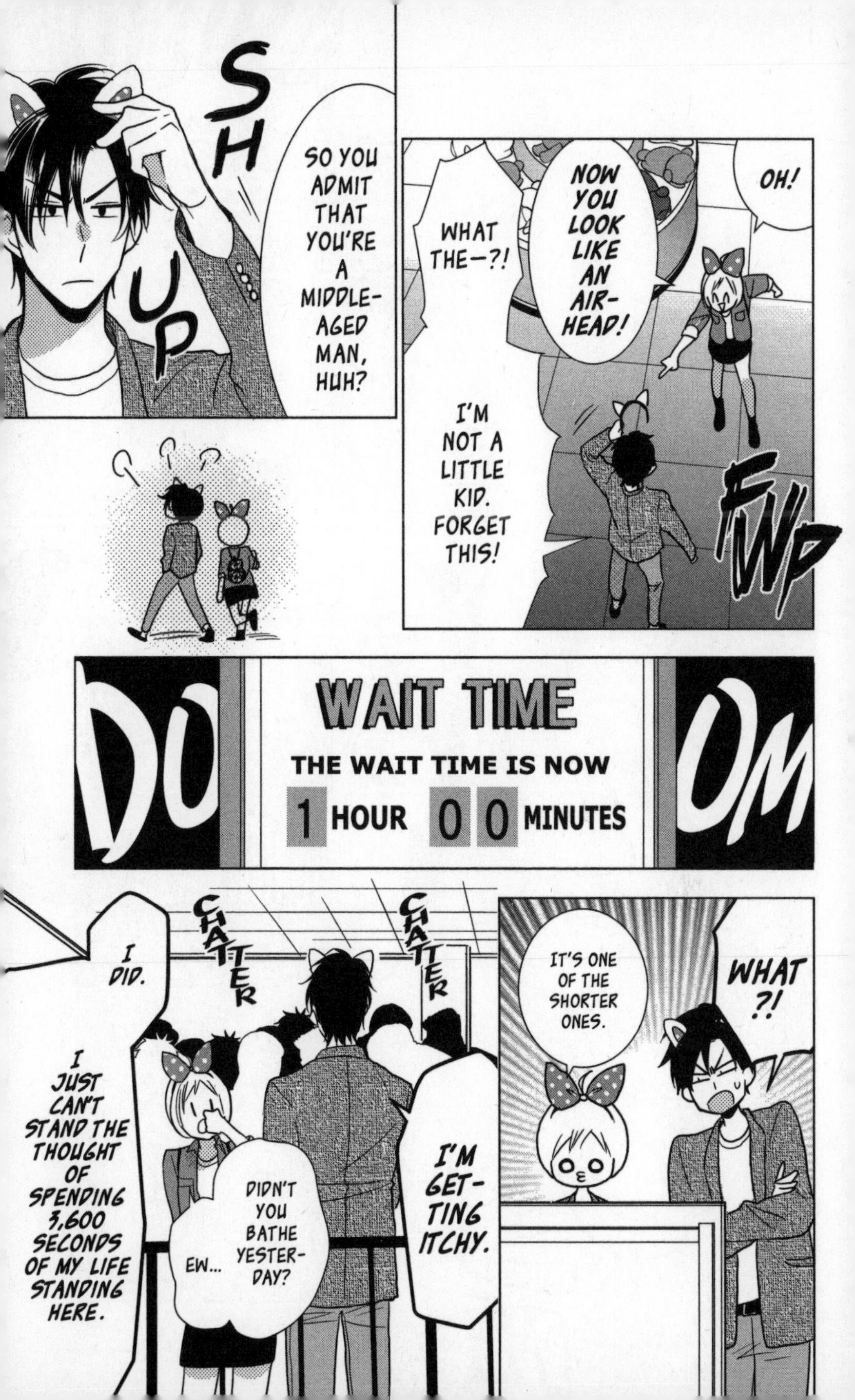
OH!
NOW YOU LOOK LIKE AN AIR-HEAD!
WHAT THE—?!
I'M NOT A LITTLE KID. FORGET THIS!
FWP
SHUT UP
SO YOU ADMIT THAT YOU'RE A MIDDLE-AGED MAN, HUH?
DO
WAIT TIME
THE WAIT TIME IS NOW
1 HOUR 0 0 MINUTES
OM
WHAT?!
IT'S ONE OF THE SHORTER ONES.
CHATTER
CHATTER
I DID.
I'M GETTING ITCHY.
DIDN'T YOU BATHE YESTERDAY?
EW...
I JUST CAN'T STAND THE THOUGHT OF SPENDING 3,600 SECONDS OF MY LIFE STANDING HERE.

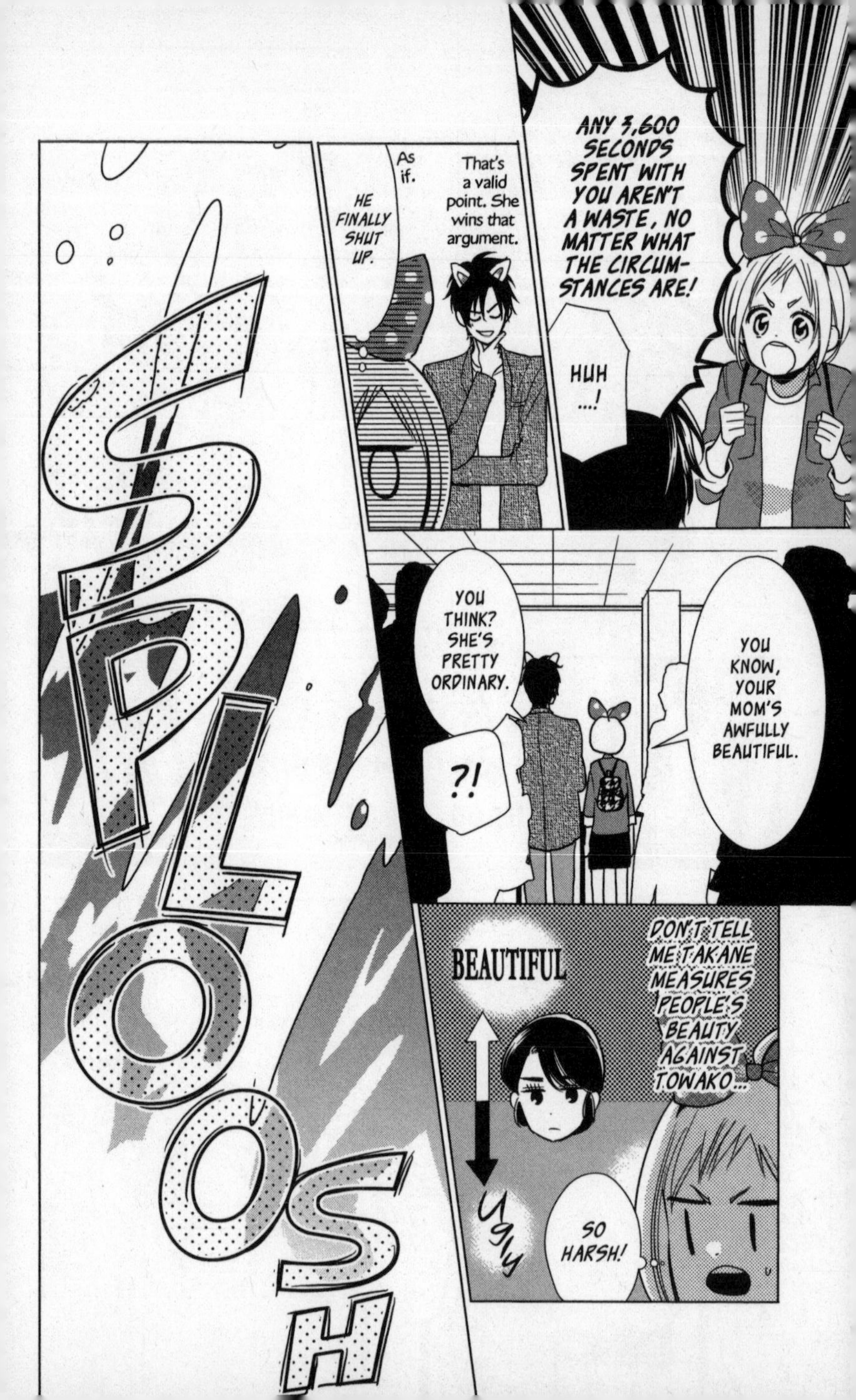
ANY 3,600 SECONDS SPENT WITH YOU AREN'T A WASTE, NO MATTER WHAT THE CIRCUM-STANCES ARE!
HUH ...!
That's a valid point. She wins that argument.
As if.
HE FINALLY SHUT UP.
YOU KNOW, YOUR MOM'S AWFULLY BEAUTIFUL.
YOU THINK? SHE'S PRETTY ORDINARY.
?!
DON'T TELL ME TAKANE MEASURES PEOPLE'S BEAUTY AGAINST TOWAKO...
BEAUTIFUL
UGLY
SO HARSH!
SPLOOOSH

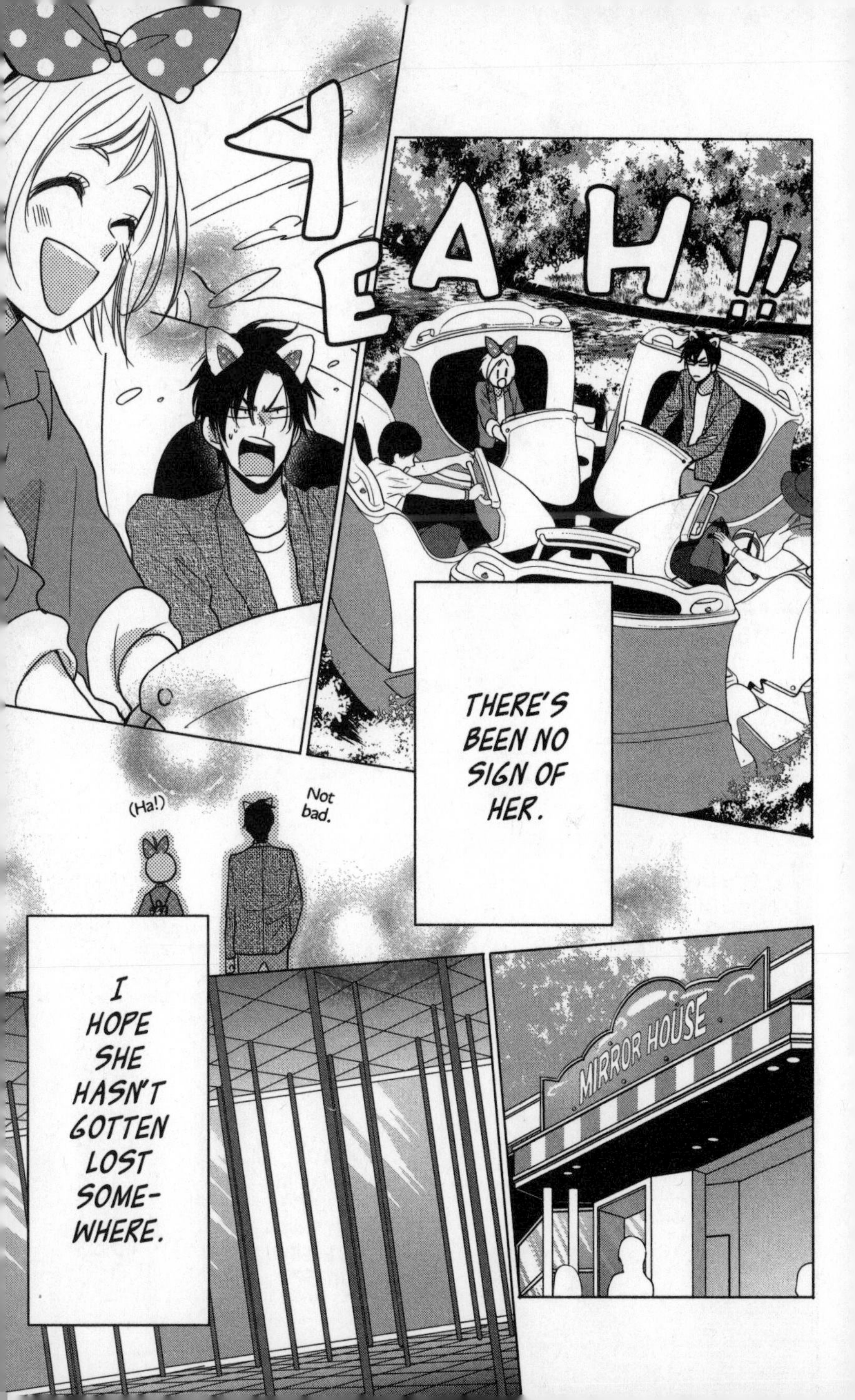

YEAH!!
THERE'S BEEN NO SIGN OF HER.
Not bad.
(Ha!)
MIRROR HOUSE
I HOPE SHE HASN'T GOTTEN LOST SOME-WHERE.

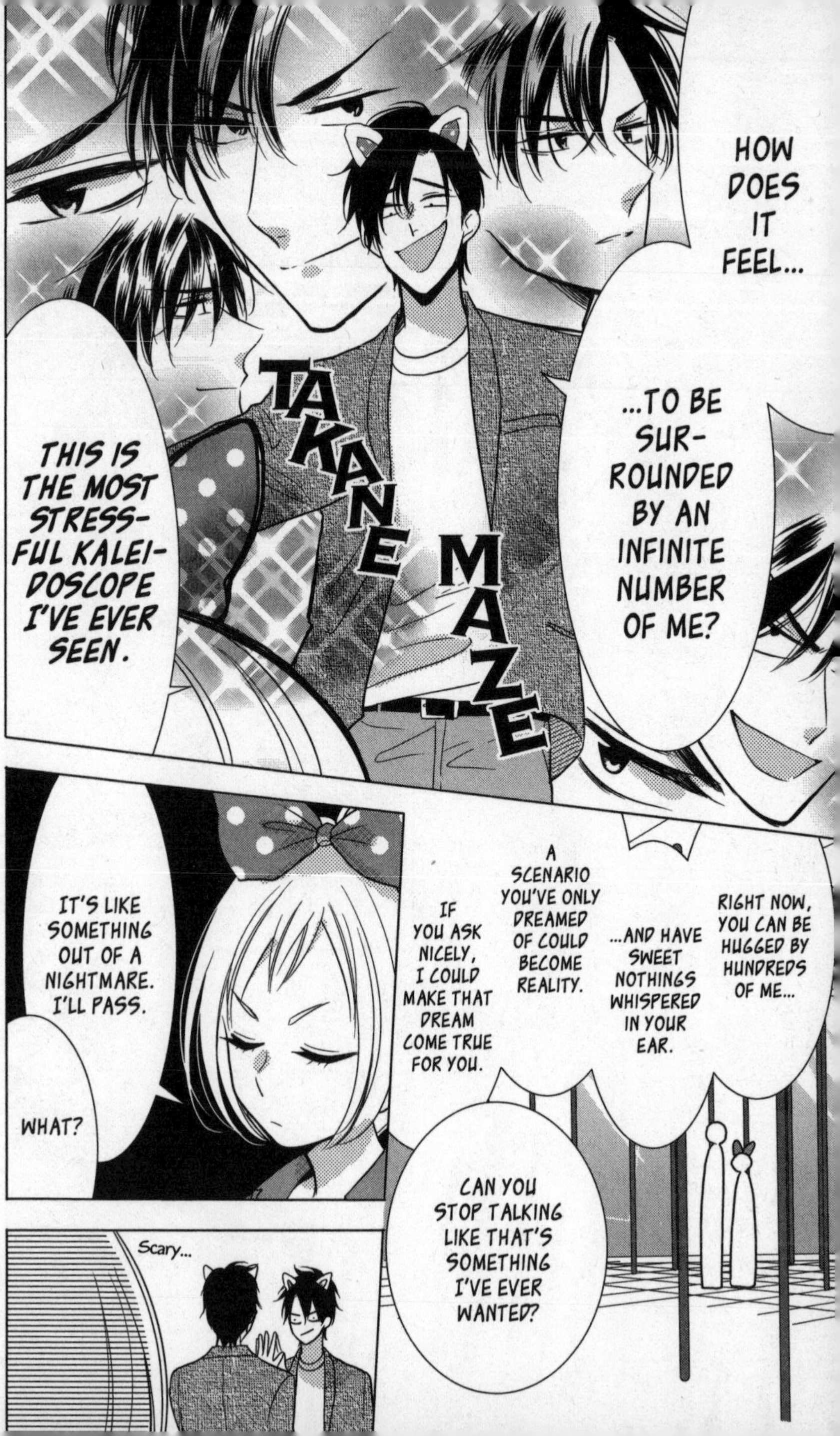
HOW DOES IT FEEL...
...TO BE SUR-ROUNDED BY AN INFINITE NUMBER OF ME?
TAKANE MAZE
THIS IS THE MOST STRESS-FUL KALEI-DOSCOPE I'VE EVER SEEN.
RIGHT NOW, YOU CAN BE HUGGED BY HUNDREDS OF ME...
...AND HAVE SWEET NOTHINGS WHISPERED IN YOUR EAR.
A SCENARIO YOU'VE ONLY DREAMED OF COULD BECOME REALITY.
IF YOU ASK NICELY, I COULD MAKE THAT DREAM COME TRUE FOR YOU.
CAN YOU STOP TALKING LIKE THAT'S SOMETHING I'VE EVER WANTED?
IT'S LIKE SOMETHING OUT OF A NIGHTMARE. I'LL PASS.
WHAT?
Scary...

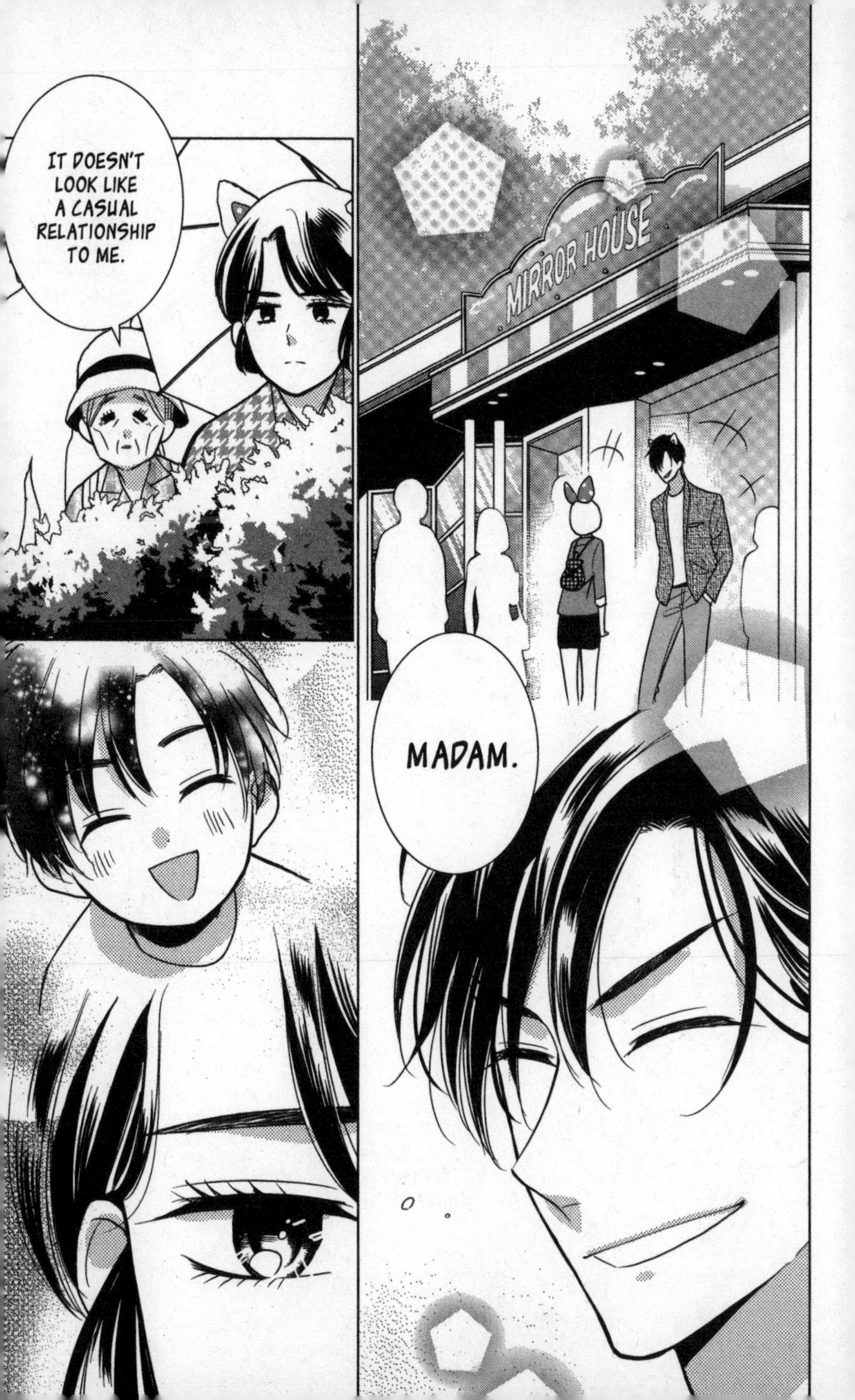
MIRROR HOUSE
MADAM.
IT DOESN'T LOOK LIKE A CASUAL RELATIONSHIP TO ME.

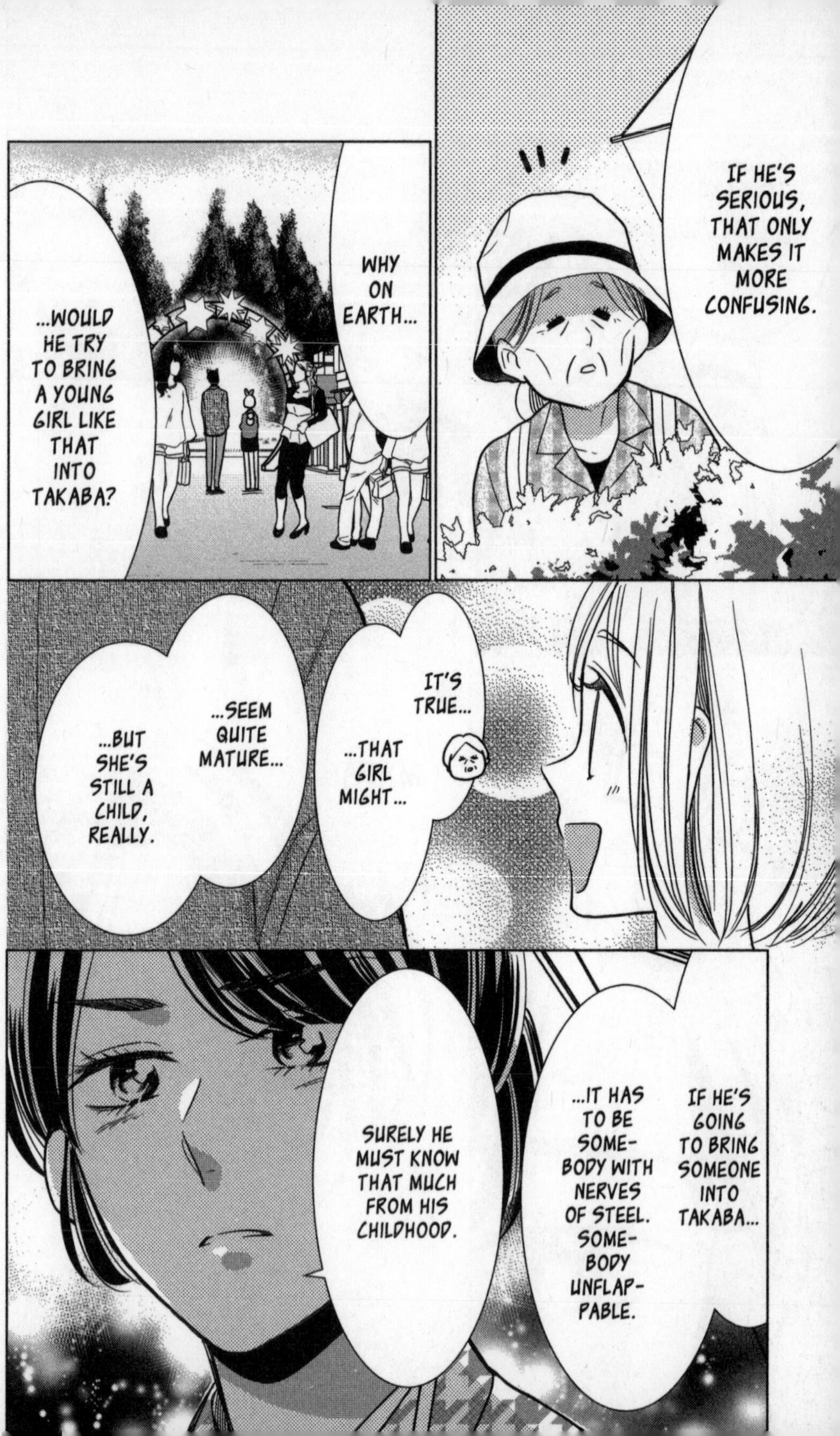
IF HE'S SERIOUS, THAT ONLY MAKES IT MORE CONFUSING.
WHY ON EARTH...
...WOULD HE TRY TO BRING A YOUNG GIRL LIKE THAT INTO TAKABA?
IT'S TRUE...
...THAT GIRL MIGHT...
...SEEM QUITE MATURE...
...BUT SHE'S STILL A CHILD, REALLY.
IF HE'S GOING TO BRING SOMEONE INTO TAKABA...
...IT HAS TO BE SOMEBODY WITH NERVES OF STEEL. SOMEBODY UNFLAPPABLE.
SURELY HE MUST KNOW THAT MUCH FROM HIS CHILDHOOD.

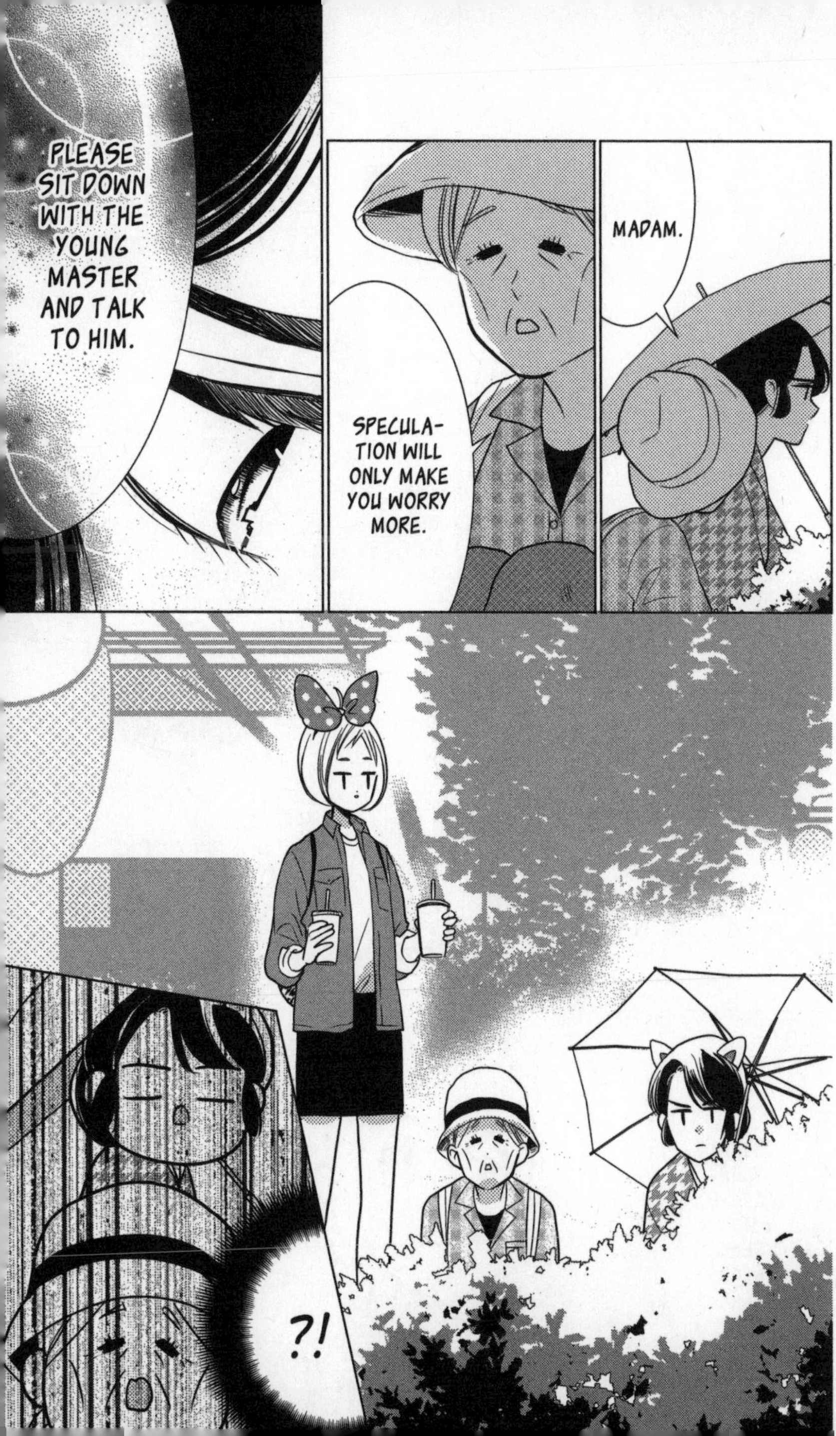
MADAM.
SPECULA-TION WILL ONLY MAKE YOU WORRY MORE.
PLEASE SIT DOWN WITH THE YOUNG MASTER AND TALK TO HIM.
?!

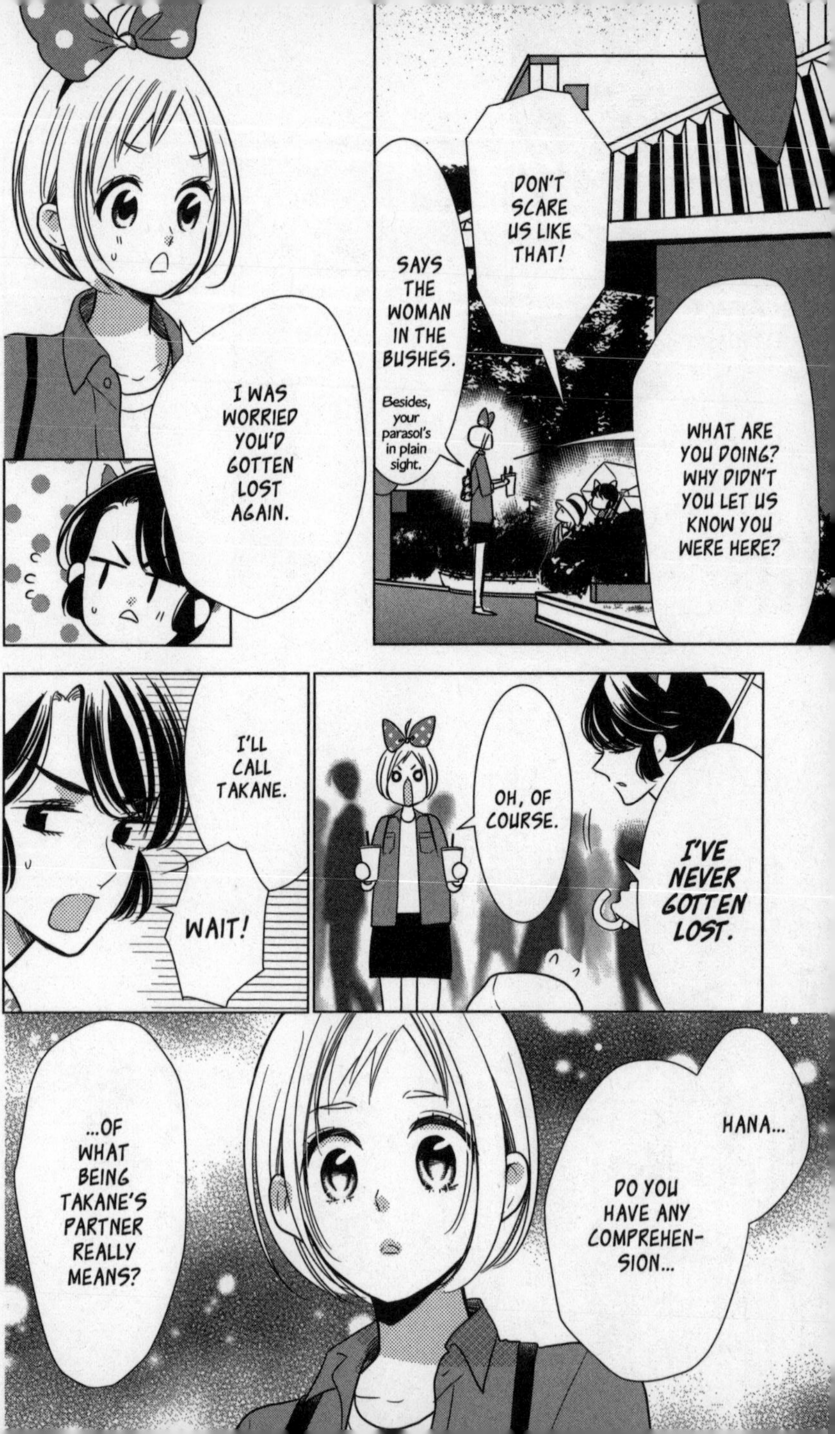
WHAT ARE YOU DOING? WHY DIDN'T YOU LET US KNOW YOU WERE HERE?
DON'T SCARE US LIKE THAT!
SAYS THE WOMAN IN THE BUSHES.
Besides, your parasol's in plain sight.
I WAS WORRIED YOU'D GOTTEN LOST AGAIN.
I'VE NEVER GOTTEN LOST.
OH, OF COURSE.
I'LL CALL TAKANE.
WAIT!
HANA...
DO YOU HAVE ANY COMPREHEN-SION...
...OF WHAT BEING TAKANE'S PARTNER REALLY MEANS?

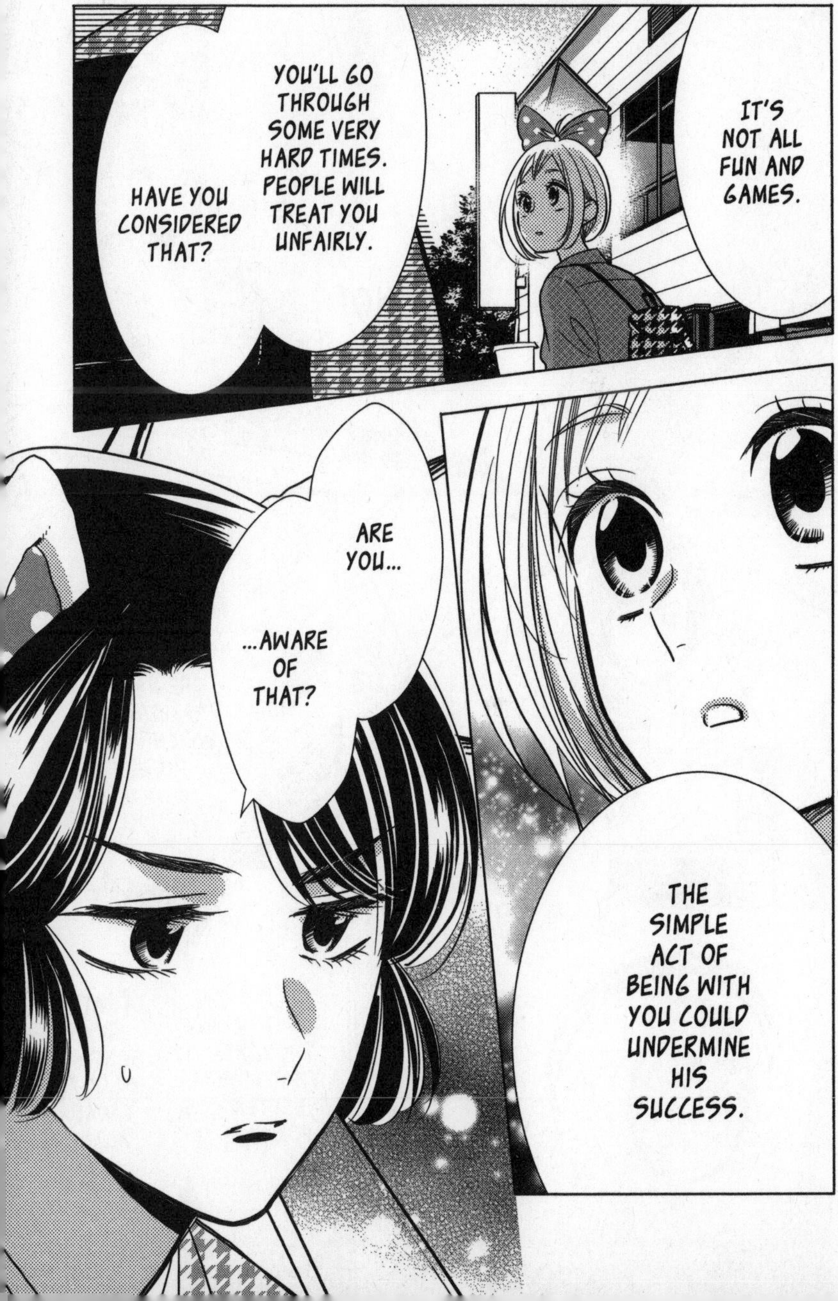
IT'S NOT ALL FUN AND GAMES.
YOU'LL GO THROUGH SOME VERY HARD TIMES. PEOPLE WILL TREAT YOU UNFAIRLY.
HAVE YOU CONSIDERED THAT?
THE SIMPLE ACT OF BEING WITH YOU COULD UNDERMINE HIS SUCCESS.
ARE YOU...
...AWARE OF THAT?

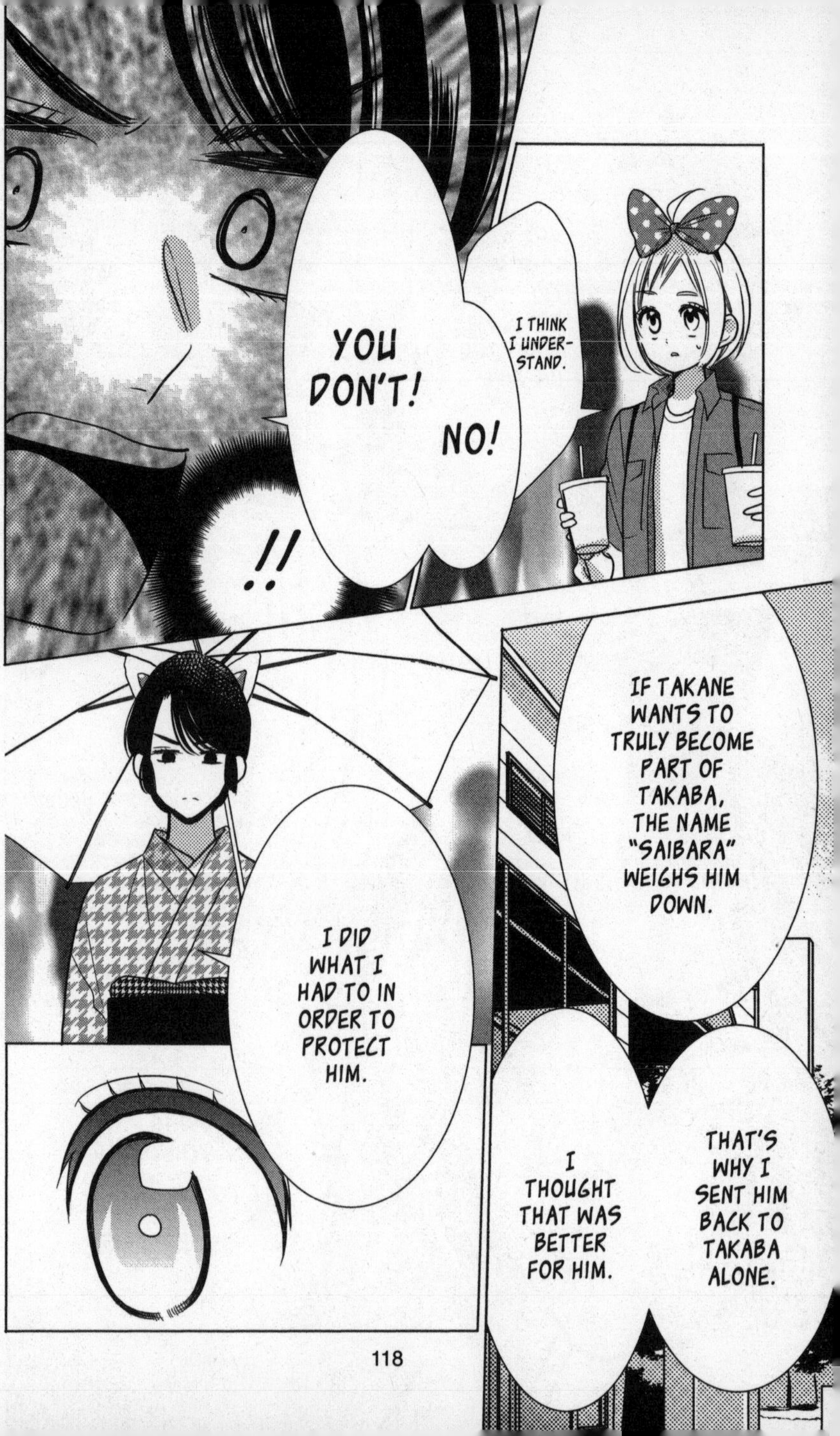
I THINK I UNDER-STAND.
NO!
YOU DON'T!
!!
IF TAKANE WANTS TO TRULY BECOME PART OF TAKABA, THE NAME "SAIBARA" WEIGHS HIM DOWN.
I DID WHAT I HAD TO IN ORDER TO PROTECT HIM.
THAT'S WHY I SENT HIM BACK TO TAKABA ALONE.
I THOUGHT THAT WAS BETTER FOR HIM.

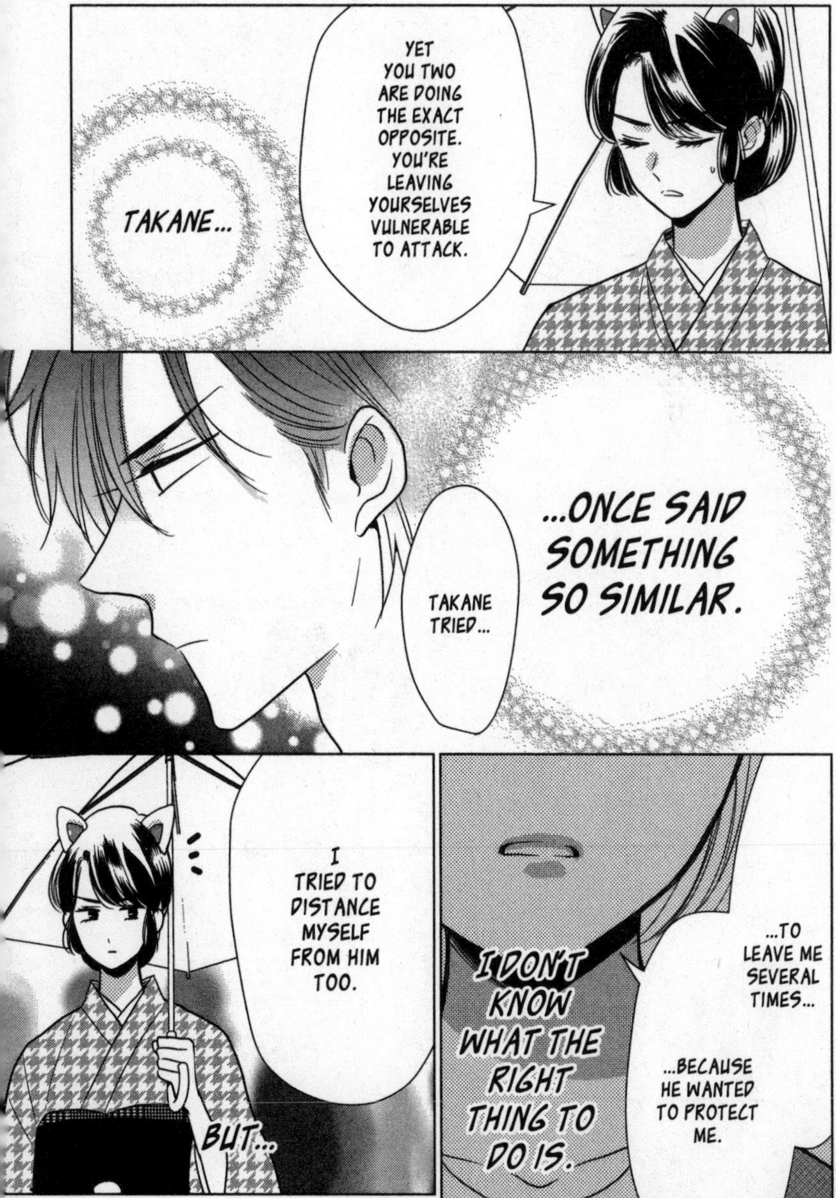
YET YOU TWO ARE DOING THE EXACT OPPOSITE. YOU'RE LEAVING YOURSELVES VULNERABLE TO ATTACK.
TAKANE...
...ONCE SAID SOMETHING SO SIMILAR.
TAKANE TRIED...
...TO LEAVE ME SEVERAL TIMES...
...BECAUSE HE WANTED TO PROTECT ME.
I DON'T KNOW WHAT THE RIGHT THING TO DO IS.
I TRIED TO DISTANCE MYSELF FROM HIM TOO.
BUT...

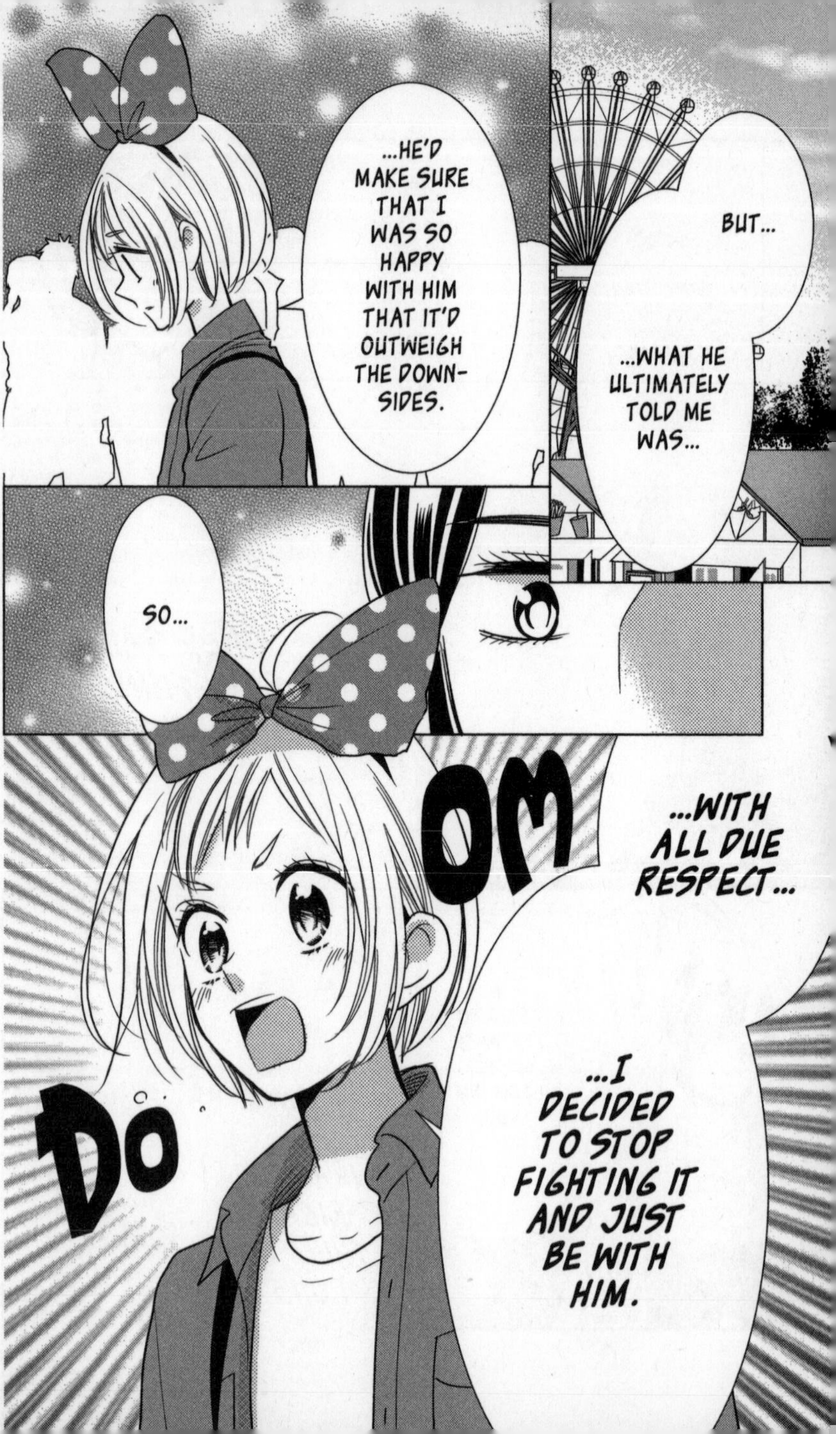
BUT...
...WHAT HE ULTIMATELY TOLD ME WAS...
...HE'D MAKE SURE THAT I WAS SO HAPPY WITH HIM THAT IT'D OUTWEIGH THE DOWN-SIDES.
SO...
OM
...WITH ALL DUE RESPECT...
...I DECIDED TO STOP FIGHTING IT AND JUST BE WITH HIM.
DO

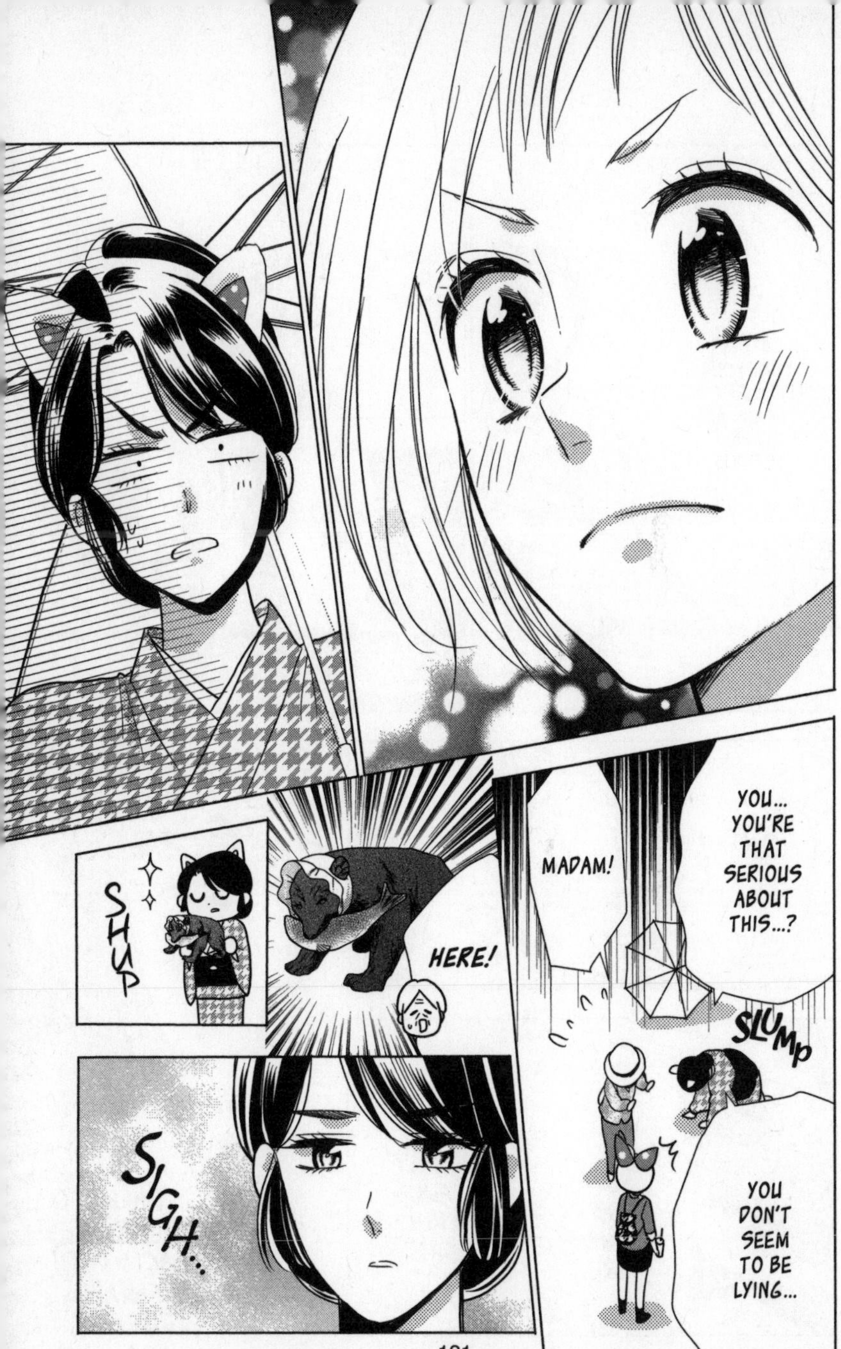
YOU... YOU'RE THAT SERIOUS ABOUT THIS...?
MADAM!
SLUMP
YOU DON'T SEEM TO BE LYING...
HERE!
SHUP
SIGH...

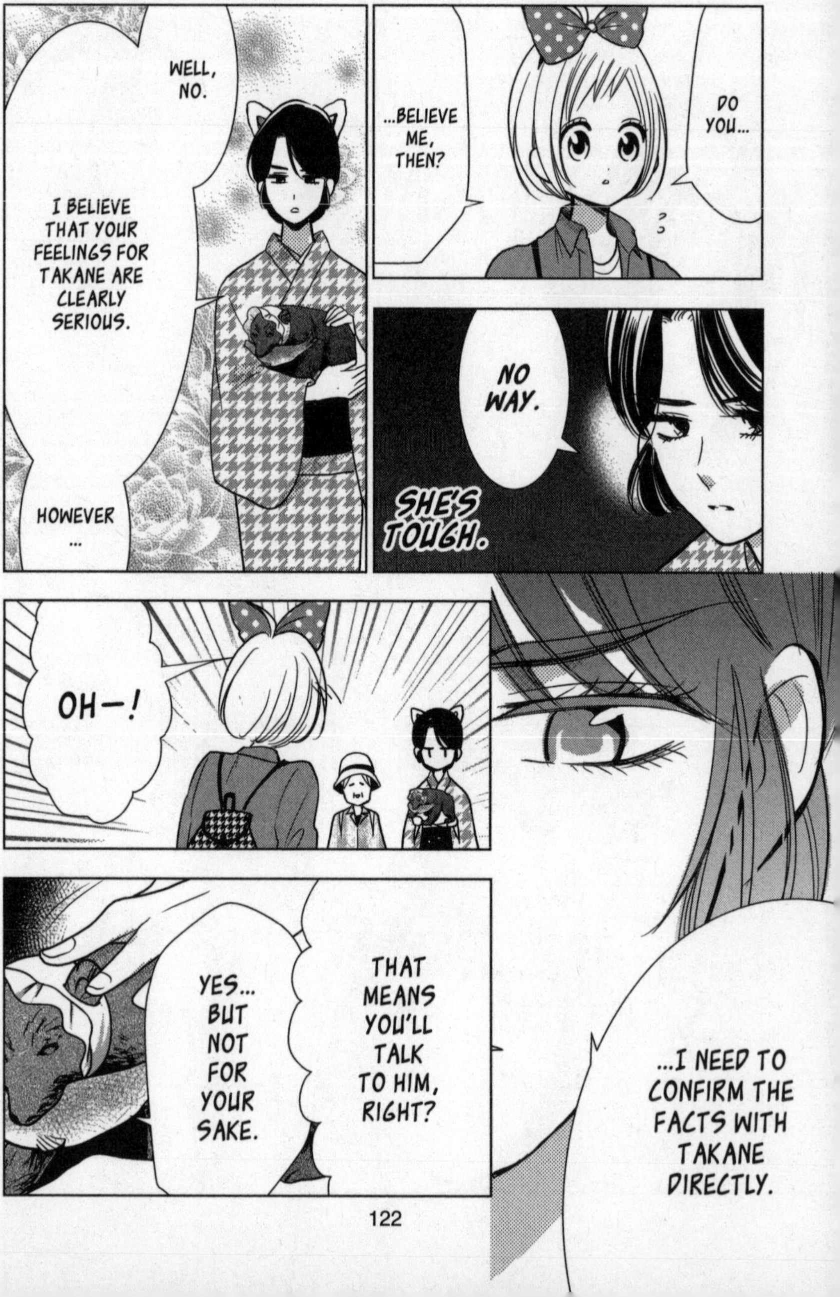
DO YOU...
...BELIEVE ME, THEN?
NO WAY.
SHE'S TOUGH.
WELL, NO.
I BELIEVE THAT YOUR FEELINGS FOR TAKANE ARE CLEARLY SERIOUS.
HOWEVER...
...I NEED TO CONFIRM THE FACTS WITH TAKANE DIRECTLY.
OH—!
THAT MEANS YOU'LL TALK TO HIM, RIGHT?
YES... BUT NOT FOR YOUR SAKE.

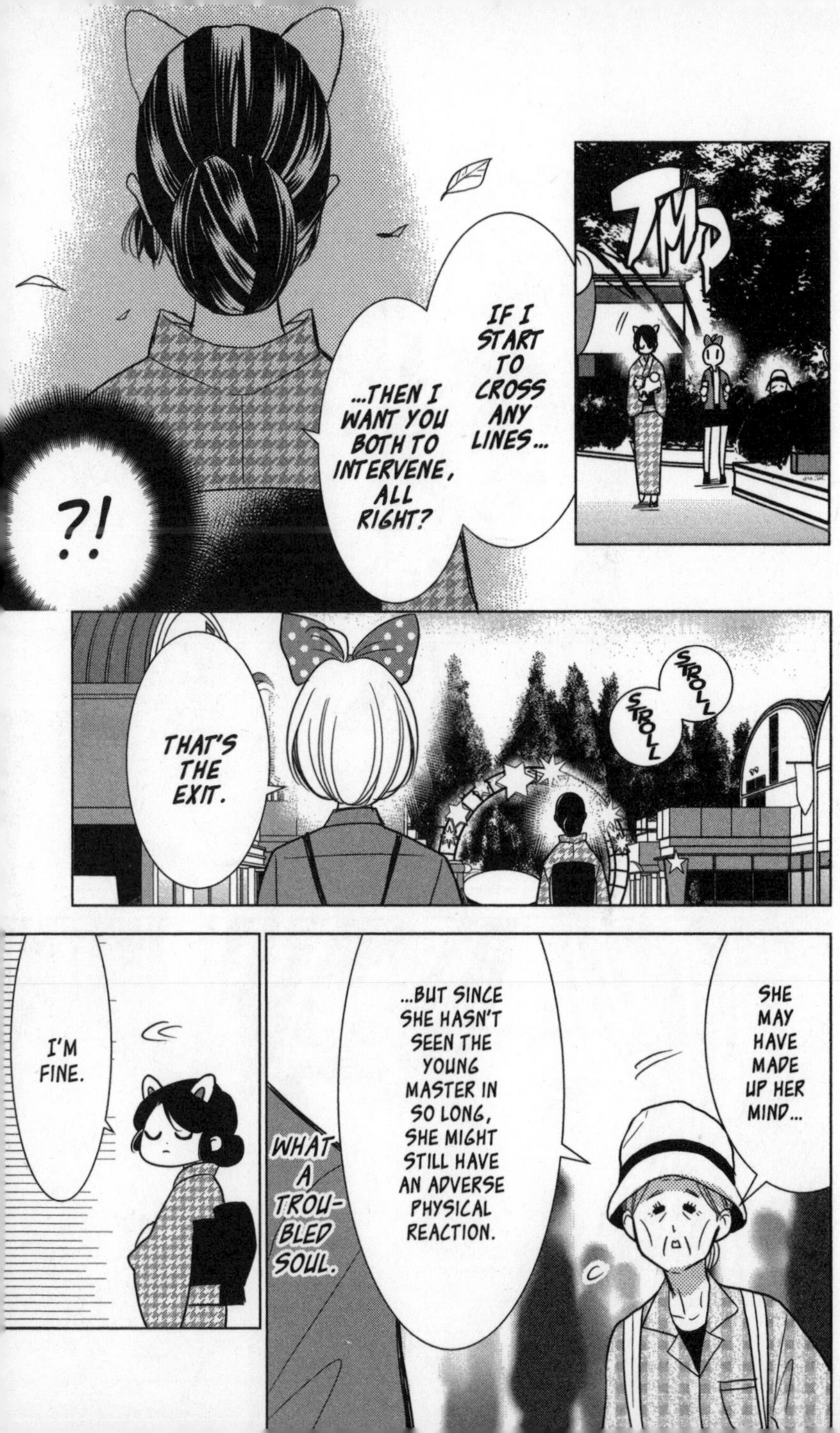
TMP
IF I START TO CROSS ANY LINES...
...THEN I WANT YOU BOTH TO INTERVENE, ALL RIGHT?
?!
SKROLL
SKROLL
THAT'S THE EXIT.
SHE MAY HAVE MADE UP HER MIND...
...BUT SINCE SHE HASN'T SEEN THE YOUNG MASTER IN SO LONG, SHE MIGHT STILL HAVE AN ADVERSE PHYSICAL REACTION.
WHAT A TROUBLED SOUL.
I'M FINE.

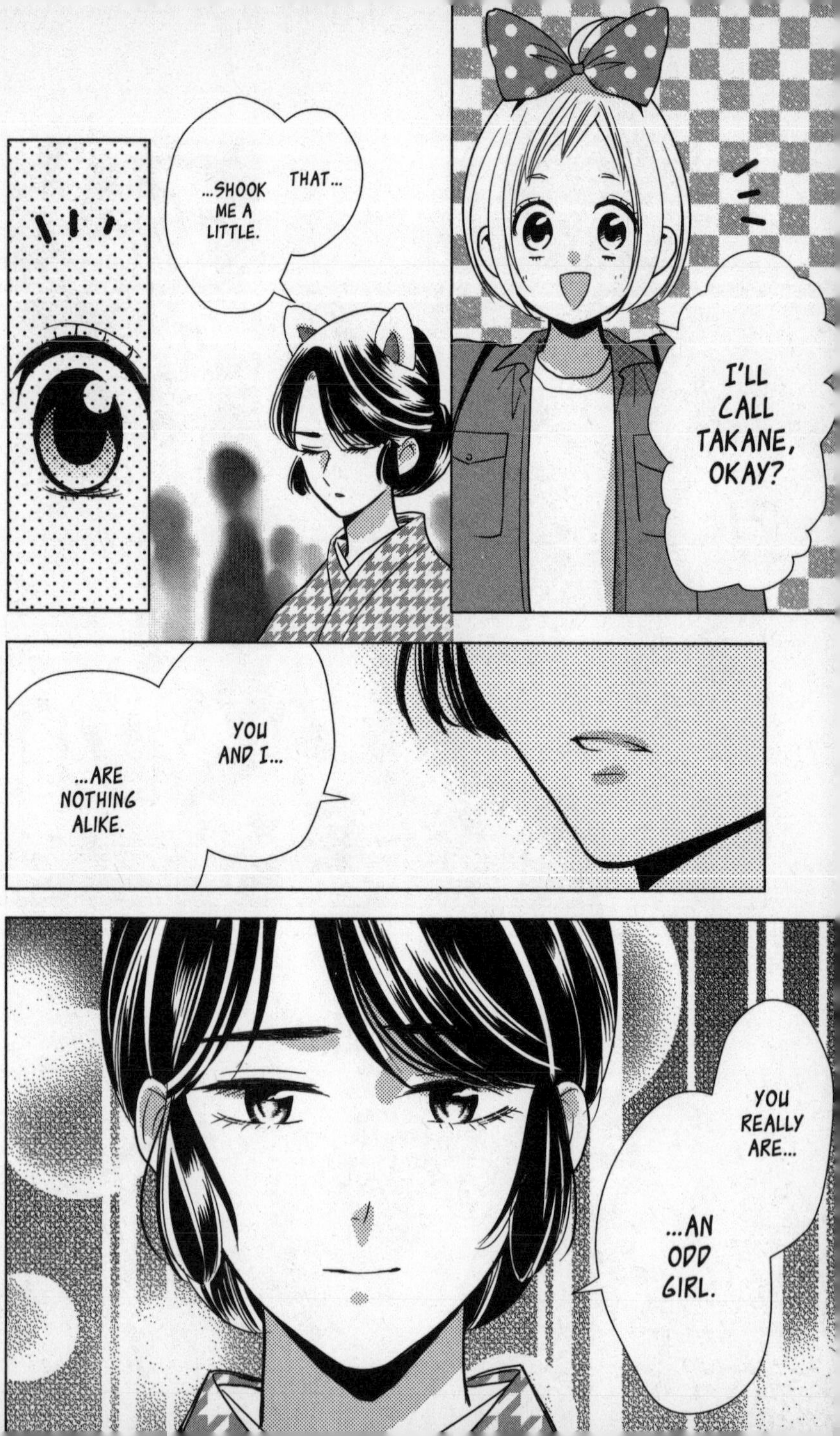
I'LL CALL TAKANE, OKAY?
THAT...
...SHOOK ME A LITTLE.
YOU AND I...
...ARE NOTHING ALIKE.
YOU REALLY ARE...
...AN ODD GIRL.

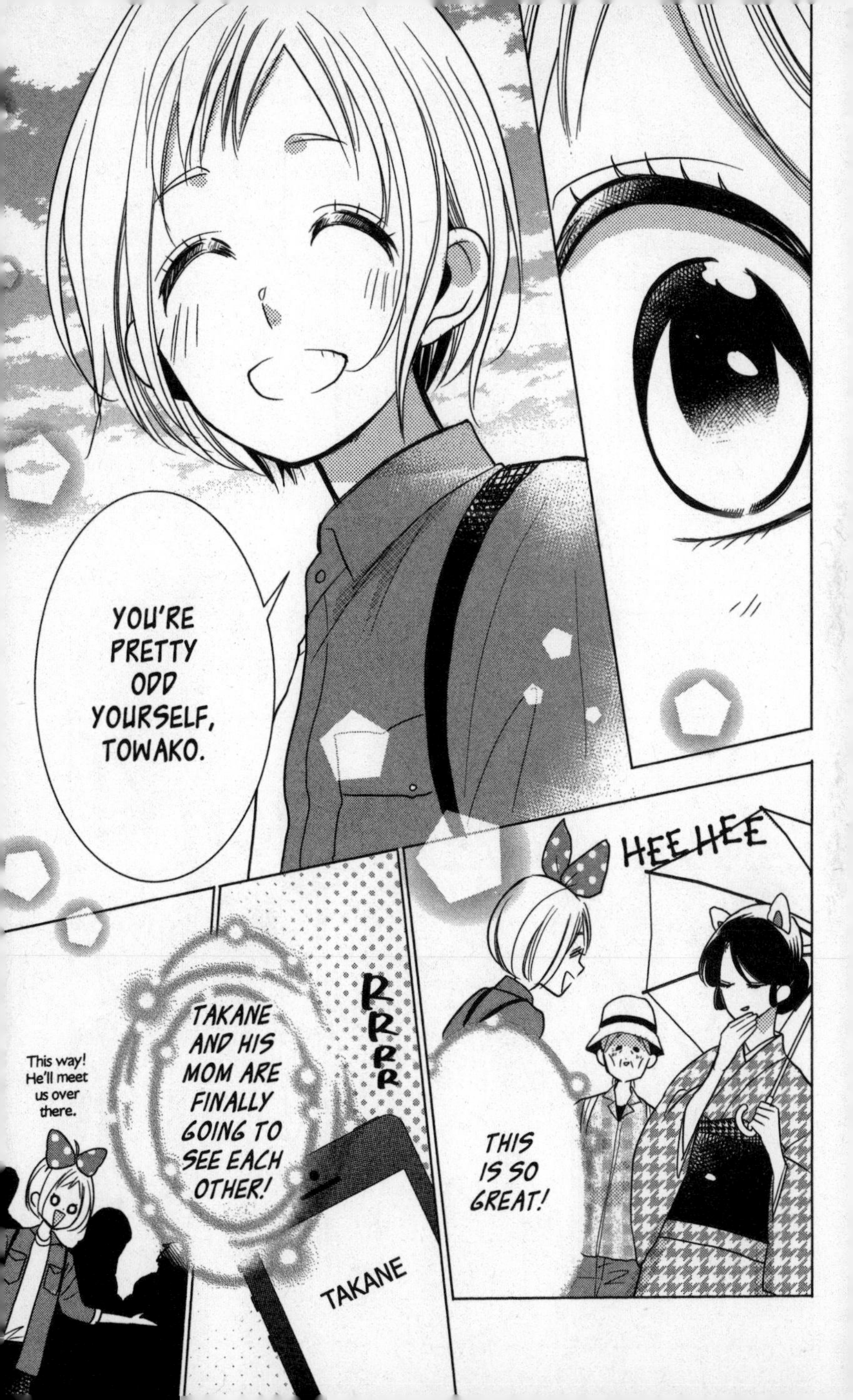
YOU'RE PRETTY ODD YOURSELF, TOWAKO.
HEE HEE
THIS IS SO GREAT!
RRRR
TAKANE AND HIS MOM ARE FINALLY GOING TO SEE EACH OTHER!
This way! He'll meet us over there.
TAKANE

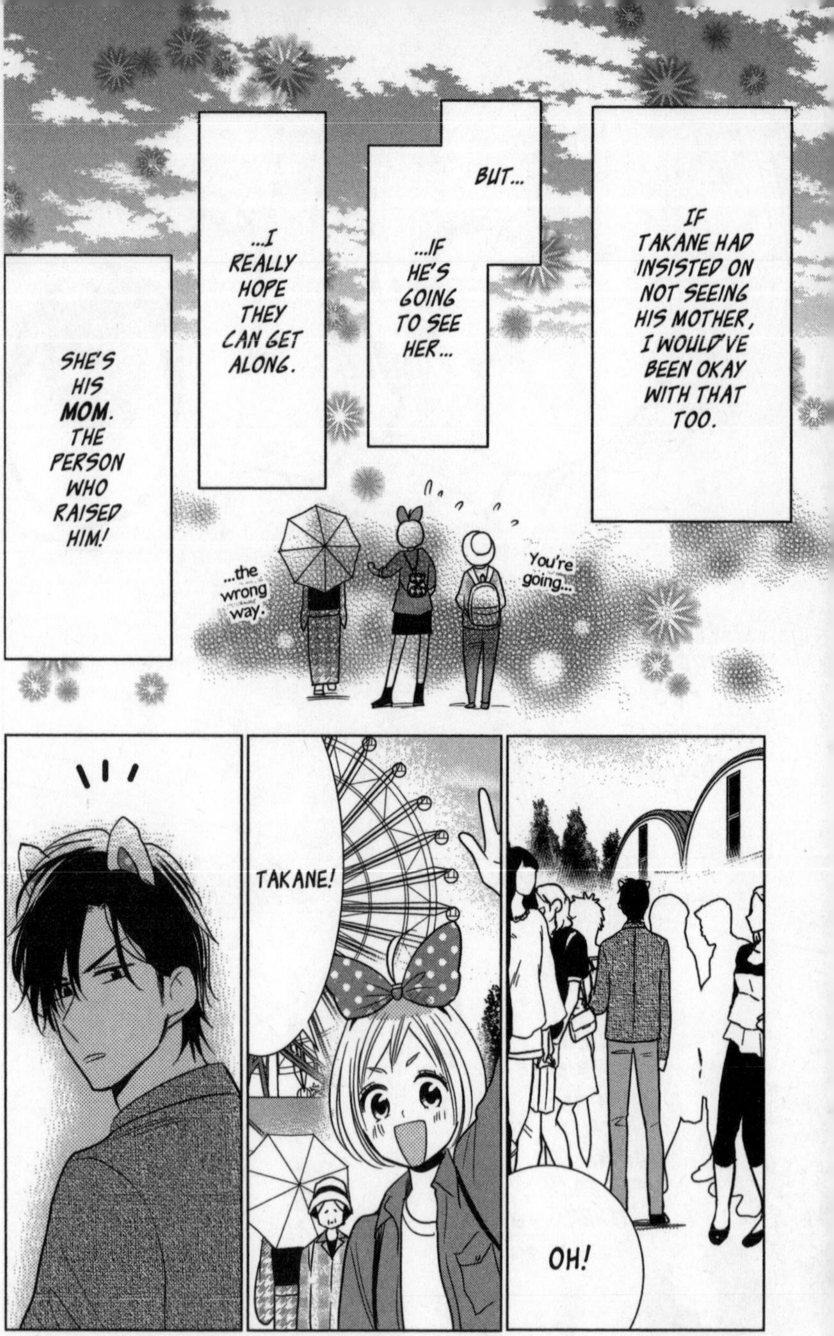

IF TAKANE HAD INSISTED ON NOT SEEING HIS MOTHER, I WOULD'VE BEEN OKAY WITH THAT TOO.
BUT...
...IF HE'S GOING TO SEE HER...
...I REALLY HOPE THEY CAN GET ALONG.
SHE'S HIS MOM. THE PERSON WHO RAISED HIM!
You're going...
...the wrong way.
OH!
TAKANE!

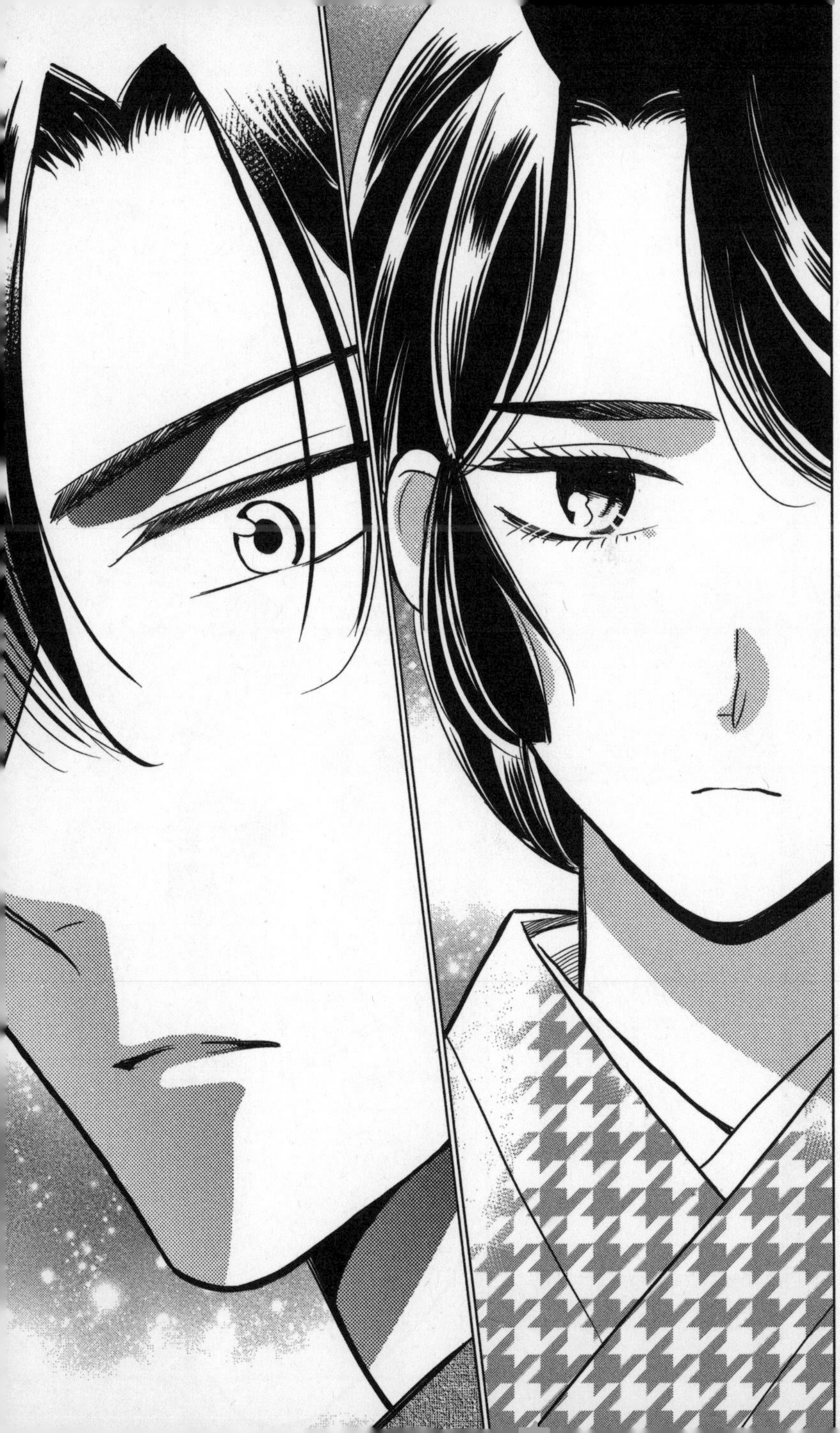

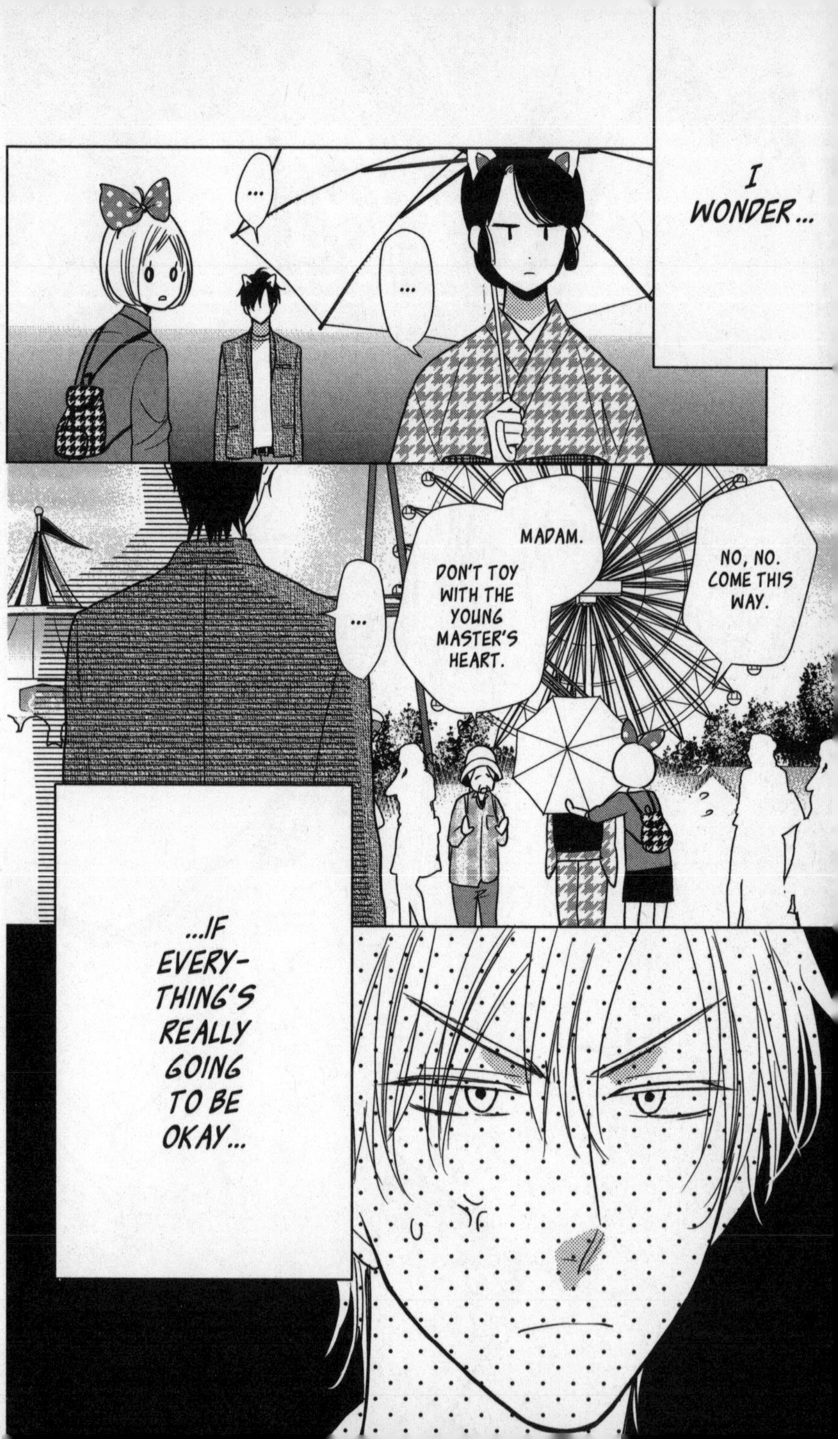
I WONDER...
...
...
NO, NO. COME THIS WAY.
MADAM.
DON'T TOY WITH THE YOUNG MASTER'S HEART.
...
...IF EVERY-THING'S REALLY GOING TO BE OKAY...

Chapter 84

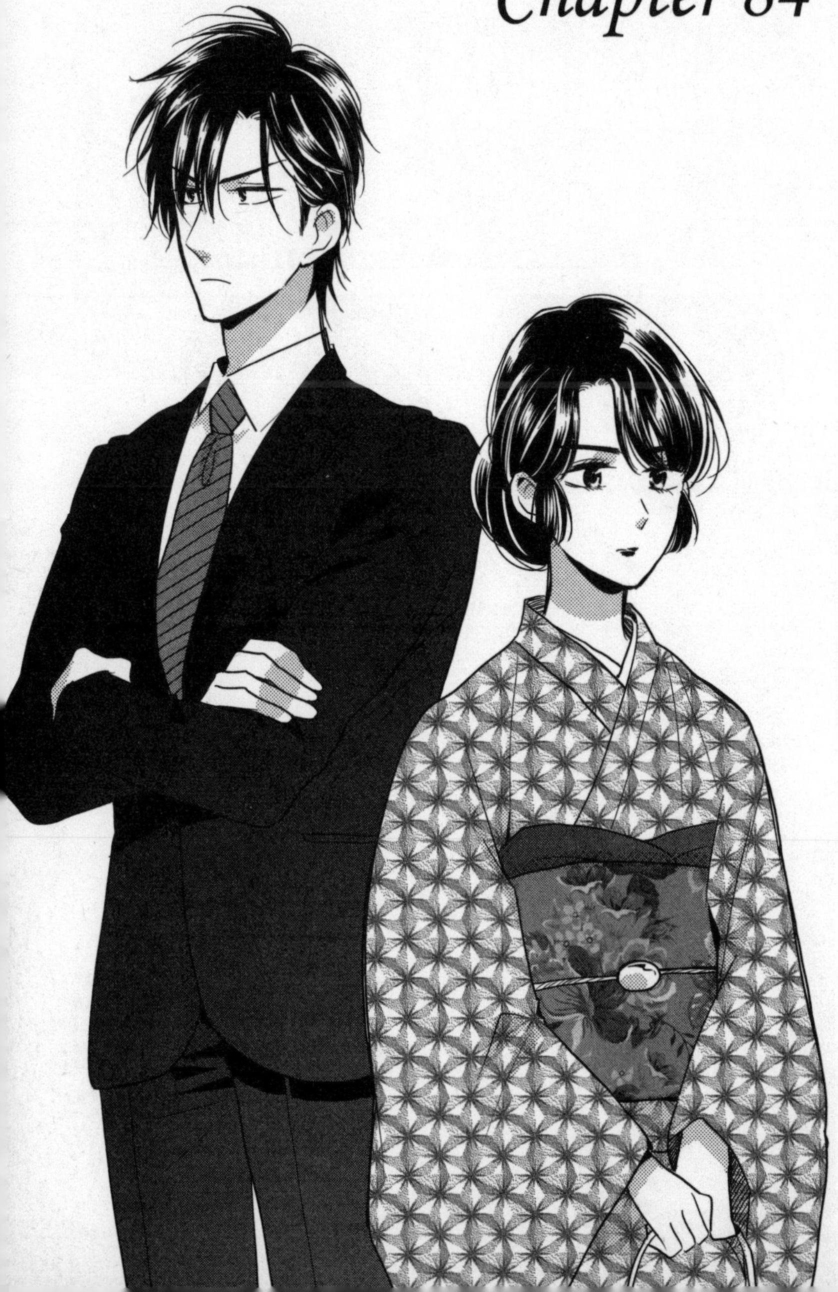

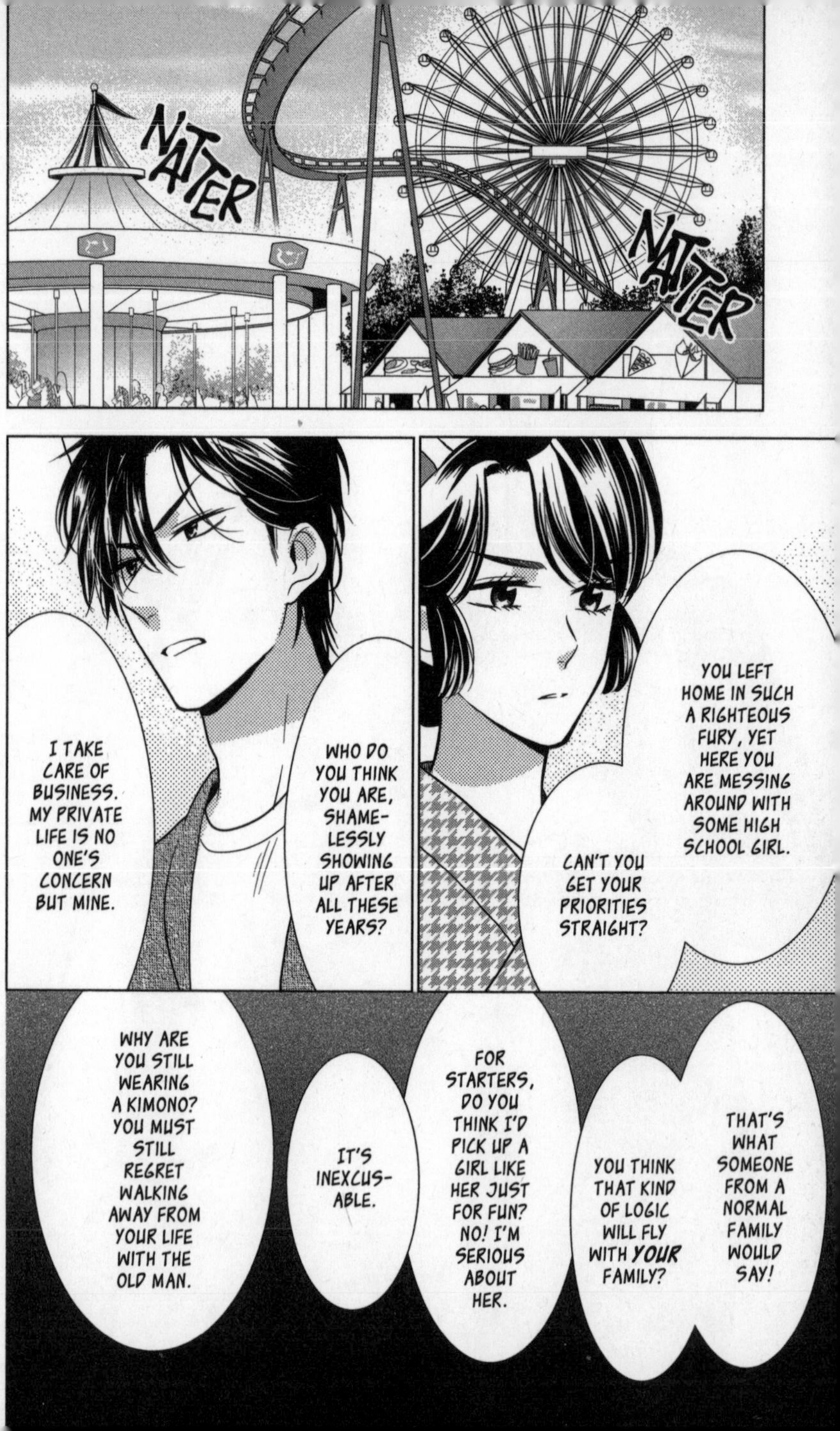
NATTER
NATTER
YOU LEFT HOME IN SUCH A RIGHTEOUS FURY, YET HERE YOU ARE MESSING AROUND WITH SOME HIGH SCHOOL GIRL.
CAN'T YOU GET YOUR PRIORITIES STRAIGHT?
WHO DO YOU THINK YOU ARE, SHAME-LESSLY SHOWING UP AFTER ALL THESE YEARS?
I TAKE CARE OF BUSINESS. MY PRIVATE LIFE IS NO ONE'S CONCERN BUT MINE.
THAT'S WHAT SOMEONE FROM A NORMAL FAMILY WOULD SAY!
YOU THINK THAT KIND OF LOGIC WILL FLY WITH *YOUR* FAMILY?
FOR STARTERS, DO YOU THINK I'D PICK UP A GIRL LIKE HER JUST FOR FUN? NO! I'M SERIOUS ABOUT HER.
IT'S INEXCUS-ABLE.
WHY ARE YOU STILL WEARING A KIMONO? YOU MUST STILL REGRET WALKING AWAY FROM YOUR LIFE WITH THE OLD MAN.

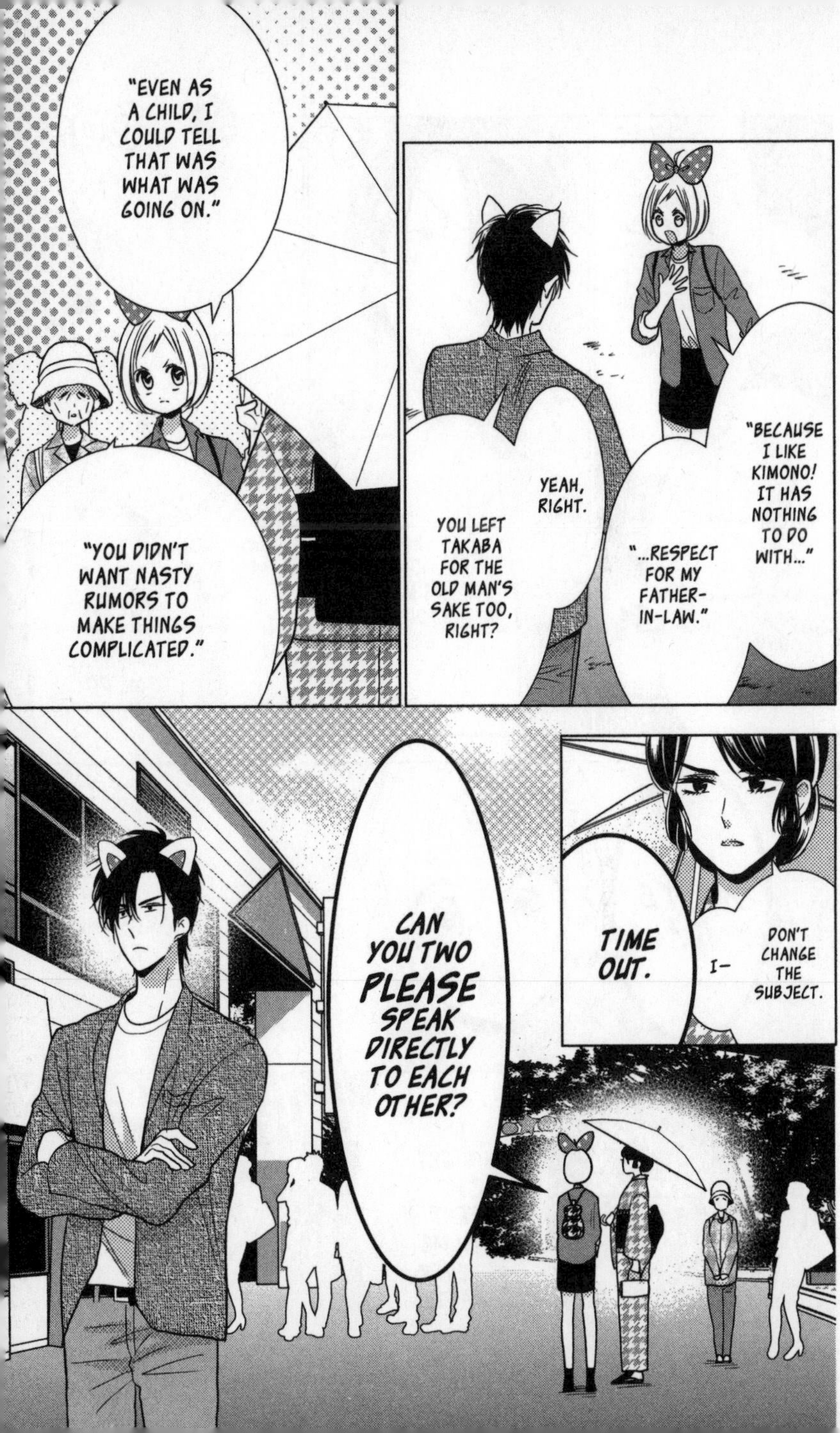
"BECAUSE I LIKE KIMONO! IT HAS NOTHING TO DO WITH..."
"...RESPECT FOR MY FATHER-IN-LAW."
YEAH, RIGHT.
YOU LEFT TAKABA FOR THE OLD MAN'S SAKE TOO, RIGHT?
"EVEN AS A CHILD, I COULD TELL THAT WAS WHAT WAS GOING ON."
"YOU DIDN'T WANT NASTY RUMORS TO MAKE THINGS COMPLICATED."
DON'T CHANGE THE SUBJECT.
I—
TIME OUT.
CAN YOU TWO PLEASE SPEAK DIRECTLY TO EACH OTHER?

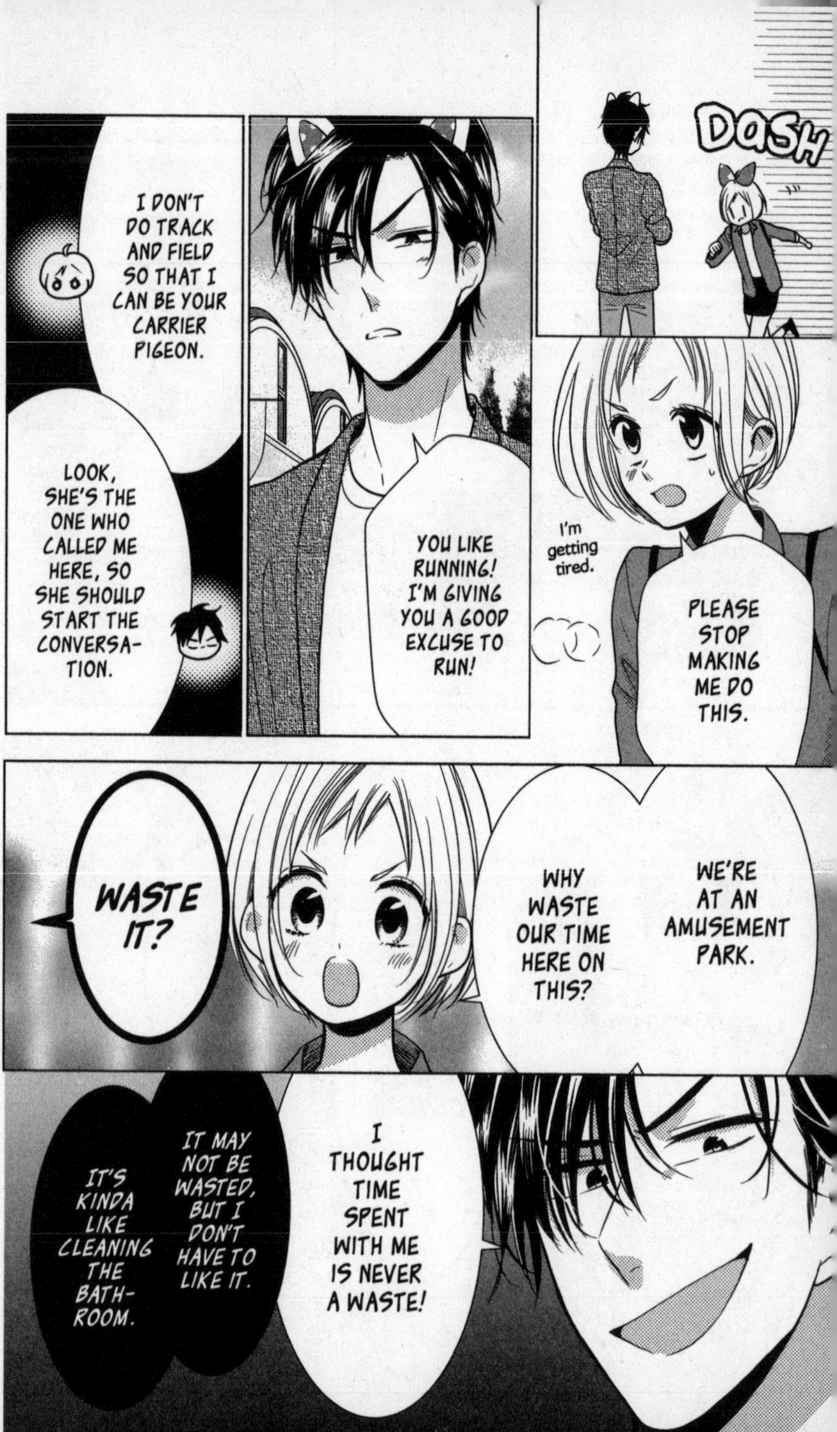
DASH
I'm getting tired.
PLEASE STOP MAKING ME DO THIS.
YOU LIKE RUNNING! I'M GIVING YOU A GOOD EXCUSE TO RUN!
I DON'T DO TRACK AND FIELD SO THAT I CAN BE YOUR CARRIER PIGEON.
LOOK, SHE'S THE ONE WHO CALLED ME HERE, SO SHE SHOULD START THE CONVERSA-TION.
WE'RE AT AN AMUSEMENT PARK.
WHY WASTE OUR TIME HERE ON THIS?
WASTE IT?
I THOUGHT TIME SPENT WITH ME IS NEVER A WASTE!
IT MAY NOT BE WASTED, BUT I DON'T HAVE TO LIKE IT.
IT'S KINDA LIKE CLEANING THE BATH-ROOM.

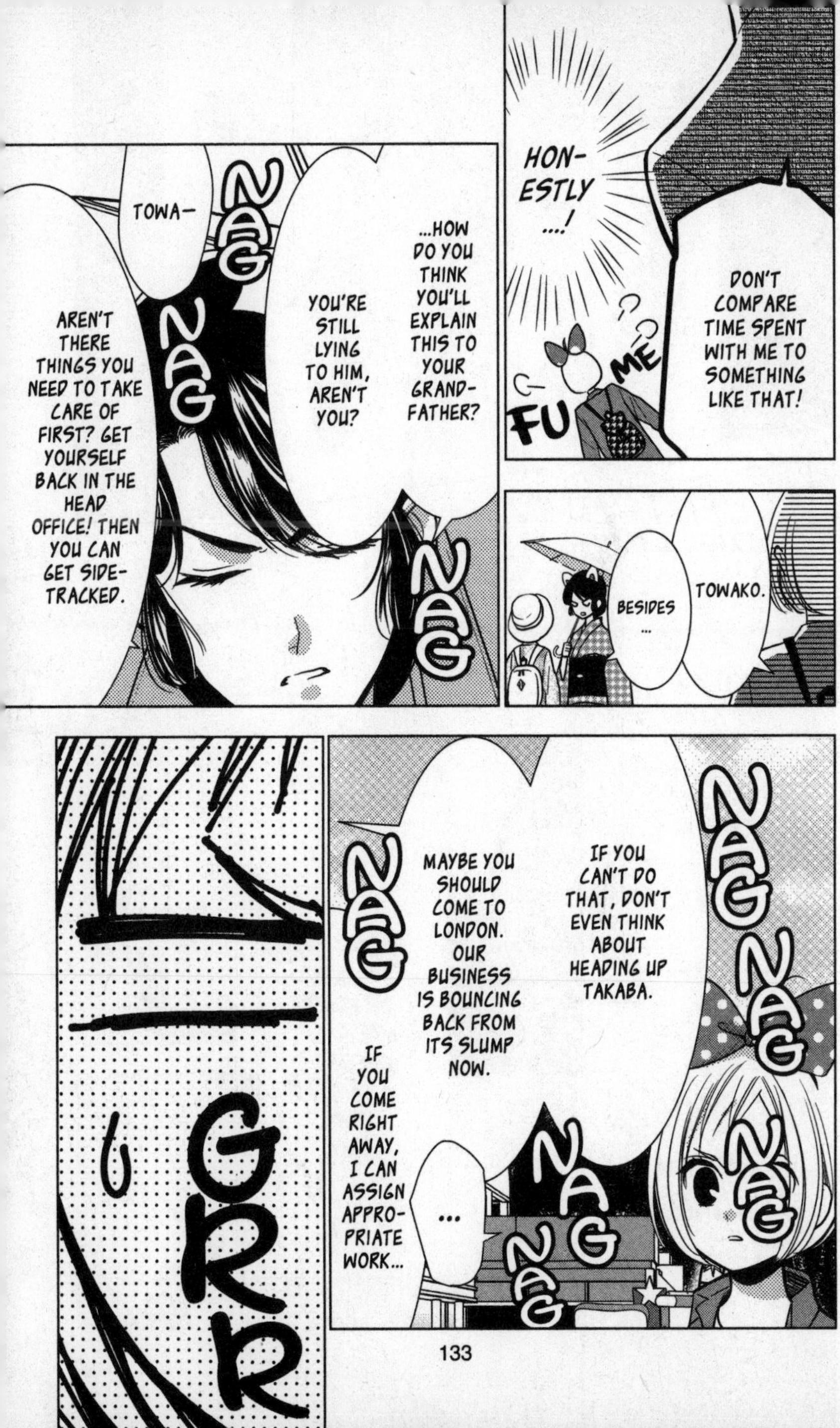
HON-ESTLY ...!
DON'T COMPARE TIME SPENT WITH ME TO SOMETHING LIKE THAT!
FU ME
TOWAKO.
BESIDES ...
...HOW DO YOU THINK YOU'LL EXPLAIN THIS TO YOUR GRAND-FATHER?
YOU'RE STILL LYING TO HIM, AREN'T YOU?
NAG
TOWA—
NAG
NAG
AREN'T THERE THINGS YOU NEED TO TAKE CARE OF FIRST? GET YOURSELF BACK IN THE HEAD OFFICE! THEN YOU CAN GET SIDE-TRACKED.
NAG
NAG
IF YOU CAN'T DO THAT, DON'T EVEN THINK ABOUT HEADING UP TAKABA.
MAYBE YOU SHOULD COME TO LONDON. OUR BUSINESS IS BOUNCING BACK FROM ITS SLUMP NOW.
NAG
IF YOU COME RIGHT AWAY, I CAN ASSIGN APPRO-PRIATE WORK...
NAG
NAG
NAG
...
GRR

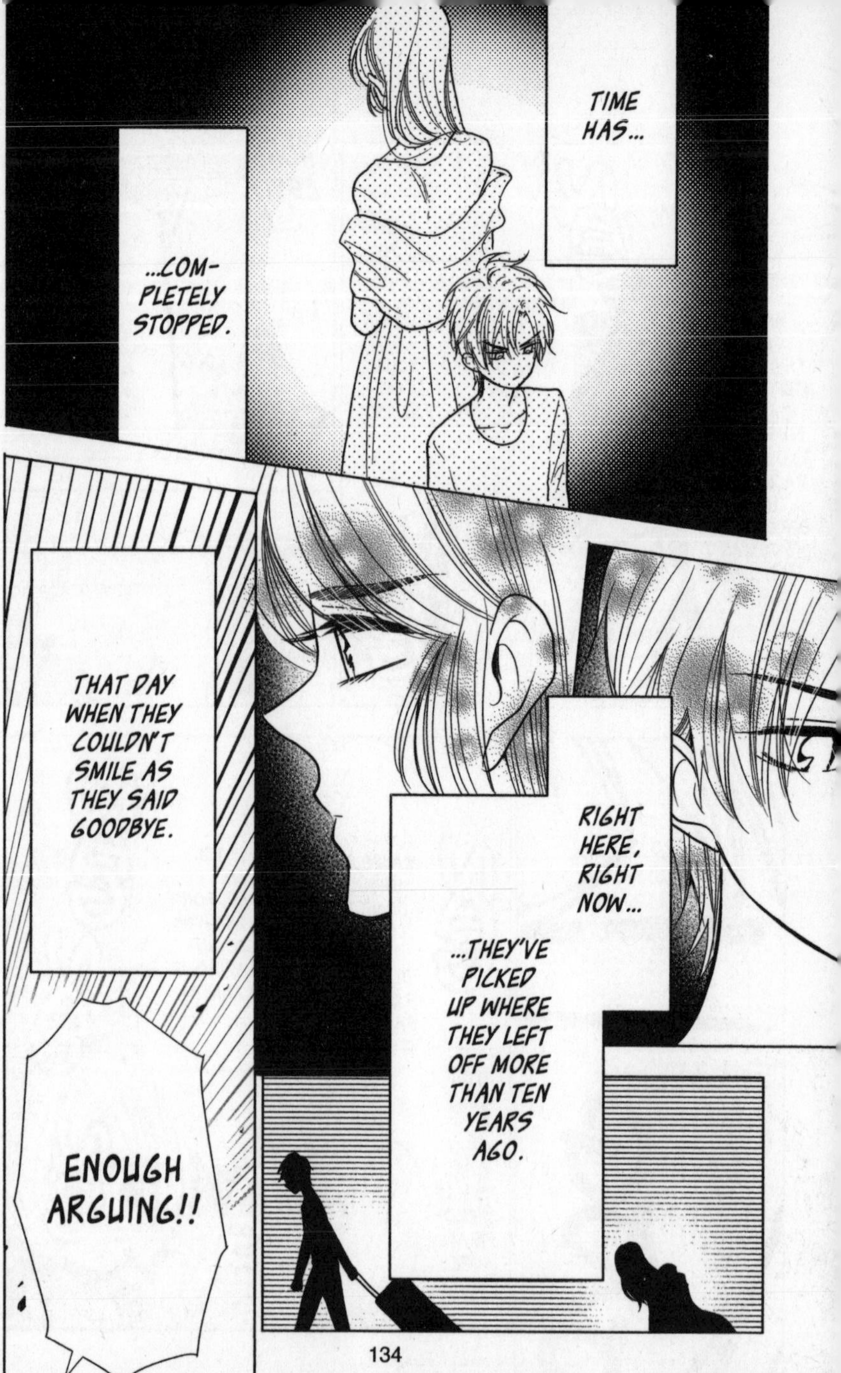
TIME HAS...
...COM-PLETELY STOPPED.
RIGHT HERE, RIGHT NOW...
...THEY'VE PICKED UP WHERE THEY LEFT OFF MORE THAN TEN YEARS AGO.
THAT DAY WHEN THEY COULDN'T SMILE AS THEY SAID GOODBYE.
ENOUGH ARGUING!!

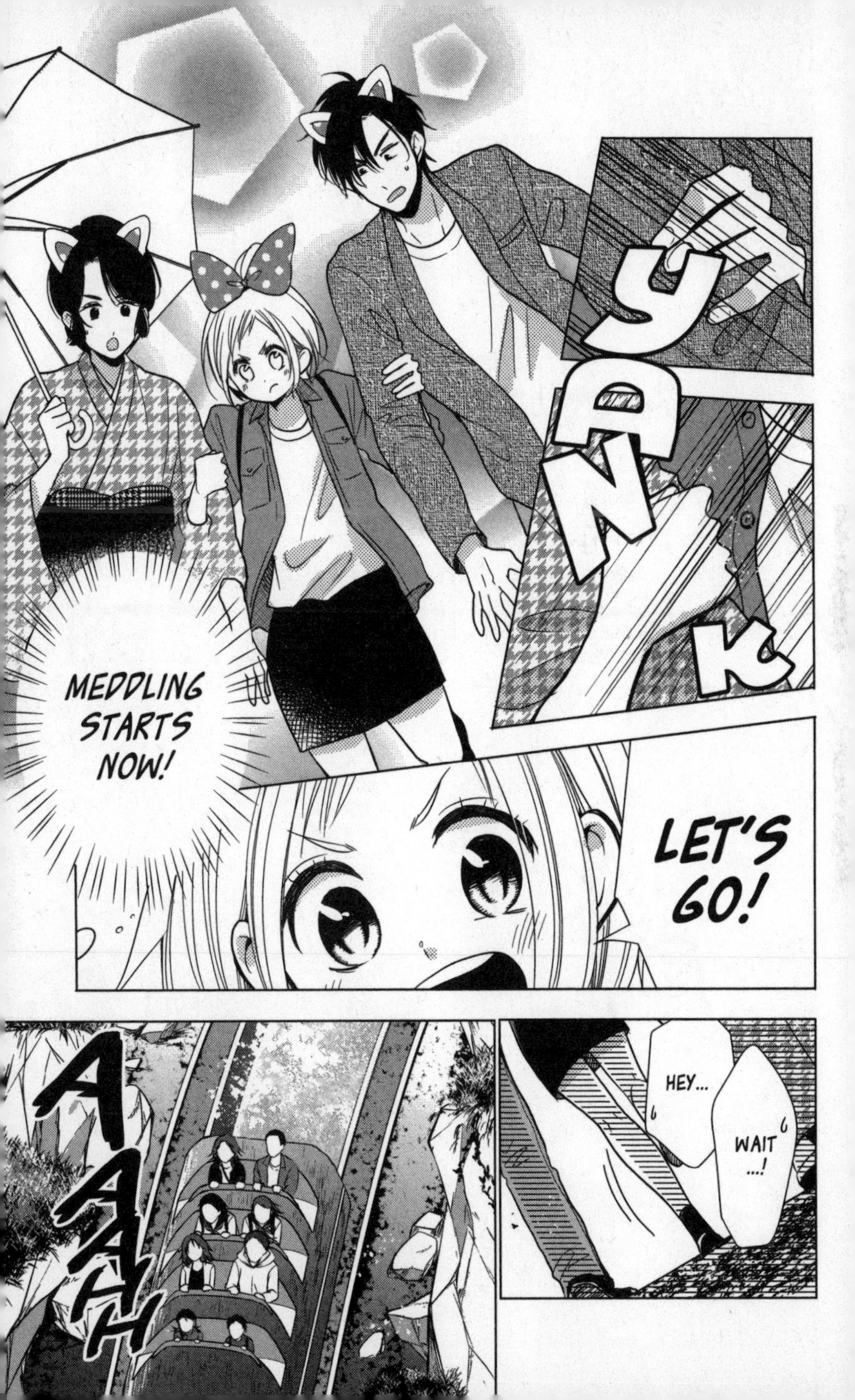
YANK
MEDDLING STARTS NOW!
LET'S GO!
HEY...
WAIT ...!
AAAH

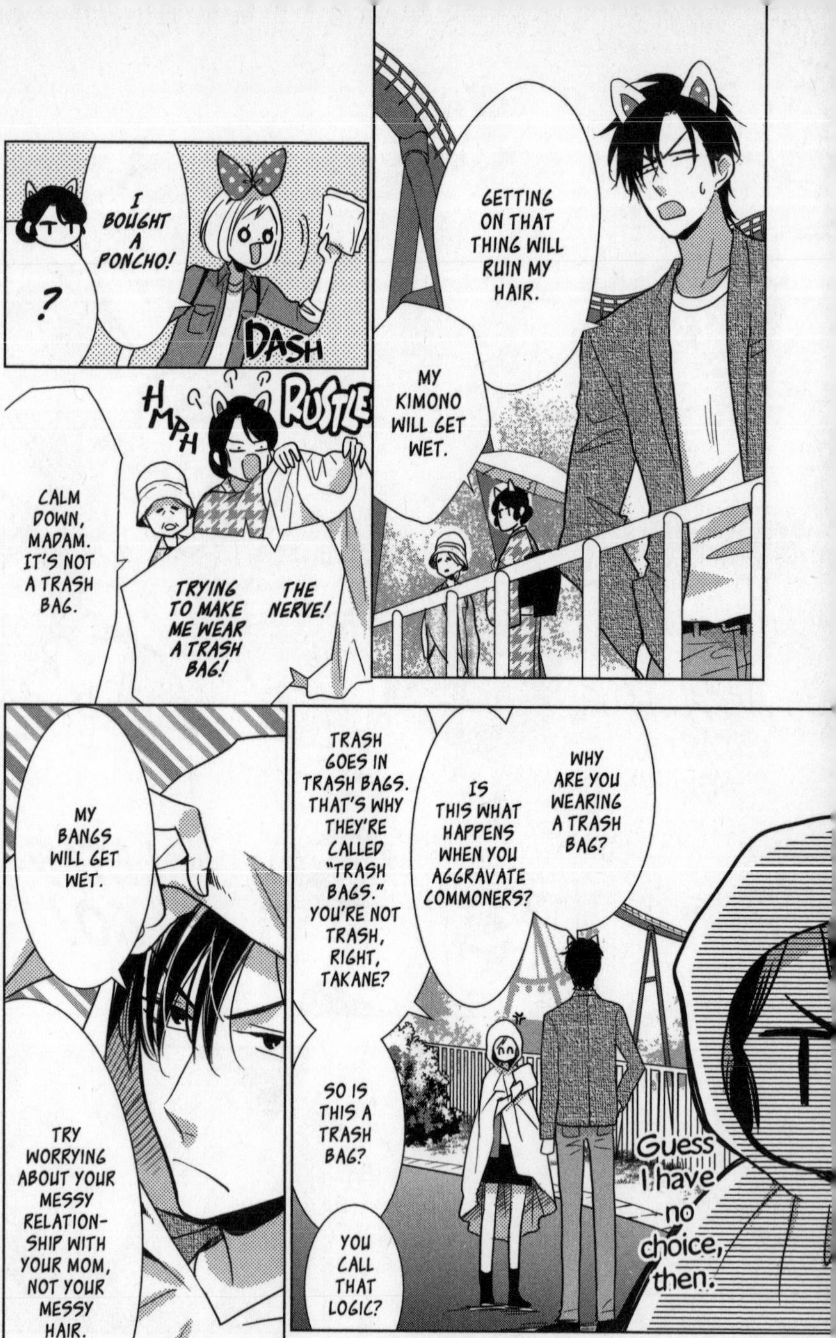
GETTING ON THAT THING WILL RUIN MY HAIR.
MY KIMONO WILL GET WET.
I BOUGHT A PONCHO!
?
DASH
RUSTLE
HMPH
THE NERVE!
TRYING TO MAKE ME WEAR A TRASH BAG!
CALM DOWN, MADAM. IT'S NOT A TRASH BAG.
Guess I have no choice, then.
WHY ARE YOU WEARING A TRASH BAG?
IS THIS WHAT HAPPENS WHEN YOU AGGRAVATE COMMONERS?
TRASH GOES IN TRASH BAGS. THAT'S WHY THEY'RE CALLED "TRASH BAGS." YOU'RE NOT TRASH, RIGHT, TAKANE?
SO IS THIS A TRASH BAG?
YOU CALL THAT LOGIC?
MY BANGS WILL GET WET.
TRY WORRYING ABOUT YOUR MESSY RELATION-SHIP WITH YOUR MOM, NOT YOUR MESSY HAIR.

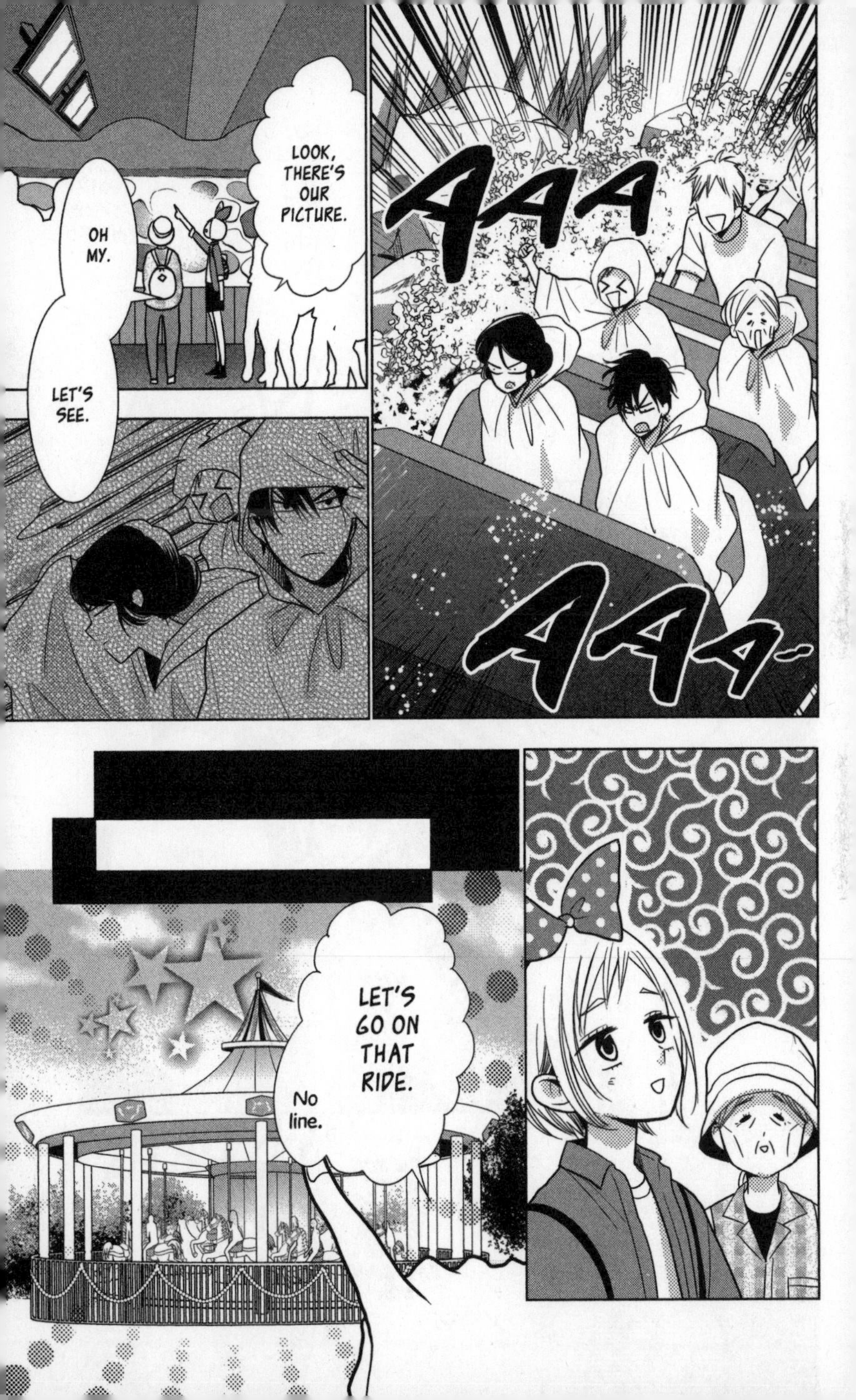
AAA
AAAA-
LOOK, THERE'S OUR PICTURE.
OH MY.
LET'S SEE.
LET'S GO ON THAT RIDE.
No line.

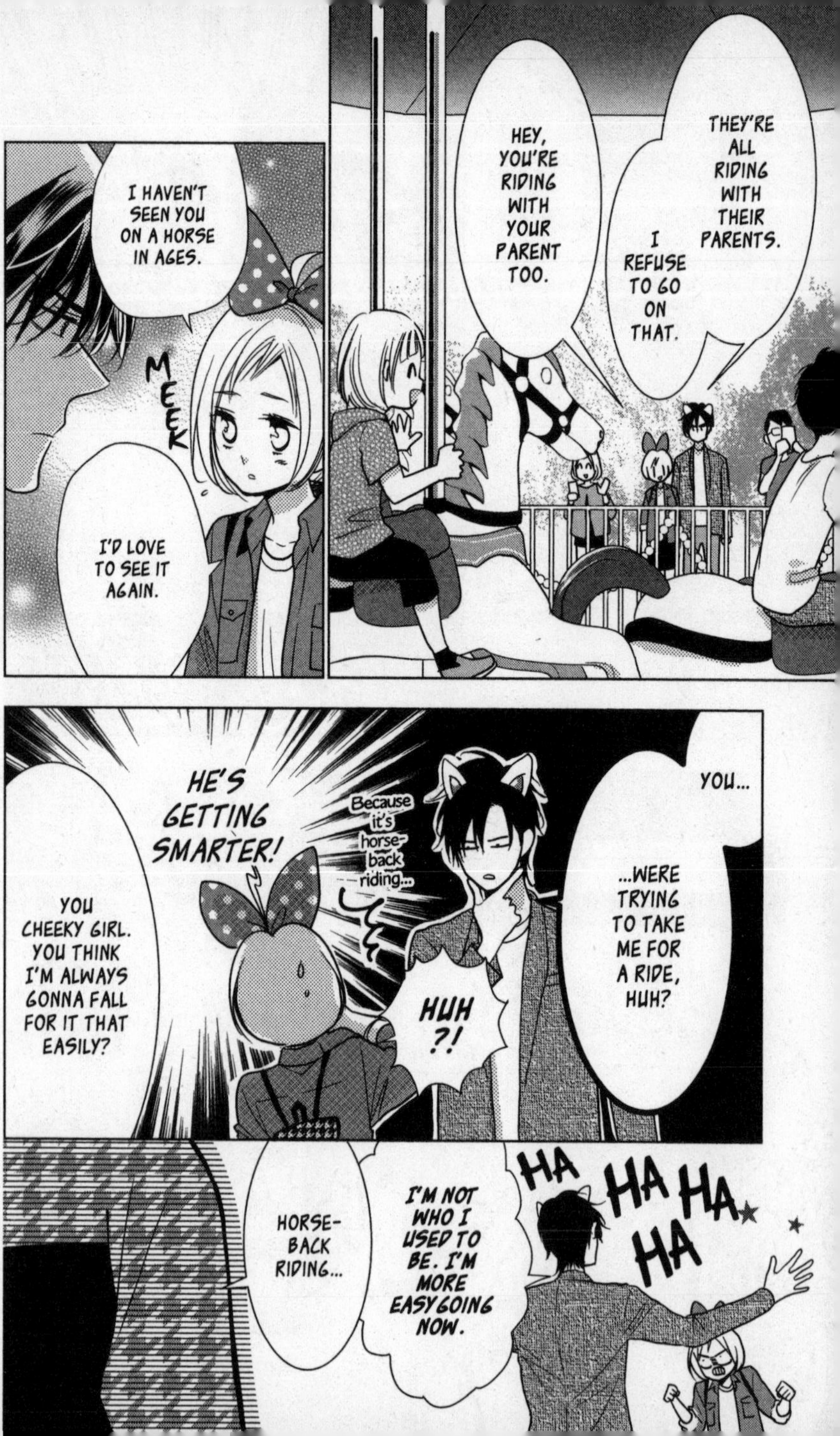
THEY'RE ALL RIDING WITH THEIR PARENTS.
I REFUSE TO GO ON THAT.
HEY, YOU'RE RIDING WITH YOUR PARENT TOO.
I HAVEN'T SEEN YOU ON A HORSE IN AGES.
MEEK
I'D LOVE TO SEE IT AGAIN.
YOU...
...WERE TRYING TO TAKE ME FOR A RIDE, HUH?
HUH?!
Because it's horse-back riding...
HE'S GETTING SMARTER!
YOU CHEEKY GIRL. YOU THINK I'M ALWAYS GONNA FALL FOR IT THAT EASILY?
HA HA HA HA HA
I'M NOT WHO I USED TO BE. I'M MORE EASYGOING NOW.
HORSE-BACK RIDING...

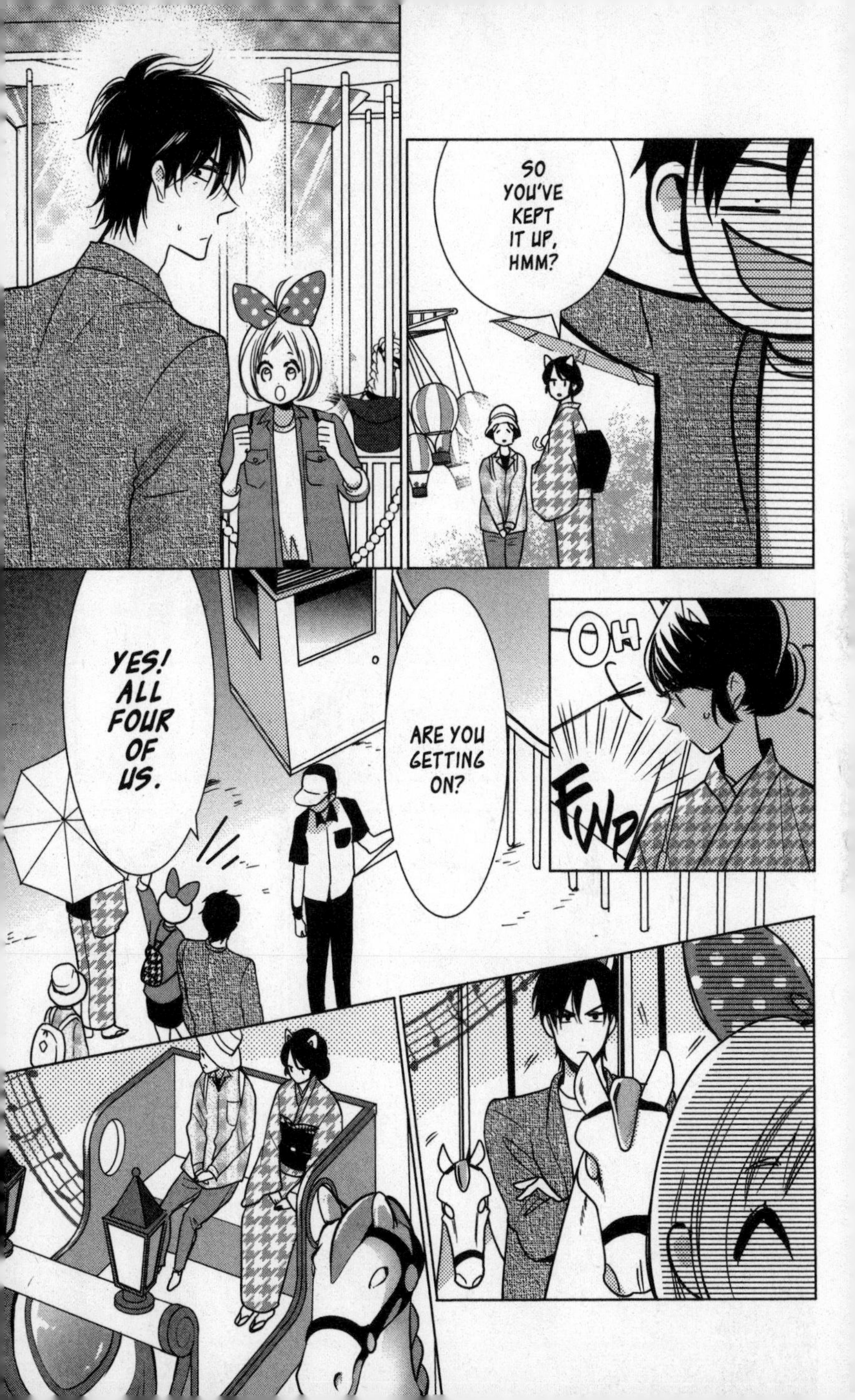
SO YOU'VE KEPT IT UP, HMM?
OH
FWP
ARE YOU GETTING ON?
YES! ALL FOUR OF US.

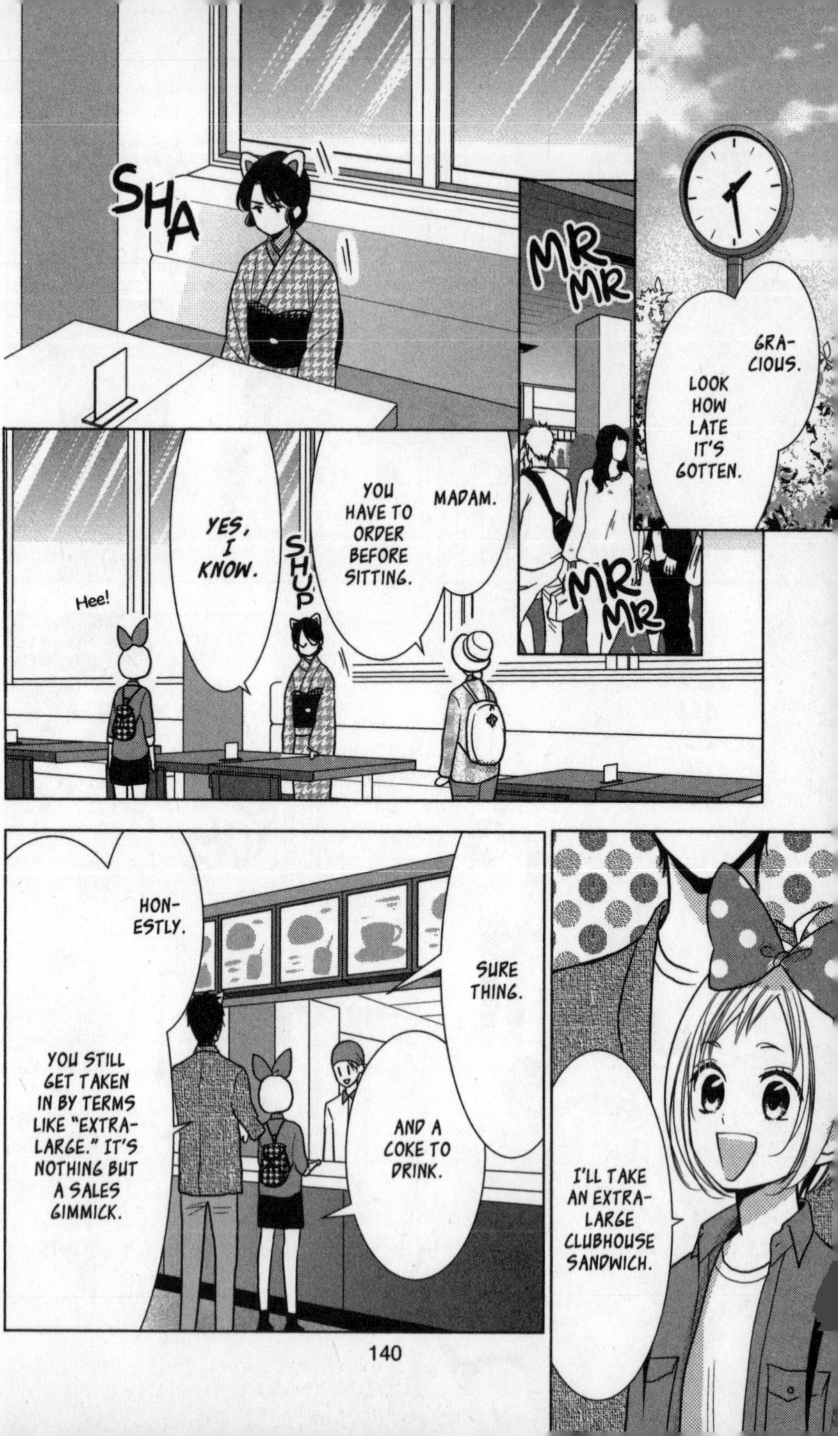
GRA-CIOUS.
LOOK HOW LATE IT'S GOTTEN.
MR MR
MR MR
SHA
MADAM.
YOU HAVE TO ORDER BEFORE SITTING.
SHUP
YES, I KNOW.
Hee!
I'LL TAKE AN EXTRA-LARGE CLUBHOUSE SANDWICH.
AND A COKE TO DRINK.
SURE THING.
HON-ESTLY.
YOU STILL GET TAKEN IN BY TERMS LIKE "EXTRA-LARGE." IT'S NOTHING BUT A SALES GIMMICK.

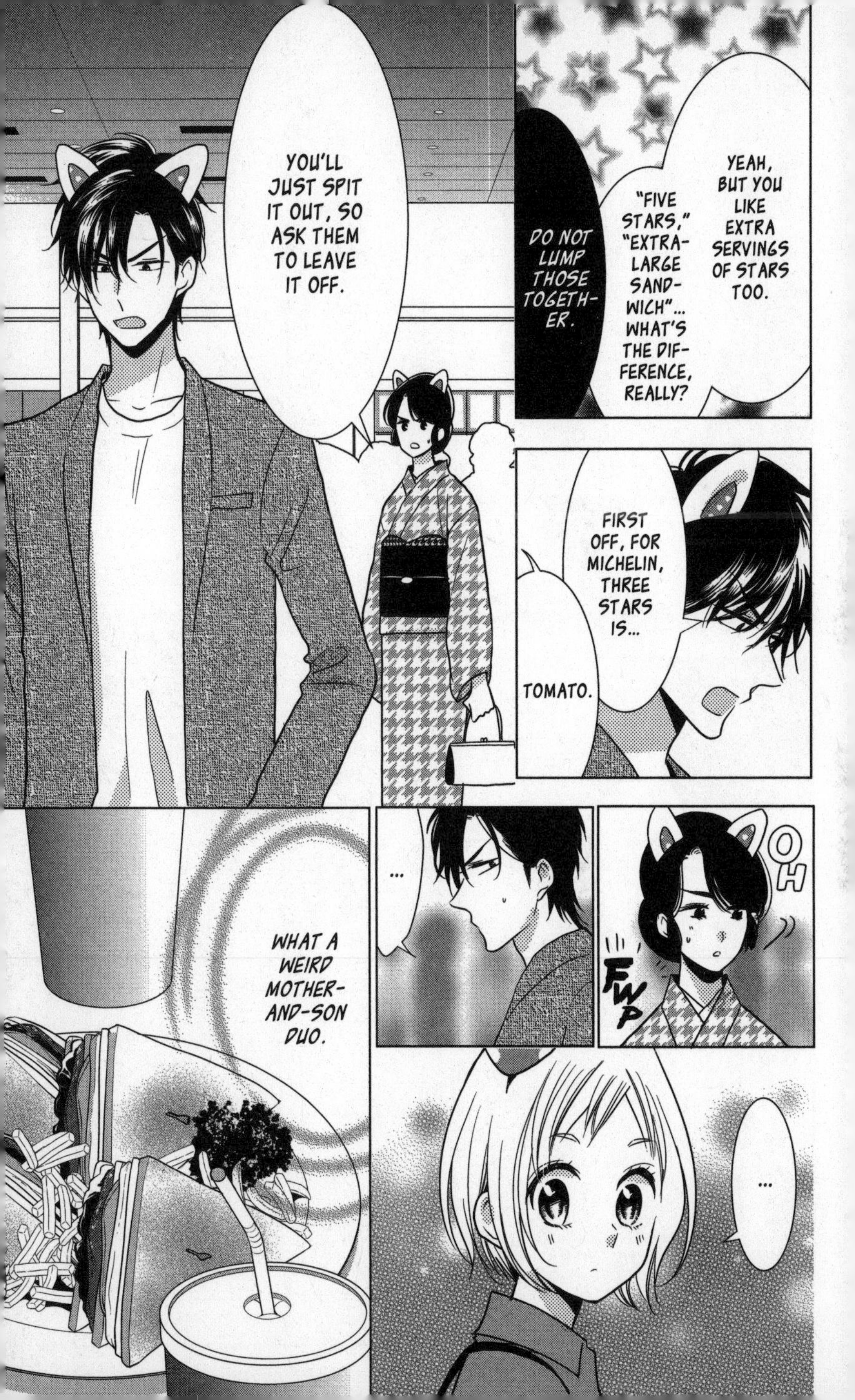
YEAH, BUT YOU LIKE EXTRA SERVINGS OF STARS TOO.
"FIVE STARS," "EXTRA-LARGE SANDWICH"... WHAT'S THE DIFFERENCE, REALLY?
DO NOT LUMP THOSE TOGETHER.
FIRST OFF, FOR MICHELIN, THREE STARS IS...
TOMATO.
YOU'LL JUST SPIT IT OUT, SO ASK THEM TO LEAVE IT OFF.
OH
FWP
...
...
WHAT A WEIRD MOTHER-AND-SON DUO.

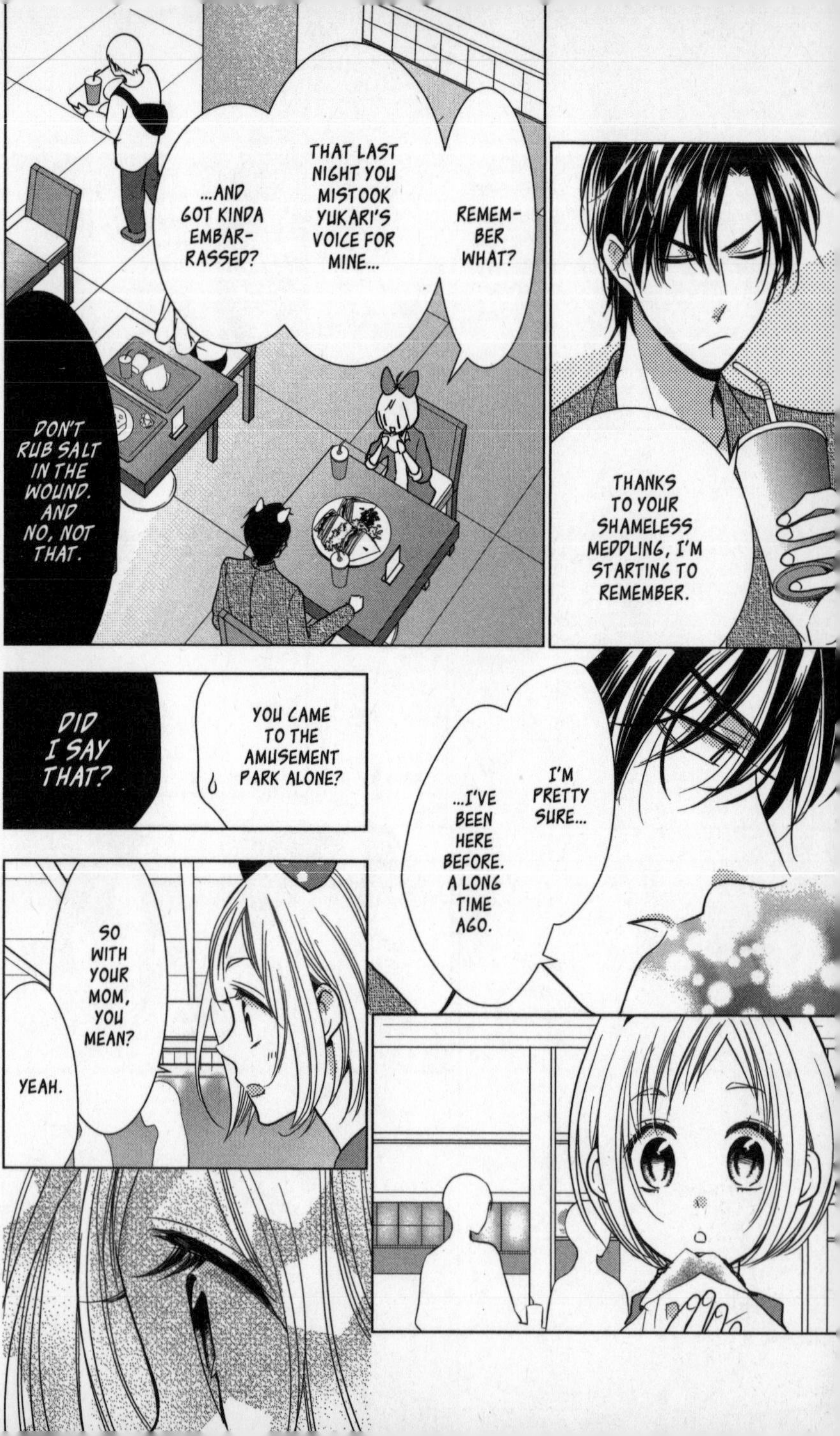
THANKS TO YOUR SHAMELESS MEDDLING, I'M STARTING TO REMEMBER.
REMEMBER WHAT?
THAT LAST NIGHT YOU MISTOOK YUKARI'S VOICE FOR MINE...
...AND GOT KINDA EMBARRASSED?
DON'T RUB SALT IN THE WOUND. AND NO, NOT THAT.
I'M PRETTY SURE...
...I'VE BEEN HERE BEFORE. A LONG TIME AGO.
YOU CAME TO THE AMUSEMENT PARK ALONE?
DID I SAY THAT?
SO WITH YOUR MOM, YOU MEAN?
YEAH.

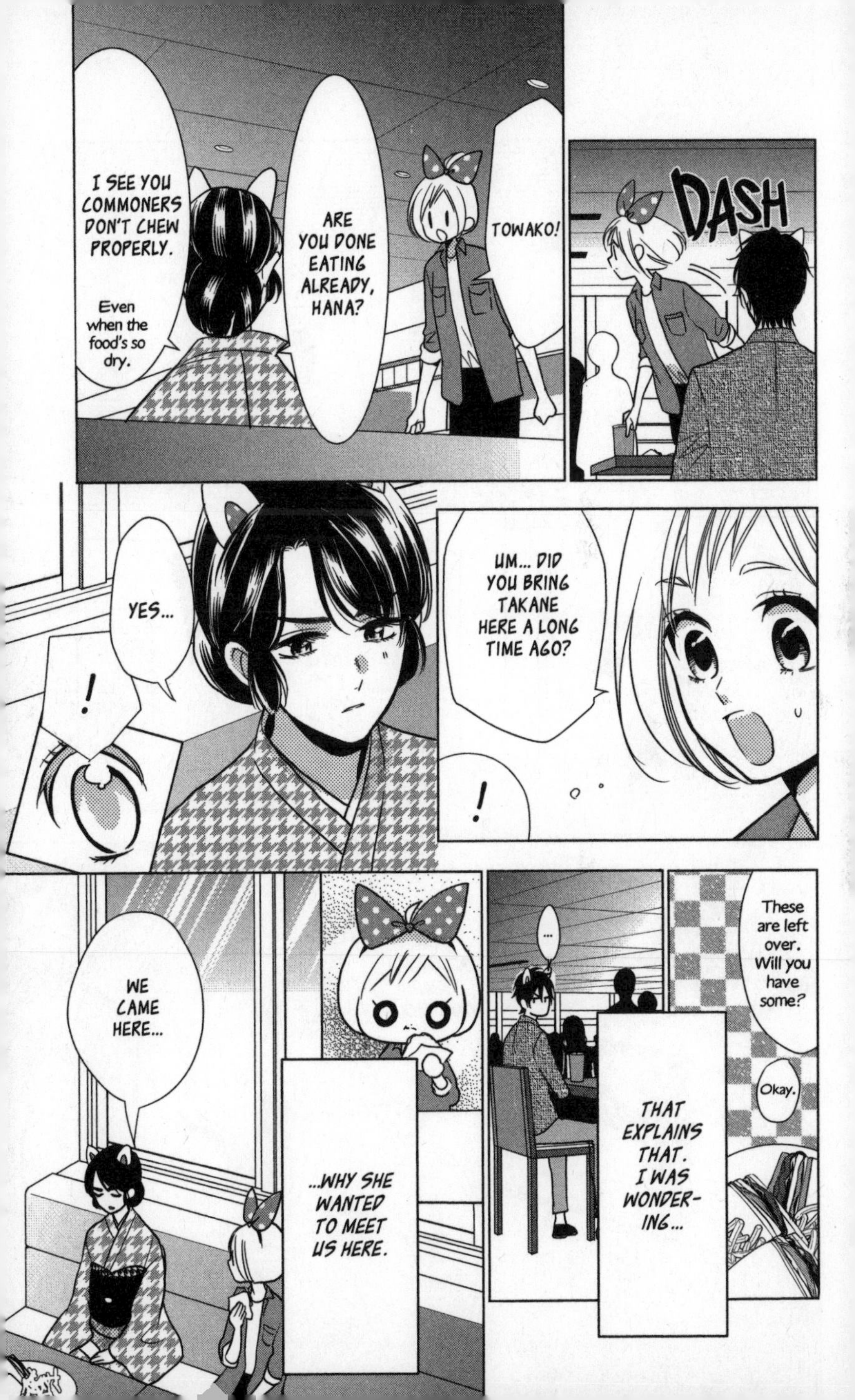
DASH
TOWAKO!
ARE YOU DONE EATING ALREADY, HANA?
I SEE YOU COMMONERS DON'T CHEW PROPERLY.
Even when the food's so dry.
UM... DID YOU BRING TAKANE HERE A LONG TIME AGO?
!
YES...
!
These are left over. Will you have some?
Okay.
...
THAT EXPLAINS THAT. I WAS WONDERING...
...WHY SHE WANTED TO MEET US HERE.
WE CAME HERE...

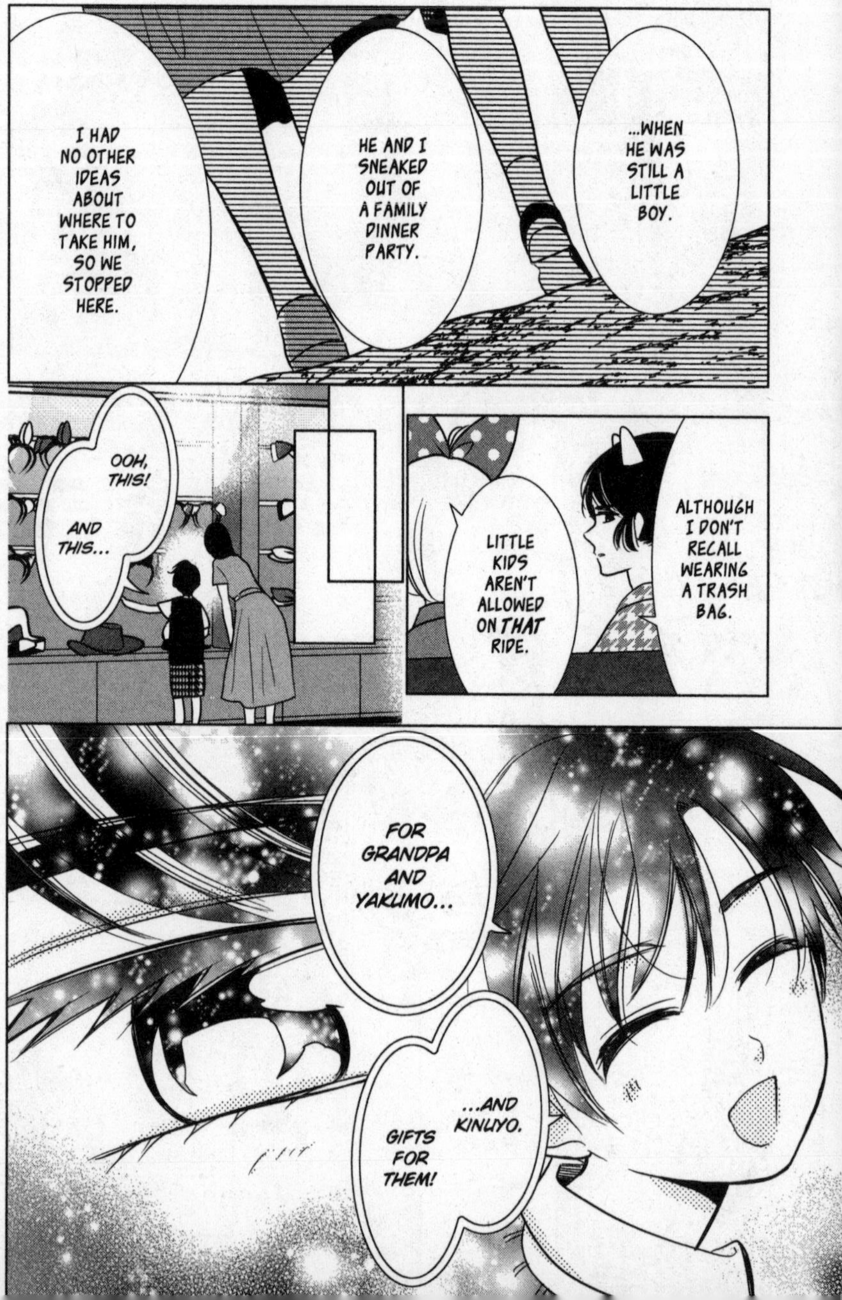
...WHEN HE WAS STILL A LITTLE BOY.
HE AND I SNEAKED OUT OF A FAMILY DINNER PARTY.
I HAD NO OTHER IDEAS ABOUT WHERE TO TAKE HIM, SO WE STOPPED HERE.
ALTHOUGH I DON'T RECALL WEARING A TRASH BAG.
LITTLE KIDS AREN'T ALLOWED ON *THAT* RIDE.
OOH, THIS!
AND THIS...
FOR GRANDPA AND YAKUMO...
...AND KINUYO.
GIFTS FOR THEM!

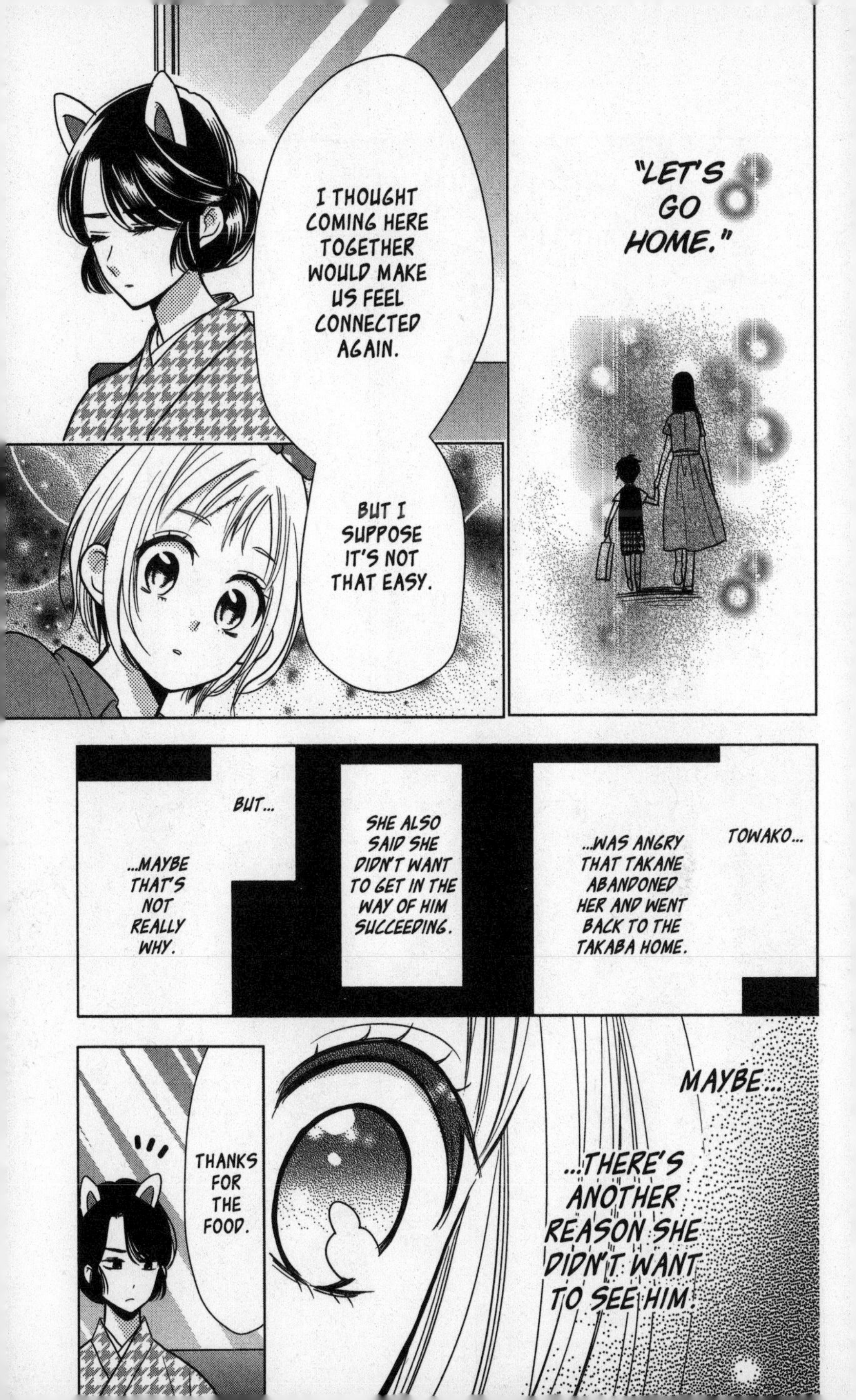
"LET'S GO HOME."
I THOUGHT COMING HERE TOGETHER WOULD MAKE US FEEL CONNECTED AGAIN.
BUT I SUPPOSE IT'S NOT THAT EASY.
TOWAKO...
...WAS ANGRY THAT TAKANE ABANDONED HER AND WENT BACK TO THE TAKABA HOME.
SHE ALSO SAID SHE DIDN'T WANT TO GET IN THE WAY OF HIM SUCCEEDING.
BUT...
...MAYBE THAT'S NOT REALLY WHY.
MAYBE...
...THERE'S ANOTHER REASON SHE DIDN'T WANT TO SEE HIM.
THANKS FOR THE FOOD.

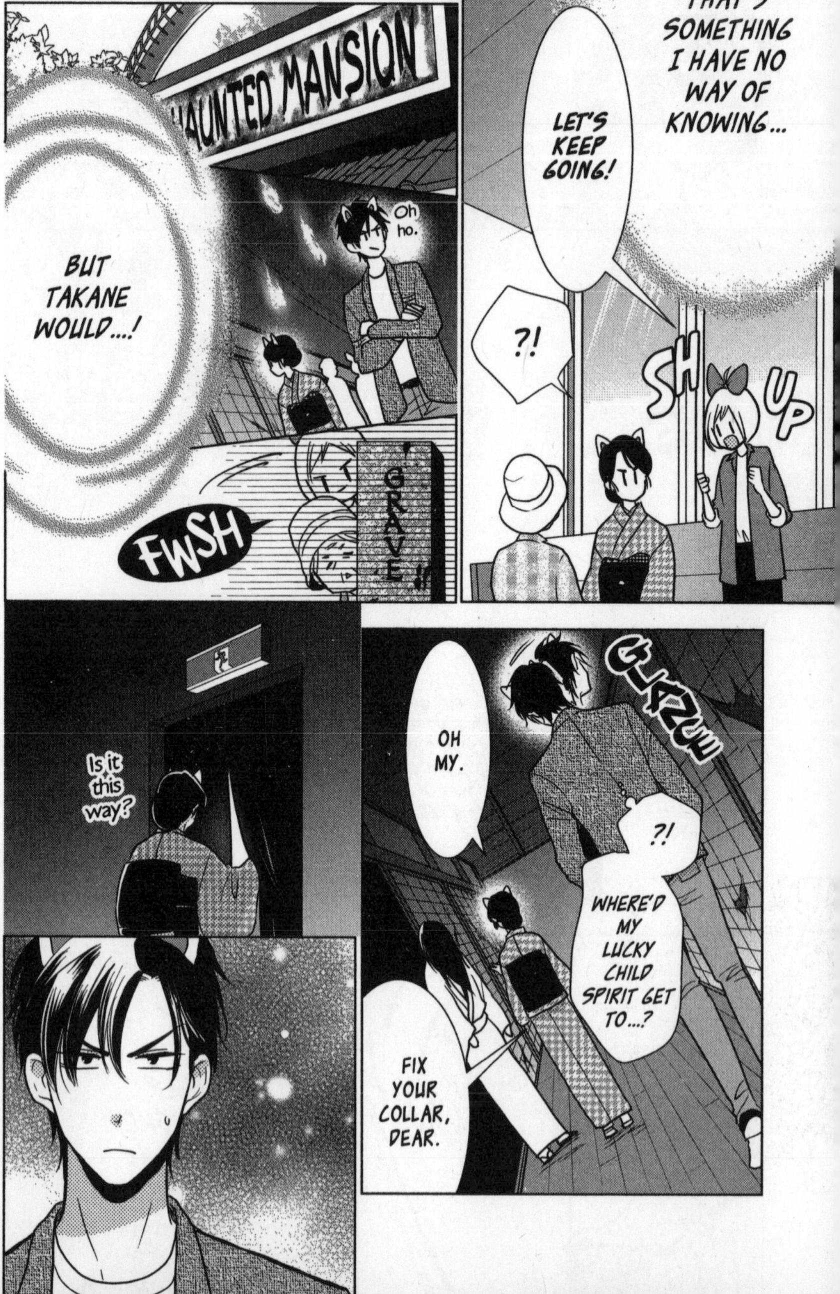
THAT'S SOMETHING I HAVE NO WAY OF KNOWING...
LET'S KEEP GOING!
?!
SH UP
HAUNTED MANSION
BUT TAKANE WOULD...!
Oh ho.
GRAVE
FWSH
GLAZE
OH MY.
?!
WHERE'D MY LUCKY CHILD SPIRIT GET TO...?
FIX YOUR COLLAR, DEAR.
Is it this way?

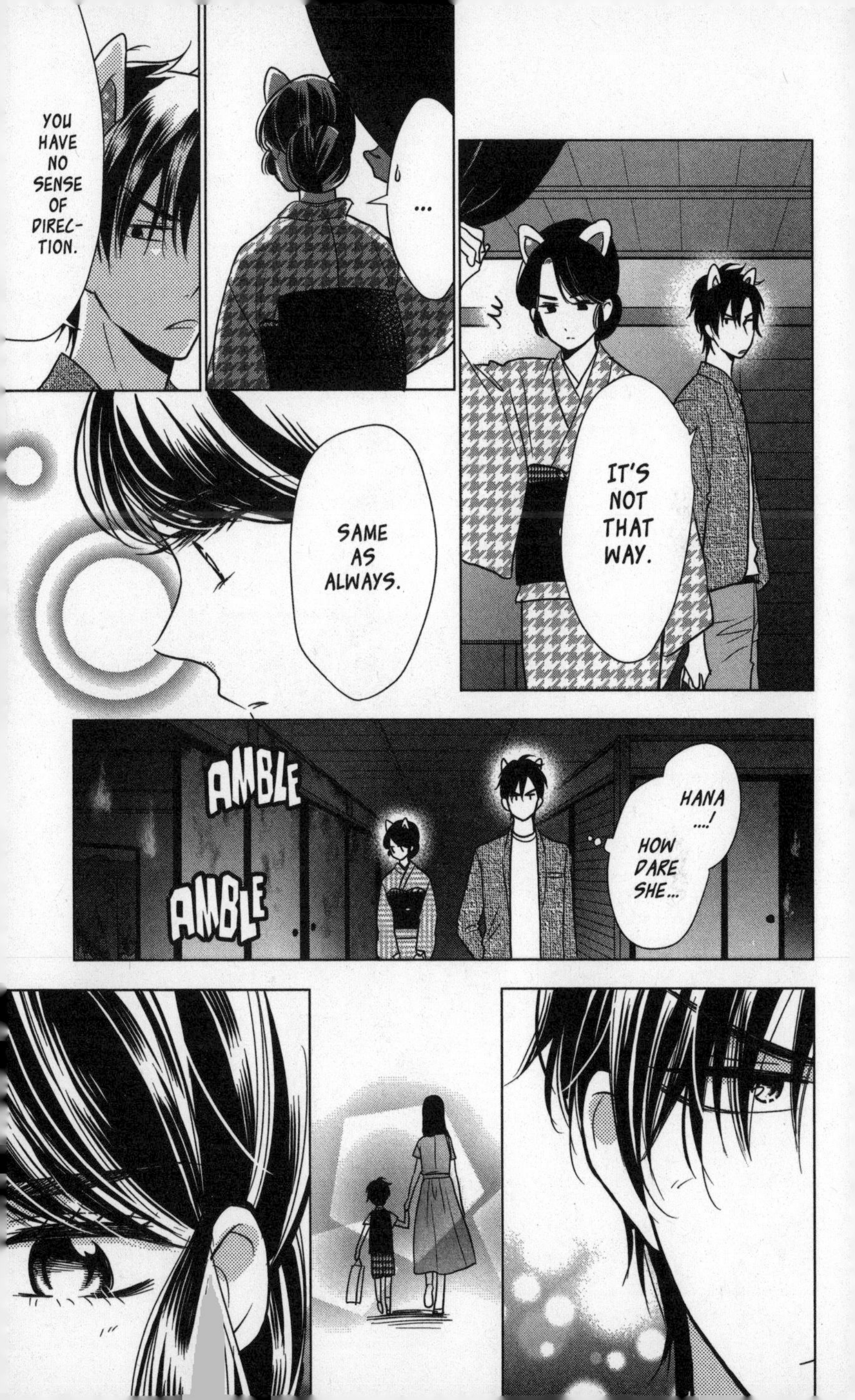
IT'S NOT THAT WAY.
...
YOU HAVE NO SENSE OF DIRECTION.
SAME AS ALWAYS.
HANA...! HOW DARE SHE...
AMBLE
AMBLE

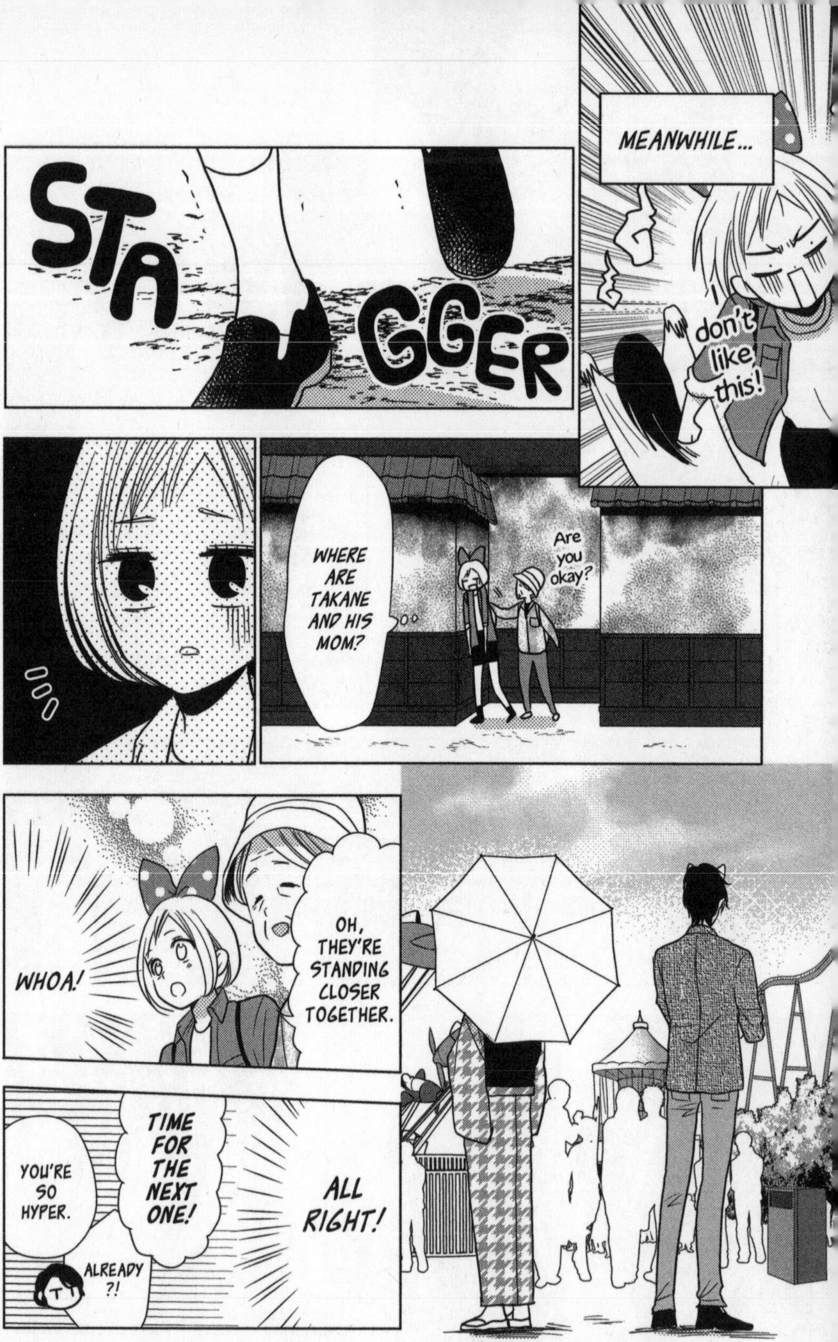
MEANWHILE...
I don't like this!
STAGGER
Are you okay?
WHERE ARE TAKANE AND HIS MOM?
OH, THEY'RE STANDING CLOSER TOGETHER.
WHOA!
ALL RIGHT!
TIME FOR THE NEXT ONE!
YOU'RE SO HYPER.
ALREADY?!

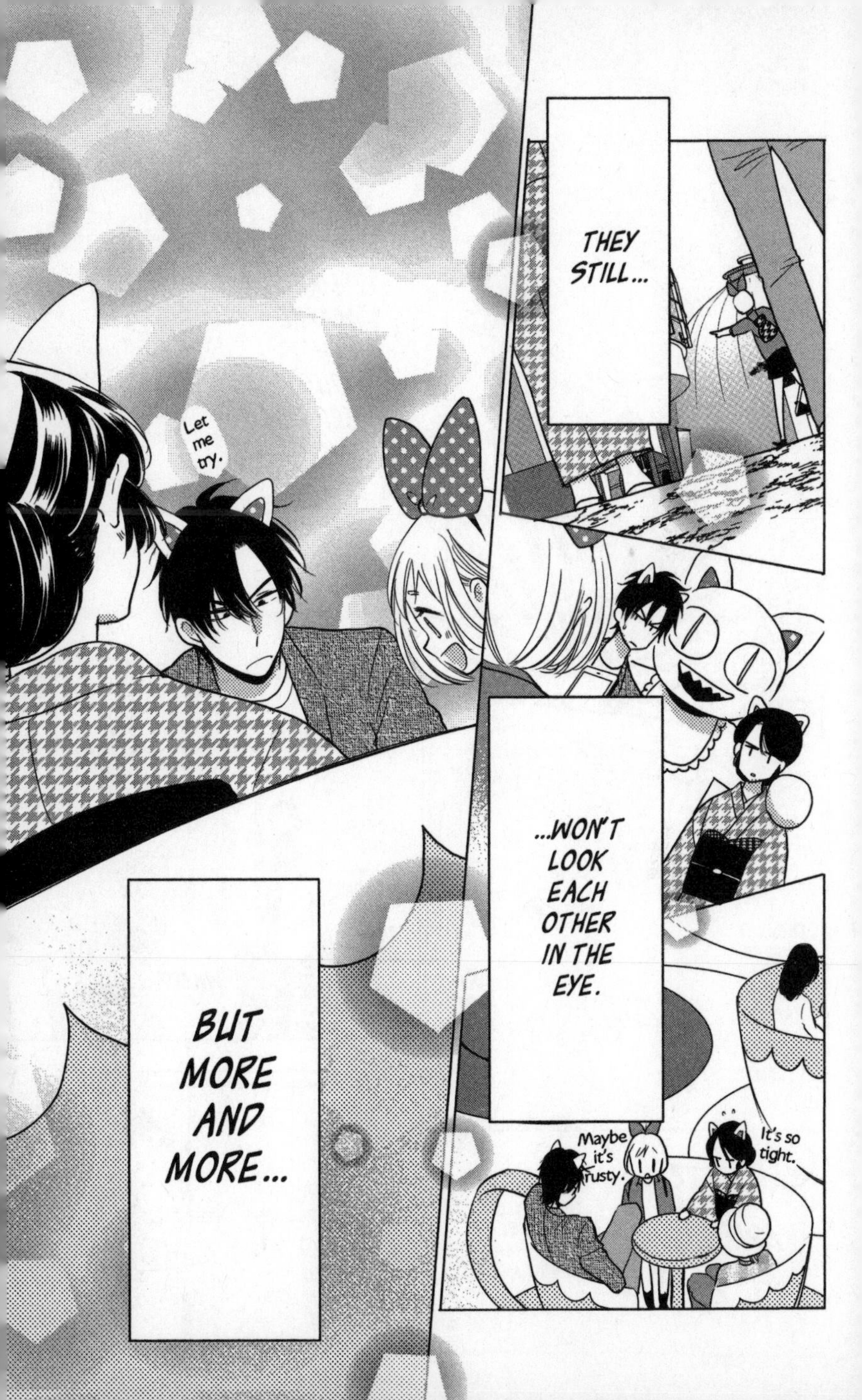
THEY STILL...
...WON'T LOOK EACH OTHER IN THE EYE.
It's so tight.
Maybe it's rusty.
Let me try.
BUT MORE AND MORE...

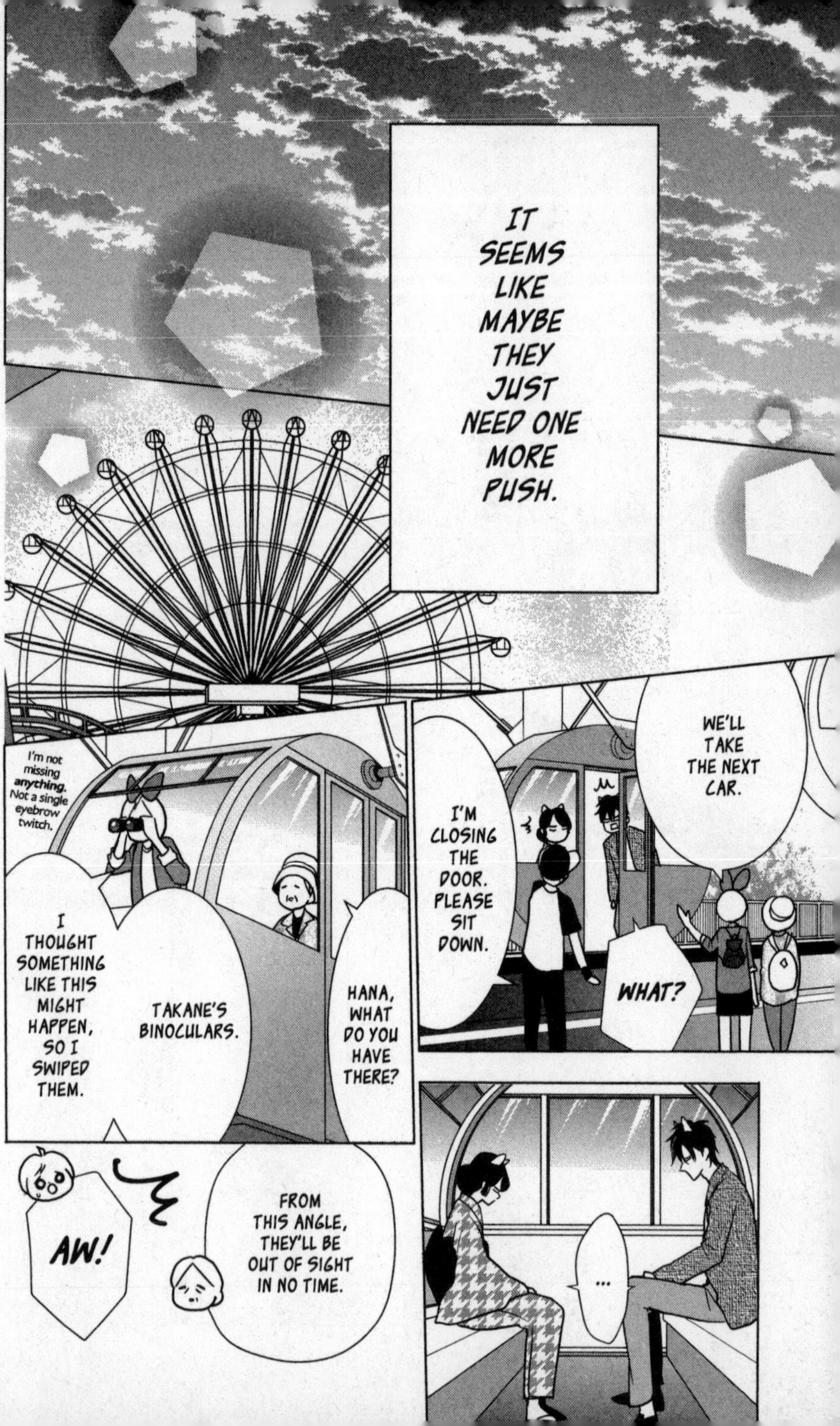
IT SEEMS LIKE MAYBE THEY JUST NEED ONE MORE PUSH.
WE'LL TAKE THE NEXT CAR.
I'M CLOSING THE DOOR. PLEASE SIT DOWN.
WHAT?
HANA, WHAT DO YOU HAVE THERE?
TAKANE'S BINOCULARS.
I THOUGHT SOMETHING LIKE THIS MIGHT HAPPEN, SO I SWIPED THEM.
I'm not missing **anything.** Not a single eyebrow twitch.
...
FROM THIS ANGLE, THEY'LL BE OUT OF SIGHT IN NO TIME.
AW!

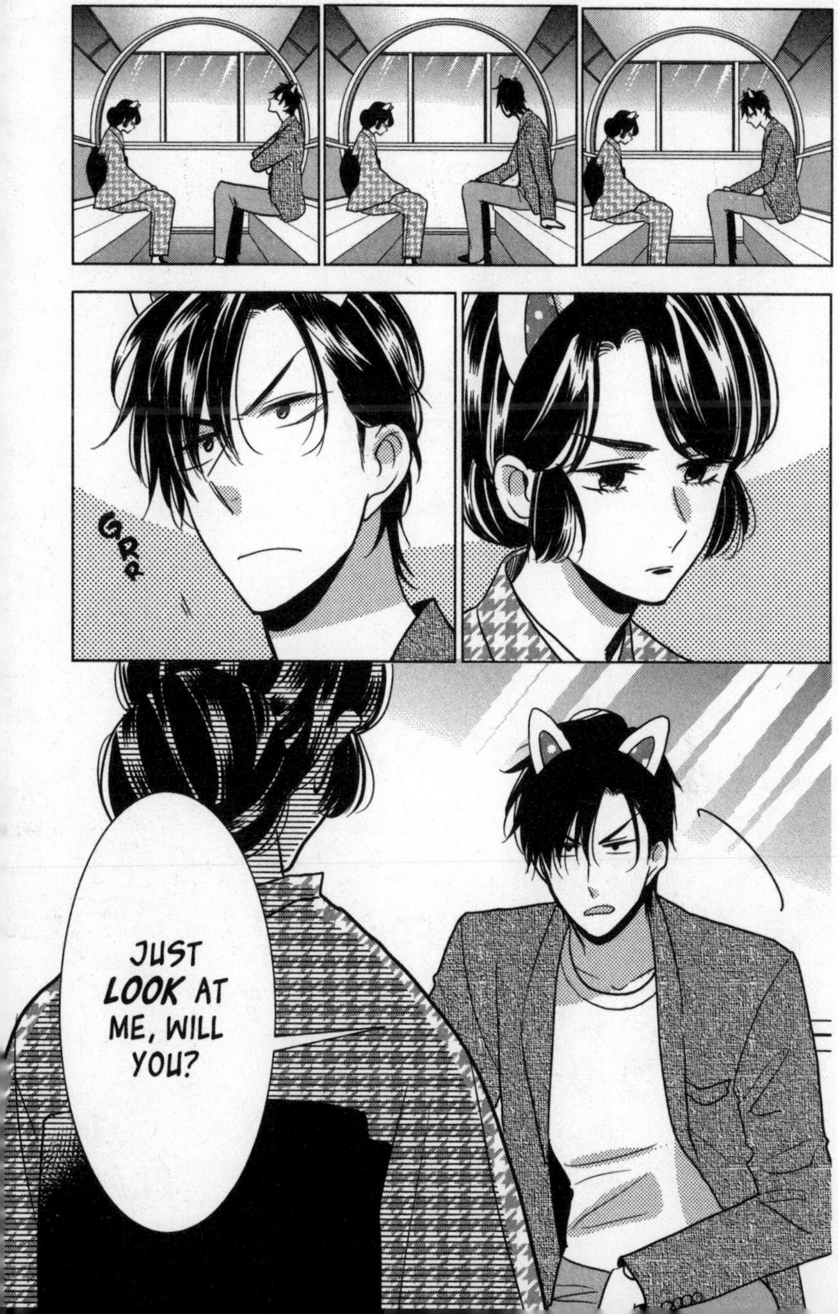
GRR
JUST LOOK AT ME, WILL YOU?

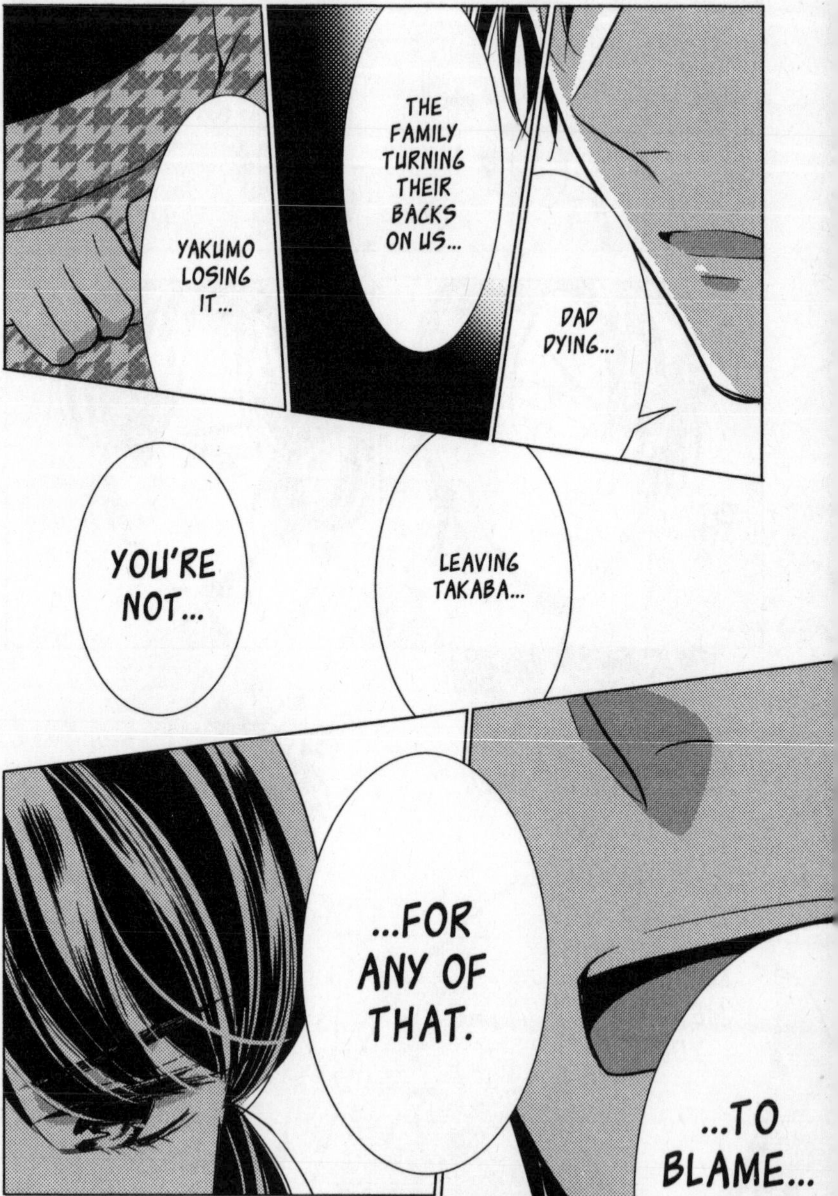
DAD DYING...
THE FAMILY TURNING THEIR BACKS ON US...
YAKUMO LOSING IT...
LEAVING TAKABA...
YOU'RE NOT...
...TO BLAME...
...FOR ANY OF THAT.

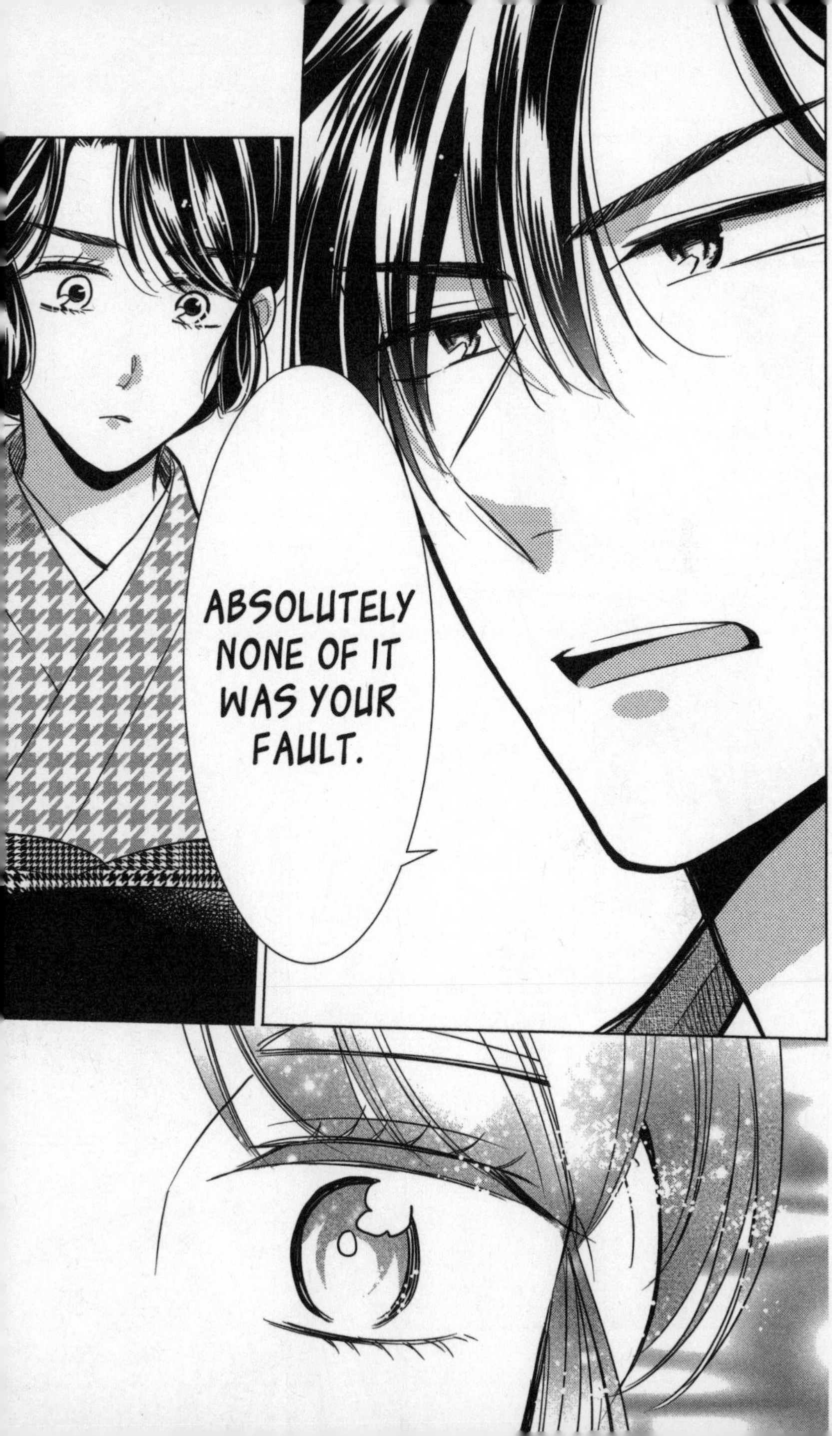
ABSOLUTELY NONE OF IT WAS YOUR FAULT.

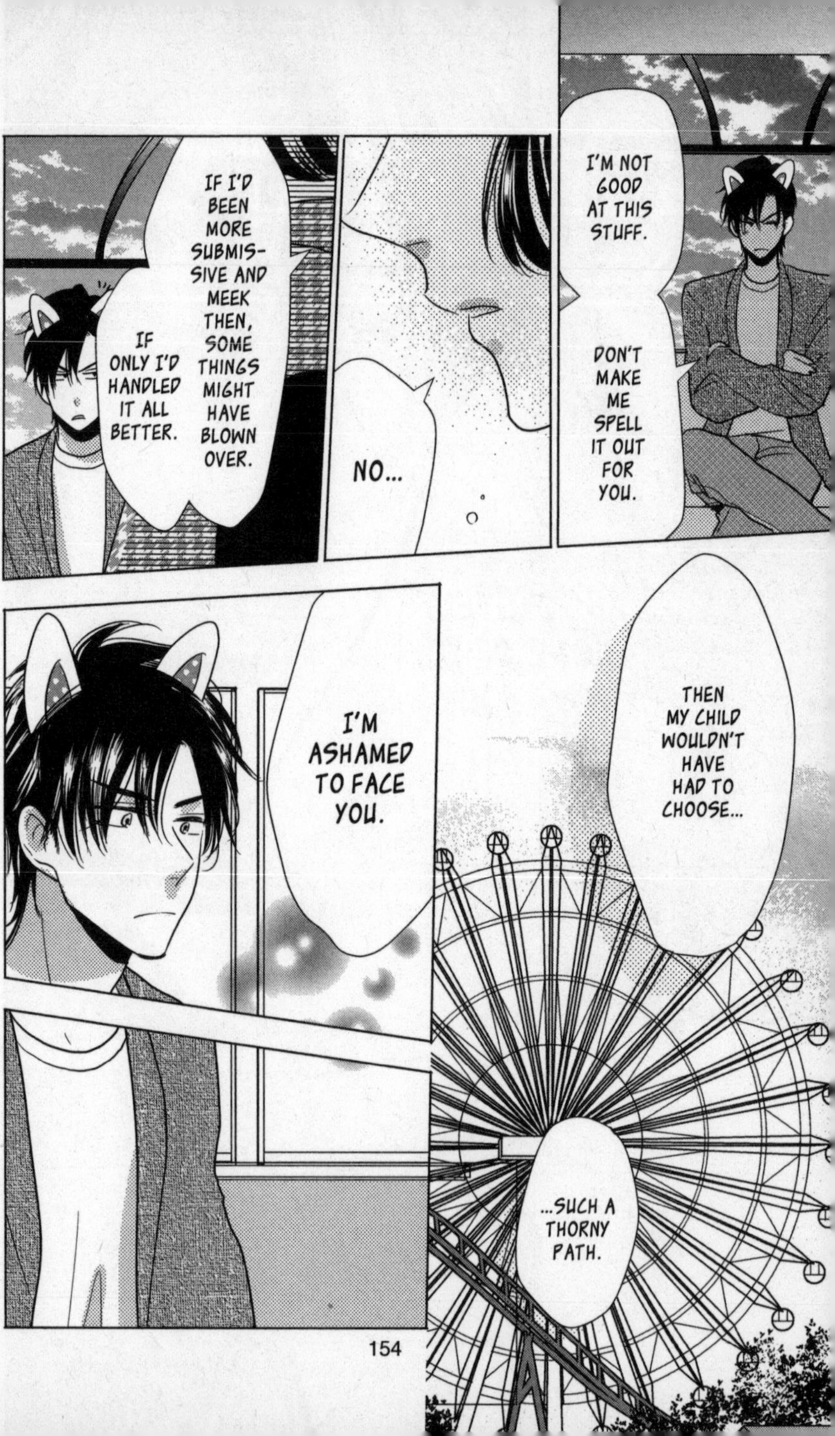

I'M NOT GOOD AT THIS STUFF.
DON'T MAKE ME SPELL IT OUT FOR YOU.
NO...
IF I'D BEEN MORE SUBMIS-SIVE AND MEEK THEN, SOME THINGS MIGHT HAVE BLOWN OVER.
IF ONLY I'D HANDLED IT ALL BETTER.
THEN MY CHILD WOULDN'T HAVE HAD TO CHOOSE...
...SUCH A THORNY PATH.
I'M ASHAMED TO FACE YOU.

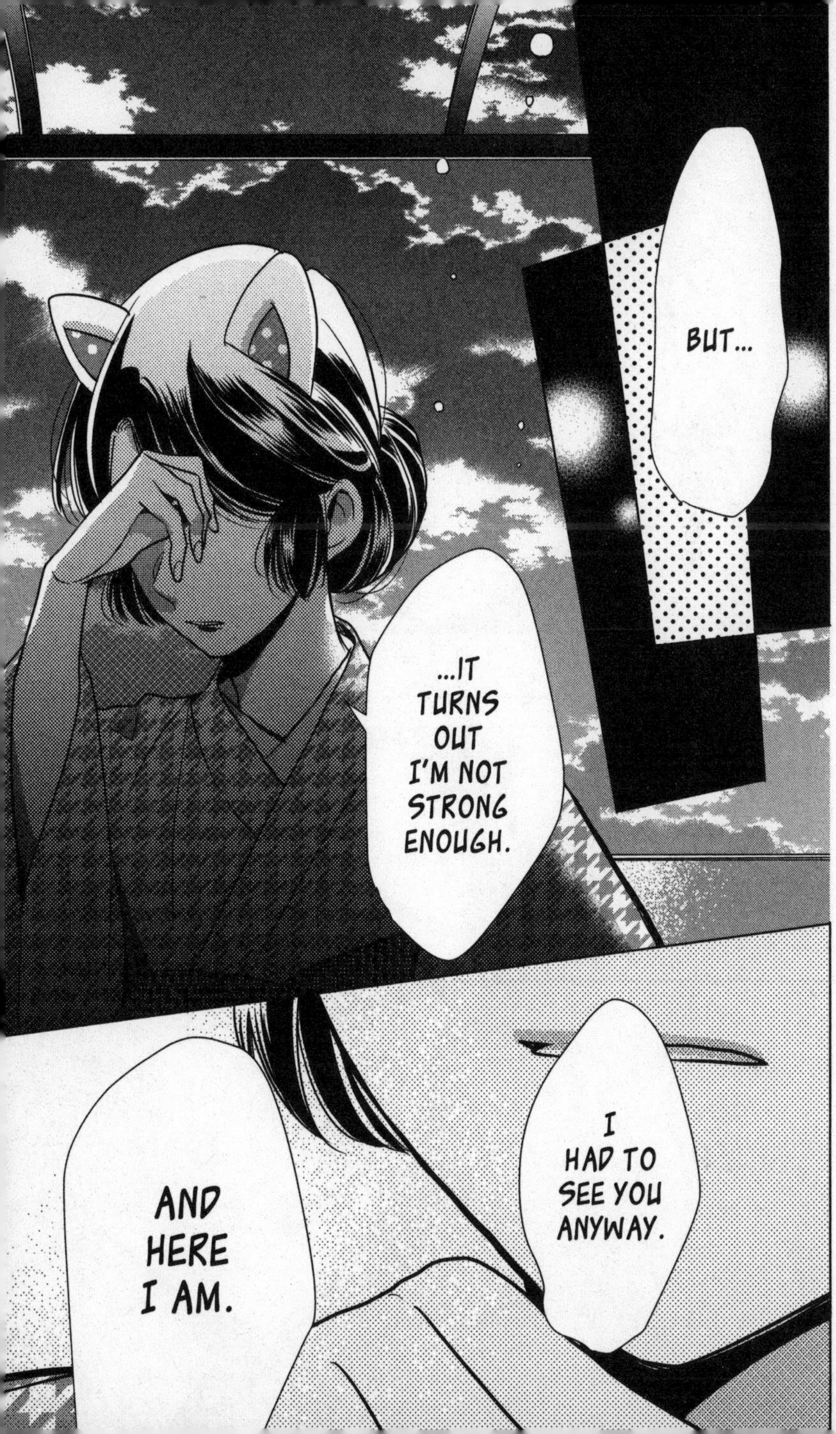
BUT...
...IT TURNS OUT I'M NOT STRONG ENOUGH.
I HAD TO SEE YOU ANYWAY.
AND HERE I AM.

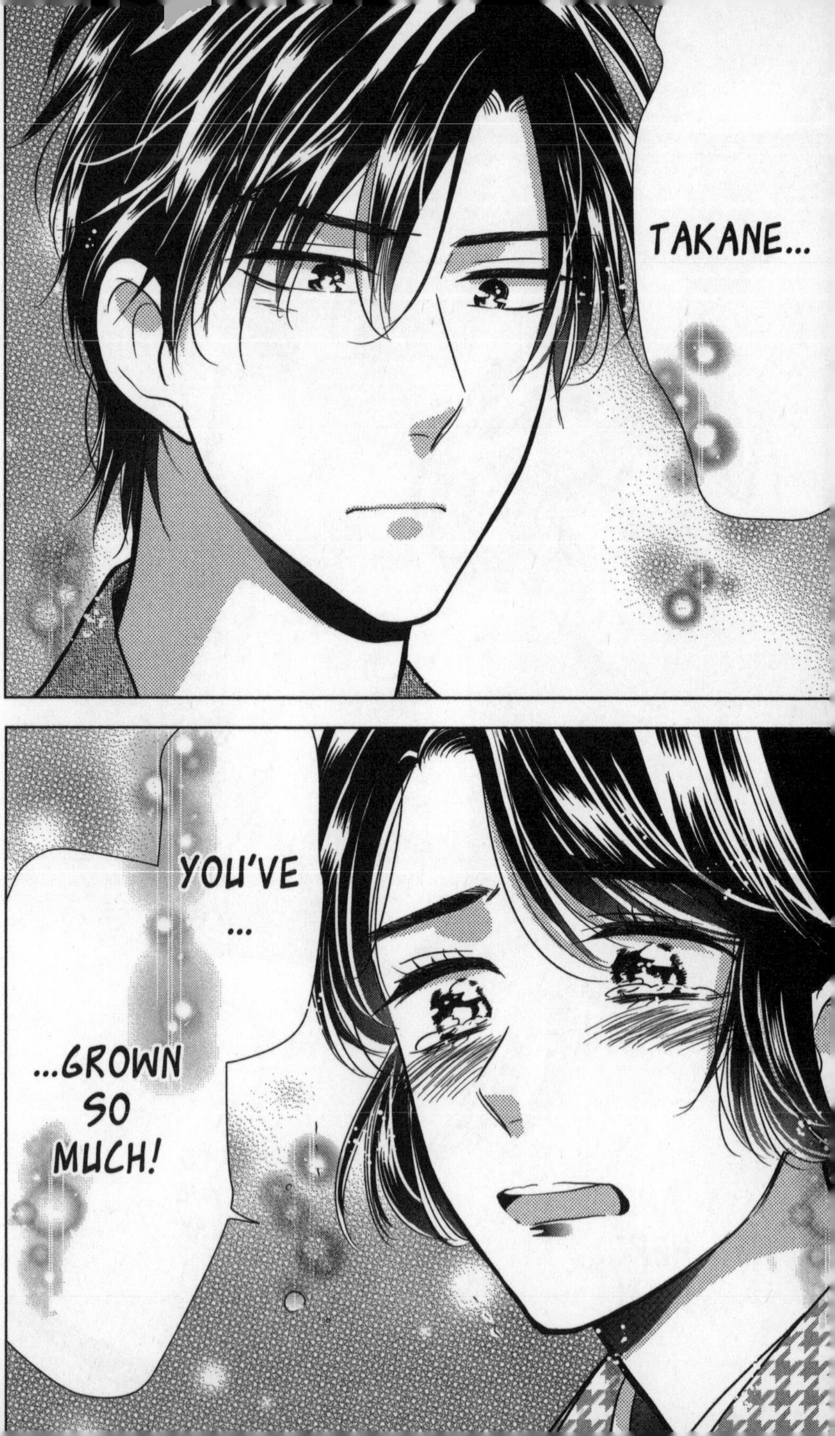
TAKANE...
YOU'VE ...
...GROWN SO MUCH!

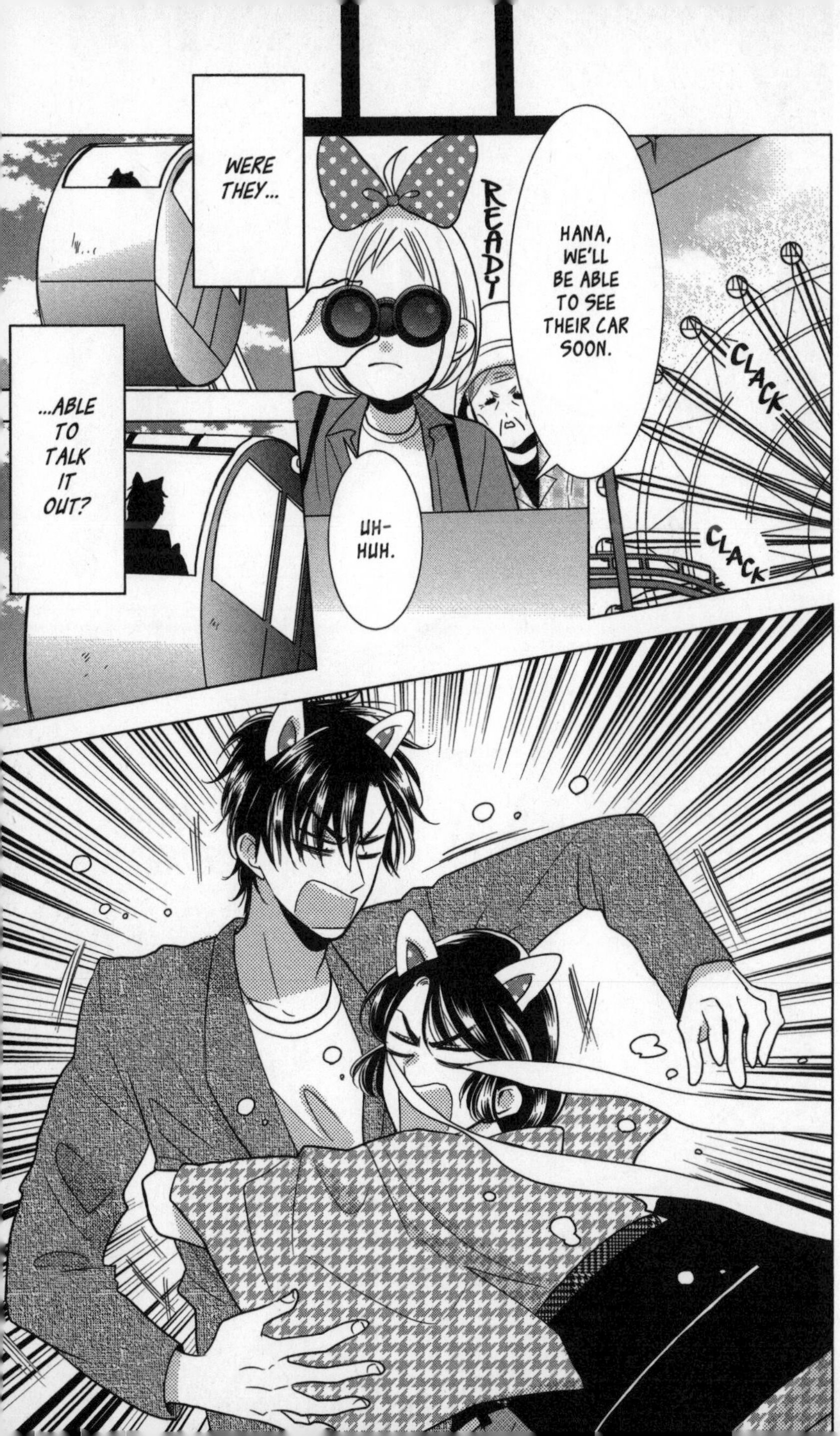
HANA, WE'LL BE ABLE TO SEE THEIR CAR SOON.
CLACK
CLACK
READY
UH-HUH.
WERE THEY...
...ABLE TO TALK IT OUT?

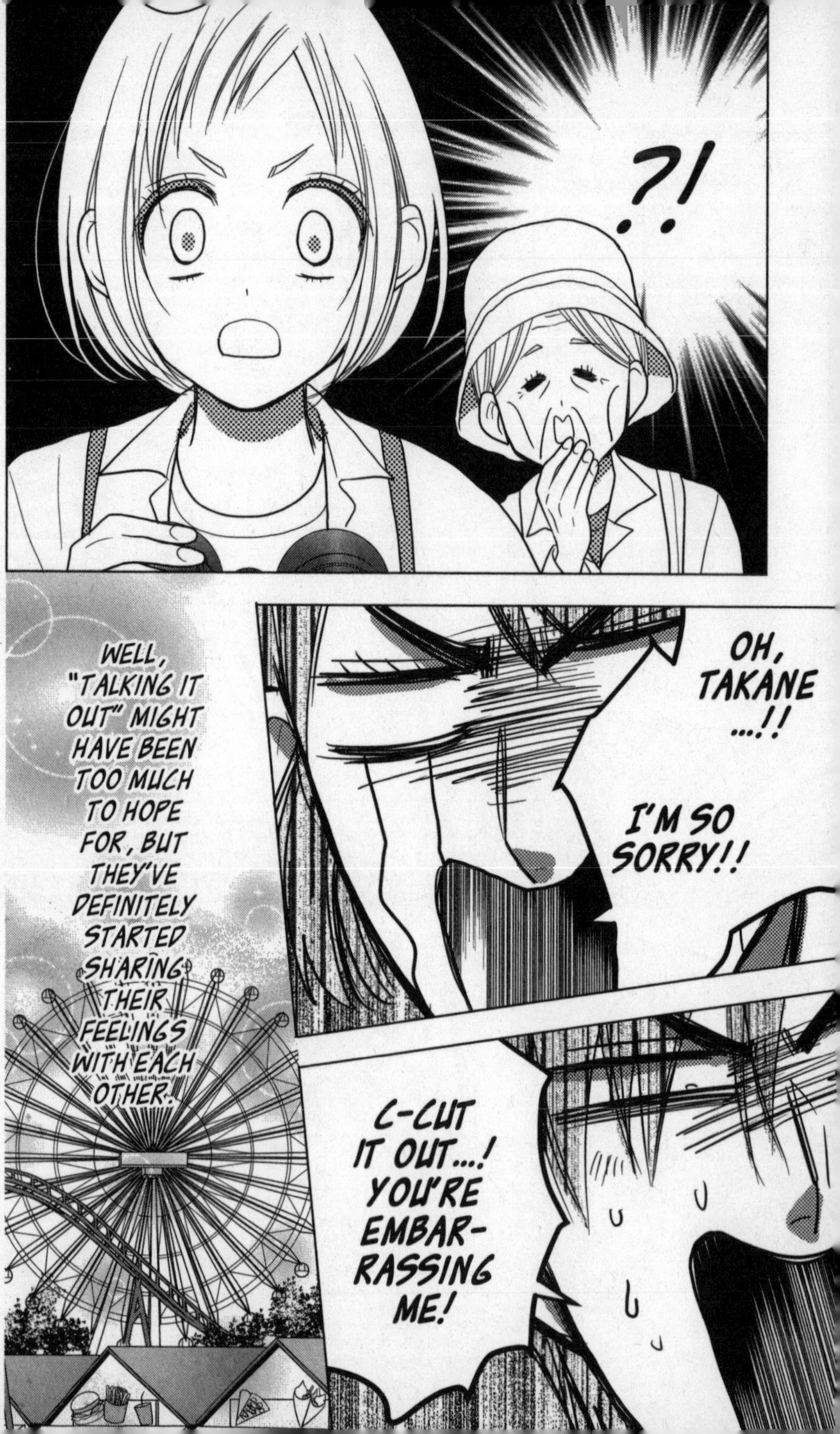
?!
OH, TAKANE ...!!
I'M SO SORRY!!
C-CUT IT OUT...! YOU'RE EMBAR-RASSING ME!
WELL, "TALKING IT OUT" MIGHT HAVE BEEN TOO MUCH TO HOPE FOR, BUT THEY'VE DEFINITELY STARTED SHARING THEIR FEELINGS WITH EACH OTHER.

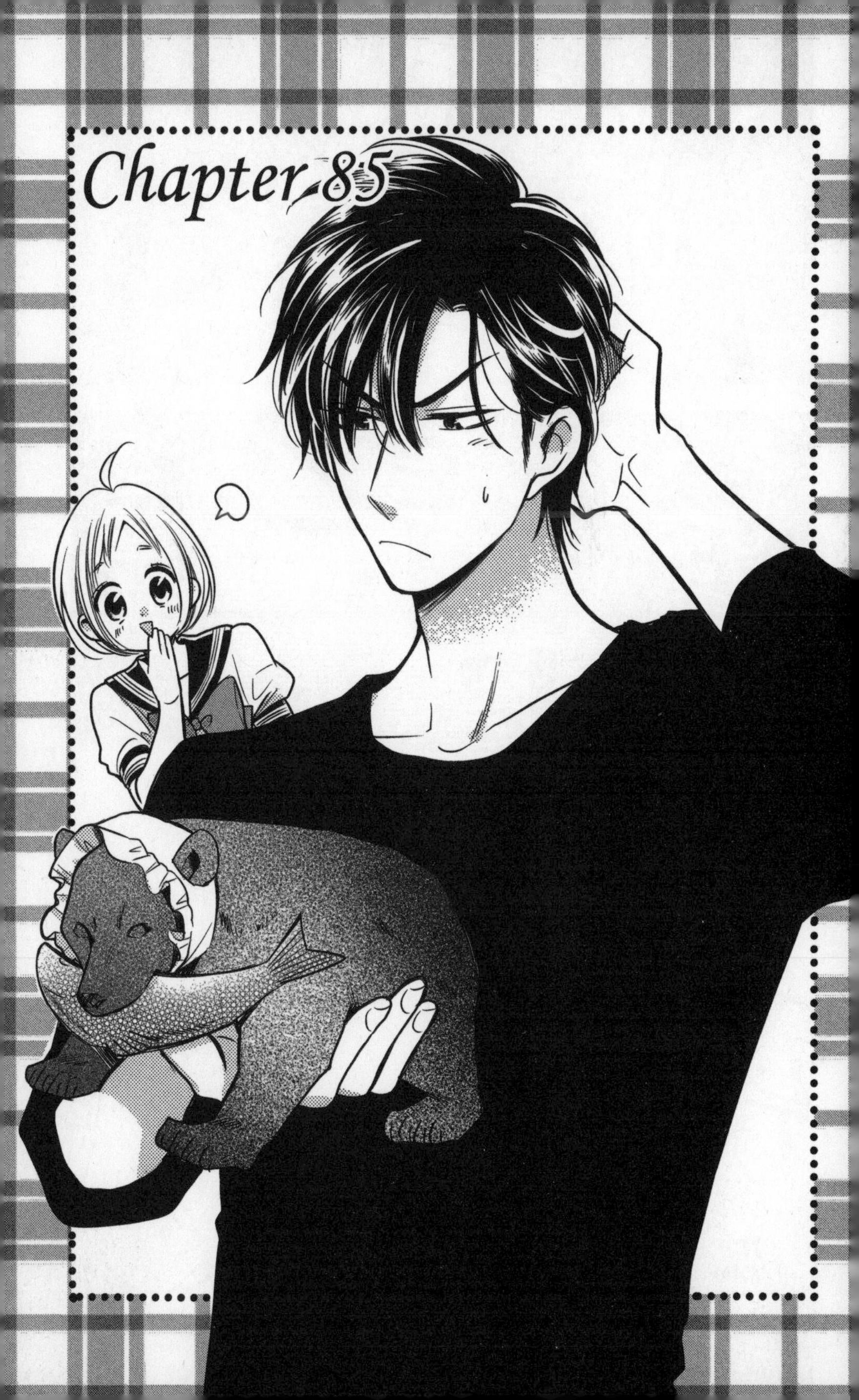
Chapter 85

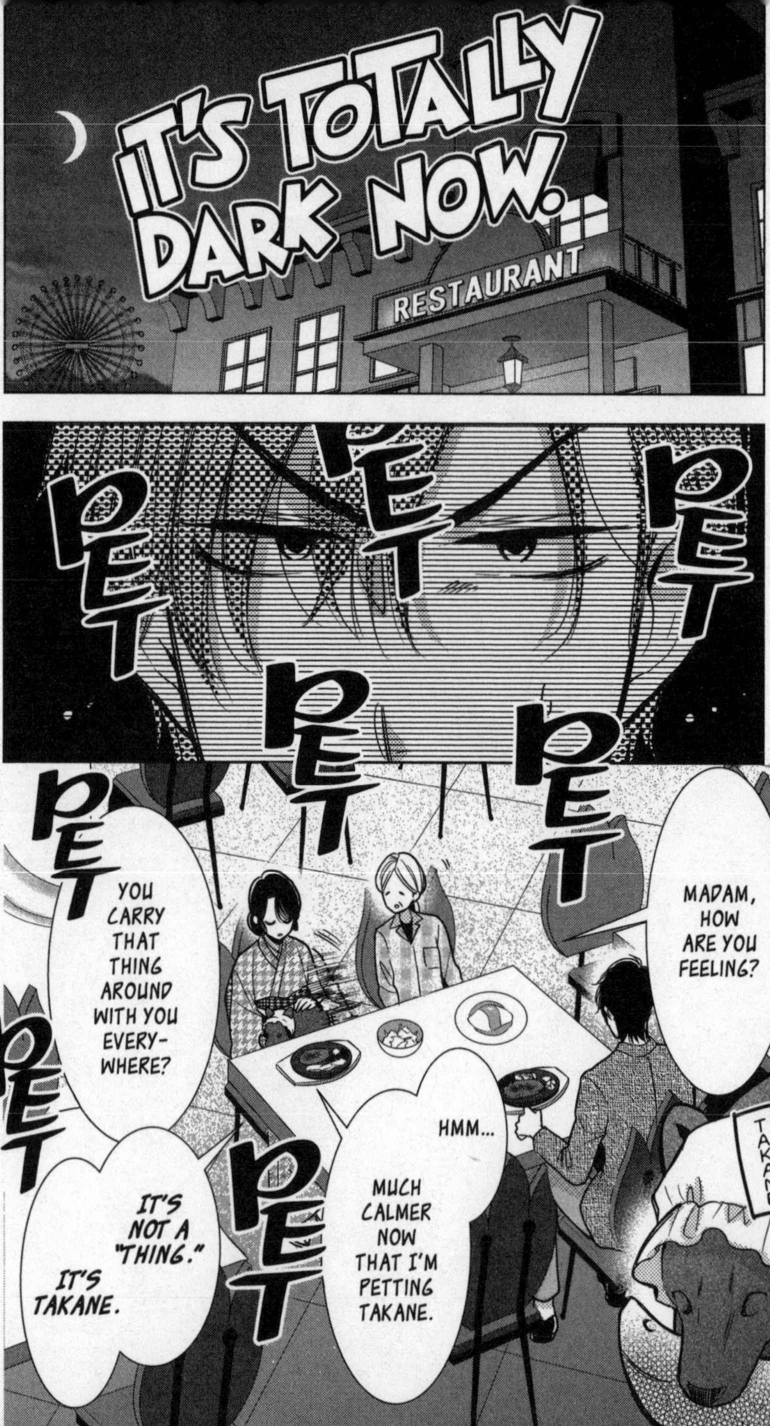

IT'S TOTALLY DARK NOW.
RESTAURANT
PET PET PET
PET PET
MADAM, HOW ARE YOU FEELING?
PET PET
TAKANE
HMM...
MUCH CALMER NOW THAT I'M PETTING TAKANE.
YOU CARRY THAT THING AROUND WITH YOU EVERY-WHERE?
IT'S NOT A "THING."
IT'S TAKANE.
PET

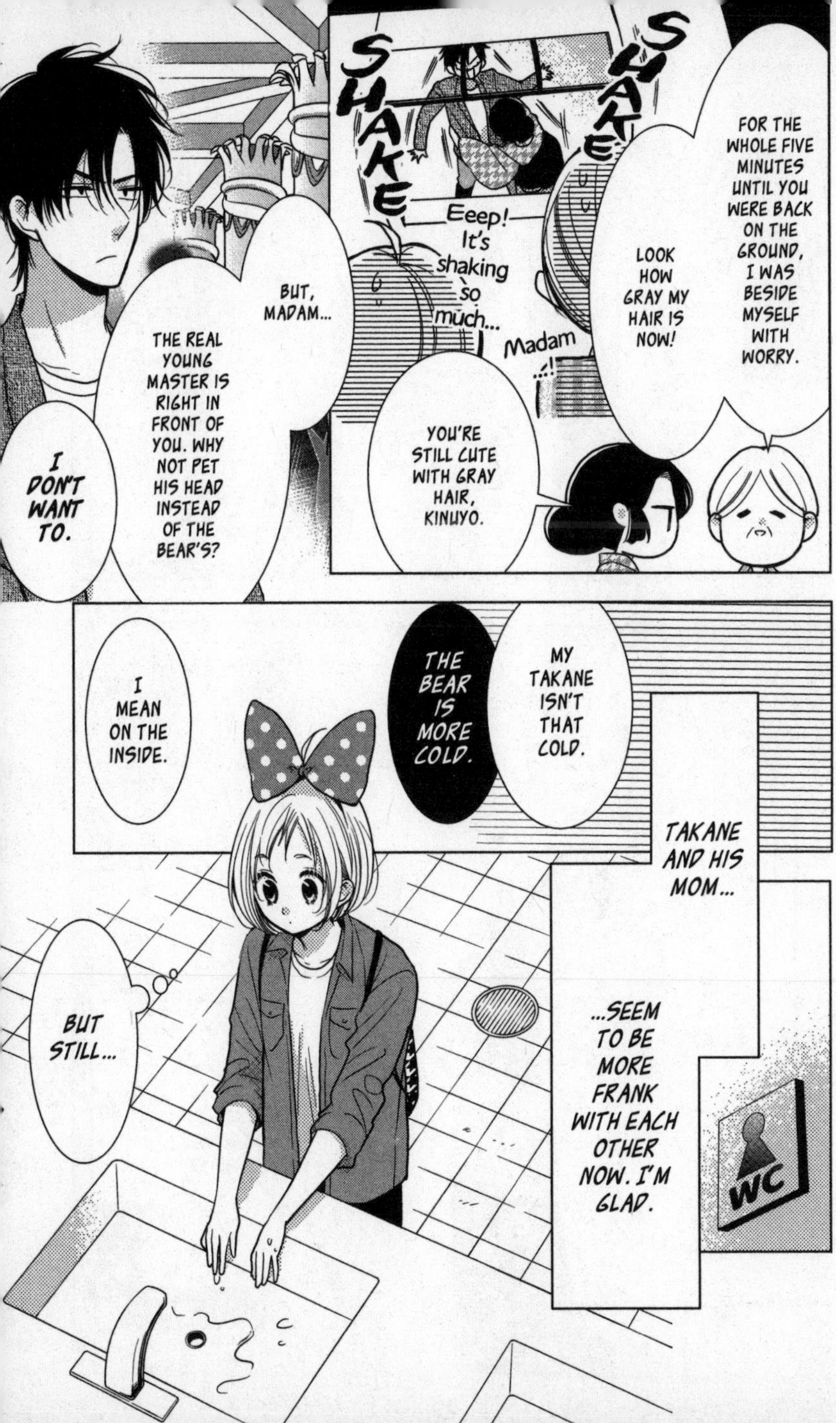
SHAKE
SHAKE
Eeep! It's shaking so much...
FOR THE WHOLE FIVE MINUTES UNTIL YOU WERE BACK ON THE GROUND, I WAS BESIDE MYSELF WITH WORRY.
LOOK HOW GRAY MY HAIR IS NOW!
Madam...!
YOU'RE STILL CUTE WITH GRAY HAIR, KINUYO.
BUT, MADAM...
THE REAL YOUNG MASTER IS RIGHT IN FRONT OF YOU. WHY NOT PET HIS HEAD INSTEAD OF THE BEAR'S?
I DON'T WANT TO.
MY TAKANE ISN'T THAT COLD.
THE BEAR IS MORE COLD.
I MEAN ON THE INSIDE.
TAKANE AND HIS MOM...
...SEEM TO BE MORE FRANK WITH EACH OTHER NOW. I'M GLAD.
WC
BUT STILL...

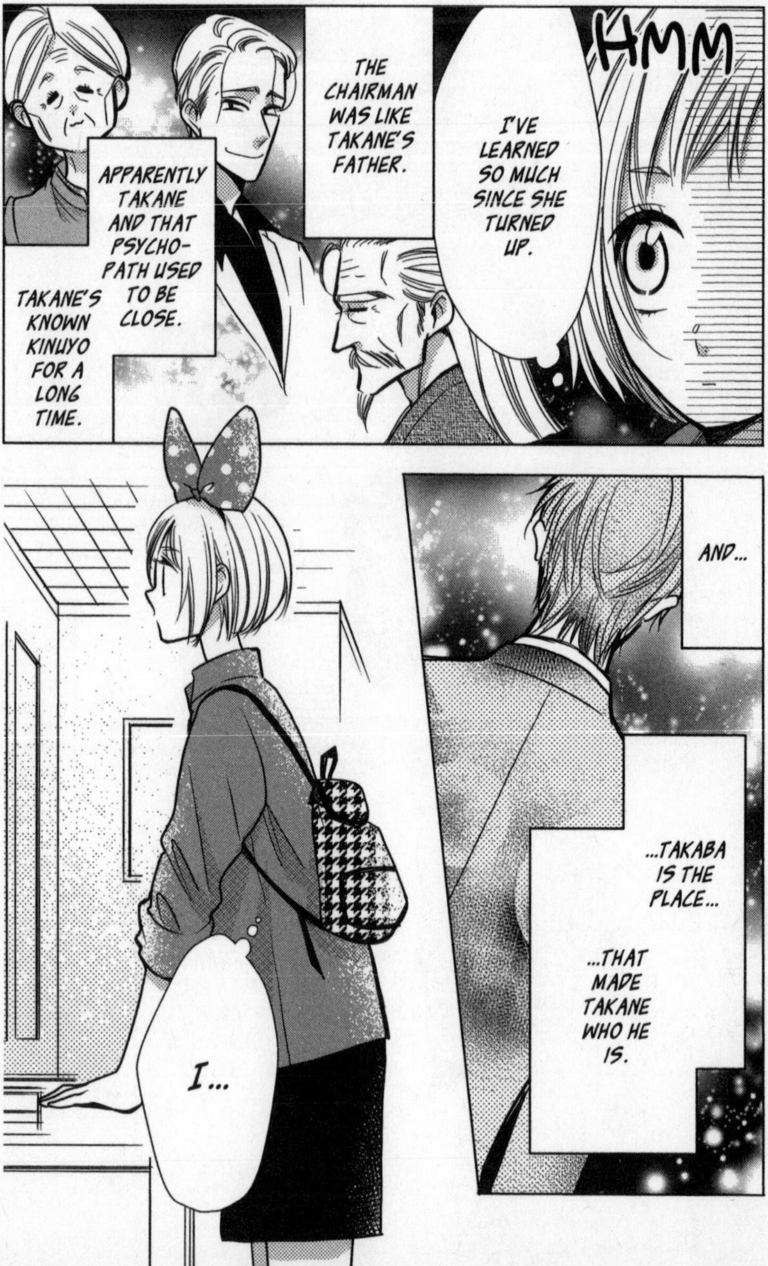
HMM
I'VE LEARNED SO MUCH SINCE SHE TURNED UP.
THE CHAIRMAN WAS LIKE TAKANE'S FATHER.
APPARENTLY TAKANE AND THAT PSYCHO-PATH USED TO BE CLOSE.
TAKANE'S KNOWN KINUYO FOR A LONG TIME.
AND...
...TAKABA IS THE PLACE...
...THAT MADE TAKANE WHO HE IS.
I...

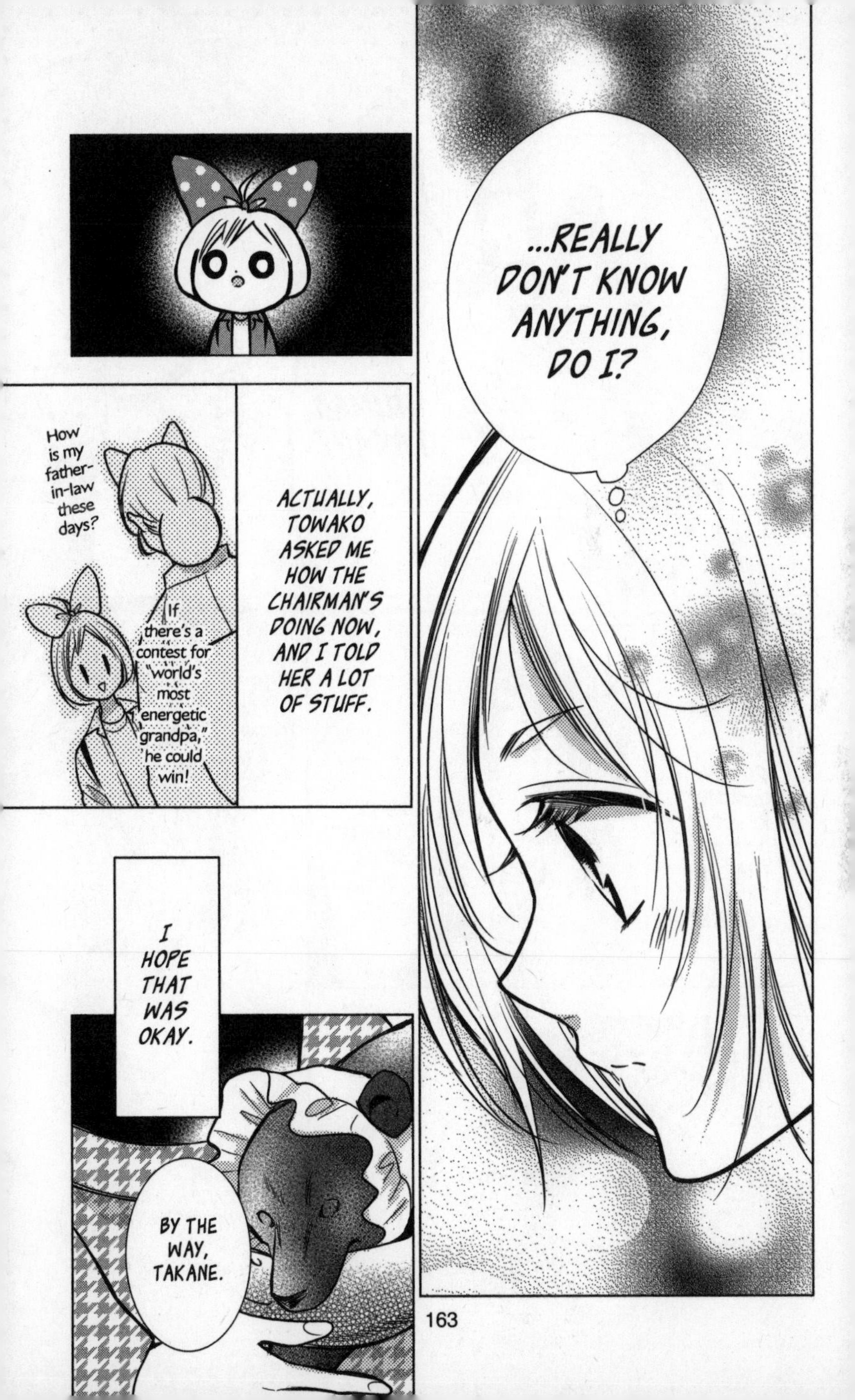
...REALLY DON'T KNOW ANYTHING, DO I?
ACTUALLY, TOWAKO ASKED ME HOW THE CHAIRMAN'S DOING NOW, AND I TOLD HER A LOT OF STUFF.
How is my father-in-law these days?
If there's a contest for "world's most energetic grandpa," he could win!
I HOPE THAT WAS OKAY.
BY THE WAY, TAKANE.

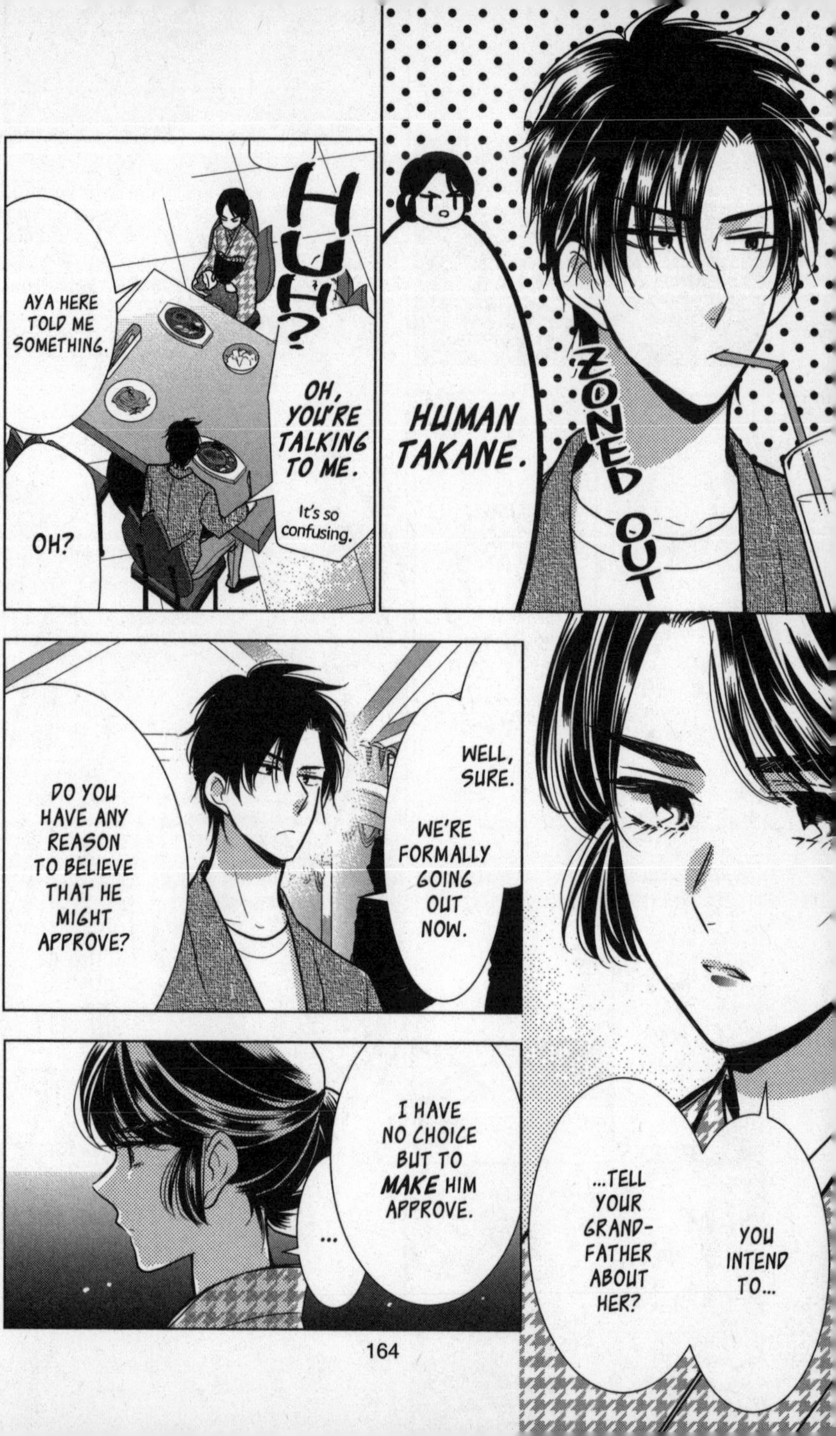
ZONED OUT
HUMAN TAKANE.
HUH?
OH, YOU'RE TALKING TO ME.
It's so confusing.
AYA HERE TOLD ME SOMETHING.
OH?
YOU INTEND TO...
...TELL YOUR GRANDFATHER ABOUT HER?
WELL, SURE.
WE'RE FORMALLY GOING OUT NOW.
DO YOU HAVE ANY REASON TO BELIEVE THAT HE MIGHT APPROVE?
I HAVE NO CHOICE BUT TO *MAKE* HIM APPROVE.
...

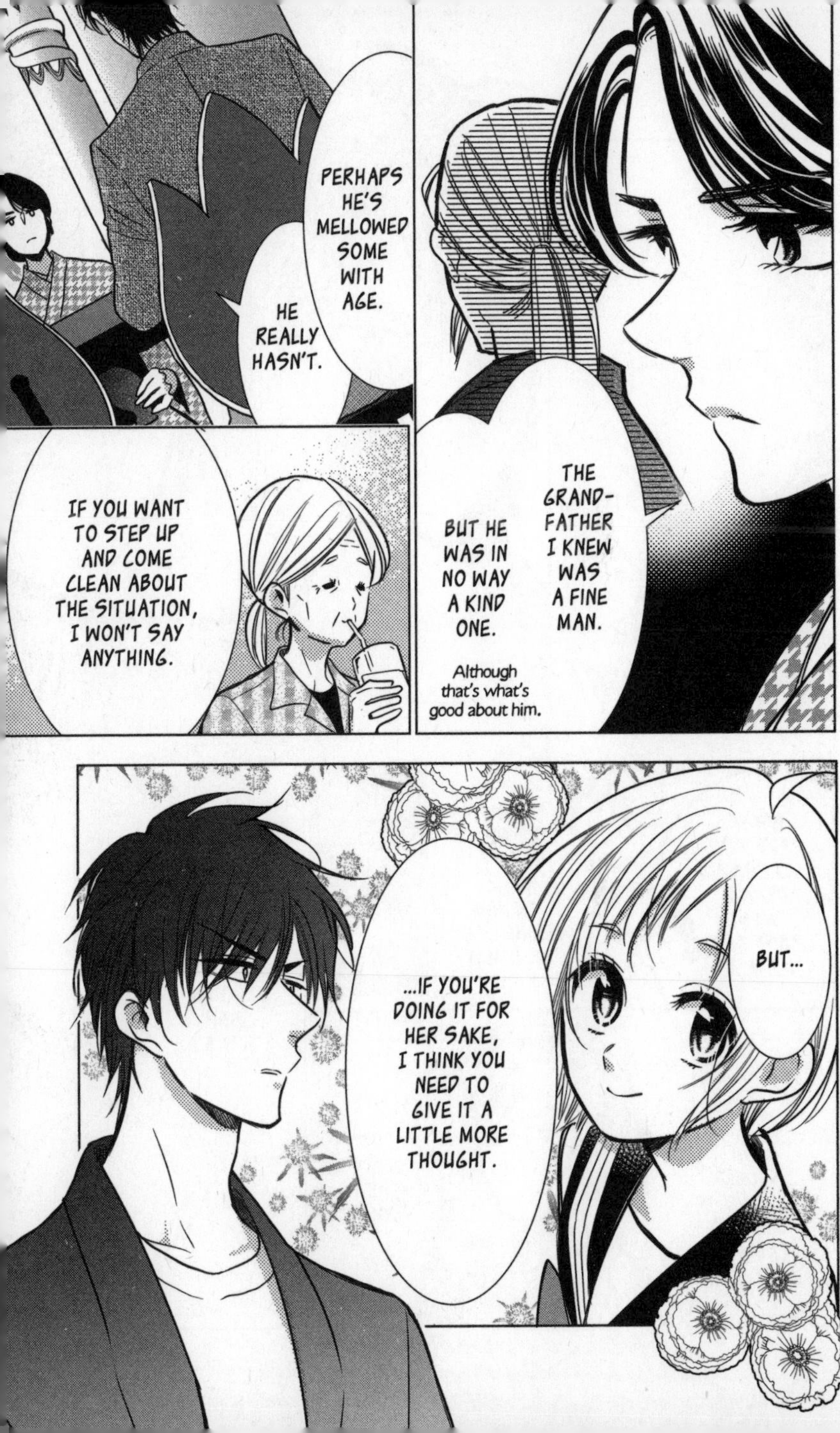
THE GRAND-FATHER I KNEW WAS A FINE MAN.
BUT HE WAS IN NO WAY A KIND ONE.
Although that's what's good about him.
PERHAPS HE'S MELLOWED SOME WITH AGE.
HE REALLY HASN'T.
IF YOU WANT TO STEP UP AND COME CLEAN ABOUT THE SITUATION, I WON'T SAY ANYTHING.
BUT...
...IF YOU'RE DOING IT FOR HER SAKE, I THINK YOU NEED TO GIVE IT A LITTLE MORE THOUGHT.

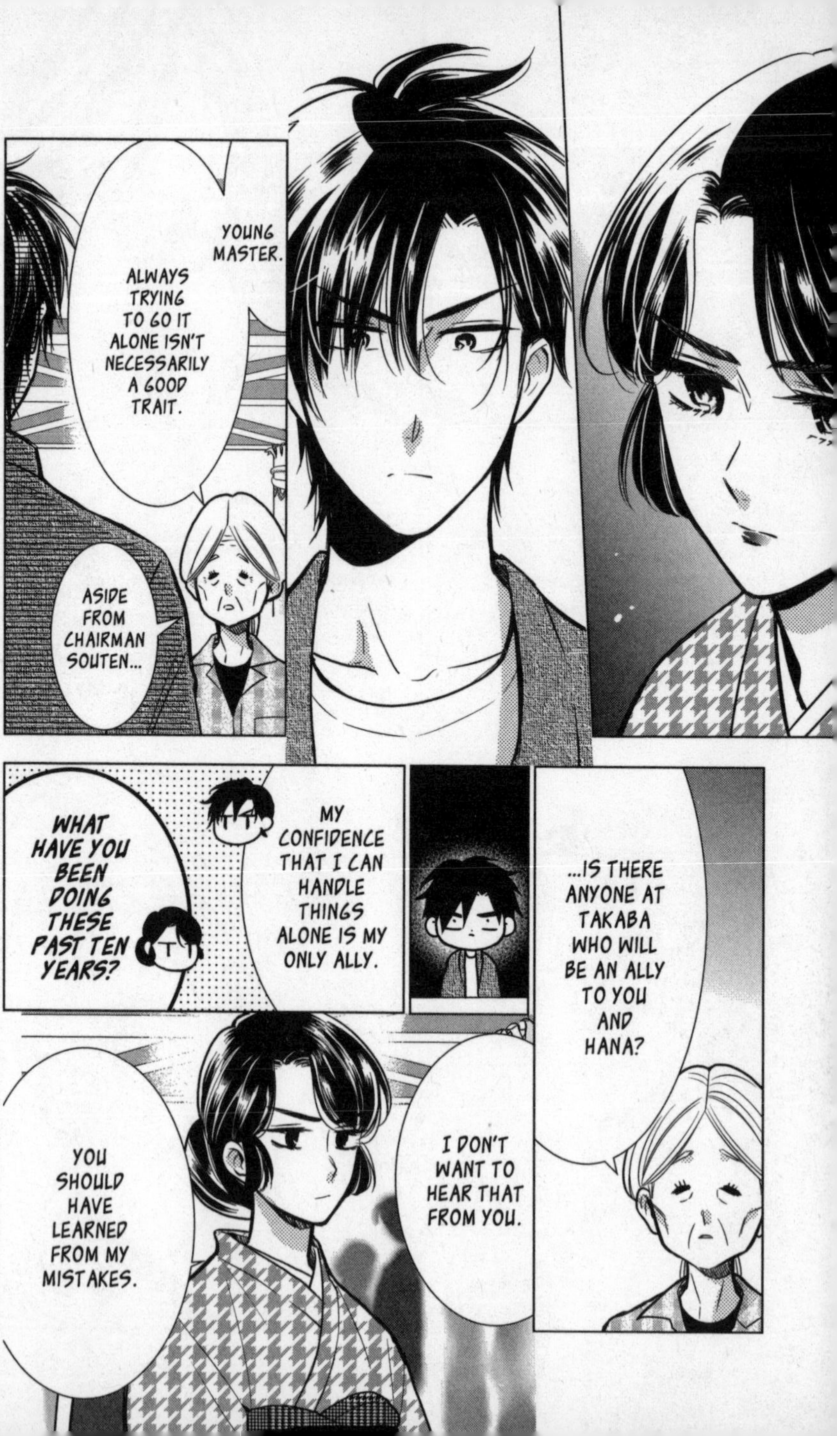
YOUNG MASTER.
ALWAYS TRYING TO GO IT ALONE ISN'T NECESSARILY A GOOD TRAIT.
ASIDE FROM CHAIRMAN SOUTEN...
...IS THERE ANYONE AT TAKABA WHO WILL BE AN ALLY TO YOU AND HANA?
MY CONFIDENCE THAT I CAN HANDLE THINGS ALONE IS MY ONLY ALLY.
WHAT HAVE YOU BEEN DOING THESE PAST TEN YEARS?
I DON'T WANT TO HEAR THAT FROM YOU.
YOU SHOULD HAVE LEARNED FROM MY MISTAKES.

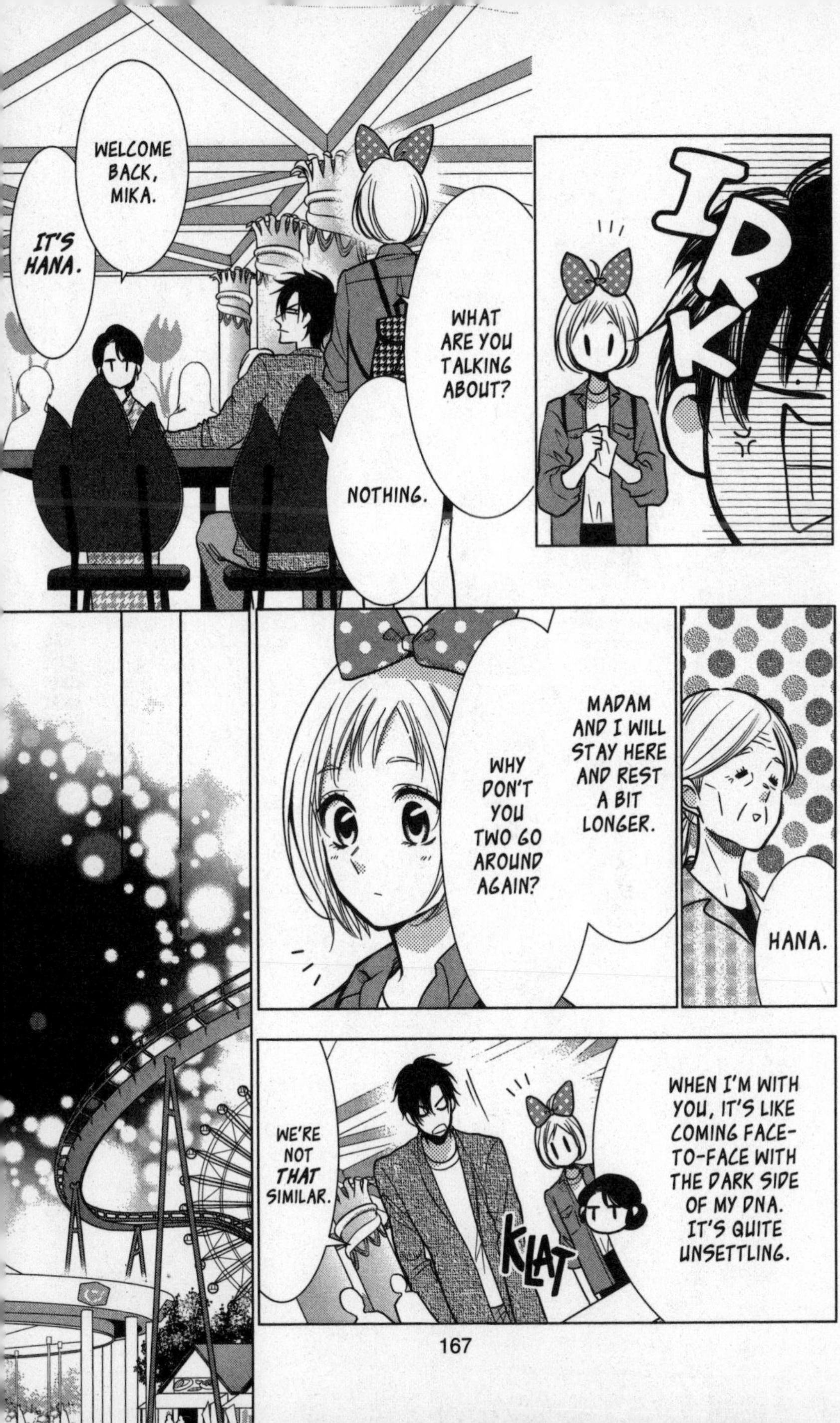
WELCOME BACK, MIKA.
IT'S HANA.
IRK
WHAT ARE YOU TALKING ABOUT?
NOTHING.
HANA.
MADAM AND I WILL STAY HERE AND REST A BIT LONGER.
WHY DON'T YOU TWO GO AROUND AGAIN?
WHEN I'M WITH YOU, IT'S LIKE COMING FACE-TO-FACE WITH THE DARK SIDE OF MY DNA. IT'S QUITE UNSETTLING.
KLAT
WE'RE NOT *THAT* SIMILAR.

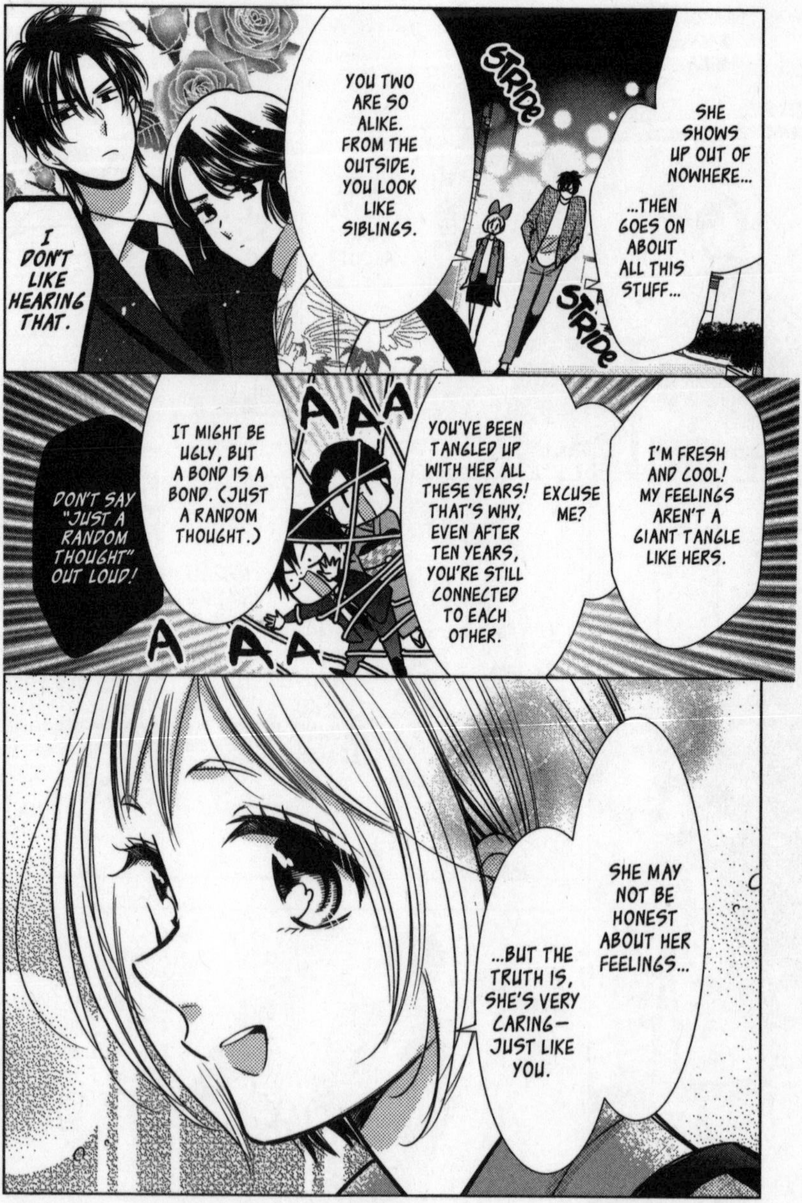
STRIDE
SHE SHOWS UP OUT OF NOWHERE...
...THEN GOES ON ABOUT ALL THIS STUFF...
STRIDE
YOU TWO ARE SO ALIKE. FROM THE OUTSIDE, YOU LOOK LIKE SIBLINGS.
I DON'T LIKE HEARING THAT.
I'M FRESH AND COOL! MY FEELINGS AREN'T A GIANT TANGLE LIKE HERS.
EXCUSE ME?
YOU'VE BEEN TANGLED UP WITH HER ALL THESE YEARS! THAT'S WHY, EVEN AFTER TEN YEARS, YOU'RE STILL CONNECTED TO EACH OTHER.
AAA
IT MIGHT BE UGLY, BUT A BOND IS A BOND. (JUST A RANDOM THOUGHT.)
DON'T SAY "JUST A RANDOM THOUGHT" OUT LOUD!
A AA
SHE MAY NOT BE HONEST ABOUT HER FEELINGS...
...BUT THE TRUTH IS, SHE'S VERY CARING—JUST LIKE YOU.

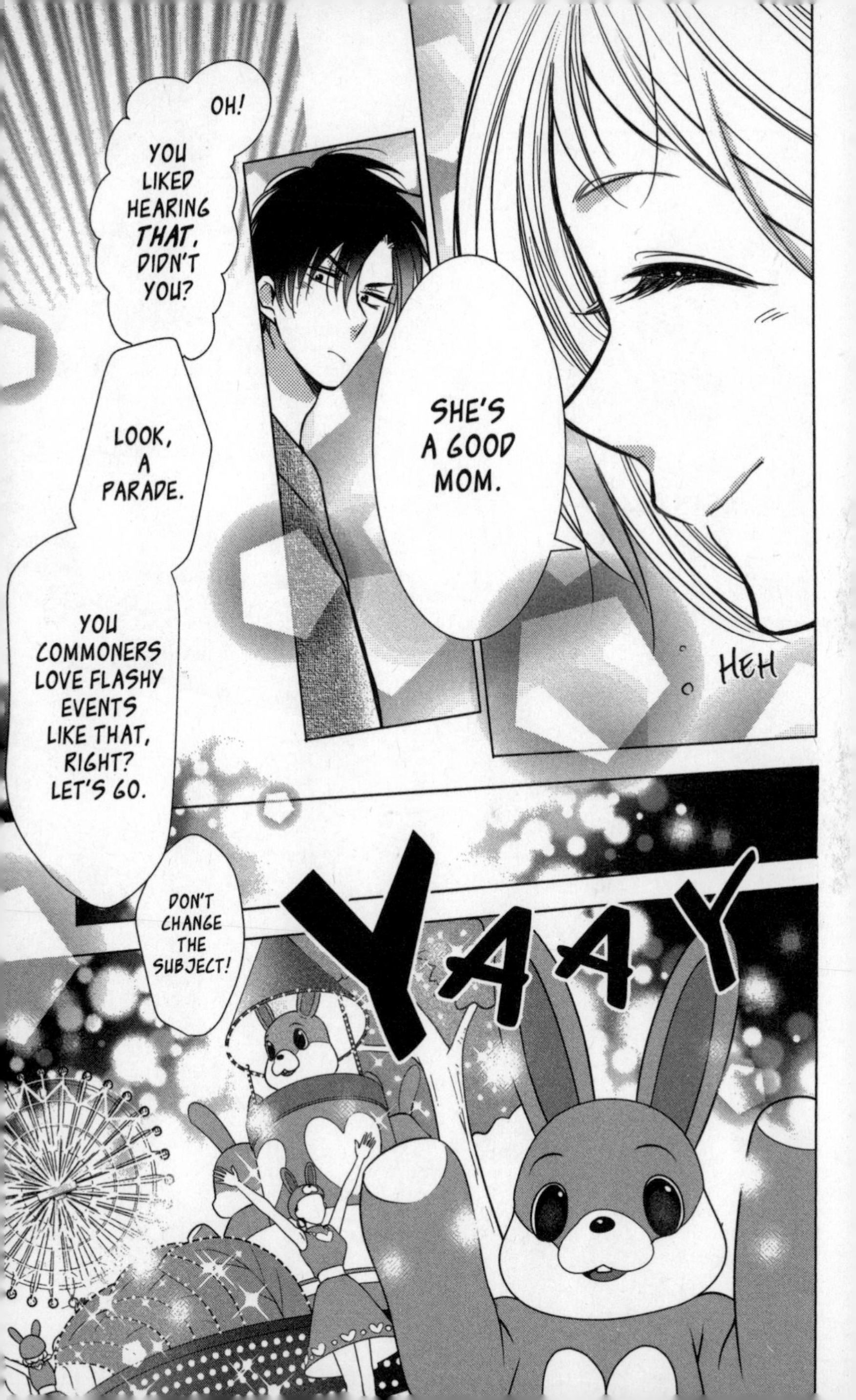
SHE'S A GOOD MOM.
HEH
OH!
YOU LIKED HEARING THAT, DIDN'T YOU?
LOOK, A PARADE.
YOU COMMONERS LOVE FLASHY EVENTS LIKE THAT, RIGHT? LET'S GO.
YAAY
DON'T CHANGE THE SUBJECT!

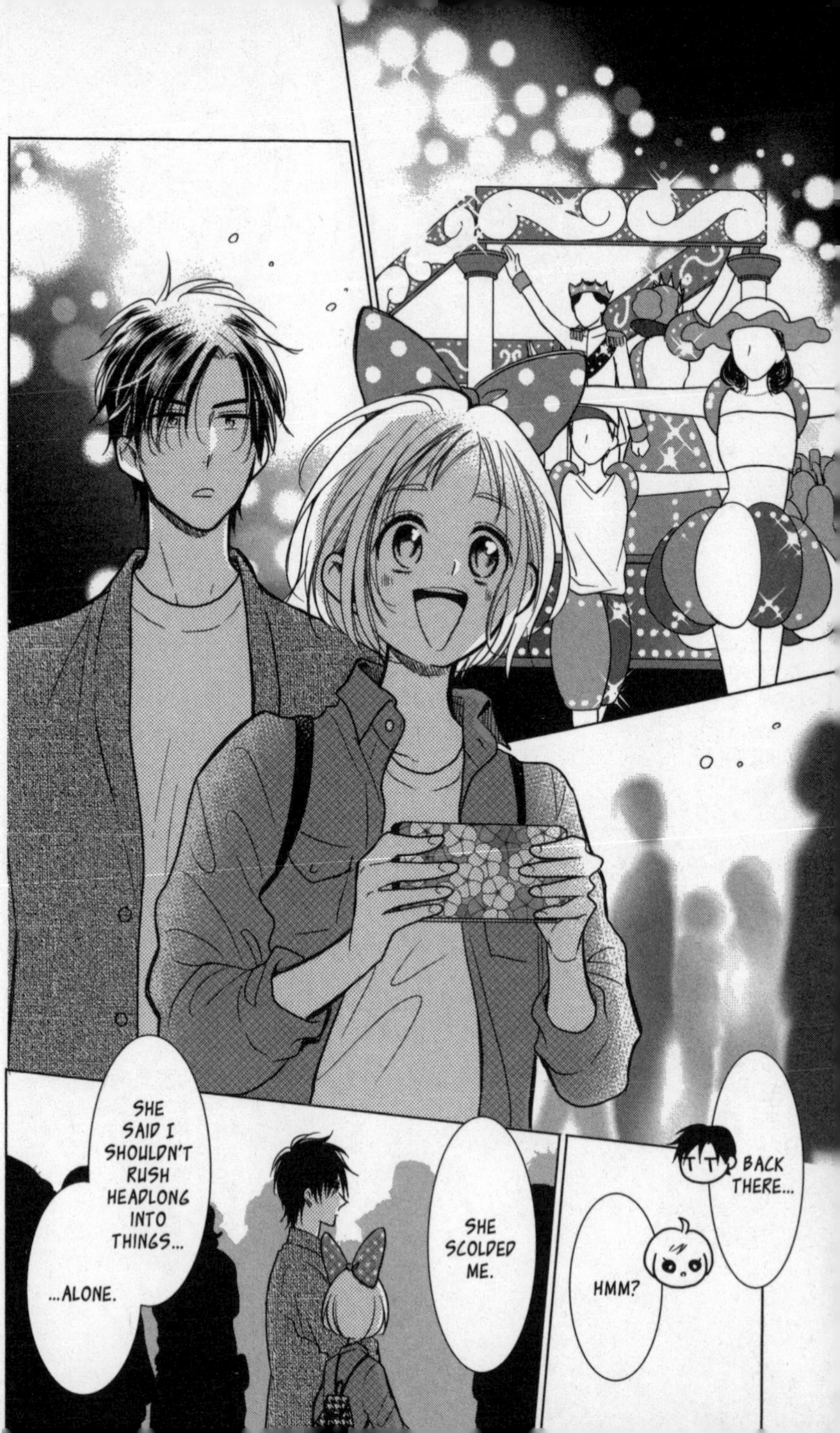
BACK THERE...
HMM?
SHE SCOLDED ME.
SHE SAID I SHOULDN'T RUSH HEADLONG INTO THINGS...
...ALONE.

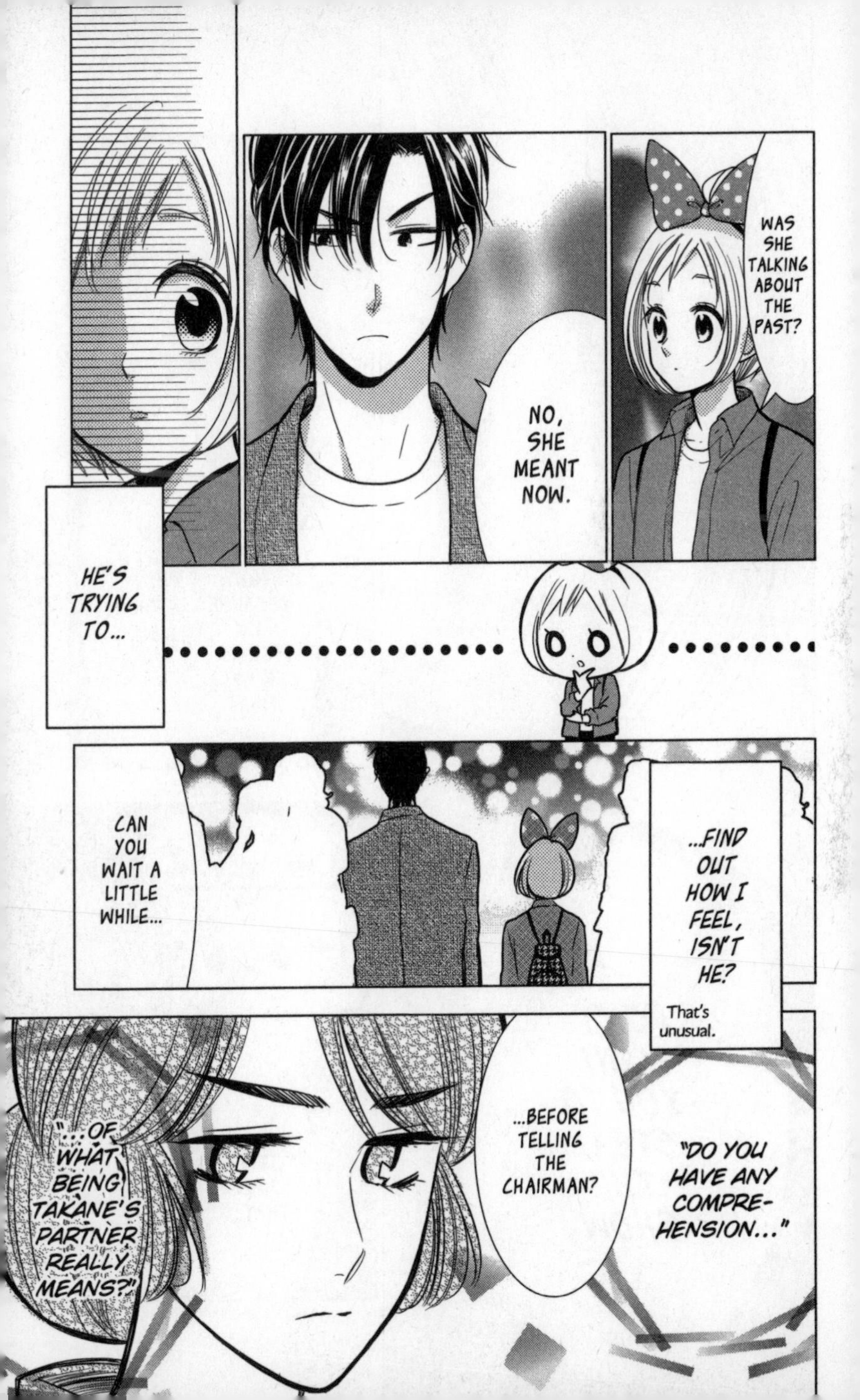
WAS SHE TALKING ABOUT THE PAST?
NO, SHE MEANT NOW.
HE'S TRYING TO...
...FIND OUT HOW I FEEL, ISN'T HE?
That's unusual.
CAN YOU WAIT A LITTLE WHILE...
...BEFORE TELLING THE CHAIRMAN?
"DO YOU HAVE ANY COMPRE-HENSION..."
"...OF WHAT BEING TAKANE'S PARTNER REALLY MEANS?"

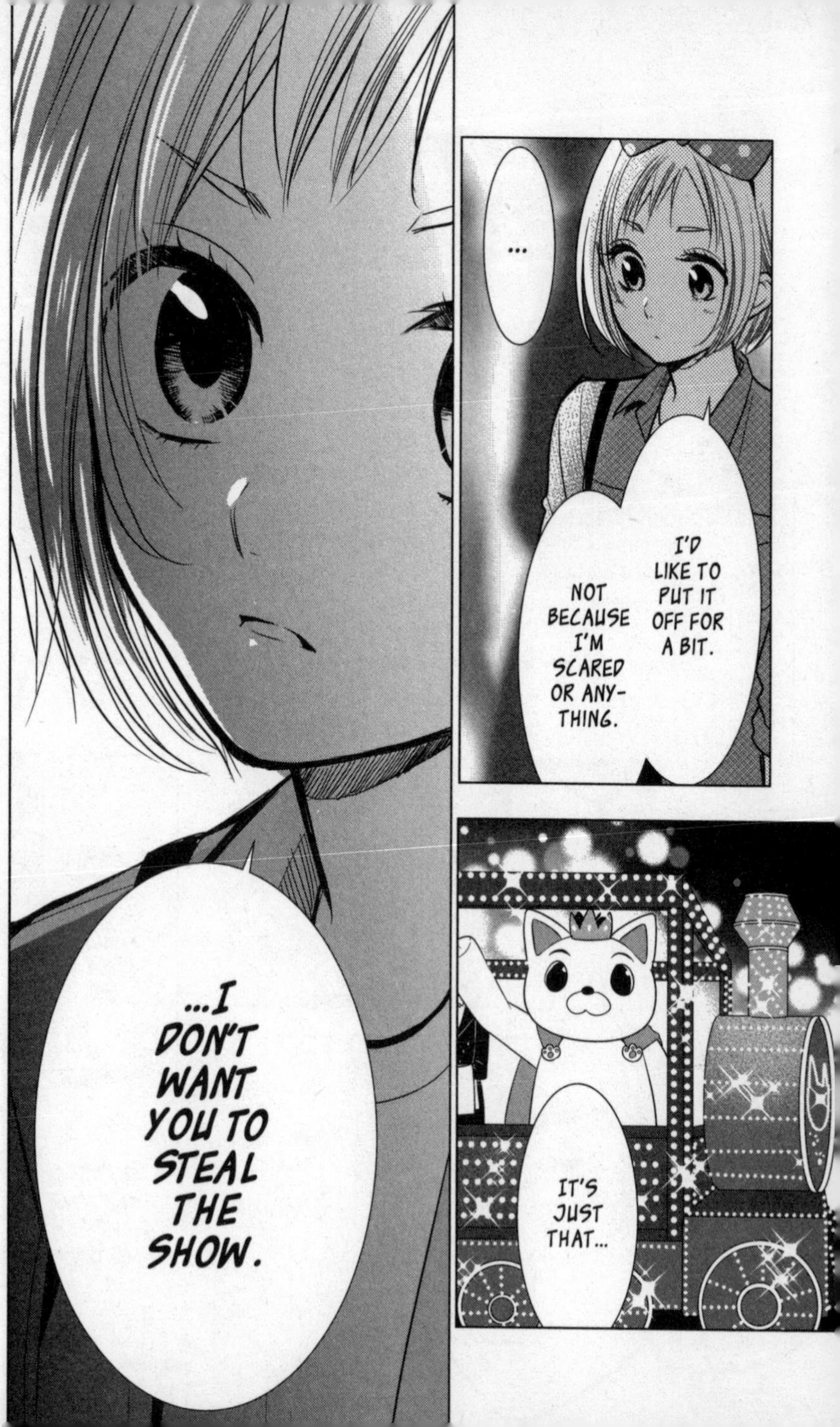
...
I'D LIKE TO PUT IT OFF FOR A BIT.
NOT BECAUSE I'M SCARED OR ANY-THING.
IT'S JUST THAT...
...I DON'T WANT YOU TO STEAL THE SHOW.

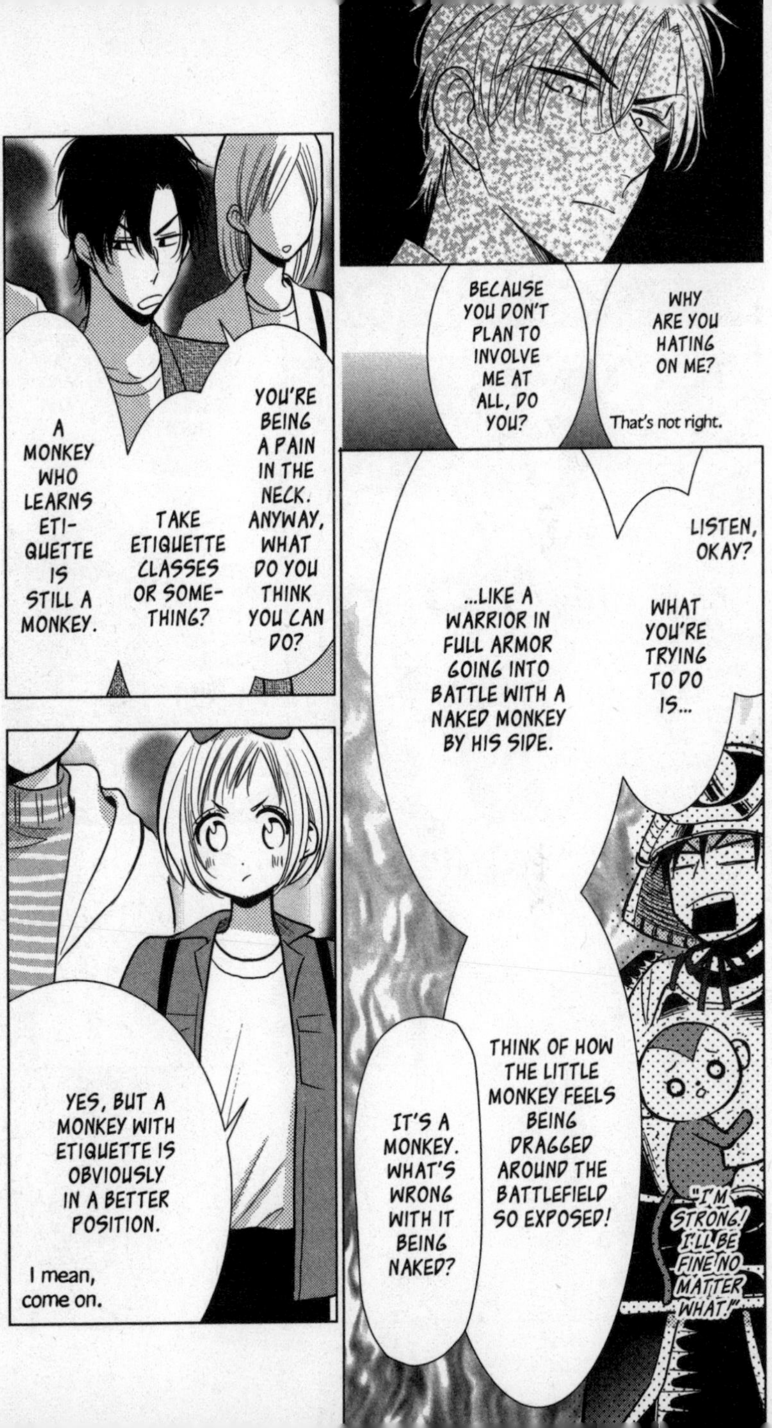
WHY ARE YOU HATING ON ME?
That's not right.
BECAUSE YOU DON'T PLAN TO INVOLVE ME AT ALL, DO YOU?
LISTEN, OKAY?
WHAT YOU'RE TRYING TO DO IS...
...LIKE A WARRIOR IN FULL ARMOR GOING INTO BATTLE WITH A NAKED MONKEY BY HIS SIDE.
"I'M STRONG! I'LL BE FINE NO MATTER WHAT!"
THINK OF HOW THE LITTLE MONKEY FEELS BEING DRAGGED AROUND THE BATTLEFIELD SO EXPOSED!
IT'S A MONKEY. WHAT'S WRONG WITH IT BEING NAKED?
YOU'RE BEING A PAIN IN THE NECK. ANYWAY, WHAT DO YOU THINK YOU CAN DO?
TAKE ETIQUETTE CLASSES OR SOMETHING?
A MONKEY WHO LEARNS ETI-QUETTE IS STILL A MONKEY.
YES, BUT A MONKEY WITH ETIQUETTE IS OBVIOUSLY IN A BETTER POSITION.
I mean, come on.

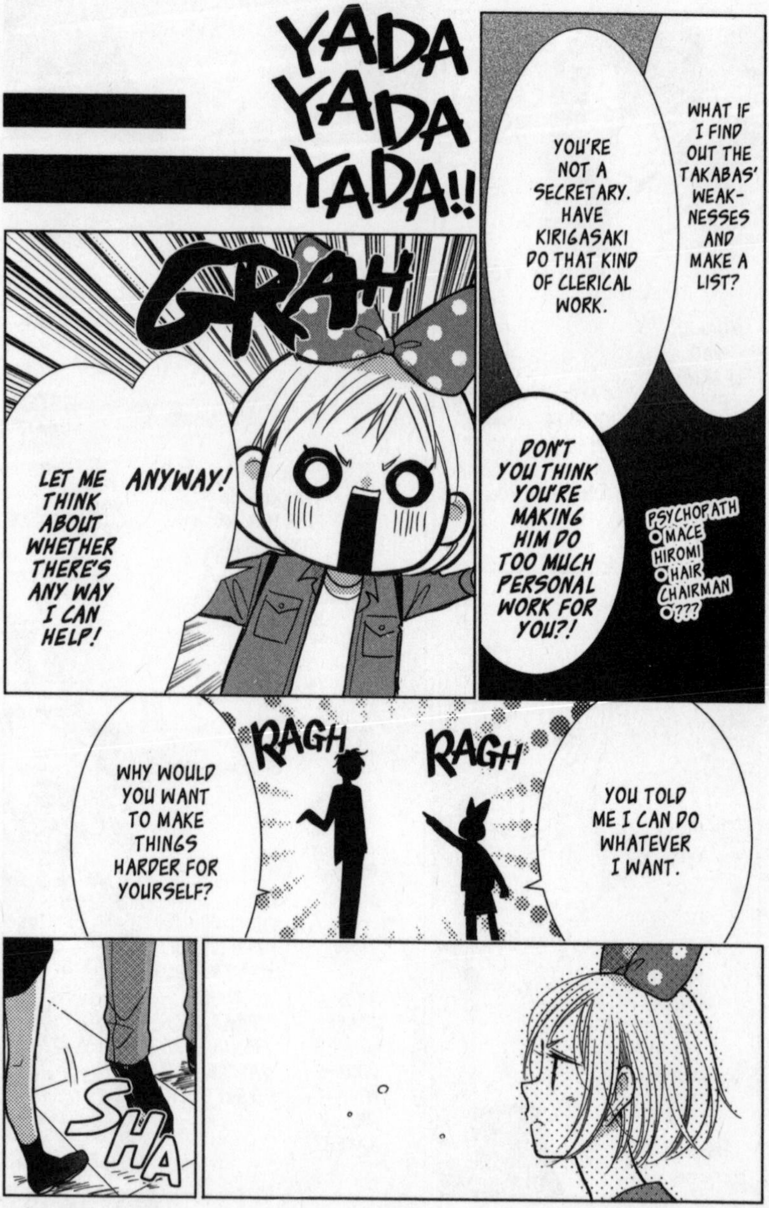
WHAT IF I FIND OUT THE TAKABAS' WEAK-NESSES AND MAKE A LIST?
YOU'RE NOT A SECRETARY. HAVE KIRIGASAKI DO THAT KIND OF CLERICAL WORK.
PSYCHOPATH
MACE
HIROMI
HAIR
CHAIRMAN
???
DON'T YOU THINK YOU'RE MAKING HIM DO TOO MUCH PERSONAL WORK FOR YOU?!
YADA YADA YADA!!
GRAH
ANYWAY!
LET ME THINK ABOUT WHETHER THERE'S ANY WAY I CAN HELP!
YOU TOLD ME I CAN DO WHATEVER I WANT.
RAGH
RAGH
WHY WOULD YOU WANT TO MAKE THINGS HARDER FOR YOURSELF?
SHA

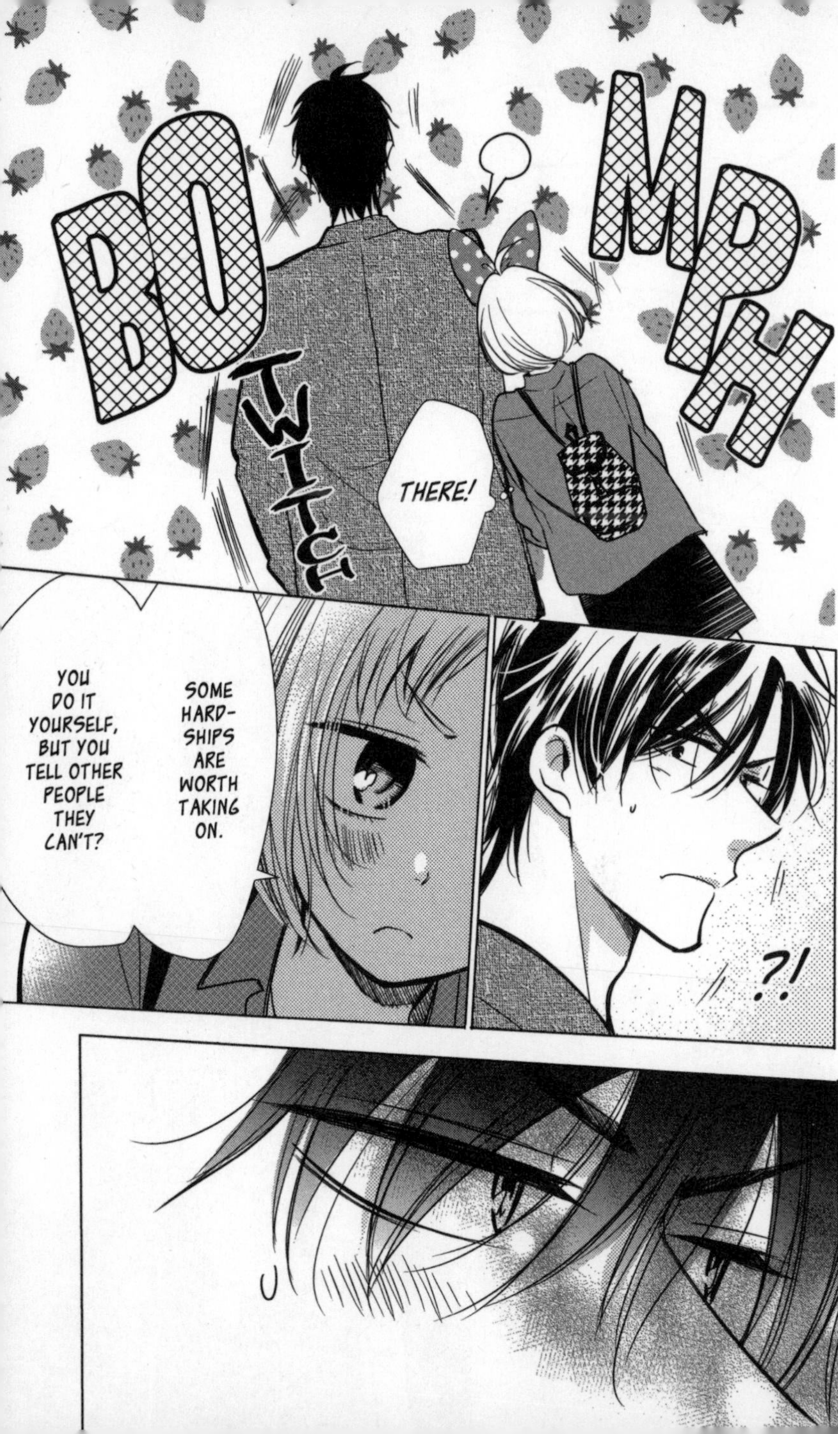
BOMPH
TWITCH
THERE!
?!
SOME HARD-SHIPS ARE WORTH TAKING ON.
YOU DO IT YOURSELF, BUT YOU TELL OTHER PEOPLE THEY CAN'T?

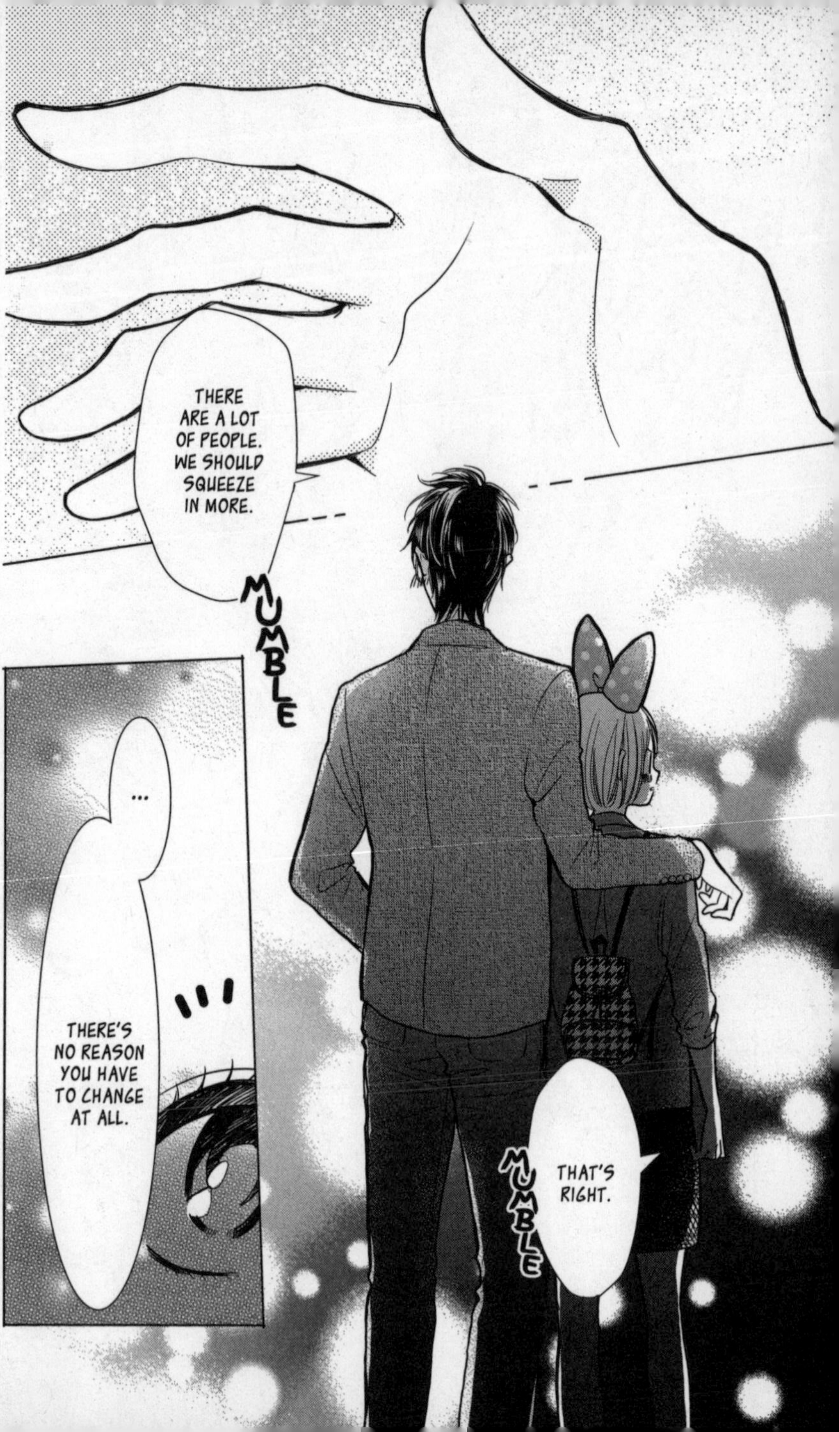
THERE ARE A LOT OF PEOPLE. WE SHOULD SQUEEZE IN MORE.
MUMBLE
THAT'S RIGHT.
MUMBLE
...
THERE'S NO REASON YOU HAVE TO CHANGE AT ALL.

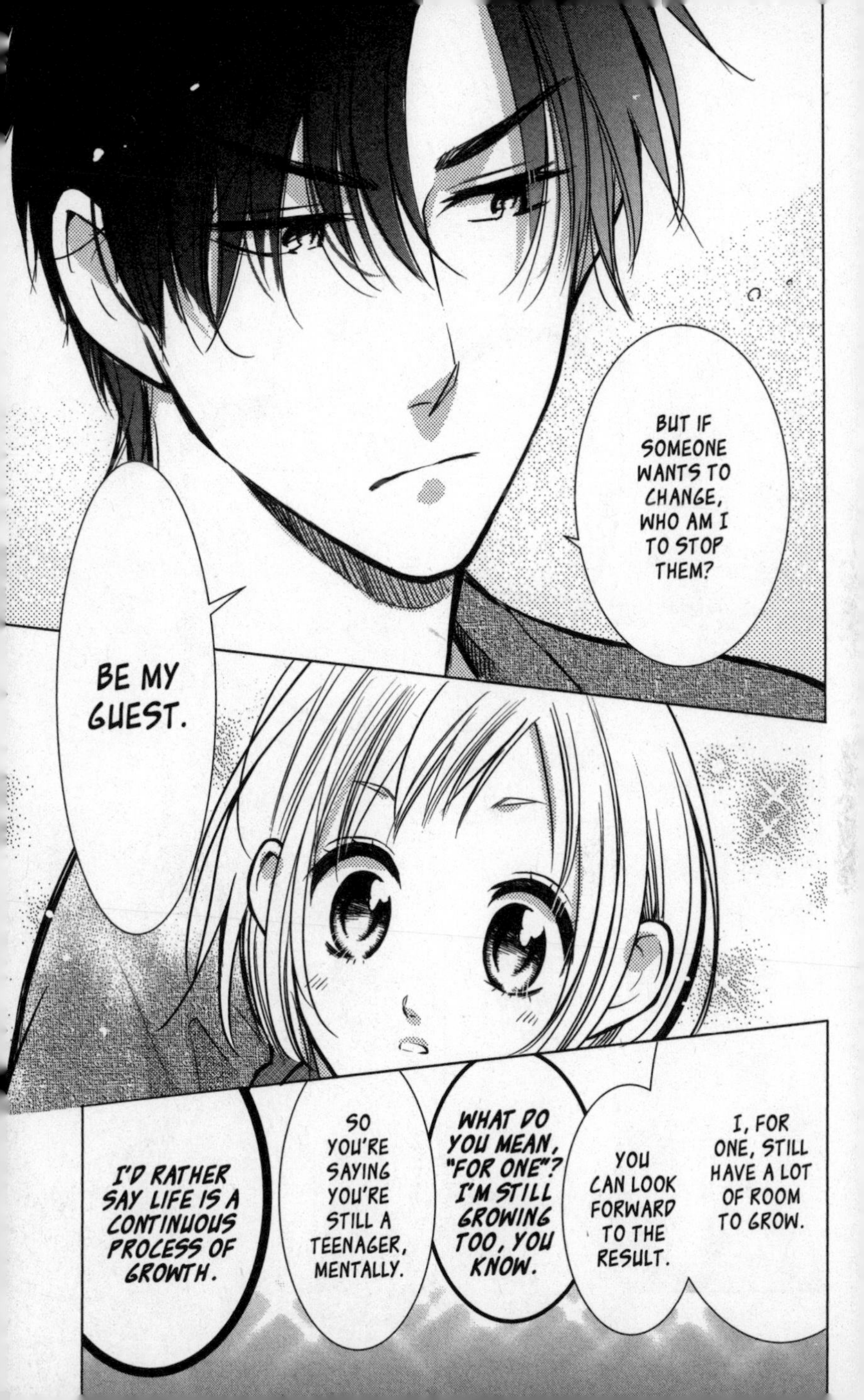
BUT IF SOMEONE WANTS TO CHANGE, WHO AM I TO STOP THEM?
BE MY GUEST.
I, FOR ONE, STILL HAVE A LOT OF ROOM TO GROW.
YOU CAN LOOK FORWARD TO THE RESULT.
WHAT DO YOU MEAN, "FOR ONE"? I'M STILL GROWING TOO, YOU KNOW.
SO YOU'RE SAYING YOU'RE STILL A TEENAGER, MENTALLY.
I'D RATHER SAY LIFE IS A CONTINUOUS PROCESS OF GROWTH.

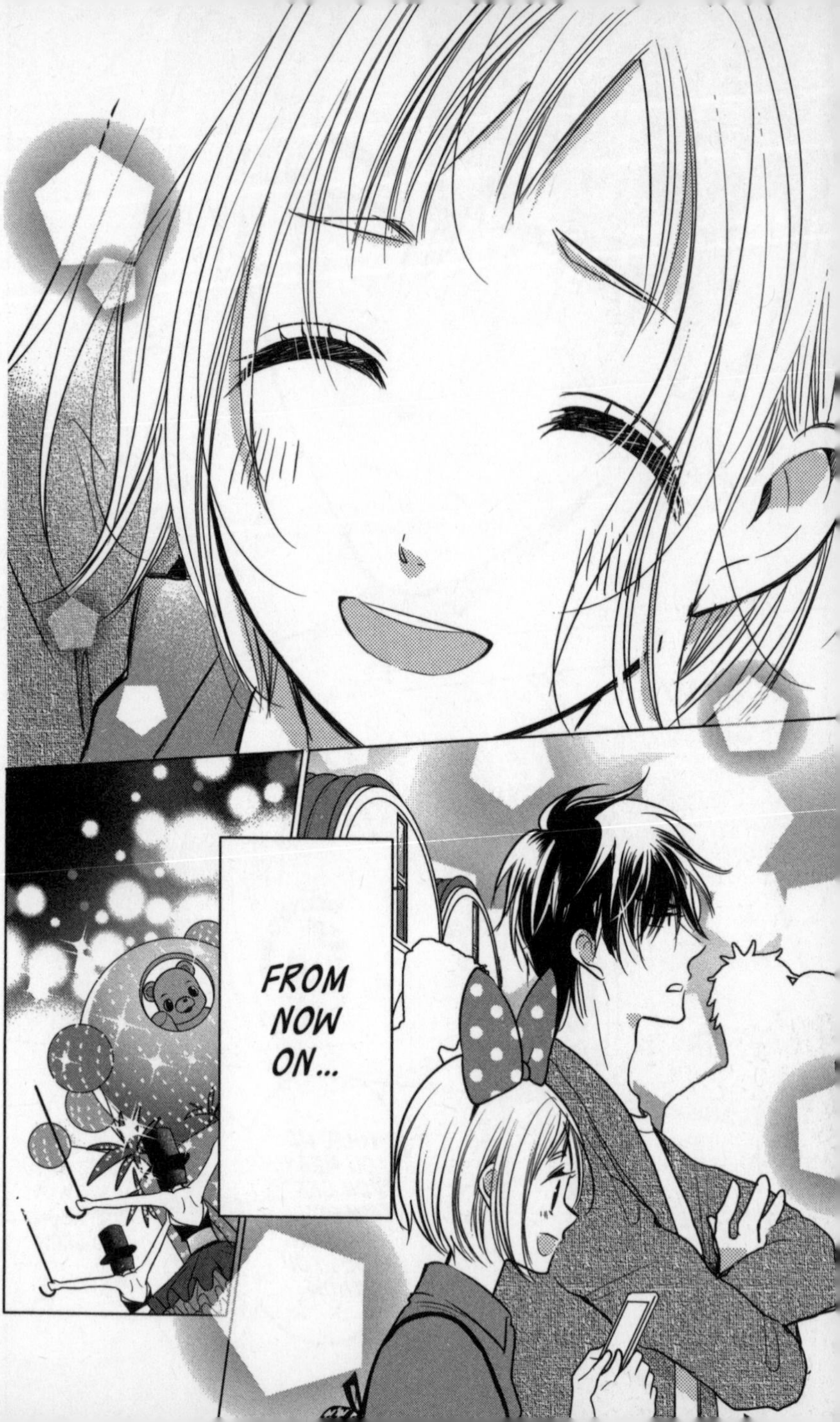
FROM NOW ON...

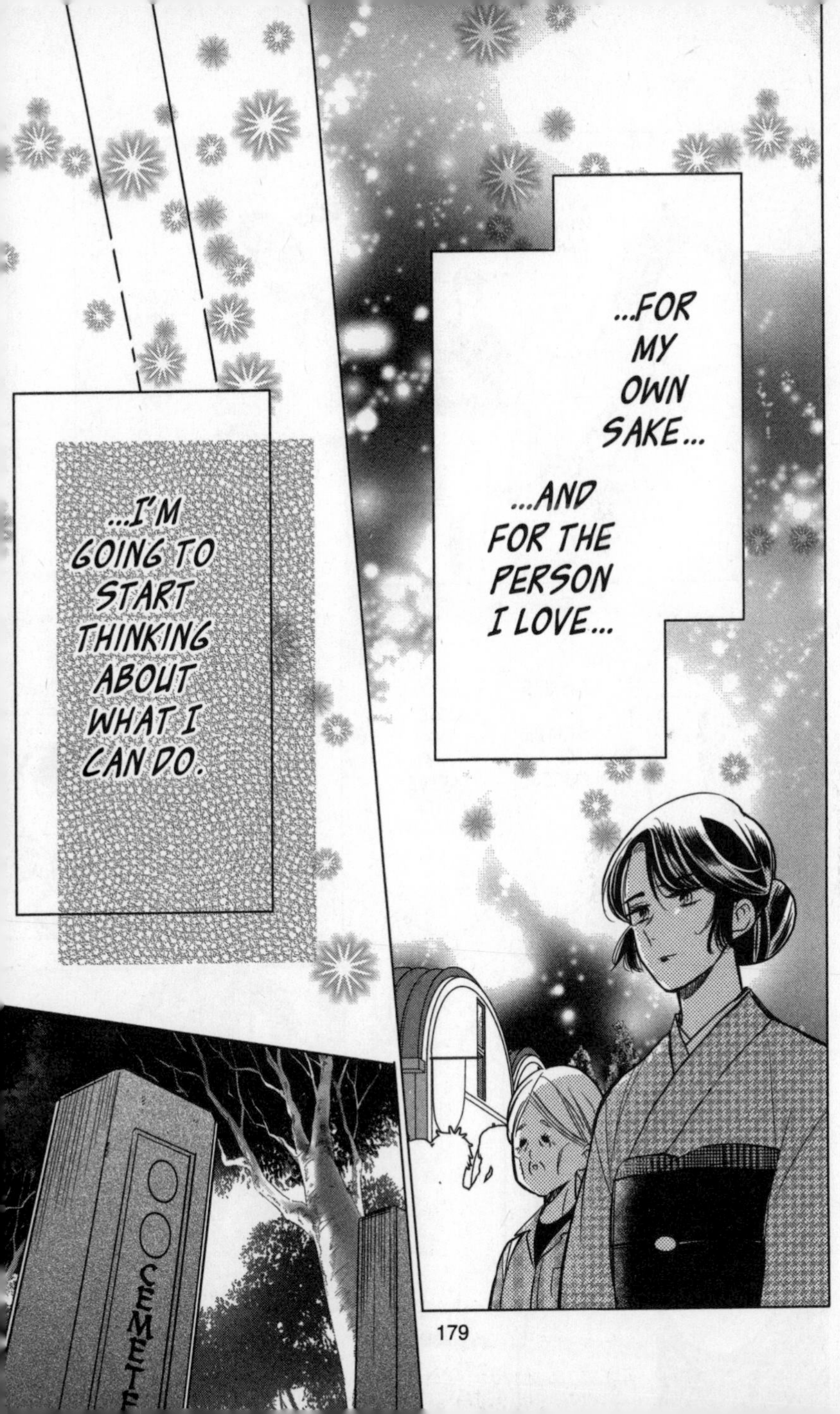
...FOR MY OWN SAKE...
...AND FOR THE PERSON I LOVE...
...I'M GOING TO START THINKING ABOUT WHAT I CAN DO.
CEMETE

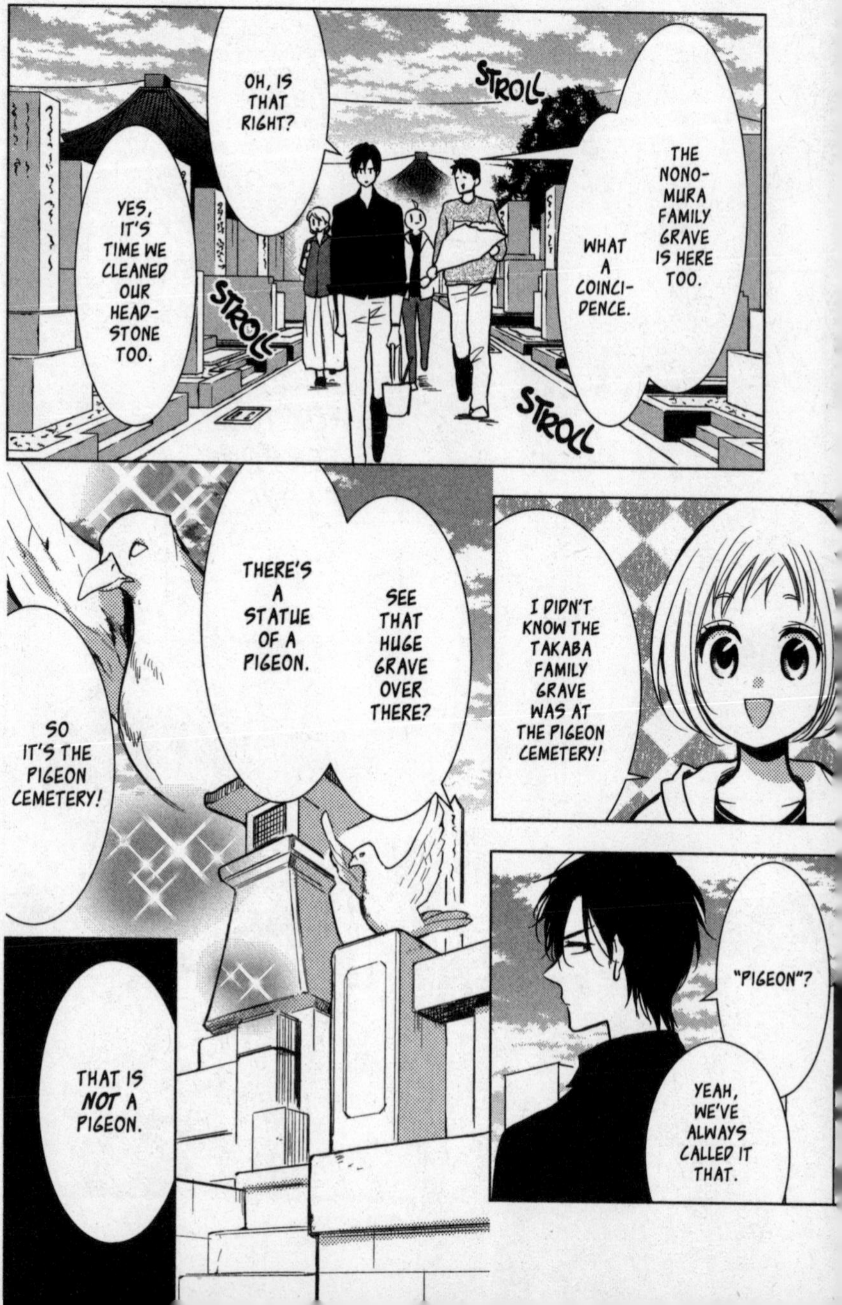
THE NONOMURA FAMILY GRAVE IS HERE TOO.
WHAT A COINCIDENCE.
STROLL
OH, IS THAT RIGHT?
YES, IT'S TIME WE CLEANED OUR HEADSTONE TOO.
STROLL
STROLL
I DIDN'T KNOW THE TAKABA FAMILY GRAVE WAS AT THE PIGEON CEMETERY!
"PIGEON"?
YEAH, WE'VE ALWAYS CALLED IT THAT.
SEE THAT HUGE GRAVE OVER THERE?
THERE'S A STATUE OF A PIGEON.
SO IT'S THE PIGEON CEMETERY!
THAT IS *NOT* A PIGEON.

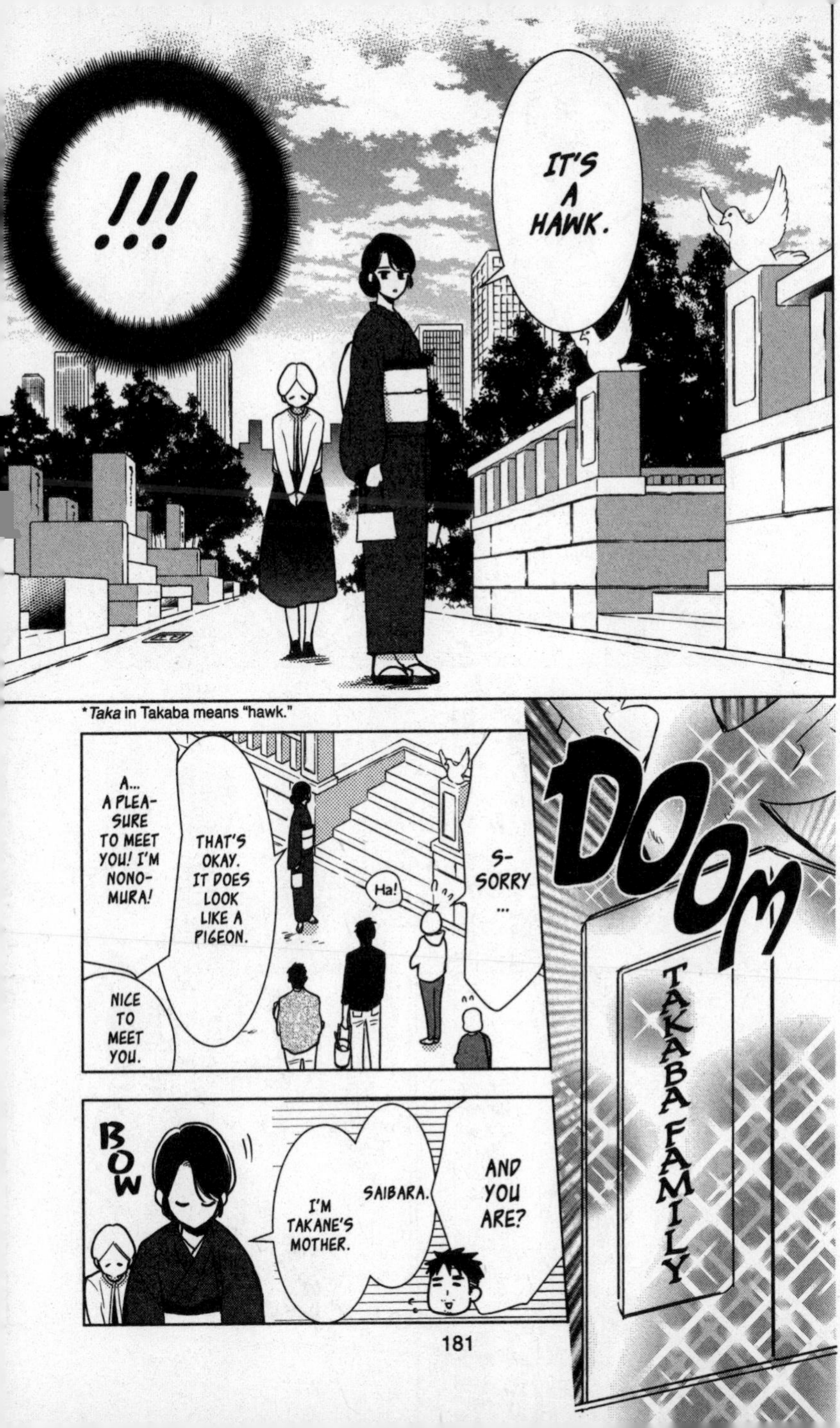
IT'S A HAWK.
!!!
DOOM
TAKABA FAMILY
S-SORRY...
Ha!
THAT'S OKAY. IT DOES LOOK LIKE A PIGEON.
A... A PLEASURE TO MEET YOU! I'M NONOMURA!
NICE TO MEET YOU.
AND YOU ARE?
SAIBARA.
I'M TAKANE'S MOTHER.
BOW

*_Taka_ in Takaba means "hawk."

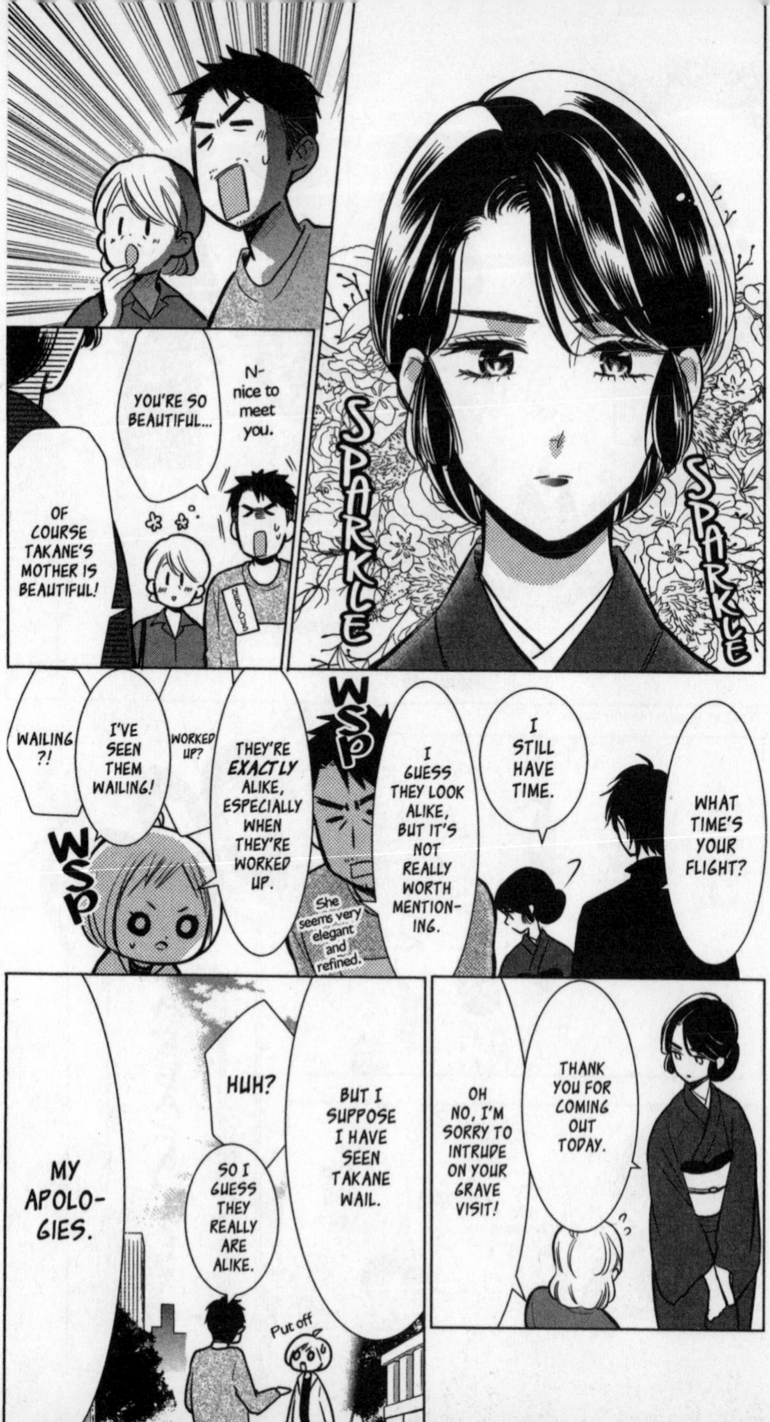
SPARKLE
SPARKLE
N- nice to meet you.
YOU'RE SO BEAUTIFUL...
NERVOUS
OF COURSE TAKANE'S MOTHER IS BEAUTIFUL!
WHAT TIME'S YOUR FLIGHT?
I STILL HAVE TIME.
I GUESS THEY LOOK ALIKE, BUT IT'S NOT REALLY WORTH MENTIONING.
WSP
She seems very elegant and refined.
THEY'RE *EXACTLY* ALIKE, ESPECIALLY WHEN THEY'RE WORKED UP.
WORKED UP?
I'VE SEEN THEM WAILING!
WAILING?!
WSP
THANK YOU FOR COMING OUT TODAY.
OH NO, I'M SORRY TO INTRUDE ON YOUR GRAVE VISIT!
BUT I SUPPOSE I HAVE SEEN TAKANE WAIL.
HUH?
SO I GUESS THEY REALLY ARE ALIKE.
Put off
MY APOLOGIES.

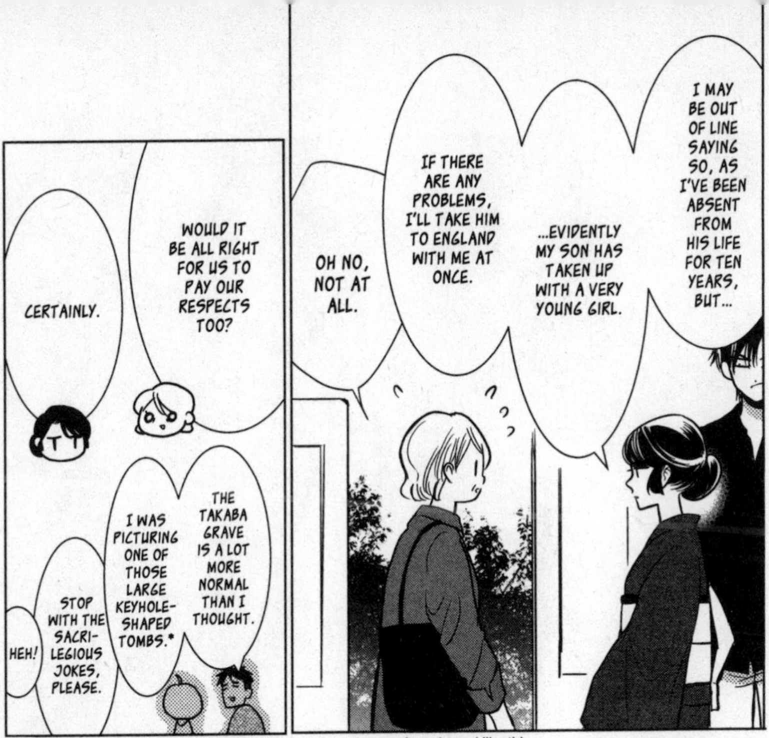
I MAY BE OUT OF LINE SAYING SO, AS I'VE BEEN ABSENT FROM HIS LIFE FOR TEN YEARS, BUT...
...EVIDENTLY MY SON HAS TAKEN UP WITH A VERY YOUNG GIRL.
IF THERE ARE ANY PROBLEMS, I'LL TAKE HIM TO ENGLAND WITH ME AT ONCE.
OH NO, NOT AT ALL.
WOULD IT BE ALL RIGHT FOR US TO PAY OUR RESPECTS TOO?
CERTAINLY.
THE TAKABA GRAVE IS A LOT MORE NORMAL THAN I THOUGHT.
I WAS PICTURING ONE OF THOSE LARGE KEYHOLE-SHAPED TOMBS.*
STOP WITH THE SACRILEGIOUS JOKES, PLEASE.
HEH!

*Tombs of the members of ruling class in ancient Japan were often shaped like this.

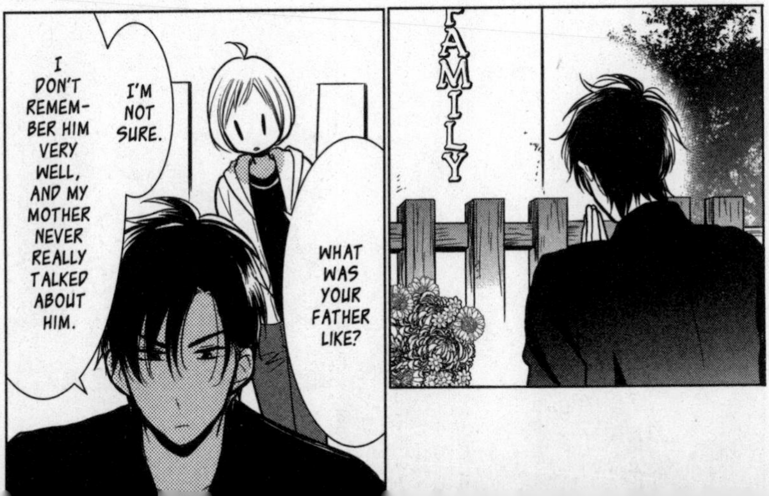
FAMILY
WHAT WAS YOUR FATHER LIKE?
I'M NOT SURE.
I DON'T REMEMBER HIM VERY WELL, AND MY MOTHER NEVER REALLY TALKED ABOUT HIM.

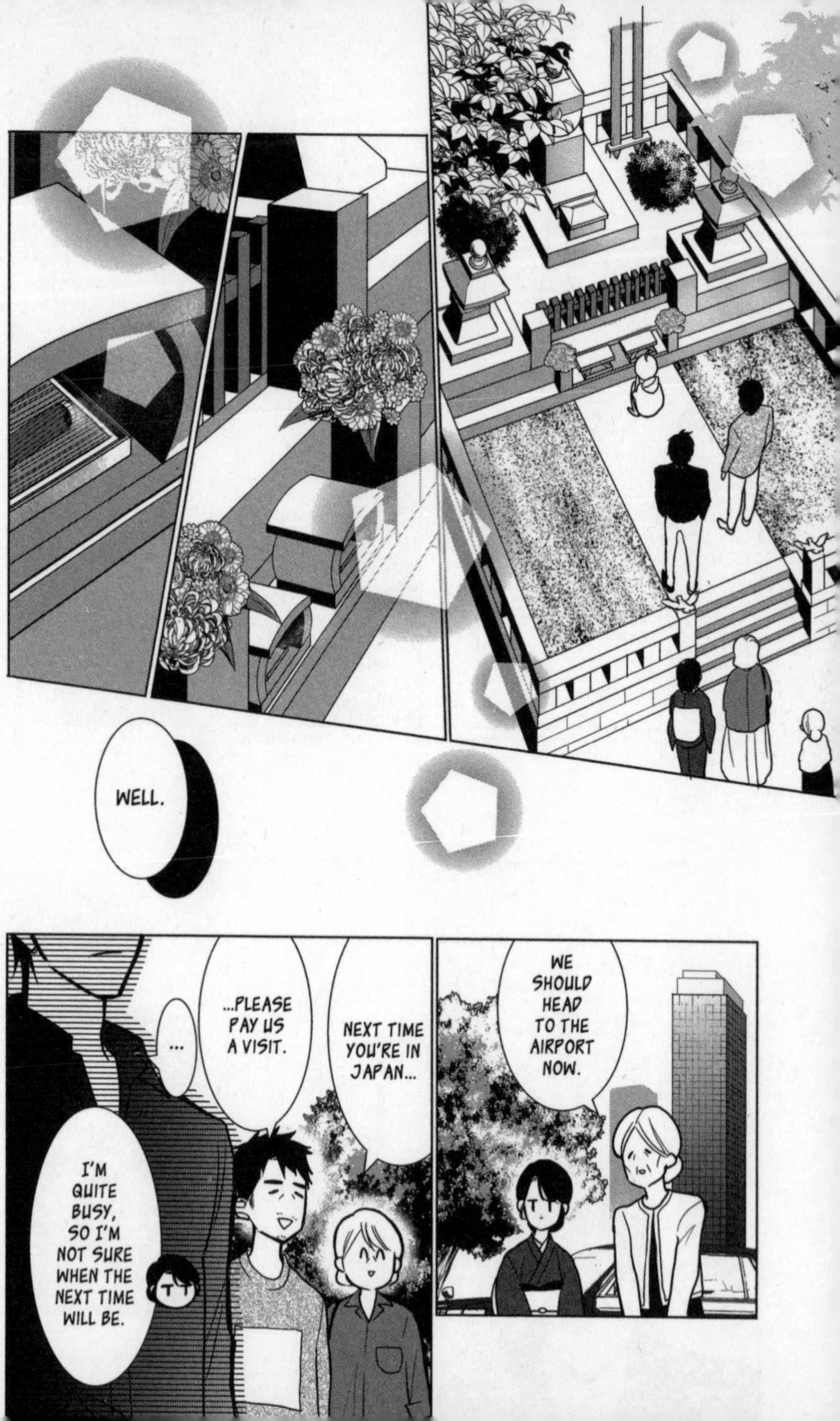
WELL.
WE SHOULD HEAD TO THE AIRPORT NOW.
NEXT TIME YOU'RE IN JAPAN...
...PLEASE PAY US A VISIT.
...
I'M QUITE BUSY, SO I'M NOT SURE WHEN THE NEXT TIME WILL BE.

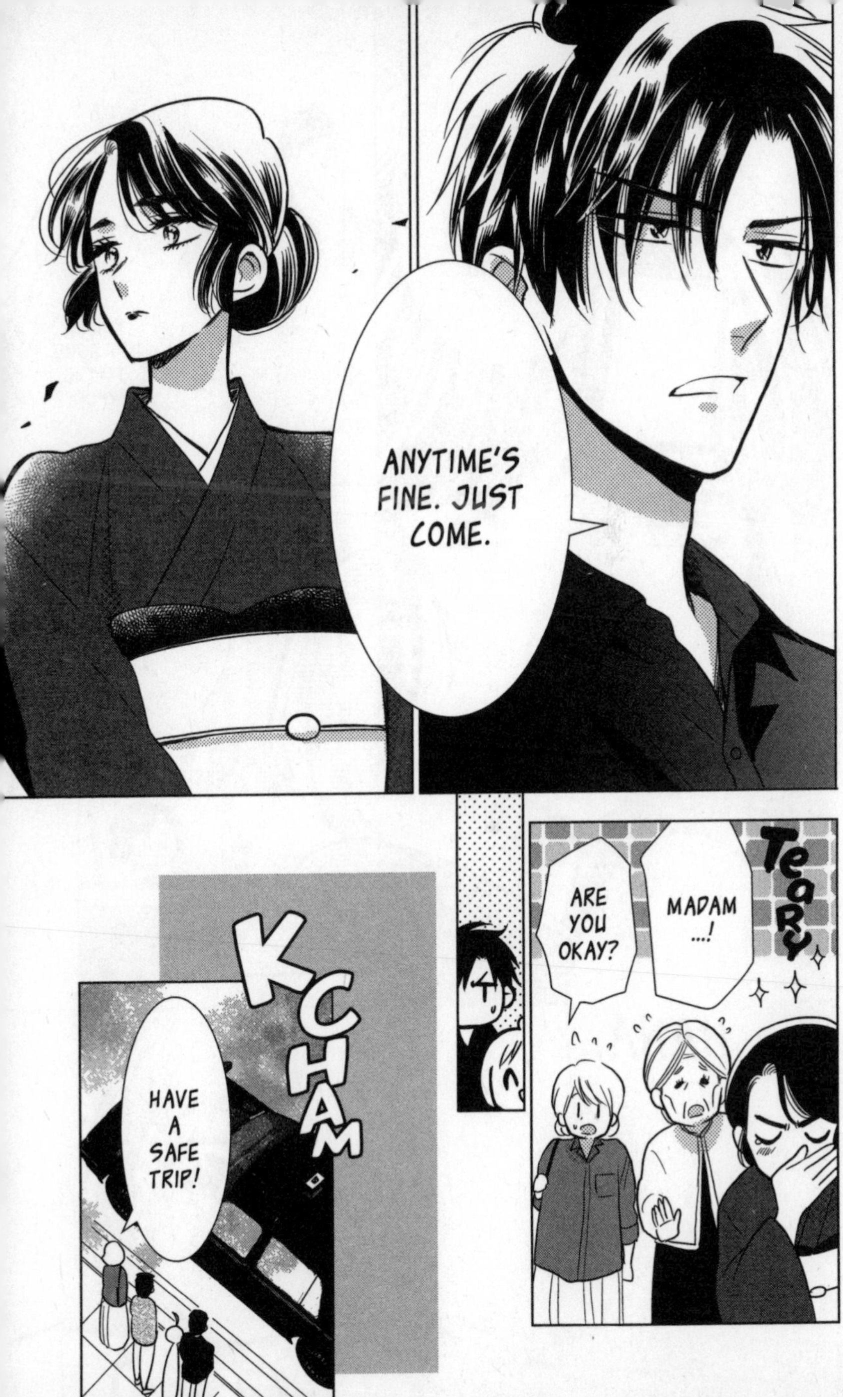
ANYTIME'S FINE. JUST COME.
TEARY
MADAM ...!
ARE YOU OKAY?
KCHAM
HAVE A SAFE TRIP!

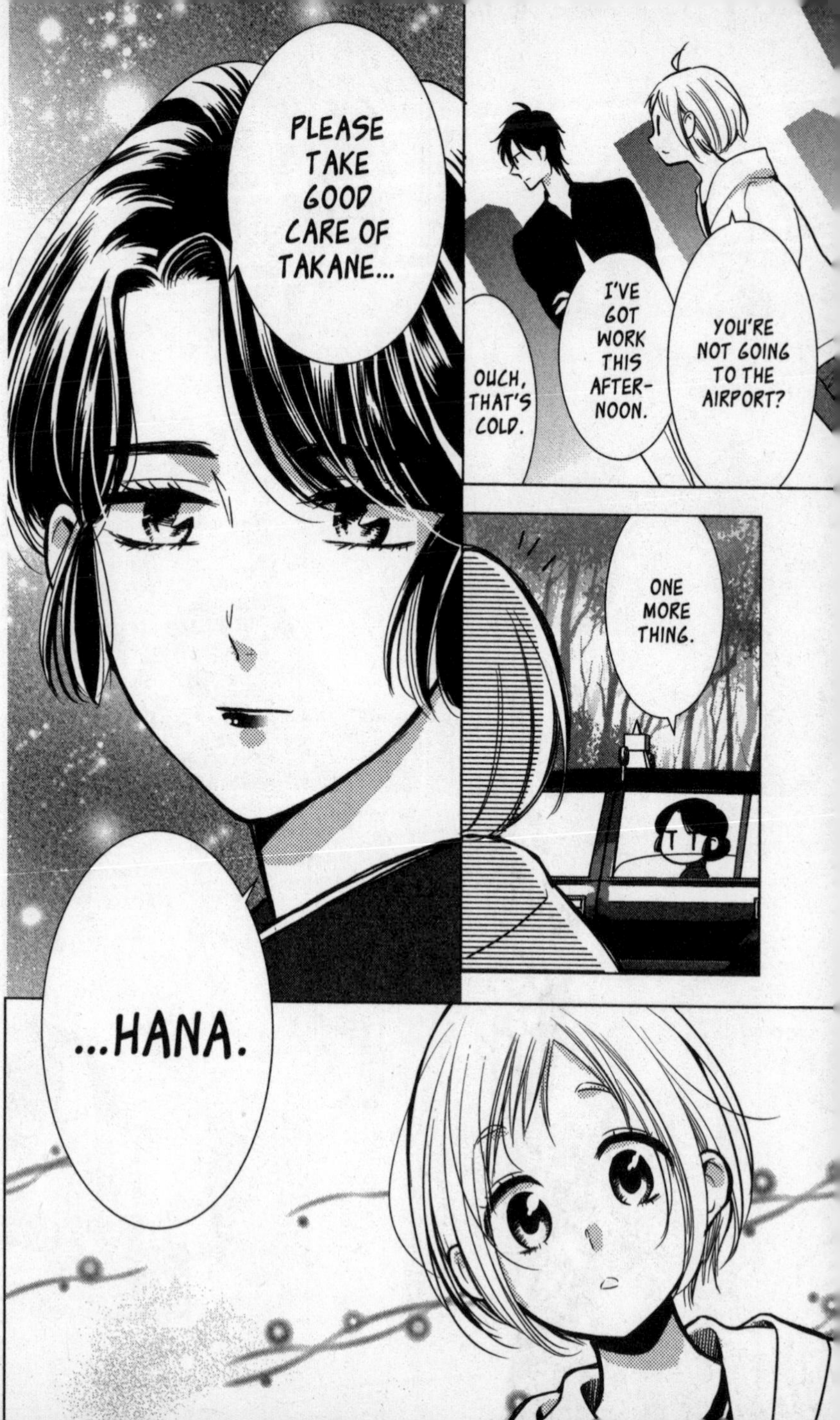
YOU'RE NOT GOING TO THE AIRPORT?
I'VE GOT WORK THIS AFTER-NOON.
OUCH, THAT'S COLD.
ONE MORE THING.
PLEASE TAKE GOOD CARE OF TAKANE...
...HANA.

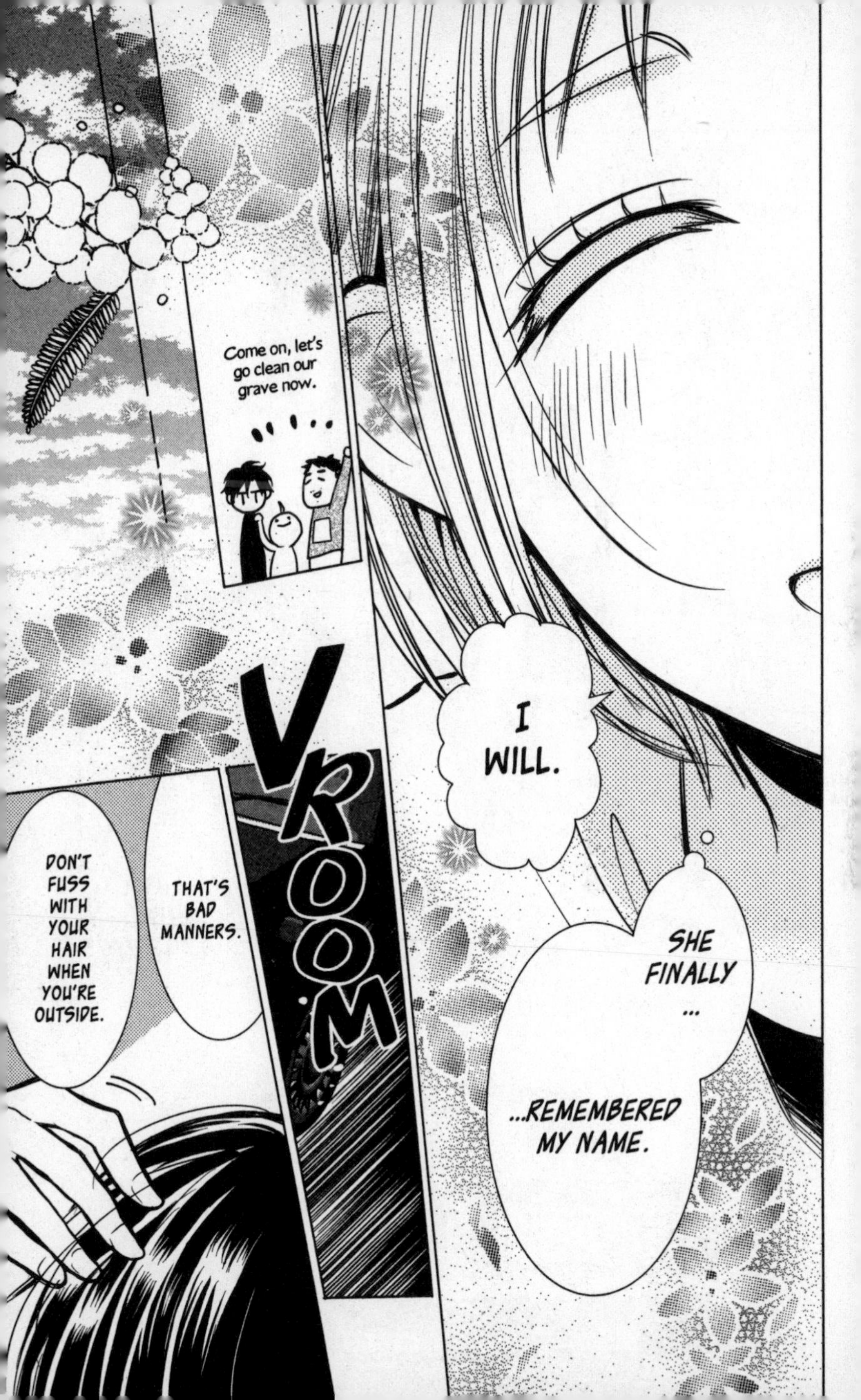
I WILL.
SHE FINALLY ...
...REMEMBERED MY NAME.
Come on, let's go clean our grave now.
VROOM
THAT'S BAD MANNERS.
DON'T FUSS WITH YOUR HAIR WHEN YOU'RE OUTSIDE.

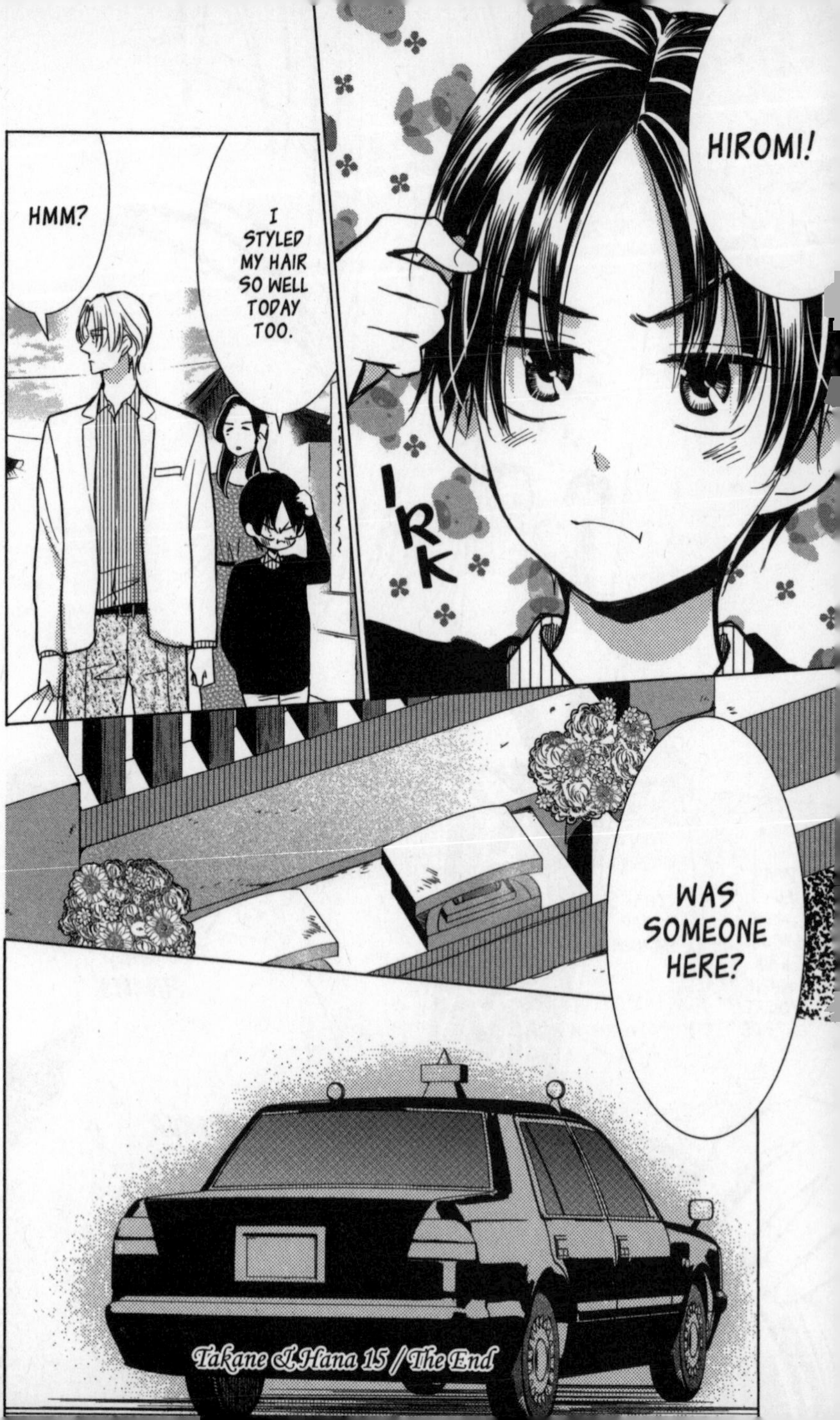
HIROMI!
IRK
I STYLED MY HAIR SO WELL TODAY TOO.
HMM?
WAS SOMEONE HERE?
Takane & Hana 15 / The End

Towako Saibara

I thought long and hard about her appearance and personality. She's Takane's mother, after all! I wanted her to be unique!

At first I envisioned her as a female Takane and thought of making her into a nasty mother-in-law type, but I wanted her to have some charm, so that's how she came to be. She's different from Takane, but I feel like I was able to create a character who's not outdone by him.

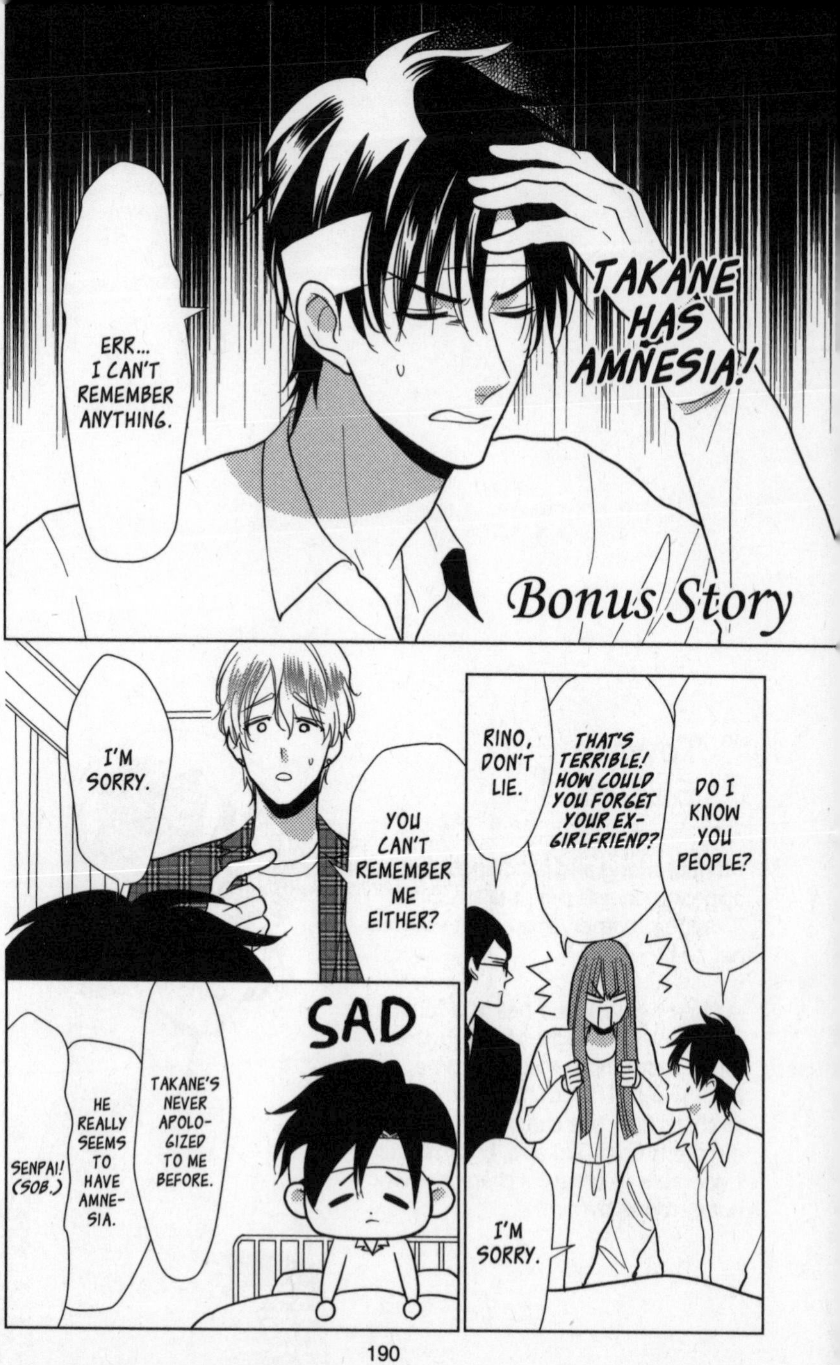
TAKANE HAS AMNESIA!
Bonus Story
ERR... I CAN'T REMEMBER ANYTHING.
DO I KNOW YOU PEOPLE?
THAT'S TERRIBLE! HOW COULD YOU FORGET YOUR EX-GIRLFRIEND?
RINO, DON'T LIE.
I'M SORRY.
YOU CAN'T REMEMBER ME EITHER?
I'M SORRY.
SAD
TAKANE'S NEVER APOLOGIZED TO ME BEFORE.
HE REALLY SEEMS TO HAVE AMNESIA.
SENPAI! (SOB.)

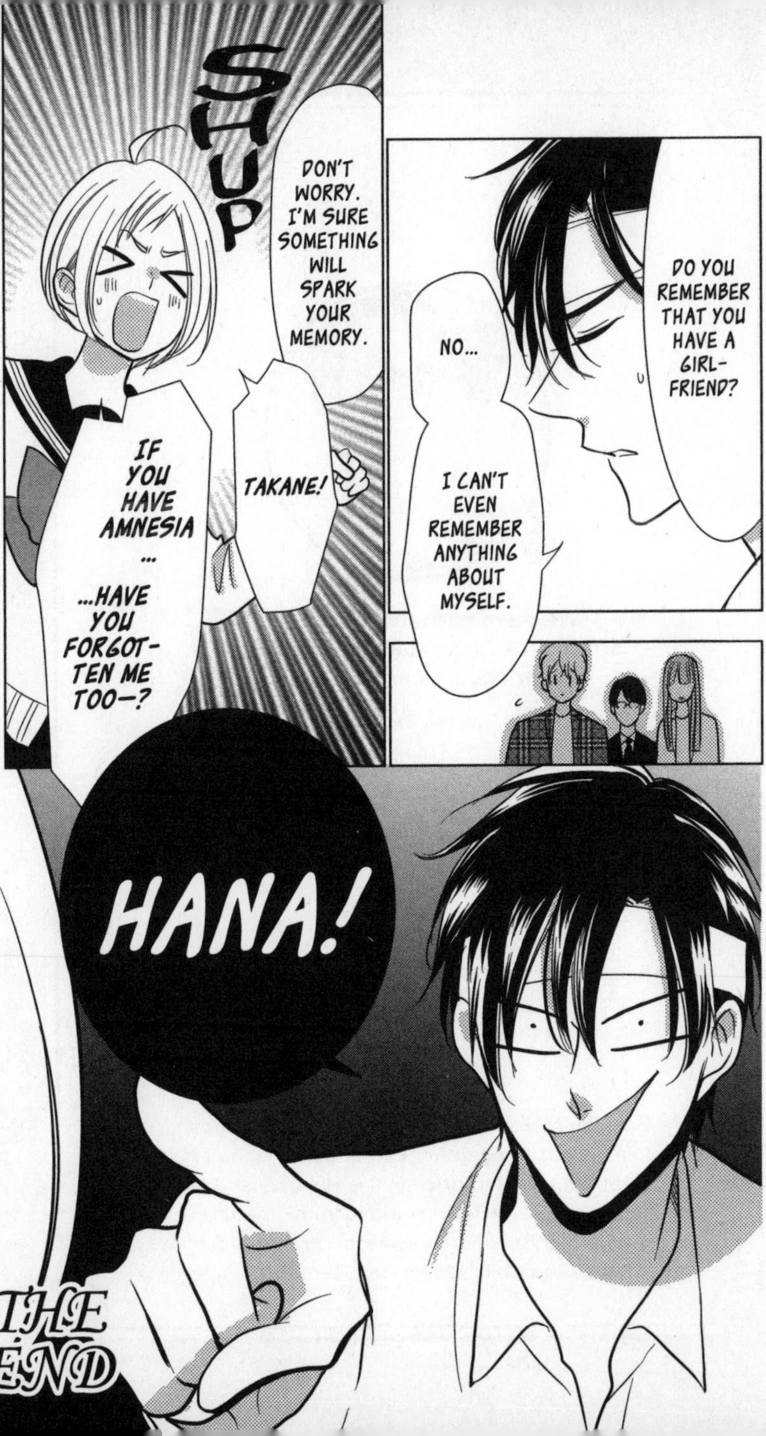
DO YOU REMEMBER THAT YOU HAVE A GIRLFRIEND?
NO...
I CAN'T EVEN REMEMBER ANYTHING ABOUT MYSELF.
DON'T WORRY. I'M SURE SOMETHING WILL SPARK YOUR MEMORY.
SHUP
TAKANE!
IF YOU HAVE AMNESIA...
...HAVE YOU FORGOTTEN ME TOO—?
HANA!
THE END

We have carnations this time.
Some covers can be deceiving, while
other covers can be spoilers.

—YUKI SHIWASU

Born on March 7 in Fukuoka Prefecture, Japan,
Yuki Shiwasu began her career as a manga artist
after winning the top prize in the Hakusensha Athena
Newcomers' Awards from *Hana to Yume* magazine. She
is also the author of *Furou Kyoudai* (Immortal Siblings),
which was published by Hakusensha in Japan.

Takane & Hana

VOLUME 15
SHOJO BEAT EDITION

STORY & ART BY **YUKI SHIWASU**

ENGLISH ADAPTATION **Ysabet Reinhardt MacFarlane**
TRANSLATION **JN Productions**
TOUCH-UP ART & LETTERING **Annaliese Christman**
DESIGN **Shawn Carrico**
EDITOR **Amy Yu**

First published in Japan in 2019 by HAKUSENSHA, Inc., Tokyo.
English language translation rights arranged with HAKUSENSHA, Inc., Tokyo.

Printed in the U.S.A.

Published by VIZ Media, LLC
P.O. Box 77010
San Francisco, CA 94107

10 9 8 7 6 5 4 3 2 1
First printing, July 2020

ratings.viz.com RATED T TEEN

PARENTAL ADVISORY
TAKANE & HANA is rated T for Teen and is recommended for ages 13 and up. This volume contains suggestive themes.

VIZ MEDIA
viz.com

Shojo Beat
shojobeat.com

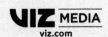

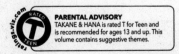

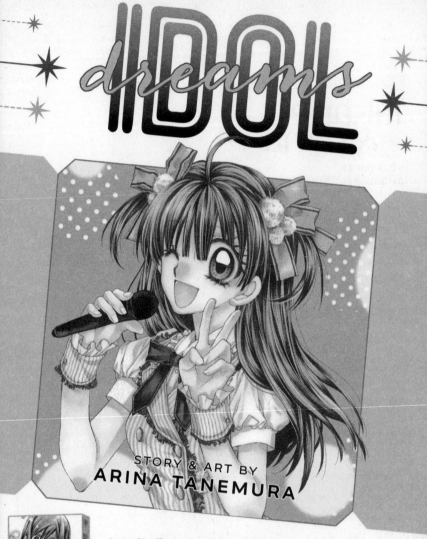

IDOL *dreams*

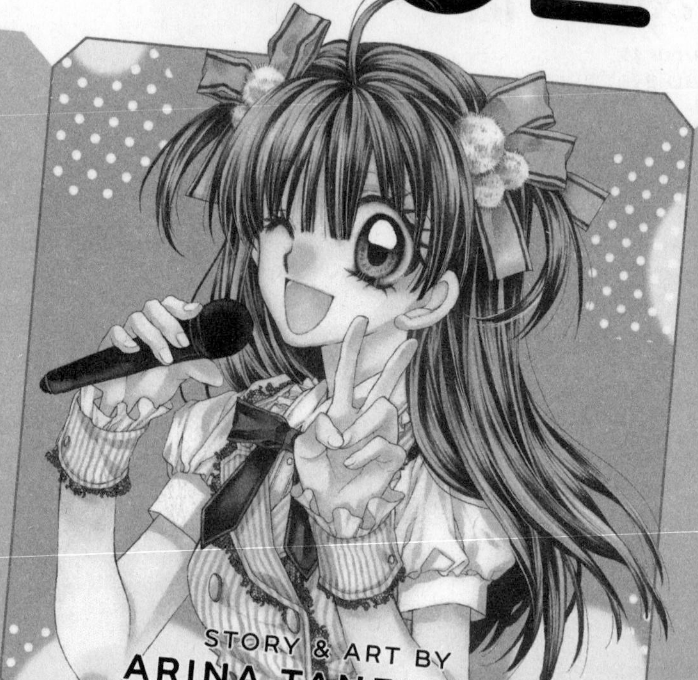
STORY & ART BY
ARINA TANEMURA

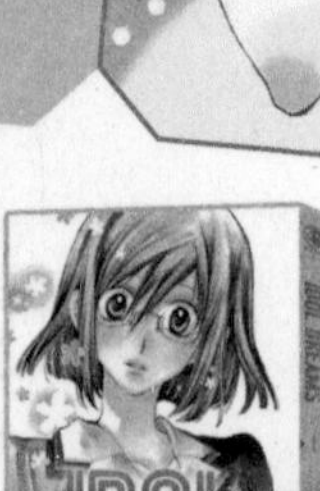
IDOL DREAMS
IDOL dreams
1
ARINA TANEMURA

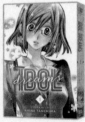

At age 31, office worker Chikage Deguchi feels she missed her chances at love and success. When word gets out that she's a virgin, Chikage is humiliated and wishes she could turn back time to when she was still young and popular. She takes an experimental drug that changes her appearance back to when she was 15. Now Chikage is determined to pursue everything she missed out on all those years ago—including becoming a star!

Shojo Beat VIZ T

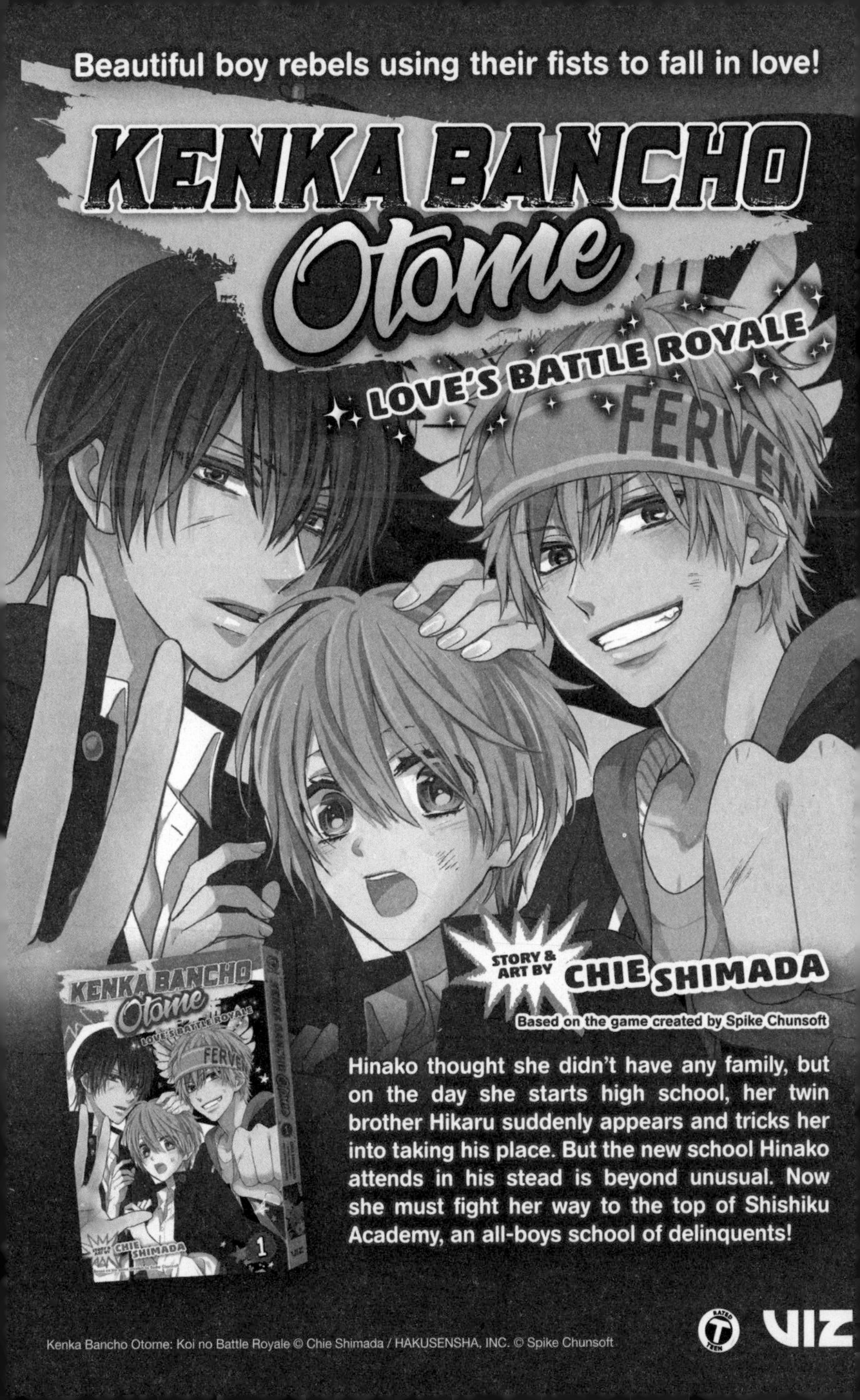
Beautiful boy rebels using their fists to fall in love!
KENKA BANCHO Otome
LOVE'S BATTLE ROYALE
FERVENT
STORY & ART BY CHIE SHIMADA
Based on the game created by Spike Chunsoft
Hinako thought she didn't have any family, but on the day she starts high school, her twin brother Hikaru suddenly appears and tricks her into taking his place. But the new school Hinako attends in his stead is beyond unusual. Now she must fight her way to the top of Shishiku Academy, an all-boys school of delinquents!
KENKA BANCHO Otome
LOVE'S BATTLE ROYALE
FERVENT
CHIE SHIMADA
1
T RATED TEEN
VIZ
Kenka Bancho Otome: Koi no Battle Royale © Chie Shimada / HAKUSENSHA, INC. © Spike Chunsoft

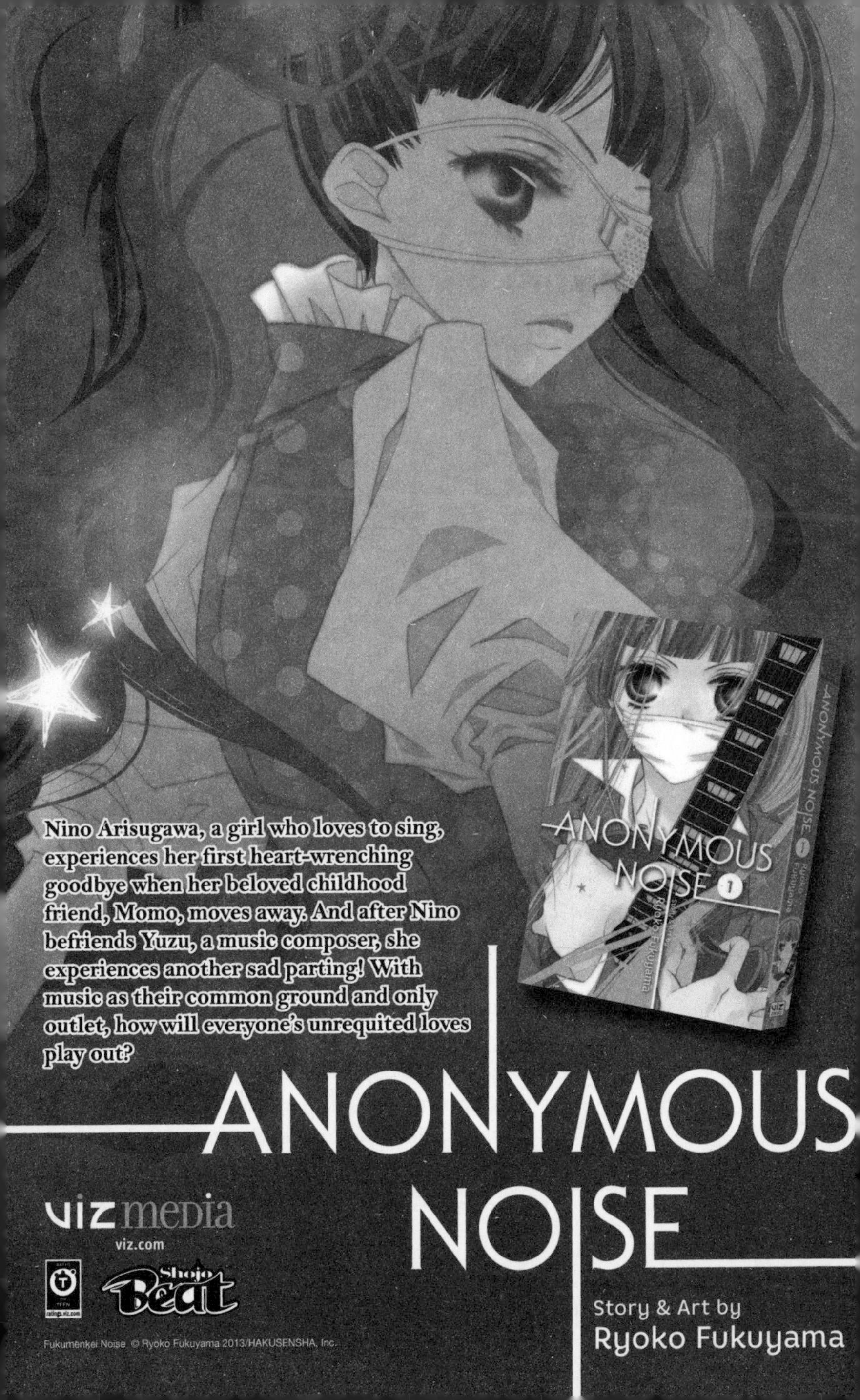
Nino Arisugawa, a girl who loves to sing, experiences her first heart-wrenching goodbye when her beloved childhood friend, Momo, moves away. And after Nino befriends Yuzu, a music composer, she experiences another sad parting! With music as their common ground and only outlet, how will everyone's unrequited loves play out?
ANONYMOUS NOISE
Story & Art by
Ryoko Fukuyama
viz media
viz.com
Shojo Beat
Fukumenkei Noise © Ryoko Fukuyama 2013/HAKUSENSHA, Inc.

Behind the Scenes!!

STORY AND ART BY BISCO HATORI

From the creator of *Ouran High School Host Club*

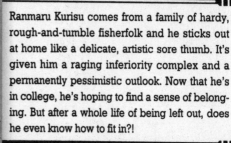

Ranmaru Kurisu comes from a family of hardy, rough-and-tumble fisherfolk and he sticks out at home like a delicate, artistic sore thumb. It's given him a raging inferiority complex and a permanently pessimistic outlook. Now that he's in college, he's hoping to find a sense of belonging. But after a whole life of being left out, does he even know how to fit in?!

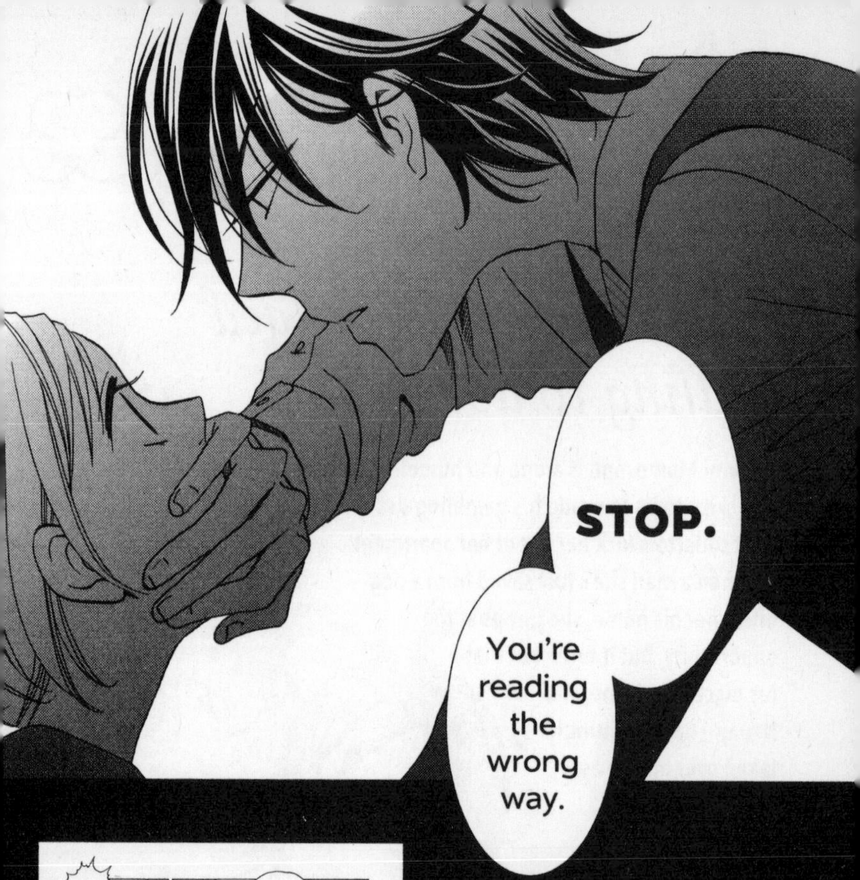
STOP.
You're reading the wrong way.

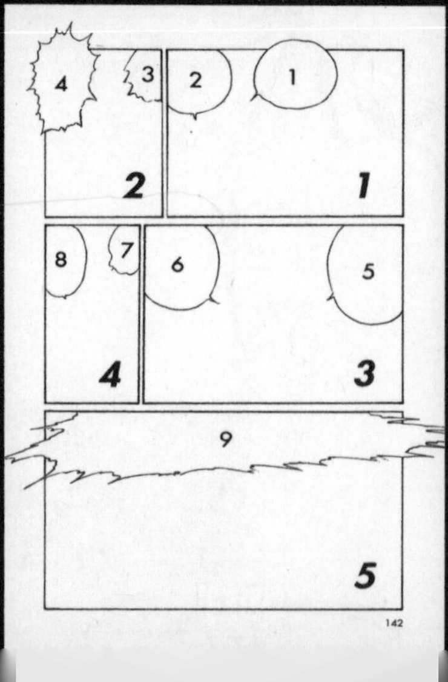
1
2
3
4
1
2
5
6
7
8
3
4
9
5
142

In keeping with the original Japanese comic format, this book reads from right to left—so action, sound effects and word balloons are completely reversed to preserve the orientation of the original artwork.

Check out the diagram shown here to get the hang of things, and then turn to the other side of the book to get started!